MW00438721

NO ONE TO MEET

NO ONE TO MEET

Imitation and Originality in the Songs of Bob Dylan

RAPHAEL FALCO

THE UNIVERSITY OF ALABAMA PRESS

Tuscaloosa

The University of Alabama Press
Tuscaloosa, Alabama 35487-0380
uapress.ua.edu

Inquiries about reproducing material from this work should
be addressed to the University of Alabama Press.

Typeface: Arno Pro

Cover image: "Bob Dylan and his Olivetti"; © Ted Russell, 1964
Cover design: Lori Lynch

Cataloging-in-Publication data is available from the Library of Congress.
ISBN: 978-0-8173-2141-3
E-ISBN: 978-0-8173-9423-3

In Memory of Pete Lentini
Magician

Ogni pittore dipinge sé
—Tuscan proverb

CONTENTS

FIGURES

ACKNOWLEDGMENTS

Mark Davidson, Mitch Blank, Elijah Wald, Sean Latham, Brian Hosmer, Scott Marshall, Michael Chaiken, Jeff Rosen and the staff of the Bob Dylan office, Tim Noakes (Stanford University Special Collections), Laura Mahony (at the Gagosian Art Gallery), Michael Shulman (Magnum Photos), Andrew Holter, Christopher Corbett, Kevin Wisniewski, Clayton Vogel, Timothy Phin, David J. Rothman, Kenneth Daley, Michele Osherow, Tim Ford, Ryan Bloom, Marsha Scott, Selena Chang, Anne Marie MacInnes, and the students of my Dylan seminar.

My co-editors at the *Dylan Review*, Lisa Sanders O'Neill, Paul Haney, and Nicole Font. I am especially grateful to Nicole Font for her help in compiling the discography.

The Bob Dylan Archive for permission to quote from the collection and to print images of documents.

The UMBC Dresher Humanities Center for a Summer Faculty Fellowship to travel to the Bob Dylan Archive and to help fund other aspects of the project.

Dan Waterman, my editor at the University of Alabama Press, for his support and belief in the book.

Joanna Jacobs and Irina du Quenoy for their intelligent, attentive copyediting.

Lauren Bernofsky for musical guidance from the embryonic to the final stages of this project. And Julia Irmscher (with her perfect pitch) for telling me what I was really hearing.

Ani and Christoph, *sine quos nihil*. In "Fourth Time Around" (*Blonde on Blonde*), Dylan sings, "I never asked for your crutch / Now don't ask for mine." But I'm proud to reveal my crutch—my two crutches. Without Christoph Irmscher, I wouldn't have been able to write this book. He has been my guide and paragon for many years.

And then there's Ani, my other crutch. I could describe her loyalty and bemused patience in detail, but, really, does any Dylan fan need to say more than thanks a lot to Saint Ani?

Finally, in a special category of acknowledgment is Dan Epstein, who, for the last fifty years, has listened to Bob Dylan's music with me. But this is not exactly a thank you, since half the time Dan wanted me to change the record.

A NOTE ON LYRICS

There is no standard print edition of Dylan's lyrics. The published lyrics are a vexing problem: the official website (bobdylan.com) is supposed to contain the definitive lyrics, but often there are conflicts between the website and published editions, including those released by Dylan, between the published versions of the lyrics and Dylan's many performances of a song, and between the website or the published editions and what listeners hear on the albums.

I have written this book for a broad audience, for lovers and scholars of Dylan's work (and with the hope that, by the end of it, readers, if they aren't yet, will be both). Even if Dylan's texts weren't in flux, a standard system of scholarly referencing would defeat my overall purpose. Throughout this book, I take the source of the lyrics to be their first release on the albums, or, in special cases, in bootleg performances saved from recording sessions or captured by someone sitting in a club. I have indicated these sources either parenthetically when introducing individual songs or in discussion of the different versions. Sometimes I have also used endnotes to clarify variations introduced in Dylan's performances, indicating when Dylan changes the lyrics in concert or on unreleased tracks. But, for the most part, I cite what I hear on the albums. The discography at the end of the book contains complete information on all official releases.

INTRODUCTION

Imagine:

The speaker stands and adjusts his doctor's bonnet. Dim lights from Clare College across the lawn fill the window. An anxious murmur comes from the audience, the rustle of language, but he ignores it. John Richardson, B.A., M.A., B.D., D.D., Cantab., Master of Trinity College, sweeps his robe behind him and steps to the deal oak podium. He begins without ceremony: "I am honored to stand before you, *in loco consilii, to announce the award of the 1615 Nobel Prize in Literature to Mr. William Shakespeare.*"

First nothing, a pure hush, then a sudden intake of breath tenses the distinguished audience. Then the quiet disturbance, the confusion. Who is he? An actor? A playwright? A popular entertainer, a song-and-dance man? S'blood, he's nearly a vagabond, that provincial mushroom. He even purchased a coat of arms last year, I know the scoundrel herald who sold it to him. It's a scandal any way you look at it.

And what literature? *Shakespeare's only published a handful of sonnets. Not Lucrece, surely?*

The babel of voices goes silent, as if struck dumb with incredulity.

The plays? They can't count plays! Plays aren't literature! They've gone mad. Do they think he's Sophocles?

What has the Nobel committee done?

They've set a precedent.

They've ruined the precedent.

It's a scandal any way you look at it.

———

This imaginary scene, preposterously anachronistic and utterly impossible in the Jacobean context, is meant only as a rough analogy to the reaction among contemporary literati to Dylan's Nobel Prize. Shakespeare's art, though recognized as remarkable in his time, was by no means held to the same standard as traditional forms of poetry—not even by Shakespeare himself, incidentally, who only published his sonnets and conventional poetry, never his plays (not least because he didn't own them). Poets laboring to imitate the Virgilian rota (wheel) of pastoral, georgic, and epic poetry garnered genuine esteem, while playwrights, though they wrote in blank verse, rarely if ever published their plays and therefore were never *read* per se. Just as they performed on the fringes of the city, in the so-called Liberties, they also inhabited a literary No Man's Land. To give a Nobel Prize to a Jacobean playwright would be the equivalent in our day to giving it—well, to a rock star.

Dylan's distinction lies in his capacity to merge performative virtuosity with a syncretic genius unlike any in contemporary poetry, let alone among folk or rock composers. The controversy and subsequent literary justifications surrounding Dylan's prize are ultimately moot arguments, a storm in a teacup. He is an artist by any measure, and he's a literary artist too, if of a different mold. Why bother defining what Dylan long ago redefined for himself? If, in his Nobel speech, he asks now whether his songs are literature, that is probably because the literature he sees as fundamental to his formation is drawn from the traditional school curriculum—Homer, Melville, Remarque—and his attitude toward it is both humble and maybe even a bit banal.[1] Yet, without rejecting those influences, which evidently he carried along from his schooldays, Dylan absorbed, reenvisioned, and wrote himself into the tradition; through the sheer force of his creativity, he translated the traditional American poetic genius from the page to the rock stage. Although Dylan's literary art originated not in the mainstream but in the tributary current of American blues and folk, that unlikely source became—"I can't help it if I'm lucky"—a flood. And if today we're all "down in the flood," it's because Bob Dylan brought us here.

Yet, yet, yet, to begin in the right mode, I will invoke a fundamental disclaimer: Dylan's songs, his performances, his recordings—none of this work exists primarily on the page. Every word we read rings in our mind with what Christopher Ricks called that "voice that can't be ignored and that ignores nothing."[2] As Dylan himself has so often pointed out, he too is a poet of the stage. His language lives in the "delivery" (his word), even if his 2017 gallery exhibition *Mondo Scripto* might suggest that he also recognizes that his words have authority on the page.[3] For most of his career, however, Dylan has avoided being judged among traditional poets of the page. For example, on a typescript draft of the liner notes for *World Gone Wrong*—"so here's what these songs mean to me (sort of)"—there's a bit of marginalia written neatly in Dylan's hand in blue ink: "Billy Joel visited me backstage in Milan recently and asked why there weren't notes to my records. Anymore. [It] seems that self-appointed connasiurs [*sic*] of modern & my music might have a hard time with this set of songs [*World Gone Wrong*] who have attempted to take my music apart . . . in hopes to see hidden meaning explaining away the intent in seemingly endless monologue (as if the whole story isn't in the delivery)."[4]

But that isn't the whole story and never will be. In preparing this book, I spent time at the Bob Dylan Archive in Tulsa, Oklahoma. The archive is new and large and will change the way we approach Dylan studies in the future, as much in terms of Dylan's compositional method as of his biography. I pored through box after box of isolated lyrics and drafts of entire songs, including many fascinating stanzas that never saw the light of day. One of my favorites is an early draft of the album *Oh Mercy*'s "Shooting Star" (1989), handwritten on pinkish Regency Hotel stationery. Utterly unlike the recorded version, this draft tells the story of Esau and Jacob:

1. Esau was a dangerous man
He hated his brother, his brother ran
His father said to *him*, go possess the land
Do what you gotta do
Seen a—[a shooting star tonight and I thought of you]

2. Esau founded Rome & Rome never fell
He was a man of experience, a man of hell
Think about it when you hear the next church bell
It ain't ringing for the chosen few
Seen a—

3. Some people say a man will betray your trust
That he sleeps with the devil & he's buried in lust
Weird strange mixture of breath and dust
Hard to tell who is who
Seen—[5]

Two verses before these are x-ed out and ten verses follow, with one "Xtra verse." The marvel of this strange reflection on lust and power and betrayal is that, despite its alien lyric (to anyone who knows the song), we cannot read it without hearing Dylan singing the version we know. This is what makes the archive such a delight. Despite merely *reading* all those words typed and corrected by Dylan; preserved in his autograph cursive on ordinary foolscap, hotel stationery, notepads, and family memo paper; or scribbled on matchbooks and ticket stubs and envelopes—all those words gathered from a half-century of industry and inspiration—despite reading rather than hearing them, I was able to imagine Dylan's performance lifting off the page.

I have worked in many archives around the world in pursuit of Renaissance and early modern textual gems. Usually, finding a text is its own reward. There is an autotelic element to the discovery: that is, reading a newly unearthed archival item, whether it is written in fifteenth-century Neo-Latin or seventeenth-century English—a poem, a play, or even a sermon—is largely an end in itself. But the Dylan archive produces something more. Every textual discovery contains a true bonus: even in a few lyrics scribbled on a sheet of notepaper we hear the voice and guitar, the harmonica, and the various backing bands. Because so many Dylan songs already preexist as sounds replaying in our memories, the archival discoveries carry a resonance I've never experienced in any other kind of documentary research.

My experience at the archive confirmed my long-standing belief in the necessity of a book analyzing Dylan's compositional method. This method is the key not only to understanding his predecessors' influence and his genre-bending lyrical experimentation but above all to comprehending his performative originality. I would have liked to insert links to Dylan's "delivery" at every quotation, or somehow to make the book more interactive, allowing readers to summon the recordings whenever I mention them. Yet, despite the versatile capabilities of electronic publication, print remains print, without sound or magical links to a complementary set of prelisted recordings.[6] I can only urge readers to keep their music-delivery device handy so they can play the lines and stanzas as I quote them.

Speaking of quotation—by long established convention, critics tend to weave bits of Dylan songs into their prose without quotation marks, often with Procrustean force. This tendency can quickly become annoying or mawkish, and I hope that when I indulge in it (which I can't resist doing from time to time) the result is trenchant, amusing, and apt. To which end: let me echo a very early song and begin by asserting that I don't want to biographize, taxonomize, petrify, or psychoanalyze Bob Dylan. Nothing so ambitious. Nor—and this is underscored—do I want to justify or provide excuses for what many critics, bloggers, and scholars have labeled borrowing or plagiarism.

This is a study of Dylan's method of imitation, which inevitably evokes the question of violations and excessive (unattributed) borrowing. Judgments on this question tend to divide along party lines, with the Dylan apologists defending the master's hand and the Dylan skeptics (who are legion) hurling allegations all over the media and internet. For better or worse, this book is neither a defense of Dylan nor an indictment. While I occasionally refer to plagiarism, this is a study of methodology, not morality. Using my background as a scholar trained in Renaissance studies, I want to show how *imitatio* contributes to Dylan's method of composition and how that method, which is anachronistic, leads him to resist influence in the conventional, modern sense. This resistance—or, more precisely, the valence of imitatio over influence—is what distinguished Bob Dylan as an "original," a highly tendentious word whose meaning fluctuates from era to era. Originality and imitation are, at once, critical judgments and methodologies. Emphasis on judgment has obscured the importance, and even the existence, of methodology.

But originality is only as good as its origin. Dylan claimed often to be seeking the "sound of the street" in his music, and it's not unreasonable to conclude that his lyrics, in striving to complement that sound, reproduce the artistic mélange of the Village—but translated to a world historical scale: "Shakespeare, *he's* in the alley . . ." ("Stuck Inside of Mobile with the Memphis Blues Again," 1966); "Mona Lisa must have had the highway blues" ("Visions of Johanna," 1966); "Madame Butterfly she lulled me to sleep" ("Someone's Got a Hold of My Heart" [*Infidels* outtake, 1983]); recorded on *Empire Burlesque* as "Tight Connection to My Heart," 1985); "it's like I'm stuck inside a painting / That's hanging in the Louvre" ("Don't Fall Apart on Me Tonight," 1983); "Michelangelo could've carved out your features" ("Jokerman" 1983); "Ezra Pound and T. S. Eliot fighting in the Captain's Tower" ("Desolation Row" 1965); and effectively all of "When I Paint My Masterpiece" (1966–67 [recorded with the Band at Big Pink]; 1971, *Greatest Hits Vol. II*; 1975, *Basement Tapes*). But it is not merely the artistic or literary icons integrated into a song that merge posterity and the street. Myriad fictional characters are given parity with those icons, from Cinderella, Ophelia, Romeo, and "Nero's Neptune" (whoever he is)—all appearing in "Desolation Row"—to Odysseus strapped to the mast ("Seeing the Real You at Last" 1985) and such obscurities as the 1966 "Sad-Eyed Lady" reference to John Steinbeck: "With your sheet-metal memory of Cannery Row."

Many of Dylan's musical quotations and variations, allusions, referential narratives (such as refitted ballads), and recast forms are readily familiar, especially to initiated listeners: among the most prominent are "Hard Rain" (a refitted "Lord Randall") and "Masters of War" ("Nottamun Town") from *Freewheelin'* (1963), along with "I Dreamed I Saw Saint Augustine" ("Joe Hill") from *John Wesley Harding* (1968). There are also less familiar and less obvious recastings, some of which raise eyebrows, such as the 2020 "False Prophet" from *Rough and Rowdy Ways*, which uses a guitar lead from the 1954 "If Lovin' Is Believin'" by Billy "The Kid" Emerson.[7] Dylan's songs are like tropes of the older ones, turning an earlier, largely inapplicable cultural meaning into a newly pertinent lyric or riff. This is by no means Dylan's literary invention, even if he was among the first to demonstrate his skill at it. Like all artists, Dylan refigures what he cites, taking command of and conspicuously resituating images, characters, and musical accompaniment. These refigurations can shift from predictable borrowings to arbitrary displacements in the flash of a verse, or even a line.

> Cinderella she seems so easy
> "It takes one to know one," she smiles
> And puts her hands into her back pocket
> Bette Davis style
> And Romeo comes in moanin'
> "You Belong to Me," I believe
> And someone turns to him
> And says, "You better leave."
> ("Desolation Row")

This is more than simply an aggregation of allusions. The verse logic of these lines is associative rather than surrealistic, more Rimbaud's "opéra-comique" than Breton's shattered imagery. Despite critics' claims regarding the Surrealism of the mid-sixties' lyrics, Dylan does not in fact follow Breton and Jean Schuster in declaring he has banished clarity (*J'ai banni le clair*); nor do his lyrics deliberately confound and frustrate (*déconcerter*); nor, above all, do they seek "to ring in the riot" (*sonner l'émeute*).[8] On the contrary, Dylan's lyrics are *associative* rather than confounding. Eschewing a call to riot, the songs strive for coherence amid the cultural jumble. The Surrealist arrogance of purposefully undermining sense and fomenting aesthetic riot are a far cry from Dylan's imitations and extensions of the traditional past. The Surrealists break with the past absolutely: this is how they banish clarity. Dylan rearranges and supersedes the past predominantly to extend clarity, leavening his effort with a ludic mask of the opéra-comique: Einstein playing an electric violin. This is his charm and arrogance.

In the stanza from "Desolation Row" quoted above, Dylan not only gestures toward fairy tales, Hollywood movies, and Shakespeare. He also inserts a self-referential element, adding his own song "She Belongs to Me" (1965) to the mix—a poetic device he deploys from time to time throughout his work: in "Dark Eyes" (1985) for instance, there's the line "Oh, the French girl, she's in paradise," which irresistibly alludes to the French girl speaking to Shakespeare in "Stuck Inside of Mobile." The richness of Dylan's allusive pattern, his self-imitation, and the constant quotation from traditional American blues and folk music together provide the material basis for my book. As he gets older, Dylan sophisticates his ludic associations, and, with an unparalleled mnemonic intuition, interweaves discoveries from a vastly increased trove of traditional song, poetry, drama, film, and the plastic arts.

The Myth before the Myth

Dylan's compositional method, as Richard Thomas and others have shown, cannot be reduced to one practice. It would be impossible to wall off pre-Romantic, let alone premodern, imitation from Dylan's compositional style. While his work has strong and unexplored affinities with pre-Romantic imitatio, it simultaneously combines intertextuality, collage, and high-Modernist, avant-garde forms of allusion. Mimesis—the imitation of nature rather than of precursor artists—also plays a part in Dylan's compositions: in the verisimilitude of "Highlands" (1997), for example, the "natural" is heightened to the point almost of banality; much earlier, in "Mama, You Been on My Mind" (1964), Dylan adds a playful inversion to the "mirror up to nature" (Hamlet's Aristotelian definition of mimesis):

> When you wake up in the mornin,' baby, look inside your mirror
> You know I won't be next to you, you know I won't be near
> I'd just be curious to know if you can see yourself as clear
> As someone who has had you on his mind.

This is the last stanza of the song. Here the speaker shifts the responsibility for holding up the mirror and creating a personality to his addressee. What she or he sees in the mirror will be the new mimetic creation.

In "Chimes of Freedom" Dylan sings of "the poet and the painter / Behind their rightful time"—at least he sings that line on *Another Side* (1964). In contrast, in his 1964 Royal Albert Hall performance, not untypically, he completely changes the lines: "Tolling . . . for the poet and the painter / Who lights up his rightful time." The inversion captures a paradox: the poet and the painter can fall short in cultural value to their "rightful" times, and, somehow simultaneously, they can light up those same times. It's as if the traditional *paragone*, or competition, of poetry and painting had led us to fall through the looking-glass. Maybe only there, in a new reality of parallel artistic interdependence, with an active mimesis, do the chimes of freedom toll.

Writing about Dylan's "Desolation Row," Frank Kermode speaks of "deliberate cultural jumble" and "history seen flat," of "so much unreality against the background of Desolation Row, the flat and dusty truth, the myth before the myth began."[9]

Like so many Dylan compositions, "Desolation Row" seems to combine hotchpotch with portent. Kermode, in any case, is referring to Wallace Stevens's "Notes toward a Supreme Fiction," an incomparably capacious poem:

> But the first idea was not to shape the clouds
> In imitation. The clouds preceded us
>
> There was a muddy centre before we breathed.
> There was a myth before the myth began,
> Venerable and articulate and complete.[10]

The speaker of the poem instructs an "ephebe" (youth) to "Begin . . . by perceiving the idea / Of this invention, this invented world." And Kermode places Dylan's speaker in the same puzzling place as the ephebe, trying to perceive "the idea / Of this invention." Imitation, according to Stevens, is not the first idea. Imitation, it would seem, is the myth that proceeds from the precursor myth of the muddy center. "The flat and dusty truth, the myth before the myth began," is tantamount, for Kermode, to Dylan's "Notes toward a Supreme Imitation."

For Dylan, art is a double-edged sword, offering on one side an escape from the drudgery of Maggie's Farm and, on the other, from the trap of the Captain's Tower. It requires a Janus-faced figure to transfigure the past: only such a figure can capture "the myth before the myth began" and remythicize the future by transcending what Kermode calls "history seen flat."

The Janus-faced image characterizes this book. In bringing a subject that has usually been reserved for scholarly investigation to Dylan studies, I look back to the past and into the future by opening the topic of Renaissance imitatio to a larger contemporary audience. For decades, literary scholars were unable to do what the Nobel Committee did in one stroke—to make Dylan part of the canon. And Dylan's new literary status makes it possible for this book to create a new audience, one that combines scholars and fans, literary and folk culture. Written accessibly, for intellectually sophisticated readers, this new argument fits premodern imitatio into the sphere of contemporary cultural studies. This would not have been possible at any other time. But with the advent of the Dylan archive and the awarding of the Nobel Prize in 2016, Dylan studies are in flux: scholars and critics, journalists, essayists, online researchers, and bloggers are coming together in unexpected ways.

Dylan's earliest recorded performances and his earliest composition intimate a commitment to recreating America as experienced through what was at the time a marginalized musical culture. This has been said in many ways over the years, and in any case, this commitment alone would not distinguish him—others in the fifties and sixties had similar aims. But Dylan is different from the others in the copiousness of his commitment and in his imitation of those earlier marginalized musical cultures. From the sharecropper songs to Delta blues to highway ballads, the chameleonlike Dylan adapted and adopted—and some might say colonized—the authority of African American musical innovation, grafting it to the preexisting revival of English folk ballads. Dylan's originality in doing this outstripped his contemporaries, especially once he began writing songs.

This book is important now, I believe, because it spans what was until the present a gulf between popular and scholarly culture. I will demonstrate how, even in his most demotic modes, Dylan practiced a form of "proto-mythmaking" as a form of imitatio, the technique of "invention" (or discovery) practiced by ancient and Renaissance poets in adapting predecessors' work. Imitatio is the means by which poets like Dylan manifest originality in the word's literal sense, deriving from a source, or *origo*. But imitatio also allows poets to express originality—in the modern sense of creativity—through new combinations and revisions of past works. The poetic practice of imitation, which extends to the other arts, predates the Romantic perspective on originality and creative imagination. Imitation evades influence, even if at times the line between them is blurred.

Dylan's lyrical postures might suggest a consummately post-Romantic, "avant-garde" consciousness, for which being "original," in the eighteenth-century sense of the word, means being inspired from within. But, on the contrary, Dylan's creative methodology more closely resembles that of classical and Renaissance (early modern) authors who sought truth and beauty externally and historically, in the absorption and transfiguration of their sources.

The companion to imitatio is, inevitably, poetic genealogy, and Dylan's attitude toward artistic permanence grows out of an ideal of originality by which he raises his virtuoso status to the plane of his most admired predecessors. His sense of legacy, his palpable struggle against and collaboration with his lyrical and musical forebears, has resonated since his first album, when he said farewell to Woody Guthrie (something I discuss in chapter 1). The intuitively revisionary drive of his lyrics and performances, while dazzling in its newness, inevitably reveals his effort to affix himself to a traditional, and highly selective, literary-musical genealogy. And, at his best, he strives in his music to supersede that genealogy and to establish his art, in all its mutability, as equal to and woven into the wider cultural tapestry of creative media. This is a lofty goal for a songwriter and rock star, but Dylan's imitative technique has helped him fashion a poetics of performative originality to warrant his ambition.

The Turning of the Key

A patently nostalgic movement, the second folk revival survived as a concatenation of role-playing postures, a pride of stylists. It was a matter of seeming rather than being. The revival depended for its bona fides on the renewed authenticity of embracing supposedly purer musical forms and of making the "roots" your own, even when your connection to the traditional canon was one of choice rather than birth and environment. Lead Belly was dead, and the living originals among roots musicians—such as Mississippi John Hurt, Lightnin' Hopkins, or Doc Watson—appeared on the Newport stages like superannuated artifacts excavated from the American earth. Woody Guthrie lay traveled out and nearly dead in a New Jersey hospital. His Dust Bowl pedigree was unquestioned and every folk singer shared the myth of Woody's purity, but his presence as a performer had evaporated. His songs lived on in an American vault, for all intents and purposes petrified in the folk repertoire. He too had become an artifact and, honoris causa, the folk revival had consigned him permanently to its private Rushmore.

In effect, the shepherd of the folk revival was Pete Seeger, who, as Benjamin Filene says, "was the archetypal folk stylist, moving from privileged background to become the personification of folk music to millions of Americans."[11] Seeger represented—or posed as—a virtual icon of authenticity, the faithful transmitter of *pure* folk music. Authenticity was, however, the myth on which the folk myth was founded. Seeger and his peers were merely the culmination of half a century of racially and culturally segregated music: ironically the motivation of their social activism, their promise to deliver "roots" folk music, was born of an academic distillation of purportedly pure racial and ethnic songs from commercial pop songs. But this distinction didn't truly reflect the character of Southern music, which, in its ventriloquized transformations, formed the bedrock of the folk revival.

The folkloric basis of Seeger's revival is an indictment of his and his father's generation of authenticity-mongers, men and women who manufactured a racially divided Southern canon. Karl Hagstrom Miller, in a brilliant landmark study, has identified the sources of what he calls "segregating sound." His analysis of minstrelsy authenticity and folkloric authenticity has a bearing on the folk music world into which Dylan arrived. According to Miller, "Minstrelsy taught that authenticity was performative. Genuine black music emerged from white bodies . . . Minstrel authenticity was not rooted in history, heritage, or collective memory. It was founded on consensus. Like visitors to P. T. Barnum's museum, minstrel fans decided to embrace the blackface humbug."[12] In contrast to this consensus, "Folkloric authenticity maintained that truthful music came from outside the marketplace. Music primarily was a form of expression, not only of individual feelings or collective culture but also of essential racial characteristics, capacities, and stages of evolution."[13] Miller's categories might seem polarized, but they set the groundwork for the second folk revival and seem proleptic in regard to Dylan's ability to combine genres and traditions.

Let me quote a bit more of Miller's contrast between marketplace consensus and folkloric "purity." The mark—or mask (or masque)—of authenticity is, after all, a crucial critical bugbear in Dylan studies. "Folklore," Miller points out, "located authenticity in isolation from modern life and modern media. Minstrelsy, on the other hand, suggested that musical authenticity was a product of racial contact and interaction through the market. Music was not primarily a form of self-expression but a method of play-acting. If minstrel authenticity maintained the mutability of racial identity, folkloric authenticity posited its fixity."[14] But Miller quickly shows the hollowness of the notion of folkloric fixity. "People's music worlds," he asserts, "were less defined by who they were—in terms of racial, class, or regional identity—than by what music they had the opportunity to hear. . . . the mass-produced music that flooded the South in the last decades of the nineteenth century did not necessarily cause crises of identity or disrupt long-honored musical folkways." But here's the rub. Miller continues, explaining how folklore undermined its own supposed aims: "Most observers agree that black and white southerners sang mass-produced pop songs. The fact that this music has not played a prominent role in histories of southern music, it seems, can be explained in one of two ways. Either southern people repudiated it, refused to contaminate their regional music with its presence, or chroniclers of southern music dismissed commercial pop as immaterial to southern culture. Evidence supports the latter conclusion."[15] This is not the place (nor am I equipped) to engage Miller's study fully. But his premise supports the paradox of the American folk revivals. They inverted the order of things. While appearing to rescue traditional music through performance, they in fact suppressed it by creating a scholarly version of the musical past. Predictably, this version of the past, like all cultural genealogies, was created in its own image—which, at bottom, is a form of self-creation risen from the ashes of pedantry.

Whether he realized it or simply intuited it, Dylan's mixed style mirrored the eclectic mixture of genres performed by blues artists like Robert Johnson. Discussing Dylan's *Love and Theft*, an album named after one of his books, Eric Lott reminds us that Dylan "generated more than one mask to handle the cultural mash he advanced, where, as he put it in an interview, the original influences are represented but not anymore in the original form, like barley into whiskey."[16] As the song goes, "You can come back but you can't come back all the way" ("Mississippi"); Dylan's distillation of his influences, which chapter 1 explores in terms of imitatio, transforms them without losing their shape.

This is Dylan's style of originality, which, as Lott puts it, "often involves trafficking in someone else's stuff." But Lott clarifies this "trafficking" in no uncertain terms: "Authenticity," he insists, "is a ludicrous, even pernicious, category, but that doesn't mean the dilemmas of cultural appropriation are easy to ford. If Dylan's version of this mash is a little sour, it's because it's so fully aged. Dylan could only have made [*"Love and Theft"*] at sixty, not just because it showcases a ripped and ragged voice but also because of its incredible range, literary, musical, and philosophical."[17] Lott might have added that only Dylan could have made this album, not because he is the most authentic (or ever was), but because only he has the poetic and musical memory to rival the great vatic poets of the past, as 2020's *Rough and Rowdy Ways* brings to the fore.

Lott's suggestion that authenticity is a pernicious category highlights the difference between Woody Guthrie and Pete Seeger in Dylan's early days on the folk music scene. Contrary to the prevailing view, Dylan's great Other was not Woody Guthrie. It was and could only have been Pete Seeger, because it was Seeger, not Guthrie, who was trying to establish his and his colleagues' authenticity as folk singers—just as Seeger's father and his generation of folklorists had blunderingly tried to establish the category of "authentic folk song." Guthrie was a genealogical precursor, an undisputed original. Seeger, however, was a transplant from a different class. He was more than just a figurehead like Woody, Son House, Mississippi John Hurt, and the others: he was an active propagator of the music his father's generation had deemed "roots" music.

Seeger sang with the fury of the convert and became a vibrant, proselytizing embodiment of the traditional way. Unfortunately, and enduringly, the so-called "tradition" he helped to forge was the result of a tendentious academic project of musical segregation. His rectitude and popularity, his patrician bearing and his folklore pedigree, stood out as beacons of light to the folk revival, while, ironically, casting long shadows over imitators of the younger generation. A Harvard dropout, scion of a wealthy family, and son of academic folklorist Charles Seeger, Seeger strummed a twanging banjo and sang with as much ungrammatical conviction as he could muster. For example,

> I'm bound to go where there ain't no snow
> Where the sleet don't fall
> And the wind don't blow
> In the Big Rock Candy Mountain.

This song not only mimics a hobo's speech—it also taps the Depression-era Tom Joad experience of hard traveling, freight trains, railroad enforcers, and jailhouses. Seeger had in fact experienced a bit of hard traveling as a young man—by choice, not necessity—but "Big Rock Candy Mountain" still sounds theatrical on the privileged Seeger's tongue.

Yet his sincerity left no doubt, which made his outsider status rare as well as ambiguous. Unlike minstrel singers "playing stylized versions of African American songs" or "singing cowboys . . . from Mount Vernon, New York; Fresno, California, and Cincinnati," Seeger identified with his music.[18] He bifurcated theatrical pretense (stylizing) with sincere feeling. This bifurcation became the hallmark of the folk music world Dylan emerged from. With Lee Hayes and other fellow travelers of the Weavers, Seeger delivered the message of peace and resistance to the masses. For more than half a century no one doubted his idealism, his leftist politics, or his social commitment. And his admiration for the music of the Folk, though slightly paternalistic, never faltered, something he proved in concerts, introductions to singers, in articles and books, and one recording after another. But, while this might seem heretical to say, Seeger's quirky adaptations of different vernacular registers finally add up to acting a part ham-fistedly, even if in a good cause. Just listen sometime to his "Black Girl." Accompanied by the guitar's heavy bass rhythm, his voice starts out low, then catches (unconvincingly) with high bluesy notes as he sings the old lament:

> Black girl, black girl, don't lie to me,
> Tell me, where did you stay last night?
>
> In the pine, in the pine, where the sun never shine,
> And I shivered the whole night through.

"Never shine," a predicate construction drawn from Black idiolect, sounds absurd in Seeger's crisp enunciation. The whole performance is a frank attempt to imitate the style of Lead Belly, from whom he took guitar lessons in the 1940s: similar chords and the chunky downstroke-strumming between stanzas recall the master like recognizable brushstrokes. Maybe this imitation was meant as homage, but the inadequacy of the interpretation only highlights the distance in class and experience between the performers: Seeger sounds like Seeger, a derivative and watered-down version of a true American original.

Not a few folk stylists coarsened their voices with bluesy gruffness and hoked-up their diction with countrified, sharecropper idioms. For every imitator of the smooth Kingston Trio, there was, in contrast, a Karen Dalton, Dave Van Ronk, or Mark Spoelstra. As Timothy Hampton says, "Dylan was surrounded by singers trying different styles: the queen of folk music, Joan Baez, sang ancient ballads in an angelic voice; Dave Van Ronk, an early mentor, specialized in Blues and early ragtime tunes; Mike Seeger and The New Lost City Ramblers sang in the accents of Appalachia; John Hammond Jr. became a blues specialist."[19] Bob Dylan was simply a more persuasive stylist than most: he performed those "pure" forms better than Pete Seeger and more persuasively than the predominantly white, mostly middle-class singers on MacDougal street—not only, as Marcus puts it, more "powerfully and more nakedly" but also with a renewed sense of lost originality.[20] Hampton adds that Dylan chose a "set of characteristics for his songwriting persona," and that he focused on "the theme of mobility" and "the implications of that theme for language, space, and identity," ultimately giving it "symbolic and even political meaning."[21]

This is another way of describing Dylan's approach to imitation: the act of choosing from among different styles (past and present), digesting those styles, and producing a unique blend in performance and composition. As he absorbed influences, even openly acknowledged them, he somehow "naturalized" the songs he performed and wrote. "This [was] an art," as Shakespeare's Polixenes puts it, "which does not mend nature—change it rather—but / The art itself is nature."[22] Dylan's irresistible magnetism forged from an already receptive audience a dedicated group of followers: they turned toward him with a kind of charisma-hunger, a need fulfilled by Dylan's "nakedly" desophisticated performances. Especially as he began writing and performing his own incomparable early songs, his charismatic-musical authority grew. He became Seeger's "pride and hope," the ewe lamb of the second folk movement.[23] According to Marcus,

> after "A Hard Rain's A-Gonna Fall," "With God on Our Side," and "The Times They Are A-Changin,'" he was no longer merely a singer, or a songwriter, or even a poet, let alone simply a folk musician. In a signal way, he was the Folk, and also a prophet. As he sang and wrote he was the slave on the auction block, the whore chained to her bed, a questioning youth, an old man looking back in sorrow and regret. As the familiar standards of the folk revival faded from his repertoire, he became the voice left after the bomb had fallen, the voice of the civil rights movement; then he became the voice of his times and the conscience of his generation. The sound of his hammered acoustic guitar and pealing harmonica became a kind of free-floating trademark, like the peace symbol, signifying determination and honesty in a world of corruption and lies.[24]

Marcus's short-form curriculum vitae is perceptive: Dylan inhabited his songs and interpreted them at the same time; his vocal distinctiveness of phrasing and breath control resulted in what Harold Bloom would call a "strong misreading" of the traditional canon. Although Dylan was quickly unveiled as a middle-class Jewish striver, no one at the time (which is the time that counts) seems to have been as exercised about his roughened voice and Dust Bowl posturing as the legions of later critics. This in and of itself is a lesson in belatedness.

Dylan's approach to the traditional canon consisted of more than vocal restylings and "strong misreading." His syncretism began early, before he began adding modern poetry to old tunes. He reinvented the canon itself by his performances, characteristically mystifying and satisfying audiences at the same time. His originality seemed simultaneously to embrace and defy the influence of the past. *Influence* implies an imposition of the past on the present. In contrast, Dylan embodied the past through imitation: as James Ackerman puts it, "Imitation stressed community, the solidarity that the maker of the present experiences with his ancestors and teachers."[25] The ideal of the folk tradition was (and is) precisely this, a solidarity with the past. As the most persuasive "maker of the present," Dylan performed the past, not as a schoolroom exercise in the Lomax-Seeger mode but as a vital demonstration of solidarity. Because he, too, was white and middle-class, his detractors said that for all his originality he was still a fraud, a con man, a snake oil merchant (and there was sometimes a patina of anti-Semitism in the remarks). But Dylan conveyed a relation to his predecessors that superseded the patronizing posture of the self-appointed discoverers, rescuers, and conservators. This assimilation and *transformation* of tradition distinguished Dylan from the most prevalent (and pedigreed) delusion among his early peers—that is, that the traditional music of the past could be reproduced exactly. In other words, Dylan rejected slavish imitation as a futile aim. Instead, he "imitated perfect," which meant that he digested and deliberately transformed everything he assimilated. Thus, through perfect or proper imitation, Dylan's models live and thrive.

Transformation involves more than assimilation, as Ackerman recognizes: the "maker," he notes, through imitation engages his or her "ancestors . . . in a contest of skill and imagination."[26] But this notion of "contest," while reminiscent of Bloom's brilliant description of the *agon* the modern poet experiences as a result of the influence of the past, describes a patently different dynamic. Speaking of premodern times, Ackerman explains: "The main difference is that imitation was . . . an explicit principle of creative formation and procedure, while influence has been a relationship that has oppressed the modern maker."[27] In this distinction lies Dylan's uniqueness, or at least his perceived uniqueness: he is not oppressed by the past. On the contrary, in style and composition, Dylan merges with the past, instantaneously (and persuasively) conveying a genealogical rather than an agonistic relationship to his predecessors.

Another Side: Idolatry versus Imitatio

Although finished with idol worship himself, as he points out in his jacket notes to *Joan Baez in Concert, Part 2* (1963), Dylan acknowledges the crucial need for a stepping-stone in his—and presumably others'—artistic development. Perhaps this is the key to his sense of genealogical development:

> But I learned t' choose my idols well
> T' be my voice an' tell my tale
> An' help me fight my phantom brawl

He is describing a kind of collaborative ventriloquism and the development of an aesthetic based on his idols' subjects:

> An' my first idol was Hank Williams
> For he sang about the railroad lines
> An' the iron bars an' rattlin' wheels
> Left no doubt that they were real
> An' my first symbol was the word "beautiful"[28]

The last line contains a surprisingly linguistic remark, parsing a poetics of shifted registers and revealing Dylan's technical facility ("technical" in the sense of *technē*, craft). In terms of idols, the passage is clear: selectively imitating Hank Williams's symbols ("railroad lines . . . iron bars an' rattlin' wheels") produced more than merely a borrowed set of railroad symbols. It produced a sense of aesthetic perfection so real that Dylan recategorized a descriptor, "beautiful," as a symbol.[29]

> For the railroad lines were not beautiful
> They were smoky black an' gutter-colored
> An' filled with stink an' soot an' dust
> An' I'd judge beauty with these rules
> An' accept it only 'f it was ugly
> An' if I could touch it with my hand
> For it's only then I'd understand
> An' say "yeah this's real"

There's something both callow and self-confident in the pat inversion of conventional beauty and ugliness—but, of course, he was so much older then and also younger than that at the same time. The self-confidence grows as, in his poetic imagination, he breaks away from his idols:

> In later times my idols fell
> For I learned that they were only men
> An' had reasons for their deeds
> 'F which weren't mine not mine at all
> An' no more on them could I depend
> But what I learned from each forgotten god
> Was that the battlefield was mine alone
> An' only I could cast my stone[30]

The Davidic image stands out, painting the lone traveler as the toppler of Goliaths down the road and underscoring the narrative's agonistic theme: early phrases like "phantom brawl" and "the battlefield was mine alone" tie up with the final refrain, "I'll sing my song like a rebel child."

Written as they are in an Iron Range, Guthriesque *Kunstsprache*—Dylan's 1963 faux-Oklahoma "bop prosody"—the jacket notes are lengthy and ostensibly autobiographical. They record the construction of a fortified and personal ars poetica and proceed to detail how the walls came tumbling down when finally Baez's voice came bursting through. He begins with personal rivalry, the agon between representatives of two utterly different kinds of beauty, remembering others' praise for Baez's voice:

> "A thing a beauty" people said
> "Wondrous sounds" writers wrote
> "I hate that kind a sound" said I
> "The only beauty's ugly, man
> The crackin' shakin' breakin' sounds're
> The only beauty I understand"[31]

But the ground of the debate shifts and Dylan's strict opposition between ugliness and beauty collapses in an instant when, "In Woodstock at a painter's house . . . I lit a cigarette an' laughed / An' gulped red wine . . . An' the room it whirled an' twirled an' sailed."[32] How significant is the painter's house? It might be that casting this sibling artist as the host is meant to signal, or literally represent, the new ground of the debate. Possibly, the agon between ugliness and conventional beauty (Bob's aesthetic versus Joan's) has been transformed into a traditional paragone—a battle between painters and poets—or an engagement between the sibling arts, because in that instant when the autobiographical speaker's hostility melts away, he recognizes the value not only of another artist but arguably of another art form.

His moral resistance low after gulping red wine, the speaker finds himself "without no choice / 'Cept to listen t' her voice." Faint praise perhaps, but the result is revelatory, a unique moment of revision to Dylan's rules of beauty. His tolerance expands as his grip on sobriety weakens and suddenly Baez's voice is given an idol's weight: it is "like the others who have taught me well / Not about themselves but me."[33] This is a pardonably self-centered interpretation in an autobiography. But, significantly, the speaker makes it clear that it is the disembodied voice that teaches him, as if he is encountering a form of art different from his own—different and parallel, a patently Other art. This sibling status, if that's what it is, does not exactly include the artist, but this is where Dylan's speaker's poetics get tricky. Certainly, it is high praise to move Baez's voice (if not Baez herself) into the company of Hank Williams, Woody Guthrie, Robert Johnson, Charley Patton, Cisco and Sonny, and Lead Belly too. Significantly, Baez only seems to gain respect after the discovery that her art form, represented by her voice (as Dylan's is represented by his), might contain something of aesthetic value. Yet she is almost immediately divided from her voice, which the speaker, grateful and unexpectedly self-deprecating, experiences as the messenger of elusive beauty:

> Oh how feeble foolish small an' sad
> 'F me t' think that beauty was
> Only ugliness an' muck
> When it's really jus' a magic wand
> That waves an' teases at my mind[34]

Dylan's portrait of a young artist, complete with its redefinition of the road-poet's resources—exile and cunning, but not silence—now comes into focus. It is a consummate coming-of-age narrative, a tale of a flight inspired by rebellion and tempered by conversion. Taking the usual license afforded by fiction, the pseudo-autobiographical author engineers a perfect bridge to the past—incidentally adumbrating the same disregard for the "truth" that so exercised critics of *Chronicles, Volume One* a lifetime later. In the Baez liner notes it is as if Jack Kerouac and Woody Guthrie met Philip Sidney's *Defence of Poetry* on the new pasture of American poetic expression—a 1960s album jacket. The material text itself effects the revolution.

Based on his attitude toward his idols, the speaker redefines his personal aesthetic, using the jacket poem's refrain—"An' I walked my road an' sung my song"—as an identity marker, pitting the consistency of the repeated line against the new impressions and gradual changes of the "I." During his journey from muck to magic wand, he manages, insouciantly, to reinvent truth and beauty, those most Romantic (Keatsian) concepts. But the reinvention is not genuinely Romantic. On the contrary, as the speaker makes amply clear, his sense of beauty derives from a form of Senecan imitatio and a return to past origins—literal "origin"-ality—for the judicial plundering of idols and models. The word "reinvention" is derived from the Latin *invenire*, "to discover, to come upon," as seen in the Virgilian quotation on the Nobel Medal. Reinventing the truth-beauty conflux for the American present is tantamount to discovering it in past and present models, weaving the intertextual fabric Thomas and other critics have described so well. If, as Dylan's speaker says on the album jacket, beauty is "really jus' a magic wand / That waves an' teases," it is because the source of beauty cannot be within oneself or discovered only through one's own vision, such as the idealization of ugliness. Only the combination of models attains the magic, and the tease is the multiplicity of visions, which, like the "ghost of electricity," are often glowing, vital remnants of the dead.

No Song Unthinged

Still, not even genealogical relationships are free of conflict. Because musical and poetic genealogies are largely manufactured, they often bear the scars of competition with antecedents. Dylan's genealogical tree is no exception. It is doubtful he would have needed a primer on how to be competitive. But it adds grist to the agonistic side of things to find that he apparently possessed a 1965 anthology of poems called *A Controversy of Poets*, and that, as figure 1 shows, he scribbled notes to himself to check several pages in the volume. The title of the book almost sounds like a generic name akin to "a murder of crows" or "a pride of lions." But, in format at least, it is a typical handbook of contemporary American poets. The "controversy," it turns out, is in fact acted out by a controversy of editors in postscripts I and II. Paris Leary and Robert Kelly polarize the criteria of the collection, as if themselves setting the tone of controversy. A more overbearing editorial comment is difficult to imagine than Kelly's postscript. Yet it contains the seeds of Dylan's transformation of traditional forms and the folk idiolect. "Literally perverse to me is the presumption or fatuity of some poets who choose to hum in the measures of Donne or Herbert about important human issues to a generation that has experienced Auschwitz, Nagasaki, Algeria, and the Congo. That is pure escapism, and can catch only the saturated ears of an audience attuned to the reviews and the world of little-magazine infighting. Nor is the perversion or betrayal simply a lack of cogent responsibility to the social and political world of the poet. More deeply, it is a betrayal too of the very achievement of the masters they follow, those masters who, whatever else their businesses, sang in their own voices in their own time."[35] In this last sentence Kelly might well have used the word *imitatio*. It's noteworthy perhaps that Robert Kelly is a professor and a staggeringly prolific poet himself, with over fifty books of poetry, ironically of the academic variety. He contends that the technique of imitating "those masters who . . . sang in their own voices in their own time" involves *not* betraying them with slavish mimicry. He elaborates on this theme, still exercised about contemporary uses of the past, and still polarizing, still proscriptive. But he also offers his dream of the ideal modern poem in language Dylan might well have taken to heart: "The work of Whitman or Rimbaud . . . has at last alerted us to the possibility of a poem that means something. I mean a poem that is not, like a tune we can choose to hear or to neglect, something for the sake of something else, like a print tacked up on the wall to hide the wall. I mean a poem that means something because it is no longer *about* something but *is* something: but, and this is all-important, a poem that, as a thing does not come to exist aesthetically and in remoteness, as a thing would be in a museum, unthinged, but as a thing would exist, and possess meaning, in a world of living men."[36] Robert Kelly brings us "inside the museums," where things are "unthinged." Dylan's notion of "infinity . . . on trial" lurks here, and this passage might well have provided Dylan with his own private "map of misreading."

Dylan's imaginative engagement with his "ancestors" manifested itself almost unconsciously. Noted particularly by musicians, Dylan's playing and singing, "his hammered acoustic guitar," revealed a new and uncanny—and to all

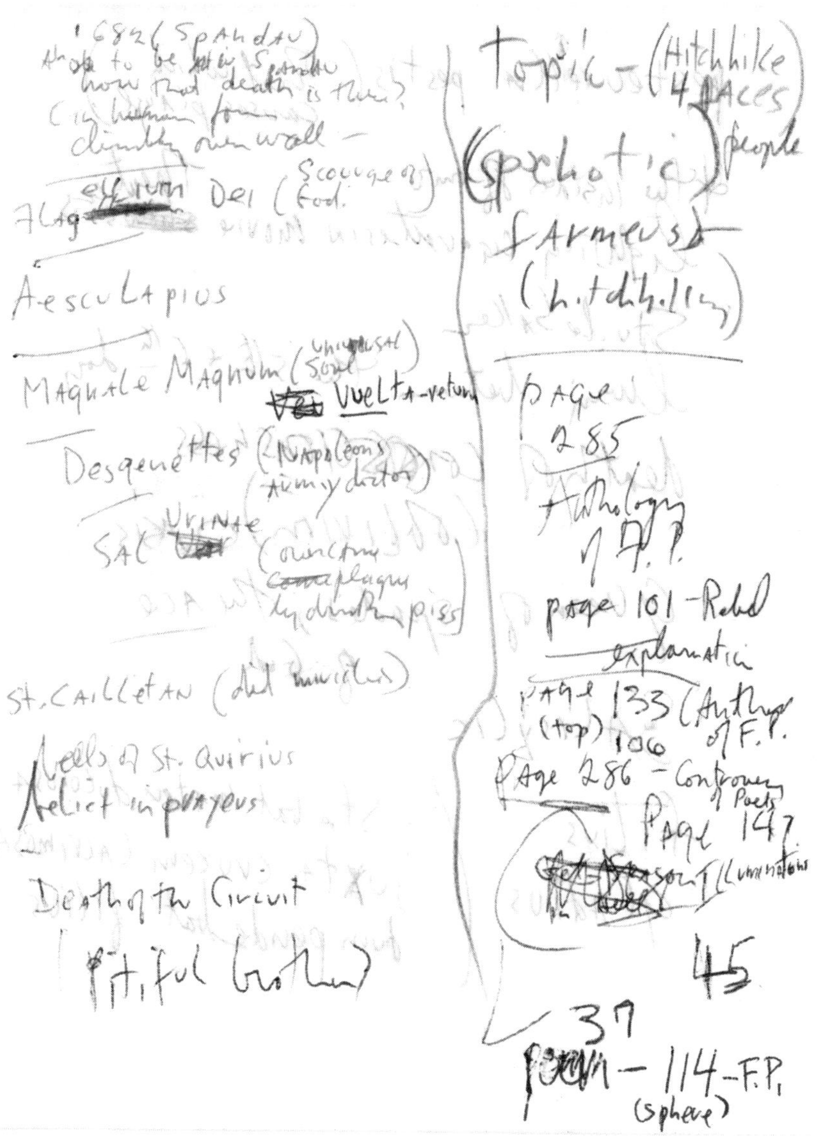

Figure 1. Dylan's notes referring to *Anthology of French Poets*. Courtesy of the Bob Dylan Archive® Collections, Tulsa, OK.

appearances unpremeditated—combination of rock rhythms with the folk idiom. Barbara Shutner saw Dylan's first performance at Gerdes Folk City on February 13, 1961: "In came this funny-looking kid one night, dressed as if he had just spent a year riding freight trains, and playing songs in a style that you could tap your feet to. Dylan's early style was a combination of blues, rock and country which caught on the very minute that he stepped on the stage at Gerde's [*sic*]."[37] The implication is that other folk singers didn't sing songs "you could tap your feet to." Shutner doesn't seem to be fooled by Dylan's bindlestiff costume; nor is she put off by it. Her remarks are interesting because, while we would no longer be surprised to hear Dylan's music described as "a combination of blues, rock and country," the innovation was striking at the time. John Bauldie casts the difference as a paradox: "Dylan just didn't sound anything like a Greenwich Village folk-singer. When he tries to sound like a folk-singer—as on 'Young but Growing' for example—he sounds slightly ridiculous; but when he sounds like a hillbilly, with his Hank Williams moans, Woody Guthrie licks, Jimmie Rodgers whoops and Little Richard cries, he makes all the regular folk-singers sound ridiculous."[38] Underlying this division between sounding ridiculous and making others sound ridiculous is the technique of imitatio. Dylan, in those earliest days, had only begun to imitate, digest, and transform his models. When Shutner and others saw his first performances, the rough edges of acquisition still showed. Dylan had yet to move from mimicry to genuine and productive imitation. But, by all accounts, he did this with uncanny speed. His technique of imitatio developed intuitively, making possible a brilliant progression of compositions, the supersession of his models, the link to parity with other artists in other media forms, and ultimately the means to debunk the myth of himself.

Whose Voice Is This?

Since Dylan first sang "Hey, Woody Guthrie, I know what you know" and "I'll know my song well before I start singing," the most common fallacy among listeners has been to conflate the homodiegetic narrator with Dylan himself. But this is mere fantasy. The separation between the narrator who also is a participant in a song should be obvious:

> While riding on a train going west
> I fell asleep to take my rest
> I dreamed a dream that made me sad
> Concerning myself and the first few friends I had
> ("Bob Dylan's Dream," 1963)

The temptation to list Dylan's "first few" early Village friends is almost irresistible, not least because Dylan uses his own (assumed) name in the song's title. But it would be more productive to isolate and distinguish the narrators in this stanza.

There are two, as always with a first-person narrative, the participant and the narrator. This is a homodiegetic text, in which both narrators are part of the same fiction. The performer of the song might suggest his or her identity with the narrators, but this identity is a mask. To insert the composer into the homodiegetic framework disrupts the narrative verisimilitude and skews the figurative balance.

The relationship of Bob Dylan the composer and performer to the usually unidentified speaker of the lyrics is important to understanding how the process of imitation functions in Dylan's songs. In a sense, biography has dogged Dylan interpretation. The Dylan-watchers, journalists, fans, and scholars—a vast panoply difficult to compare to the fanbase of any other living poet—have habitually hunted and tracked details of Dylan's life in the lyrics of the songs. This has had a deleterious effect on criticism.

Dylan does not write *chansons à clef*. Even if "it's for myself and my friends my stories are sung" ("Restless Farewell") and even if that line were genuinely autobiographical—which it patently is not, given it appears on a commercial recording—then the songs would still not be *about* "myself and my friends." As closely as scholars and Dylanologists—a distinction I make advisedly—have pored over such intimate recordings as those on *Blood on the Tracks* and *Desire*, the autobiographical parallels can only ever be wisps of speculation. As Thomas has suggested, "The most intensive meaningful variation of lyrics is found in the songs that have seemed most autobiographical, especially the songs of *Blood on the Tracks*, and particularly when the status of a relationship is at stake. It is as if Dylan is responding to biographical readings by essentially changing, and at times radically transforming, the singer's point of view."[39] Or, more accurately, underscoring that it is only the diegetic figure's point of view, and not a confessional or autobiographical expression.

A brief historical tour of the homodiegetic fallacy should prove the point. Is *Astrophil and Stella* autobiographical? Philip Sidney's Elizabethan sonnet sequence, indisputably written *à clef* for the amusement of the court, contains 132 different poems. The speaker (Astrophil) remains the same, as does the unattainable and voiceless object of his mostly foiled desire (Stella). But even in a format designed to be decoded, Astrophil's misadventures, desires, and flights of metaphorical excess could never be linked with confidence to Philip Sidney's real-life behavior. In truth, the narrative voice of *Astrophil and Stella* can never escape the delimitations of the poems' rhetorical needs. There is no Sidney in the sonnet sequence, only Sidney's characterization.

Similarly, Milton's apparently autobiographical "Methought I Saw My Late Espoused Saint" should not seduce the biographer. The homodiegetic figure may seem to collapse into the reality of the blind Milton dreaming about his second wife, recently deceased, who comes to him in a dream only to disappear "as day brought back my night." But the shock and poignancy, the moment of discovery, are fictions. Diegesis invariably prevails: Whitman's "I" in "Song of

Myself" might contain multitudes, but even if it can be lauded as American poetry's most intimate revelation of the self, it remains mediated by the nature of the poetic vehicle. The narrator can only *pose* as "Myself," which is something the ongoing revisions of the poem attest to. John Berryman, in *The Dream Songs*, is more unguarded than Whitman, closer to perforating the membrane between poet and speaker. Yet even his voice requires mediation.

Dylan embraces diegesis. He expressly rejects the identification of the speaker/singer in his lyrics with himself. As early as his interview with Gooding in 1962, Dylan had recognized the fundamental perspectival characteristic of composition, a fundamental often misunderstood by even the most sophisticated critics. Speaking of the "elephant lady" in the carnival he was pretending to have traveled with, he explains, "I wrote a song for her a long time ago. And lost it some place. It's just about speaking from first person, like here I am, and sort of like, talking to you, and it was called, 'Won't You Buy a Postcard'?"[40]

According to Tim Riley, who is by no means an apologist, "the most banal way to read Dylan songs is to link them up with his life, as though he had no greater ambition than to record his autobiography—this is the injustice his lesser profilers fall into."[41] This notion of "lesser profilers" applies not only to critics, however, but to listeners as well who think Bob Dylan, rather than his homodiegetic speaker, "is leaving tomorrow, but could leave today" or is dancing "beneath the diamond sky, one hand waving free" or finds it "not dark yet, but getting there." Riley adds that Dylan is "greater than this; his songs inhabit personas and he shifts characters so often on the large stage of rock stardom that it's clear he enjoys toying with 'Dylan.'"[42] As support for Dylan's remark to Gooding about "speaking in the first person" from another point of view, Riley's idea of character shifts might be useful. But his notion of "toying with 'Dylan'" has itself become banal: it has been a feature, if not a fetish, of Dylan's career to toy with the "Dylan" persona. Dylan himself expands on this when discussing *Renaldo and Clara* (1978) in interviews. His identity game goes way back, as far as the Halloween show at Town Hall in 1962—"I'm wearing my Bob Dylan mask"—through the white paint of *The Rolling Thunder Revue* (concert tour 1975–76). Similarly, the masks (or masque) and alter-egos of Dylan's film *Renaldo and Clara*, Larry Charles's star-studded *Masked and Anonymous* (2003), and Todd Haynes's *I'm Not There* (2007) together constitute a kind of conceptual rehash of Dylan's ludic experimentation. Dylan and his imitators seem to be reminding us, as did Lord Chesterfield, that life imitates art.[43]

Two Cultures

Although it might seem ironic that we can measure a rock 'n' roll singer by the standards of high culture, in fact Dylan has breached the walls of the artistic citadel ever since his astonishing debut. His songs lifted the pop lyric into another, utterly new realm, and critics began calling him a poet half a century ago. The

Nobel Prize doesn't represent high culture condescending to Dylan, inviting him to breathe its rarefied air. On the contrary, it underscores Dylan's career-long challenge to the boundaries between the two cultures of high and popular art. It means that in measuring Dylan against the arts traditionally regarded as high culture productions, we are, in effect, recognizing what Dylan's songs have always done. His lyricism and virtuosity have always demanded to be measured in a parallel relationship with the sister arts.

But there is an irony when we think about Dylan's place in the literary pantheon, as the Nobel Prize (if nothing else) forces us to do. It seems pointless to compare Dylan's poetic authority to that of his predecessors, despite his apparently sincere efforts to affix himself to a traditional genealogy of musicians and poets. In the sheer number of intelligent and sophisticated audience members who experience Dylan as a meaningful artist, not to mention the hordes of fanatic followers, Dylan has far exceeded the readers and listeners of all his precursors, with the probable exceptions (in the West) of Shakespeare, William Tyndale, the biblical poet of the J-texts, and Homer. Virgil, Milton, Whitman, and Woody Guthrie have never reached as many ears and minds. Yet Dylan acknowledges no perfect victory, and his sense of supersession, as seen in such songs as "Blind Willie McTell" (1983), is tempered by a palpable indebtedness and an impulse toward collaboration with the past.

This impulse, which saturates Dylan's lyrics and provides the musical architecture of his songs, has a counterpart in Dylan's approach to originality, imitation, and influence. From collaborative to syncretic can be a short step, and the songs again and again reveal the interstices of Dylan's genealogical positioning and his engagement with the figures, models, and media of the American experience. Dylan sings,

> Leave your stepping stones behind, something calls for you
> Forget the dead you've left, they will not follow you
> ("It's All Over Now, Baby Blue," 1965)

But the dead are never forgotten in Dylan's poetics. They follow him in every song, whatever calls for him. As he acknowledges in the didactic copy accompanying his painting exhibition, *The Beaten Path*, "I believe the key to the future is in the remnants of the past."[44] Ideally, the chapters of this book will trace the stepping-stones this artist never leaves behind and allow us to hear what is calling for him from the remnants of the past across time and culture and even artistic disciplines.

––––––

The seventeenth-century poet Robert Herrick, in the first poem of his collection *Hesperides*, sketched out "The Argument of His Book":

I Sing of *Brooks*, of *Blossomes*, *Birds*, and *Bowers*:
Of *April*, *May*, of *June*, and *July-Flowers*.
I sing of *May-poles*, *Hock-carts*, *Wassails*, *Wakes*,
Of *Bride-grooms*, *Brides*, and of their *Bridall-cakes*.
I write of *Youth*, of *Love*, and have Accesse
By these, to sing of cleanly-*Wantonnesse*.
I sing of *Dewes*, of *Raines*, and piece by piece
Of *Balme*, of *Oyle*, of *Spice*, and *Amber-Greece*.
I sing of *Times trans-shifting*; and I write
How *Roses* first came *Red*, and *Lillies White*.
I write of *Groves*, of *Twilights*, and I sing
The Court of *Mab*, and of the *Fairie-King*.
I write of *Hell*; I sing (and ever shall)
Of *Heaven*, and hope to have it after all.[45]

Herrick's list, mutatis mutandis, might well be an index of Dylan's poetic and musical range. Everything's there in "The Argument," presented with promise and delight in Herrick's characteristically perfect measures. We can find all those themes—encompassed, enlarged, transmogrified—somewhere in Dylan's work: blossoms, birds, Hock-cart labor, youth and love, "cleanly-Wantonness," expected rain and Gilead balms in country bowers, Mercutio's magic queen, cathedral dawns and Roman twilights, hope of heaven, and the ever-during dark. Although Herrick doesn't let his anger show, or envision rainbows in the sky, he nevertheless captures something uncannily akin to Dylan when he promises to "sing of *Times trans-shifting*." What better phrase to describe the Dylan songs that echo in our heads? From the early sixties, Dylan has sung of the "times transshifting" and he's still singing—and embodying—that theme. It's not dark yet, he reminds us, but it's getting there: the watchman lies dreaming and there's high water everywhere.

The key to singing "times trans-shifting" is to sing in a vatic voice, as a poetprophet (the original meaning of the Latin term "vates"). Dylan has always had the vatic calling, and this is what accounts for his unique status in contemporary culture. More than that of any other living poet or singer, his fame rests on the visionary, prophetic element in his songs. Certainly Rimbaud, Verlaine, Eliot, and maybe the Surrealists left their mark on Dylan's work, especially his mid-sixties songs, perhaps even to some extent as modernist visionaries. But the roots and branches of Dylan's vatic authority spring from William Tyndale, through whom Dylan heard the voices of the J-Writer of Genesis, Ezekiel, and Jeremiah. Then, most prominently, come Dante, Virgil, Milton, Blake, Whitman, Woody Guthrie, Carl Sandburg, and Allen Ginsberg—and with the same force, like a permanent backcloth, there's the language of Jesus and salvation infusing every blues lyric Dylan ever absorbed and transformed.

But behind those profoundly resonant influences, behind Dylan's transformative genius, lies the process of imitatio: the careful study of those models supplied by tradition and the maneuver-ending business of construing a vatic presence out of them, not only where one might expect it, in the anthems and protest songs, but also in virtually every blues, ballad, devotional lyric, and love song Dylan sings. As he himself memorably shouted from stage in England in 1964, "Come on, all my songs are protest songs!"

The Argument of *my* Book, therefore, comes down to this: I analyze the growth and development of Dylan's unparalleled lyrical authority through his practice of imitation, appropriation, and self-imitation. Chapter 1—"Past the Vernacular: Dylan's Technique of Originality"—describes ancient and Renaissance techniques of imitatio and their undeniable similarity to Dylan's compositional practice. Dylan's originality stems from his capacity to borrow from, digest, and transform past models, both intuitively and as a function of conscious manipulation. His borrowing has sometimes come under attack and this chapter demonstrates how true originality means returning to an origin, a source. This is Dylan's unique strength: he has the mnemonic capacity to survey and adapt a startling range of predecessors—to *imitate* them in the best sense and to supersede their language. Going "past the vernacular," which is what he calls this practice, defines his technique of originality.

What matters, though, is how much one adapts and borrows. Chapter 2—"Savage Innocence: Dylan's Art of Appropriation"—addresses the question of degree. The difference between slavish and transformative imitation is the determining factor in creative innovation. This chapter charts the nuances of Dylan's compositional techniques in the light of his appropriations: the allusive range and referential scope of Dylan's music, his songs, and his painting testify to his (predominantly) conscious effort to choose his influences and to honor and reinvent them. Confronting some of the allegations of theft leveled at Dylan's method, the chapter clarifies Dylan's commitment to selective imitation as opposed to either so-called "appropriation art" or slavish copying.

Significantly, Dylan's appropriations also extend to his own work. Chapter 3—"Self-Portrait in a Broken Glass: Dylan Imitates Dylan"—examines a compositional phenomenon unique to him. Increasingly, throughout his career, Dylan has alluded to, parodied, and transformed his own earlier music. No other artist of Dylan's rock generation—indeed no other artist I can cite in the twentieth century—has mined his or her own body of work for as much material to reintroduce, adapt, and weave into songs. Dylan has written over six hundred songs and, as his oeuvre keeps growing, he plucks from past lyrics to reimagine new narratives. This self-imitation carries a promise of renewal, reflection, and often self-confrontation. As a compositional technique, self-imitation augments the kind of transformative imitation Dylan has always practiced, but with the extraordinary added dimension of using his own productions as precursor models.

Chapter 4—"The Wizard's Curse: The American Singer as *Vates*"—is both a culmination and an expansion, closing the circle on my argument that Dylan's status as a vatic poet is unique in contemporary culture. The chapter traces Dylan's sense of inspiration, from his sometime admission of divine madness (or furor poeticus) in his songwriting to his demonstrable poetic consciousness. I trace Dylan's linguistic engagement with William Tyndale, whose language makes up the chief part of the King James Bible, and explore the complex interdependence of visionary poetics and imitation.

The book concludes with an afterword—"Every Conceivable Point of View"—where I briefly discuss Dylan's poetics of imitation in the context of his film *Renaldo and Clara* (1978). The film captures Dylan dissecting his own imitative process as the two worlds captured by the film begin to mirror each other: the sequence of Dylan's actual stage performances while on tour and the fictional narrative of imagined performances, tours, and personal entanglements causes a head-on collision of imitation and identity. Despite the verité atmosphere of the film, there's a sense of times or time *trans-shifting* throughout the narrative: the tawdry glamor and the make-believe—Joan Baez as the mysterious, unnamed Woman in White, for example—the coded conversations, the indistinguishable six-hour series of hotel rooms and performance halls, and, at the center, the mercurial rock 'n' roll prince. Despite the cinematographer's technique of rendering a true image of life, the film seems unreal, both staged and dreamlike, as if it could be taking place at Robert Herrick's Court of the Fairie-King.

1 | PAST THE VERNACULAR
Dylan's Technique of Originality

I've heard too much Lead Belly to be influenced by whirling dervishes.
—Bob Dylan in an interview

Imitatio

In presenting the 2016 Nobel Prize in Literature to Bob Dylan, Horace Engdahl not only justified the Swedish Academy's exceptional choice but also explained how Dylan's songs achieve their unique lyrical beauty:

> In itself, it ought not to be a sensation that a singer/songwriter now stands recipient of the literary Nobel Prize. In a distant past, all poetry was sung or tunefully recited, poets were rhapsodes, bards, troubadours; "lyrics" comes from "lyre." But what Bob Dylan did was not to return to the Greeks or the Provençals. Instead, he dedicated himself body and soul to 20th century American popular music, the kind played on radio stations and gramophone records for ordinary people, white and black: protest songs, country, blues, early rock, gospel, mainstream music. He listened day and night, testing the stuff on his instruments, trying to learn. But when he started to write similar songs, they came out differently. In his hands, the material changed. From what he discovered in heirloom and scrap, in banal rhyme and quick wit, in curses and pious prayers, sweet nothings and crude jokes, he panned poetry gold, whether on purpose or by accident is irrelevant; all creativity begins in imitation.[1]

It's worth repeating: "all creativity begins in imitation." Engdahl refers here to imitation as a poetic methodology, a practice both programmatic and instinctive, handed down from antiquity.

Dylan's instinct for imitation, in embryonic form, was manifest in his Hibbing rock bands and his Buddy Holly/Elvis Presley ambitions. When he arrived in New York, still legally Robert Zimmerman, he was dubbed a "Woody Guthrie Machine" because he played and replayed Woody's songs. But, if hindsight is creditable, "Mrs. Smith" chided Dylan for this, saying: "Woody is a man of his own times. Why do you try to live in his times? . . . Don't do what all the other folk singers are doing. What the hell does a boxcar mean to them? What does it mean to you? . . . Don't lose yourself in Woody's shadow."[2] Dylan heeded this advice to an extent unimaginable to his early Village friends and folk-singing contemporaries. He broke away from Woody and complicated his imitative technique, never losing sight of his precursors but always reinventing them. Much later, in 1978, he said to Jonathan Cott, "I don't try to imitate Rimbaud in my work. I'm not interested in imitation."[3] But this statement is misleading. It isn't imitation Dylan eschews. It is *slavish* imitation. In fact, his work is more technically imitative—more properly a result of imitatio—than that of any other songwriter or performer of our time. Engdahl is referring to imitatio, not slavish imitation, in saying "all creativity begins in imitation."

While Dylan's imitations might draw on traceable and familiar precursors, his imitative technique is less familiar. His ability to consume, adapt, and "write similar songs" that "came out differently" has been a perpetual puzzle for critics. As I said in the introduction, Dylan's technique of imitating predecessors itself has a predecessor, closely resembling the Renaissance practice of imitatio, the means by which poets plucked from and digested the best of their poetic antecedents. Dylan probably never fully realized his proximity in practice to that of these ancient and early modern poets, although he studied Latin at Hibbing High School and was briefly a member of the Latin Club. Richard Thomas has made a particularly convincing case for the survival of Dylan's early Latin training in his compositional imagination. And, in fact, Latin phrases appear in his drafts from the sixties. There's the phrase "occide moriturus," which comes from Apuleius's *Metamorphoses*, written in blue pen on a page of his notes for the experimental prose piece *Tarantula*.[4] Similarly, on the verso side of the sheet of notepaper from 1964–1965 citing the *Anthology of French Poets*, Dylan made a handwritten list of Latin phrases (figure 1 in the introduction).[5] Yet, despite his familiarity with Latin and his frequent recourse to translations of such authors as Virgil and Juvenal—as in his reference to the brothel keeper in "Tempest" (2012)—Dylan never indicates that he knows he is practicing a classical method of composition.

To complicate matters, he often credits divine inspiration as the source of his songs, eschewing self-consciousness altogether. But while the otherworldly has always played a part in Dylan's life, his lyrical consciousness and music-culture instinct have always manifested in his imitative technique (insofar as a technē can be instinctive, that is). From this ancient technique his virtuosity and the stunning pattern of his originality were born—an originality that, fittingly, *naturalized* folk performance and provided what I have elsewhere called "instant artifacts" in the form of newly written songs.[6]

The most celebrated articulation of the practice of imitatio is found in the Roman poet Seneca, whose formula for composition became de rigueur for poets in the Renaissance and early modern periods. Imitation of past works became the order of the day, a practice which often morphed into *emulatio*, a combination of imitation and admiration—something often ostentatiously on display in Dylan's songs (e.g., "Hey, hey, Woody Guthrie, I know that you know"; or "Nobody can sing the blues / Like Blind Willie McTell"). Seneca describes imitatio this way: "We should follow . . . the example of the bees, who flit about and cull the flowers that are suitable for producing honey, and then arrange and assort in their cells all that they have brought in; these bees, as our Vergil [*sic*] says, pack close the flowing honey, and swell their cells with nectar sweet. It is not certain whether the juice which they obtain from the flowers forms at once into honey, or whether they change that which they have gathered into this delicious object by blending something therewith and by a certain property of their breath."[7] Celebrated for millennia as the "apian metaphor," this inordinately influential passage contains, in the last sentence, an anticipation of Dylan's own understanding of his vocal identity. Seneca speaks of the "delicious object" being produced by a blending of flowers and "a certain property of breath." Dylan puts it this way: "My songs are different & i don't expect others to make attempts to sing them because you have to get somewhat inside & behind them & it's hard enough for me to do it sometimes & then obviously you have to be in the right frame of mind. But even then there would be a vague value to it because nobody breathes like me so they couldn't be expected to portray the meaning of a certain phrase in the correct way without bumping into other phrases & altering the mood, changing the understanding."[8] It isn't only Dylan's own songs that reflect this "property of breath." As Wilfrid Mellers says about Dylan's cover of "See That My Grave Is Kept Clean," from his debut album, "Dylan's control of line in relation to verbal meaning is here already *sui generis*; his extraordinary, instantly recognizable voice whispers, chuckles, grunts, growls and howls without impairing the line's musical contour."[9] Nothing could better characterize the transformation of material, musical and lyrical intertwined, than the notion that in Dylan's hands a 1920s-era blues standard becomes something sui generis, "of its own kind."

Is Dylan's recording on *Bob Dylan* a form of performative colonization, or even theft? In whispering, grunting, growling, and howling, is he trying to rip off the Black idiolect and thus the authority of Blind Lemon Jefferson and Furry Lewis? If it is as unique as Mellers suggests, then Dylan's performance of "See That My Grave Is Kept Clean" raises inevitable questions about imitation: the imitation of Blind Lemon Jefferson's cultural authority, the white performer's debt to Black blues culture, and his simultaneous absorption of that marginalized culture into a more mainstream and commercial product. The white folk and blues performers of Dylan's generation altered their accents and often strained their voices to ventriloquize an experience not only not their own but (at least in chronological terms) long past. But if they can be accused of trying to "sound Black," their vocal appropriations (most of them unsuccessful in terms of authenticity) should be considered acts of homage as much as of theft.

Janet Gezari and Charles Hartman, discussing Dylan's performances of "No More Auction Block," ask, "How did a young, white, middle-class Jewish folksinger manage to channel the age-old weariness of a freed black slave? How is it that Dylan had the courage, conviction, or simple nerve to attempt it?" They note that his performance of "No More Auction Block" is "entirely without what [James] Baldwin calls 'protective sentimentality' . . . He had captured the sound that had captivated him."[10] The sound Dylan captured not only captivated him, but also captivated—and often mesmerized—his peers. Michael Gray has argued that Dylan "worked the blues so strongly and resourcefully that he has given it something back," adding that he has never used the blues "in bad faith to the gravitas he found within it."[11] With basic guitar and harmonica and "resourcefully" nuanced vocal sensibilities, Dylan seemed able to return folk music to its origins, and he did it without the ideological patina of Pete Seeger. He disappeared into the songs utterly, or at least with an utterly convincing vocal mask.

As with "Auction Block," Dylan's audacity in vocalizing the "age-old weariness of a freed black slave" is concomitant with his nuanced taste in interpreting the lyrics. In making that song and "See That My Grave Is Kept Clean" his own, he maintains the sense of lament without suppressing or denying his source. This is imitatio practiced to a highly sophisticated degree—and practiced intuitively by the young, white, middle-class Jewish singer. If it is also a form of cultural appropriation—an attempt at "sounding Black"—then it is only that because Dylan recognized the source of his authority and was able to imitate it. He never "sounded Black" per se, but his quirky Iron Range vocalizations were clearly meant to disrupt the expectations of a white singing voice. As much as he borrowed from the melodies and lyrics whirling around him in the folk scene, he absorbed and transmuted the sounds of his vocal antecedents in the blues.

Nor were the fictionalized settings of these songs lost on him. The "gravitas" remains intact, and is often enhanced, when Dylan reworks (or rewords) an old blues song. This sense of preserving the core meaning of a song seems strongest with the blues. Other folk inheritances, such as Child ballads—an influential collection of traditional English and Scottish ballads—were utterly different from the blues, with an age and origin untouched by slavery, Civil War, manumission, and the American history of oppressing Black people.[12] Dylan recognized this difference perhaps more profoundly and, once he began writing his own songs, with more interpretive authority than any of his contemporaries. His use of blues forms and his transformative delivery of modern lyrics in those forms represents not a denial but an affirmation of his imitative models—and an homage to his sources. He rarely does this with other musical forms: exceptions might be "Hard Rain," a colossally transformative song in its own right (if for other reasons) or, later, "I Dreamed I Saw Saint Augustine," or maybe the less-weighty songs of his *Nashville Skyline* period.

Take, for example, Blind Lemon Jefferson's haunting "See That My Grave Is Kept Clean." While the song is probably not about a lynching, as some have suggested—if for no other reason than the likelihood that a lynching victim wouldn't be given the chance to ask for "one kind favor"—it nevertheless describes in minute detail the impending death and then the actual *being dead* of a young man. The "kind favor" or last wish he asks for is more commonly associated with condemned prisoners about to be executed. The two white horses (if taken as real) waiting to haul the dead body to "my burying ground" indicate a more formal execution—indeed, lynched bodies were often left to hang on the tree limbs as lessons or trophies (the horrifying strange fruit) rather than being buried at all. If, on the contrary, the white horses aren't real but phantasmagoric spiritual horses drawing the chariot to heaven, then perhaps a martyred body is the song's subject. Yet when, and why, would the "church bells tone" ("toll," in Dylan's version) for a grotesque, lawless act of savagery? It's difficult to imagine that even in the most benighted Southern town, the church would lend its imprimatur to homicidal mob rule.

The speaker of "See That My Grave Is Kept Clean" seems more like a condemned man who is about to be hanged and asks for a last wish—and then is hanged ("My heart's stopped beating / And my hands turned cold"). Some versions include the verse "See that my digger is well paid"—again, hardly a request addressed to a lynch mob. The singer asks, "Did you ever hear that coughin' sound? / Means another poor boy is underground": the "coughing sound" might describe the last truncated breath in the throat of a hanged man. But there's nothing in the song that says definitively the hanged man is being lynched. On the contrary, there's a sense of ambiguity about the hanged man's guilt, a sense that despite being condemned (rightly or wrongly) the church bells will toll, the white horses will be waiting, and his grave will (or might) be kept clean.

Another poor boy is underground: it's that word "boy" that resonates so forcefully. That link of the about-to-die "boy" with Dylan's first-person, of the homodiegetic "boy" with the baby-faced (white) twenty-year-old on the album cover of *Bob Dylan* is staggering: why would Dylan even attempt such a song on a debut album; why would he put his authenticity to the test when so much was on the line? In Blind Lemon's vocabulary, "boy" might refer to a coeval male or could echo the derogatory use by whites referring to all Black men (and Black servants). For Dylan, who would have known that latter usage, the word also echoes all the "poor boy" songs of Woody Guthrie and company. But the singer on *Bob Dylan* was demonstrably a boy, and, as listeners, we can hear in Dylan's performance the dead speaker of "See That My Grave Is Kept Clean" being reinvented from extracts of precursor "boys" as this new voice. Appropriation, accumulation, and digestion combine in Dylan's imitation of the song. His "originality" fastens him to Blind Lemon Jefferson and Woody Guthrie; it also highlights his musical and performative choices, making a combination of origins into what Dylan was so often called—an original.

The Virtuoso

This intuitive force of interpretation, heard on Dylan's first album, soon became an originality of composition, based on the same principles of imitation and emulation. As the always astute Kermode noted, Dylan is "a virtuoso executant, and since he writes the words with virtuoso performance in mind, they can't, on the page, be more than musical notes are: hints, or shadows."[13] Mellers seems to echo this in his combined interpretation of Dylan's voice (his main instrument), his lyrics, and his musical accompaniment, highlighting that "extraordinary, instantly recognizable voice" that first stunned listeners with its originality. And Betsy Bowden (a musically attentive critic) observed, "It was his voice that spoke so directly to and for each individual listener: Dylan's whining, grating, snarling voice that could drip scorn or comfort, could stretch or snap off words to disregard their literal meaning or to fulfill it."[14]

But that voice is itself the successful result of an imitative process at the foundation of Dylan's musical poetics, that "combination of blues, rock and country which caught on the very minute that he stepped on the stage at Gerde's." When Seneca describes the production of honey as an analogy to the writing of poetry, he means that, just as a bee samples and digests the pollen from a whole field of flowers to produce a new kind of honey, which is part flower and part bee, a poet produces a poem by sampling *and digesting* the best authors of the past. Dylan's imitations follow this Senecan pattern, and his best work—his most enduring work—is always part flower, part Dylan. He practices imitatio in its most ambitiously effective mode. Every self-conscious allusion or retrospective chord change represents a digestion of the past. Dylan the man might be enigmatic and elusive, but the music has few different faces, few masks, few "I-Am-Not-There" personas. There are only different sources, drawn not only from past songwriters, but also from artists in other fields. *Rough and Rowdy Ways* (2020) not only confirms but showcases a plurality of source material. To analyze Dylan's variations on his far-reaching originals is to understand the method of musical-lyrical imitation he enacts. And, to that end, Seneca's metaphor/analogy offers a valuable tool for unpacking Dylan's methodology, because it defines a truer, less Romantic idea of originality.

Dylan's imitative style takes us back beyond Shelley and Keats and Coleridge to the semantic basis of originality as it was understood in the Renaissance: to be original is to return *to the origin* and imitate sources. As Arthur Kinney explains, "The act of *imitatio* . . . seems from the beginning to be a matter not merely of *copying* but of improving, combining, transforming, and hence *creating.*" The artist (or poet) accomplishes this act of creation "by selecting many models so as to create an ideal that is at best a composite of what is before him [or her, presumably]."[15] While Seneca's metaphor of the bees generally held sway, Macrobius also influenced Renaissance theories of imitatio: "Assimilations of models result in a process that *changes* them, that produces *something new*. It is this new product, new work of art, that the artist thus *creates*, a work in which the sources have become so absorbed, or digested, as to have receded from sight so that only the newly created composite remains."[16] Joachim du Bellay, in *La*

Défense et illustration de la langue française (1549), explains how the Romans enriched their language: "In imitating the best Greek authors, transforming themselves into them, devouring them, and after having digested them well, converting them into blood and nourishment [or nurture of the mind]." Because he was concerned about the poetic inadequacies of sixteenth-century French, du Bellay recommended that his fellow poets "amplify the French language by imitation of ancient Greek and Roman authors."[17] This sense of contemporary inadequacy was not unusual. Thomas Greene points out that "the focus of England's sense of disjuncture lay most visibly in its embarrassment over its rude vernacular."[18] English poets, like the French and the Italians (earlier), turned to imitatio to remedy the imbalance they felt in confrontation with antiquity. As Greene summarizes, "The Augustan Age in Rome produced some of the greatest imitative poetry ever written. It demonstrated for future eras, including the Renaissance *and including our own*, the potential power of a poetic based on the bridging of discontinuities."[19]

Dylan composes using a method of imitation he intuitively understood would bridge discontinuities—bridge them without losing the connection to his models. As Kinney makes clear, "The successful art of imitatio is not simply the newly created composite that diverges successfully from particular features of its source(s) but one in which the audience may see the residual traces of the original, which has been the initial impulse or model. The *significatio*, that is, now lies precisely in charting *what* the divergence is (and, consequently, why and how). . . . The *divergence* itself points to the essential meaning."[20]

This notion of divergence as meaning defines Dylan's practice of imitation: we could say, in McLuhanspeak, the meaning of Dylan *is* the divergence. From his first years on the folk music scene, Dylan practiced a form of imitation that was more than a composite of his models. His music is rife with residual traces of his models and evidence of confrontations overcome. The *significatio*—if this is not too grand a word—of his music lay (and lies) in its divergence from the impulses that inspired it and the models he imitates. Ricks remarks, trenchantly, that "like the great athlete, the great artist is at once highly trained and deeply instinctual."[21] In terms of imitatio, this combination is crucial. Even so, a disclaimer might be necessary: while Dylan's compositional method mirrors ancient and early modern imitatio, I have no intention of dressing him up in period garb and pretending that an anachronistic genius wandered in, not from Hibbing but from Augustan Rome, Medicean Florence, or the Elizabethan court (my prologue notwithstanding). Dylan's Americanness is unimpeachable, as is his place as both a product and a creator of his American generation. Even his imitation of English and Scottish ballads is carried out as an American plunderer, with the inevitable effect of resituating local values and musical styles.

In an interview in *Sing Out* (1968) with John Cohen and Happy Traum, Dylan recalls his early preparation in a way that took Cohen completely by surprise:

Dylan. My thoughts weren't about reading, no . . . they were just about that feeling that was in the air. I tried to somehow get ahold of that, and write that down, and using my musical training to sort of guide it by, and in the end, have something I could do for a living.

Cohen. Training!

Dylan. Yes, training. You have to have some. I can remember traveling through towns, and if somebody played the guitar, that's who you went to see. You didn't necessarily go to meet them, you just went necessarily to watch them, listen to them, and if possible, learn how to do something . . . whatever he was doing. And usually at that time it was quite a selfish type of thing. You could see the people, and if you knew you could do what they were doing with just a little practice, and you were looking for something else, you could just move on. But when it was down at the bottom, everyone played the guitar, and when you knew that they knew more than you, well, you just had to listen to everybody. It wasn't necessarily a song; it was technique and style, and tricks and all those combinations which go together—which I certainly spent a lot of hours just trying to do what other people have been doing. That's what I mean by training.[22]

This is a perfect description of the young artist going from living flower to living flower to cadge and absorb the best "technique and style . . . tricks and combinations." According to G. W. Pigman, the apian metaphor is a "misleading topos, because it is used to present two opposed conceptions of imitation: the poet as collector (following) and the poet as maker (imitation or emulation)."[23] But this opposition between collector and maker defines Dylan, even if it has puzzled and polarized his critical audience since he began performing. And it hardly matters whether the young Dylan practiced his form of apian imitation consciously or not. "Like the great athlete, the great artist is at once highly trained and deeply instinctual."[24]

Dylan's work from the beginning revealed both training and instinctual depth: he used the imitative process as living practice, *digesting* the tricks and combinations of Woody Guthrie and the old bluesmen, the lyrics and the passions, with a forceful, quirky originality that was tantamount to an alternate folk idiom and a new poetics of performance. In the liner notes to *Biograph* (1985), Dylan describes what he considered his training: "Everybody had their particular thing that they did. I didn't much ever pay attention to that. If I liked a song, I would just learn it and sing it the only way I could play it. Part of it was a technical problem which I never had the time nor the inclination for, if you want to call it a problem. But it didn't go down well with the tight-thinking people. You know, I'd hear things like 'I was in the Lincoln Brigade' and 'the kid is really bastardising up that song.'" Dylan's insouciant attitude about making a song his own, regardless of his inability to play the guitar part exactly, constituted a strong misreading and produced what Mellers referred to as a performance sui generis. Criticized by orthodox folkies, he was creating a new style almost with every breath. "The other singers never seemed to mind," he continues in the *Biograph* liner notes. "In fact, quite a few of them began to copy my attitude in guitar phrasing and such." He adds, "Basically, I'm self taught. What I mean by that actually is that I picked it all up from other people by watching them, by imitating them. I seldom ever asked them to take me aside and show me how to do it." While he trained by imitating those around him, he himself almost instantly became a training model.

This pivotal juncture between imitator and model illustrates how the combination of creativity and imitation in Dylan's early performance style was perceived as a stunningly original product. Dylan was redefining the nature of originality for his generation of performers long before they even realized what he was doing—and probably before he was fully conscious of it himself. Often referred to as a freak in his early days, Dylan ultimately proved his genius by organizing and transmuting his newfangledness into a charisma of voice and stage presence that mesmerized his contemporaries. As Joan Baez commented, "He knocked me out completely. He seemed tiny, just tiny, with that goofy little hat on. And he was just astounding. I was totally absorbed. His style and his eyes and the whole mystical whatever it was."[25] But his charisma was not inchoate. Even as a callow newcomer Dylan had his eye on the poetics of the American songwriting tradition. Greil Marcus excerpts an interview with Al Kooper regarding the Aldon music teams (including Carole King) who worked at the famous song factory at 1650 Broadway: "'They were doing something in their own right that was just as major as what Dylan was doing,' Kooper says of the Aldon writers . . . Dylan more than anyone ended their careers as songwriters. 'You were watching silent movies,' Kooper says, speaking of the way Dylan changed what a pop song could be, of how his use of language changed the language of the song. 'And all of a sudden there was sound in them. *Ohhhh*—and that put a lot of people out of work.'" Marcus adds that "they knew it, too: there is no overstating how terrified these great writers were of Bob Dylan. Years before 'Like a Rolling Stone,' he had all but challenged them to a duel."[26] Your grandpa's cane, it turns into a sword.

That early challenge can serve as a template for one side of Dylan's attitude. But while he might have set out single-handedly to destroy Tin Pan Alley songwriting, he soon began to seek a reciprocal, syncretizing relationship to complement his competitiveness. His ability to change and adapt with astonishing speed became legendary, his first three months in New York bringing him from anonymity to a gig at Gerdes Folk City on the bill with John Lee Hooker. But, lucky as he was (and he admits his luck), there was method to the mad transformation from yokel to cultural icon, from what Dave Van Ronk called "being a hayseed" to, in Spider John Koerner's words, "something stronger than we got into, something forceful, something coming off."[27]

Past the Vernacular

Seneca said poets should copy the bees, sift whatever they have gathered, and then, "by applying the supervising care with which our nature has endowed us—in other words, our natural gifts—we should so blend those several flavors into one delicious compound *that, even though it betrays its origin, yet it nevertheless is clearly a different thing from that whence it came.*"[28] If Dylan is to be believed in his autobiographical *Chronicles*, he was precocious in understanding exactly this Senecan recipe and in seeing the nuanced relationship of imitation to originality: "It's not like you see songs approaching and invite them in. It's not that easy. You want to say something about strange things that have happened to you, strange things you have seen. *You have to know and understand something and then go past the vernacular*. The chilling precision that these old-timers used in coming up with their songs was no small thing. Sometimes you could hear a song and your mind jumps ahead. You see similar patterns in the ways that you were thinking about things" (my emphasis).[29] Dylan's conscious aim "to know and understand something and then go past the vernacular" constitutes a poetics of imitation and a pre-Romantic concept of originality. It forms the foundation of his lyrical mode. The phrase "to go past the vernacular" is as profound and enigmatic as anything in Philip Sidney's *Defence of Poetry*. Sidney says, "Only the poet, disdaining to be tied to any subjection, lifted up with the vigour of his own invention, doth grow in effect another nature, in making things . . . better than nature bringeth forth."[30]

Going past the vernacular, as Dylan describes his early ambition, is equivalent to what Sidney calls growing "another nature" and making things "better than nature." This ambition characterizes Dylan's mode of originality and elevates his songs, placing them among the sibling arts on equal terms of creative imagination. Not only poets, but painters, sculptors, musicians, and dancers, at their best and most permanent, have engaged in the practices of imitatio and emulatio. On this elite artistic plane Dylan meets his creative peers in all the arts. As scores of examples throughout Dylan's six-hundred-song oeuvre show, the encounters range from the agonistic to the admiring, but always they resonate beyond the allusive surface and reveal a uniquely Dylanesque syncretism.

As Gabriel Josipovici says, "Clearly, something has changed, and we are the inheritors of Wordsworth, not Pope. From now on every major writer will have to forge his or her own language, a language which of course lives off the vernacular of his or her own time, but to which we have to grow acclimatized."[31] This may just be a matter of semantics, or it may be that Dylan's sense of supersession is different: rather than abandon the past, he imitates and syncretizes his predecessors. He is not, strictly speaking, an inheritor of Wordsworth because his method of imitation reaches back even beyond Pope. Dylan's language might "[live] off the vernacular," in Josipovici's phrase, but only insofar as he can go "past the vernacular." Moreover, there is nothing new or Wordsworthian about having to forge one's own language: poets (and painters too) have always done this. Imitatio is the consummate method of forging one's language from the combination of external sources and internal resources. Josipovici's choice of the word "forge" suggests an ambiguity: the new "originality," born of the self as opposed to imitation, will be as much a forgery as the product of an internal kiln.

In countless attempts to "simplify and classify" Bob Dylan, critics have dubbed him a (very well-paid) troubadour, an oral poet, a song-and-dance man, and a modern minstrel. The academic journal *Oral Tradition* dedicated a special edition to him in 2007. According to the editors' introduction, "Folklore, ethnomusicology, linguistics, anthropology, literary criticism, and philology: none of these fields can be left aside in a thorough attempt to gain insight into the rich dynamics and designs of Bob Dylan's performance artistry. It is indeed in the combined views and equations of these disciplines that scholars may identify with greater precision the complex subtleties or . . . the subtle complexities of Dylan's creative breakthroughs into an art form uniquely his own and yet soundly embedded in American popular culture."[32] There's no tautology in the last sentence: each new Dylan album in the sixties so altered the musical—or musical-cultural—landscape that he seemed to produce "creative breakthroughs into an art form uniquely his own." Yet, as unique as Dylan's songs can seem, no art form is ever comprehensively one's own. It is, instead, a *blending* and emulation of precursor works and forms. One of Dylan's most significant "creative breakthroughs" was—and is—his ability to augment his musical forebears with predecessors in the other arts. No other figure of our time has manifested the "breakthrough" originality it takes to produce a new art form with cultural status equivalent to that of established, "sister-art" forms.

The Latin inscription on the Nobel medal echoes this sense of newness: "*inventus vitam iuvat excoluisse per artes*," a phrase adapted from Virgil's *Aeneid*:

> hic manus ob patriam pugnando vulnera passi,
> quique sacerdotes casti, dum vita manebat,
> quique pii vates et Pheobo digna locuti,
> *inventas aut qui vitam excoluere per artis,*
> quique sui memores alios fecere merendo.[33]

> And here are troops of men
> who had suffered wounds, fighting to save their country,
> and those who had been pure priests while still alive,
> and the faithful poets whose songs were fit for Phoebus:
> *those who enriched our lives with the newfound arts they forged*
> and those we remember well for the good they did mankind.[34]

Book 6, containing the Nobel motto, describes Aeneas's descent into Hades and the paradise-worthy accomplishments of vatic poets (*pii vates*, or pious poet-prophets). Yet the passage doesn't expand on the prophetic element of vates.

Instead, Virgil describes these poets as, in Fagles's translation, "those who enriched our lives with the newfound arts they forged," emphasizing civic or social enrichment over prophecy. The word "arts" ("artis") in the line is pivotal. Williams, in his commentary, glosses "artis" this way, using the more common spelling (*artes*): "for *artes* (not 'arts' or 'skills' but the good way of life),"and he cites Horace, *Odes* 4.15, 12, "veteres . . . artes ('the traditional way of life')."[35] This notion of the good or traditional way of life replacing "arts" or "skills" would give a different tenor to the motto. It jibes neither with the somewhat inaccurate William Morris translation quoted by Sara Danius, permanent secretary of the Swedish Academy—"and they who bettered life on earth by their newfound mastery"—nor, for example, with Thomas Palaima's more literal rendering: "it is of use (i.e., it is beneficial) to have improved life through discovered arts."[36] Not even Fagles's "newfound arts they forged" captures Williams's implied "newfound [*inventas*, discovered] *way of life*." But, while Williams's gloss favors social over aesthetic accomplishment, it would nevertheless resonate with Dylan's transformative cultural effect as *the* vatic poet of our time.

As in Josipovici's phrase, the doubling meaning of the Fagles's word "forged" offers the best insight into Dylan's method of creating—his "creativity in imitation," as Engdahl says. There is a passage in Ben Jonson's famous verse preface to Shakespeare's First Folio that offers a serendipitous comparison:

> Yet must I not give nature all: thy art,
> My gentle Shakespeare, must enjoy a part.
> For though the poet's matter nature be,
> His art doth give the fashion; and, that he
> Who casts to write a living line, must sweat,
> (Such as thine are) and strike the second heat
> Upon the muses' anvil; turn the same
> (And himself with it) that he thinks to frame,
> Or, for the laurel, he may gain a scorn;
> For a good poet's made, as well as born;
> And such wert thou.[37]

The "muses' anvil," an allusion conflating Hephaestus's forge with the Muses of poetry, recalls Fagles's translation of Virgil's line on the Nobel medal. Even in 1623 the word "forge" resonated with "forgery." Jonson's poem is resoundingly famous, not least for the equivocal praise that although he had "small Latin and less Greek," Shakespeare outshone such ancient playwrights as "thundering Aeschylus, Euripides, and Sophocles." Fagles would probably have known Jonson's poem, and—like Harold Bloom's Shakespeare reading Freud—might have given his Elysian poets Shakespearean powers to forge their poems at the muses' anvil.

Jonson might have written the same things about Dylan, who, a college dropout with "small Latin," has out-thundered the poet-performers of his own and even earlier generations. The reason for this parallel poetic authority begins with Shakespeare and Dylan's uncanny skill in reworking common expressions into verse and making them seem new—of going "past the vernacular" with what Dylan calls "the chilling precision that these old-timers used." He might as well be describing Shakespeare's achievement: no one has since been able to go past Shakespeare's language, much of which was drawn from the vernacular of his time. Nor has Dylan been superseded, though only half a century has passed in his case. The capacity to combine a new linguistic vernacular with a debt to the language of precursors—to that "chilling precision" of old-timers—is rare enough. To do it without losing the vernacular and at the same time without becoming a museum piece is rarer still.

No need to strain the comparison, however, except to underscore the combination of anvil and inspiration in both. If, as Thomas asserts, Dylan is "the supreme artist of the English language of my time," Shakespeare, as Jonson puts it, "was not of an age, but for all time." John Milton, the "great poet of the age to come," published an epitaph on Shakespeare in the commendatory poems of the Second Folio (1632).[38] For Milton, in contrast to Jonson, Shakespeare was pure inspiration, pure natural talent: "to th' shame of slow-endeavouring art, / thy easy numbers flow" (9), he says in a poem ultimately concluding that Shakespeare needs no tomb of "piled stones" (2) since he has a "livelong monument" in his verse. Although he calls Shakespeare "dear son of Memory, great heir of Fame" (5), Milton cites no genealogy and acknowledges no process nor muses' anvil in Shakespeare's accomplishment. Such a thorough denial of conscious effort has struck critics as dismissive on the part of the ferociously learned Milton, who, though he sneers at "slow-endeavouring art," eventually put all his marbles into extensive study and slow, deliberate craft. His portrait of Shakespeare as nature's child is backhanded praise from the poet who would go on to write *Paradise Lost*.

Dylan's prodigious output as a young songwriter seemed at the time to defy "slow-endeavouring art." His celebrated ability to write songs effortlessly in any situation was the marvel of everyone around him, and now we have evidence of this constant outpouring in the scores of scribbled-on napkins, matchbooks, and torn-out notebook sheets at the Tulsa archive. Dylan's "easy numbers" seemed to flow as if he, like Milton's Shakespeare, were the "dear son of Memory." Nor did the young prodigy help to define his method. Too often he credited divine intervention in the composition of his early songs, characterizing himself as merely a vessel conveying messages, "as if through trumpets" (to paraphrase Marilio Ficino): "Those early songs, I don't know where they came from."

As he grew older, Dylan acknowledged that it became much harder for him to get what he wanted in a song, owning up to the kind of agency Milton denies Shakespeare. In fact, he has focused our attention increasingly on his method of writing, both by multiplying intertextual references and by discussing the effort he makes to get a song right. He often alludes to his craft in interviews: once, when asked what he thought about, he answered, "Meter." A surprise answer, probably, because it seems so workmanlike instead of inspired (by the "Mother of Muses," Mnemosyne, the title of a song on *Rough and Rowdy Ways*). But this is the Other Side of Bob Dylan often overlooked. As David Boucher and Gary Browning point out, "Fans who were won over to Bob Dylan by the strength of his lyrics will be disappointed that [in *Chronicles*] he talks only of the *process* of writing songs, not about their content" (my italics).[39]

Which returns us to the kind of balance Jonson sees in Shakespeare, a balance of natural talent and laborious fashioning (and self-fashioning) that describes Dylan's art as well. According to Jonson, nature can't take full credit for Shakespeare (*pace* Milton): nature might have given him his inspiration (or "first heat"), but ultimately the poet gives form to nature. The forge and anvil are the poet's (metaphorical) tools, with Hephaestus in the muses' role. Reversing the old maxim, *orator fit, poeta nascitur* ("an orator is made, a poet born"), Jonson concludes "a good poet's made, as well as born." The pun in the line is pedantic. The word "poet" comes from the Greek *poiein*, "to make," so the line literally means "a good maker's made," the redundancy ably reflecting Jonson's notion that nature brings to life and inspires the poet while at the same time being the "matter" to which a poet's work *gives* life through form.

Imitatio outside the Museums

Thomas sees a contrast between Dylan's compositional mode around the time of "Hard Rain" and, much later, during the writing of *Time Out of Mind*: "Where the lines in 'Hard Rain' had come from places that even he did not understand, the Muse, that is, his memory of the whole tradition was now handing him scripts, which he integrated, orchestrated, and expanded into the song he made."[40] Thomas adds, crucially, that Dylan now "has control of a dizzying variety of fragments of traditional gospel and old songs and he knows what he wants to do with them. As the song ['Tryin' to Get to Heaven's Door'] is set out here you can read the intertexts, but what matters is what Dylan does with them."[41] According to Mellers, "The gradual sophistication of his resources in a sense represents a growth towards 'conscious' awareness; in another sense, however, electric presentation, with Dylan as with other pop artists, implies a merging of individual awareness into a communal consciousness."[42] Whether a "communal consciousness" is ever manifest in the music, Dylan divides his writing and performance into "unconscious" and "conscious" periods. Significantly, as I discuss in the next chapter, he credits his painting lessons with Norman Raeben as the watershed moment dividing these modes of working.

In an interview for a documentary, Mike Marqusee qualified Dylan's sense of folk tradition by "heightening the contrasts":

Nobody of his generation absorbed folk in greater diversity or greater depth. And he's constantly reworking it. But his understanding of folk music was not a museum piece. This is what's always important to Dylan. What he hates— at one point he says, "It's not the bomb that's gotta go, it's the museums." Bit of an extreme statement, but I know what he's getting at: that the museums *embalm* living art. And art that lives for him is art that's on the tip of people's tongues, art that's spoken on the street, art that comes from real and immediate experiences, rather than from people trying to imitate previous models. And so folk music to him is exactly not about people with period instruments taking what someone did thirty years ago or a hundred years ago and reproducing it. It's about people taking that inheritance and remaking it. And so what he does when he goes electric is to take all of those folk sources, and not abandon them, but heighten them and give it a broader musical palette.[43]

The confrontation between embalmed art in museums and "art that's spoken on the street" is significant for this book and for my thoughts about Dylan's relation to other arts—many of which are in fact embalmed in museums. But, ironically, museum art notwithstanding, Marqusee ends his statement with a reference to a "broader palette," which of course alludes to painting—not an art spoken on the street but one found principally in museums. His metaphor indicates the habitual association of diverse sibling arts and the longevity of such comparisons as Horace's *ut pictura poesis*, "as in painting, so in poetry."

Similarly, Thomas's notion of "intertexts" capitalizes on a familiar weaving or textile metaphor already built into the word *text*. Both critics describe a reworking of existing material within the diachronic plane of folk tradition, a reworking that inevitably restructures that tradition, irrupting into the synchronic plane (which is always complete). While, significantly, both critics use metaphors drawn from sibling arts, Thomas's metaphor has more currency in discussions of linguistic works, perhaps because the warp and weft of threads are more easily visualized than the overlaying of brushstrokes.[44] In any case, in the expanded metaphorical context of structuralist and poststructuralist criticism, brushstrokes would themselves be part of a larger, painterly text.

Intertextuality and imitatio are often two sides of the same coin. Imitation— if we can strip the English word of its negative connotations—inevitably results in an intertextual relationship with prior authors. The process of imitation is inextricable from the resulting intertextuality. Some authors, like James Joyce, imitate their predecessors with the ostentatious aim of producing an intertextual map for readers. Dylan too does this at times, as in "Murder Most Foul" (2020), where the juxtaposition of names begs interpretation. All art imitates other art. The intertexts a listener or critic detects in a work of art are likely to have been deliberate imitations, redeployed from predecessor works for the present work of art. Unlike cultures, artists consciously marshal their allusive and "digested" intertexts in a sophisticated practice of imitatio, intending, as Horace says, "to teach and delight."

Dylan is virtually unique as an exemplar of imitatio among songwriters. He works in his Etnan forge, fashioning songs from transformed pieces—"in his hands, the material changed," said Engdahl. For example, Dave Van Ronk tells the story of how "Bob Dylan heard me fooling around with one of my grandmother's favorites, 'The Chimes of Trinity,' a sentimental ballad about Trinity Church [in lower Manhattan] . . . He made me sing it for him a few times until he had the gist of it, then reworked it into 'Chimes of Freedom' [1964]."[45] Van Ronk quotes a few lines he remembers to illustrate where the two songs are similar. But comparing the whole first verse to Dylan's "reworking" gives a better idea of how powerfully Dylan's imitation transformed the original while keeping a palimpsest of its salvationist rhetoric:

> In a city grand and gay
> Where the mighty throng holds sway
> Stands a church whose spire points toward the sky,
> And down in the belfry tow'r
> Oft the chimes have toll'd the hour
> Many saddened hearts were charmed while passing by
>
> Many millionairs [*sic*] and ladies grand and nobleman of state,
> With outcasts from every land and monarchs grand and great,
> All have whiled the hours away
> 'Way down on old Broadway,
> As they listened to the chimes of Trinity.
>
> Tolling for the outcast tolling for the gay
> Tolling for the millionaire and friends long pass'd away
> But my heart is light and gay
> As I stroll down old Broadway
> And listen to the chimes of Trinity.[46]

In Dylan's song, the chimes "flash" and the "trinity" becomes "freedom." As the song builds toward its final stanza, the language becomes increasingly universal. It's a long song, but Dylan's methodology is clear in these excerpts:

> As the echo of the wedding bells before the blowin' rain
> Dissolved into the bells of the lightning
> Tolling for the rebel, tolling for the rake
> Tolling for the luckless, the abandoned an' forsaked
> Tolling for the outcast, burnin' constantly at stake
> An' we gazed upon the chimes of freedom flashing . . .

Tolling for the tongues with no place to bring their thoughts
All down in taken-for-granted situations
Tolling for the deaf an' blind, tolling for the mute
Tolling for the mistreated, mateless mother, the mistitled prostitute
For the misdemeanor outlaw, chased an' cheated by pursuit
An' we gazed upon the chimes of freedom flashing . . .

Tolling for the searching ones, on their speechless, seeking trail
For the lonesome-hearted lovers with too personal a tale . . .

Tolling for the aching ones whose wounds cannot be nursed
For the countless confused, accused, misused, strung-out ones an' worse
An' for every hung-up person in the whole wide universe
An' we gazed upon the chimes of freedom flashing

"Chimes of Freedom," which Mike Marqusee calls a "transitional work," has elements of an anthem or social protest song, like "The Times They Are A-Changin,'" "When the Ship Comes In," or the biting "With God on Our Side," all from *The Times They Are A-Changin'* album (1963).[47] But Dylan utterly confutes the straightforward metaphors of those earlier social protests with a diction, that, according to Timothy Hampton, "has the anthemic feel of a protest song, but . . . recasts the moralistic refrains of such tunes . . . as personal vision."[48]

In terms of imitation, the recasting affects the "Chimes of Trinity" most significantly. Dylan redirects the word "tolling" from the original: the inspiriting echo of the church bells on lower Broadway—"tolling for the outcast tolling for the gay"—translates into the vatic diction of a visionary. But whereas the chimes of Trinity are inclusive, tolling for millionaires and outcasts alike, as well as for the living and the dead, Dylan's chimes toll mostly for "the confused, accused, misused, strung-out ones and worse." As Hampton says, Dylan's song "hooks the moment of illumination to a set of scenarios of redemption, the story of the refugee, the lonesome-hearted lover, the misdemeanor outlaw."[49] The illumination comes in a visionary "flashing" of the chimes, a syncretic image that entangles sight and sound, forging from Trinity Church's "belfry tow'r" where "Oft the chimes have toll'd the hour" a self-consciously new poetic diction. Dylan transfigures his nineteenth-century model, selecting judiciously among the lines he incorporates, refracting the language of Van Ronk's grandmother's song through the prism of a modern (and perhaps Modernist) vernacular. As a cross-section of the imitative process, "Chimes of Freedom" has the advantage of providing one main source from which Dylan clearly absorbed and transformed not only specific verses but also thematic elements of social inclusion.

Imitatio is a complicated process, however, and there's a risk of oversimplifying it by demonstrating a single song-to-song development—the "tolling" might arguably have recalled for Dylan the line "Have you ever heard them church bells toll?" from "See That My Grave Is Kept Clean." From an existing tradition comprising countless melodies and lyrics, Dylan "forges" his songs—"forges" being a word that inevitably implies falsified composition. With an eye to classical imitatio (and maybe to Jonson's allusion), Fagles no doubt heard the double meaning and chose the word for his translation of Virgil—"those who enriched our lives with the newfound arts they forged." But Dylan's critics (many of whom are not scholars) have demonstrated at best mixed and at worst hostile reactions to Dylan's imitative method. Journalists, professional critics, and unblushing detractors have written about Dylan's relationship to his musical forebears and to other musical genres with at times shocking ignorance.[50]

Dylan's use of such diverse sources as twentieth-century popular music, old minstrel shows, Delta blues, and the utterly different Child ballads has sometimes been called a collage style of composition. This compositional style receives accolades in some quarters as a kind of Cubist brilliance, and bitter critiques in others for being near-plagiarism and "a form of larceny."[51] Robert Polito seems to get the measure of the criticism. There was an indignant outcry with the "discovery" of Dylan's borrowings from the nineteenth-century Southern poet Henry Timrod on his *Modern Times* album (2006), accompanied by the usual charges of plagiarism. Polito coolly and expertly defuses what he calls the "dust-up in the *Times*": "narrowing the Dylan / Timrod phenomenon . . . into possible plagiarism is to confuse, well, art with a term paper."[52]

Dylan has in fact addressed this issue, though not until recently. In frank, sometimes embittered responses to Mikal Gilmore in 2012, he not only acknowledged the volumes of accusations, but offered a succinct anatomy of his method:

> Gilmore. Before we end the conversation, I want to ask about the controversy over your quotations in your songs from the works of other writers, such as Japanese author Junichi Saga's "Confessions of a Yakuza" and the Civil War poetry of Henry Timrod. Some critics say that you didn't cite your sources clearly. Yet in folk and jazz, quotation is a rich and enriching tradition. What's your response to those kinds of charges?
>
> Dylan. Oh, yeah, in folk and jazz, quotation is a rich and enriching tradition. That certainly is true. It's true for everybody, but me. I mean, everyone else can do it but not me. There are different rules for me. And as far as Henry Timrod is concerned, have you even heard of him? Who's been reading him lately? And who's pushed him to the forefront? Who's been making you read him? And ask his descendants what they think of the hoopla. And if you think it's so easy to quote him and it can help your work, do it yourself and see how far you can get. Wussies and pussies complain about that stuff. It's an old thing—it's part of the tradition. It goes way back. These are the same people that tried to pin the name Judas on me. Judas, the most hated

name in human history! If you think you've been called a bad name, try to work your way out from under that. Yeah, and for what? For playing an electric guitar? As if that is in some kind of way equitable to betraying our Lord and delivering him up to be crucified. All those evil motherfuckers can rot in hell.

Gilmore. Seriously?

Dylan. I'm working within my art form. It's that simple. I work within the rules and limitations of it. There are authoritarian figures that can explain that kind of art form better to you than I can. It's called songwriting. It has to do with melody and rhythm, and then after that, anything goes. You make everything yours. We all do it.

Gilmore. When those lines make their way into a song, you're conscious of it happening?

Dylan. Well, not really. But even if you are, you let it go. I'm not going to limit what I can say. I have to be true to the song. It's a particular art form that has its own rules. It's a different type of thing. All my stuff comes out of the folk tradition—it's not necessarily akin to the pop world.

By the "folk tradition" Dylan probably isn't referring to a body of material, an impossibly variegated compendium of songs. Instead, he is trying to describe what Pete Seeger called "the folk process."[53] The "pop world" is different, and not only because it draws on different material—after all, many pop songs rework blues progressions and rhythms to produce their rocking backbeat. It differs because pop songs eschew the folk process of aggregation and transformation, imitation, revision, and recombination. To mistake this shared communal process for Dylan's own larcenous invention and to level accusations of theft or plagiarism reveals the ignorance of the accusers—as Dylan pointed out to Gilmore:

> Dylan. People have tried to stop me every inch of the way. They've always had bad stuff to say about me. *Newsweek* magazine lit the fuse way back when. *Newsweek* printed that some kid from New Jersey wrote "Blowin' in the Wind" and it wasn't me at all. And when that didn't fly, people accused me of stealing the melody from a sixteenth-century Protestant hymn. And when that didn't work, they said they made a mistake and it was really an old Negro spiritual. So what's so different? It's gone on for so long I might not be able to live without it now. Fuck 'em. I'll see them all in their graves.
>
> Everything people say about you or me, they are saying about themselves. They're telling about themselves. Ever notice that? In my case, there's a whole world of scholars, professors and Dylanologists, and everything I do affects them in some way. And, you know, in some ways, I've given them life. They'd be nowhere without me.[54]

He's right about that. Articles continue to appear indignantly levelling allegations of phoniness and plagiarism. It seems fair to ask, Why must he always be the thief? To return briefly to the Shakespeare comparison—no sane critic calls Shakespeare a thief, let alone a plagiarist, despite the fact that not one of his plays is "original": he took virtually every single one from other plays or novellas. Yet the Shakespeare Industry thrives and grows in academia.

Despite the naysayers, the Dylan Industry is also thriving, with new books, journals, articles, and even imitators (on YouTube) proliferating. Scholars from different disciplines continue to dig, and, like the apparently bottomless supply of biographers, will undoubtedly expand their archaeological project now that the Bob Dylan Archive is open. "Essential" interviews never cease to appear, while self-styled "completists" track down every reference in every song, not necessarily with scholarly intent (or rigor), but rather in the hope of finding and decoding a new *chanson à clef* like "Girl from the North Country" (1963) or "Ballad in Plain D" (1964) or "Idiot Wind" (1974)—not to mention "Sara" (1975). It's important to remember, however, that the necessary cause of this rage to research is Dylan's grounding in the *process* of folk music. Bob Dylan *is* the folk process. By the force of his imitative imagination, he constantly disrupts the folk tradition and, simultaneously, completes it.

Things Unattempted Yet in Prose or Rhyme

All across the telegraph people concentrate on how Dylan borrows verbatim from other authors, which has caused no end of Sturm und Drang—with the word "borrows" generally appearing in scare quotes. Yet the appropriation of others' language or others' images (as in some of Dylan's paintings) reflects a technique as common to contemporary artists as it was to poets throughout the tradition. A classic instance occurs in Milton's first invocation in *Paradise Lost*:

> I thence
> Invoke thy aid to my advent'rous song
> That with no middle flight intends to soar
> Above th' Aonian mount, while it pursues
> *Things unattempted yet in prose or rhyme.*[55]

Milton published his epic poem in 1668. The italicized line is a direct translation of a line from the beginning of Ludovico Ariosto's wildly popular chivalric epic, *Orlando Furioso*, published in 1532.

> Dirò d'Orlando in un medesmo tratto
> *cosa non detta in prosa mai, né in rima.*[56]

> I'll sing of Roland in the same way
> A thing not yet spoken in prose or rhyme.

Milton's line is so nearly a literal translation of Ariosto's that we might be tempted to call the later line a copy of the earlier. More than merely copying, however, Milton appropriates Ariosto's famous earlier verse and turns it, *by the very act of appropriation*, into an entirely different "thing."

Ironically, some translators of Ariosto copy Milton's translation, by a kind of back-formation reading his imitation into the earlier text. In Italian "cosa non detta" is singular, "a thing not said," "not "spoken," or "not told." Despite this grammatical fact, however, translators have sometimes played their own inter-textual game with *Paradise Lost*. The Penguin Classics edition from 1975 (still extant and sold on Amazon) has Barbara Reynolds's translation: "Of Orlando I will also tell / Things unattempted yet in prose or rhyme." Older translations, too, such as William Stewart Rose's popular one from 1858, repeated Milton's line: "In the same strain of Roland will I tell / Things unattempted yet in prose or rhyme."[57] Intertextuality tracks across the linguistic and temporal barriers, de-ceptively representing the "original" model while appropriating its imitation. Yet which line, Milton's or the translators', is the copy?

This sort of playful anachronism does not explain what Milton is up to. The aim of translation is to maintain an equilibrium between texts. But Milton delib-erately destabilizes the imitative relationship; at the same time, it is by no means clear he is acting playfully. In adapting Ariosto's line to his own context, Milton transforms the meaning while challenging the informed reader to decide if the use of a *repeated* line claiming to herald things "unattempted" is theft, irony, or a new truth. Ariosto sings of knights and ladies, of Roland's madness and his errant adventures returning from Charlemagne's (failed) crusade to liberate Jerusalem from the "Turks." Yet Milton also sings of "man's first disobedience" and of the Son of God who routed the rebel angels and sacrificed himself, as the second Adam, to save fallen humankind. He finally gets around to explaining the con-trast between the *Orlando Furioso* and *Paradise Lost* in book 9 of his epic poem:

> Since this first subject for heroic song
> Please me long choosing, and beginning late;
> Not sedulous by nature to indite
> Wars, hitherto the only argument
> Heroic deemed, chief mast'ry to dissect
> With long and tedious havoc fabled knights
> In battles feigned; the better fortitude
> Of patience and heroic martyrdom
> Unsung.[58]

The opposition is clear, and *these* are the things unattempted yet in prose or rhyme: "the better fortitude / Of patience and heroic martyrdom." The old for-titude of war, subject of countless epics, will pale before the true courage of the

Son's patience and martyrdom. By changing topics but keeping the poetic form, Milton in effect wrests Ariosto's line from its chivalric context and inserts it in the sacred epic that anticipates *all* epics from Homer through Ariosto and Spenser while at the same time concluding the epic line in the seventeenth-century present. There's a Miltonic wink in this timeline, not least because it scrambles the sequence of imitations.

But is Milton a plagiarist for using the line? Should he have thought up a different way to say "things unattempted yet"? It is too late to argue about this, of course, since the success of Milton's appropriation continues to have an impact (as in post-Miltonic translators of Ariosto) and the retooled theft resounds down centuries of literary tradition.

The more crucial question is how Milton can be a vatic poet and practice imitation at the same time. The magic line between divine inspiration, the Muse who "visits . . . nightly," and the all-too-human art of imitatio never seems as dubious as when the poet's words are supposed to be so original as to be prophecy.

Einstein Disguised as Robin Hood

Coterminous with imitatio is *auctoritas*, a word that combines the concepts of origination and power. Every new voice, every practitioner of imitation, must establish his or her authority to speak through an authentication process inseparable from the arts. Poets, painters, sculptors, dancers, actors, and other artists authenticate themselves through a balance of virtuosity and genealogy. No art, whether static or performed, can exist ahistorically: the appreciation of virtuoso skill is always already an appreciation of the historical development of that skill and its antecedent practitioners. For this reason, one of the primary goals in establishing artistic *auctoritas* is to link oneself to a genealogical succession, without slavish imitation of a past master.

Dylan intuited this genealogical nuance of the authentication process from his earliest performances and his first recorded composition. Yet to establish his bona fides required much more than merely linking himself to a Mount Rushmore of folk singers from an earlier generation. The folk revival into which he launched himself was already furiously engaged in imitating the music of the "folk," ranging, in Dylan's own taxonomy in the *Biograph* album notes, from Southern Mountain Blues, Southern Mountain Ballads, City Blues, Texas Cowboy songs, to English ballads (but not including bluegrass tunes or Appalachian Ballads).[59] Yet, as Mellers's unparalleled "backdrop to Bob Dylan" explains, "it is important to recognize that influences with Dylan are never more than skin deep: they mean no more than that he was alive in a world where other things happen. Everything is re-created in his performance, which is also composition; and in his composition, which is also performance."[60] Mellers is exactly right to notice that "influences with Dylan are never more than skin deep." In part this refers to a come-what-may absorption of ambient music but, more precisely, to Dylan's instant transformation of what he heard into something new. As Van Ronk and many others have noted (including Dylan himself), Dylan's capacities of absorption even of the haphazard were stunning: he was called a musical sponge in his early Village days. But it wasn't all haphazard. From the outset Dylan was determined to choose his models of imitation cannily as part of the authentication process. His opportunism complemented his race to authenticity, and his exceptional transformations of his models—the same models everyone else was imitating—gave him an authority unique among his folk-singing peers.

It is difficult to describe, let alone conjure up, Dylan's charismatic authority in the early sixties. His voice seemed to strip caprice and frivolity from songs in a way other young voices could not. Mikki Isaacson recalls Dylan's shyness, his marginality at a party, until she asked him to play: "He came out of his shell. He moved toward the group, sat on the edge of one of the chairs and began to play. He didn't even have his own guitar with him: he borrowed someone else's. And he sang a song about somebody's death, and I wept."[61] The power of this living-room performance to move a listener to tears, in a room full of professional folk singers, is evidence of what John Hammond saw in the young Dylan, which encouraged him to sign Dylan as a performer, not a singer-songwriter (a "folk" category Dylan would himself create). Dylan once observed that it was harder to sing for ten people than for a concert audience, and Isaacson's reaction underscores Mellers's chiasmus: performance is composition and composition performance.

It is not an exaggeration to say that Dylan restored nature to the American folk music of his generation, and, fleetingly, revived the folk revival. First in his performances and then in his songs, he desophisticated the folk repertoire while renaturalizing ballad styles, blues standards, and vocal registers for white diction. His performances created the "instant artifacts" I mentioned above: they seemed so genuine as to pit present-day nostalgia and artificiality against a natural origin. Walter Jackson Bate quotes Samuel Johnson's *Rasselas*: "It is commonly observed that the early writers are in possession of nature, and their followers of art: that the first excel in strength and invention, and the latter in elegance and refinement."[62] Maybe because his guitar skills were basic, but largely because he sang with such magnetic conviction, Dylan's art made him seem "in possession of nature." He conveyed, simultaneously, the "strength and invention" of early bluesmen and a new version of their sound, conveying the totally alien emotions of the blues experience despite his class, Chaplinesque act, and cherubic face, despite "porcelain pussy cat eyes" and an accent belonging to "a jive Nebraskan, or maybe a Brooklyn hillbilly."[63]

Before Dylan was ever the voice *of* his generation, if he ever was, he *had* the voice of his generation. That was the root of his charismatic appeal. His musical authority seemed to derive from a source originating before art and artifice had sullied poetry and folk song. His desophistication of the folk repertoire was a kind of primitivism reminiscent in its imitations, distortions, and caricatures of early twentieth-century European art like that of Modigliani, Brancusi, Picasso, and Braque. And although Dylan himself often protested that he could never sing or play with the authority of someone like Doc Watson, his audience created him in the image of an antecedent voice. With a new irresistible rhythm and bespoke phrasing, Dylan seemed to bridge a cultural divide. Every singer in the folk music movement reached back, nostalgically and with varying mimetic skills, hoping to recover a lost original in song. Dylan, on the other hand, seemed to embody that originality. His performances evaded nostalgia because he was never really a conventional folk singer, never a quiescent legatee of tradition. As Christophe Lebold puts it, "While the blues seemed indeed the ideal medium for Dylan's mercurial creative energy and his magpie artistic temperament, what strikes first in the artist's early years is his insubordination to the Folk Revival ethos."[64]

That insubordination fit the mood of the time, deceptively introducing a James Dean defiance to counter the slavishly refined imitations of the Village folkies. John Hinchey writes of the "combination of sweetness and aggression" that, as "an abiding feature of Dylan's temperament," characterized his "early sense of his audience": "There is a seductive conspiratorial air about Dylan's songs of this period . . . It's a quality that had a lot to do with Dylan's early popularity: At once brash and unassuming, he treated himself as one of us, and even better, he treated what was most free in our spirit as if it were what made us normal, our truest (and only) common denominator."[65] Dylan's unconventional approach utterly transformed the sounds and diction he imitated, while seeming to recuperate the raw, preventriloquized power of pure folk music. This illusion of avatar purity was so strong that, notoriously, Dylan shocked and angered his true believers when he played an electric guitar at Newport in 1965. An audience member in the throes of deluded musical chauvinism even shouted "Traitor!," and in some ways he has remained a prisoner of his acoustic career ever since: the name Bob Dylan still conjures *folk singer* among infidels.

The origin myth has had countless retellings. Like the perfect tramp, Bob Dylan "burst on the scene," as Joan Baez sings, "already a legend, / the unwashed phenomenon, the original vagabond" ("Diamonds and Rust" 1975). But Dylan was anything but "original." He was always already an imitator. John Gibbens remarks on Dylan's magpie posturing, his claim "to be from nowhere, or from everywhere," which "some saw a con from early on, but most found the show worth the suspension of belief." And Gibbens perceptively adds that while the show might seem hard to believe in hindsight, "we can easily miss how precisely Bob-Dylan-shaped was the space in people's expectations, the people who were drawn to the folk revival, and how precisely he shaped himself for it."[66] Moreover, just as Dylan satisfied the charisma hunger of his audience and milieu, he shaped not only himself but that very milieu. The phenomenon of charismatic authority is symbiotic and requires an interdependence of group and leader in the creation and sustaining of its bond.

Dylan's imitative genius nurtured the bond and carried the day. He appeared to be a disheveled harp-blowing guitar player who'd already adopted the accents and persona of the most unassailably "original" white singer of the folk pantheon, Woody Guthrie. He aped him, honored him, and visited him in the hospital. But, significantly, this last gesture distinguished Dylan from the other Village folkies, from all the other Woody imitators and admirers. It gave him a unique authenticity. As Van Ronk remembers it, "We all admired Woody and considered him a legend, but none of us was trucking out to see him and play for him. In that regard, Dylan was as stand-up a cat as I have ever known, and it was a very decent and impressive beginning for anybody's career."[67] There's even a story that during his first week in New York, on Friday, January 27, 1961, Dylan knocked on the door of Woody's house in Howard Beach, Queens. The great man wasn't in and "the babysitter wanted to send him away but I let him in," according to Arlo Guthrie (who was thirteen years old at the time); "I liked him because he was wearing boots and looked interesting. We talked for a few minutes and he showed me how to play a few tunes on the harmonica."[68] Apparently, Marjorie Guthrie arrived home later to find "a household of bubbling children."[69]

Who was that masked man, she might have asked, "unborn and unnamed"?

The sincerity of Dylan's pilgrimage and of his Guthrie-worship was indisputably genuine. The middle-class outsider from the Iron Range came knocking to pay his respects, to sing for the dying legend, and, no doubt, to receive a benediction from the hand that strummed the Machine That Killed Fascists. And, to everyone's surprise (except his own, probably), he got his foot in the door—literally. But the speed of Dylan's transformation from grateful suitor to canny insider stunned his peers and still causes critics discomfort. As Greil Marcus puts it, "Even as a folk singer, Bob Dylan moved too fast, learned too quickly, made the old new too easily; to many he was always suspect."[70] As if following Ezra Pound's maxim for poetry, Dylan *made it new*, and in making it new made it his own. No sooner had he become an insider than he began to supplant his dewy hero-worship with a burgeoning awareness of himself as a pivotal link in the American folk tradition. Daniel Karlin suggests that "Dylan's career as a songwriter was self-inaugurated . . . by 'Song to Woody,' one of the two 'original' songs on his first album, *Bob Dylan*. 'Song to Woody,' like [Robert Frost's] 'Dedication,' places itself in a line of authoritative precursors, modestly and respectfully."[71] Modestly and respectfully, yes, but also ambitiously, with its newness manifest. Amid the distinctive covers of traditional songs on the album, that sole original composition forces an agon with Woody, the living protomyth of folk revivalists, and, unexpectedly, allows Dylan to supersede his presumed idol. "At the beginning of the second verse," according to Hinchey, Dylan "sounds surprised to discover he's written a song to Woody, to find himself talking to him, and not just about him. There's more to his delight than satisfied hero worship; this is the song in which Dylan outgrows his need for a hero, his dependence on the 'other men' who pioneered the road he travels. He does it quite gently, smashing the idol while leaving the man intact."[72]

"Song to Woody" is an early genealogical marker, signaling both a link to the past and an uncompromising departure from it. The lyrics contain the young Dylan's simple heartfelt homage, credibly sung in his early Iron Range *Kunstsprache*. Yet the homage gradually becomes a farewell, and the greeting that opens the song, ostensibly bringing the speaker together with the pathbreaking icon—"Hey, Hey, Woody Guthrie"—changes by the last stanza into a rejection of Woody and his way of life:

> Here's to Sonny and Cisco and Lead Belly too
> And to all the good people that traveled with you
> Here's to the hearts and the hands of the men
> That come with the dust and are gone with the wind

The speaker's Janus-like gaze wistfully names the guitar (and harmonica) heroes of a storied Dust-Bowl past as if yearning nostalgically to join them, while in fact he already has a foot planted in another direction.

> I'm a-leavin' tomorrow, but I could leave today
> Somewhere down the road someday
> The very last thing that I'd want to do
> Is to say I've been hittin' some hard travelin' too

He has no reason to wait, nothing left to do where he is, and he could as usefully be elsewhere already.

Two genealogical actions are taking place at the same time in "Song to Woody," neither of which, typically, is completely legitimate. First, the speaker, by implication (or insinuation), affixes himself to the catalog of names, grafting his voice onto the roots-and-branches of a folk-music family tree he has chosen for himself. (This is illegitimate, or a case of sleight-of-hand, since no one chooses his or her family tree.) The second genealogical maneuver is unexpected because it occurs so quickly, although in retrospect it might seem predictable. The speaker rejects the most revered acts and suffering of his heroic antecedents: the very last thing he'd want to do is to hit the road like his forebears. But, while respectful, he probably isn't expressing awe for the sublime stamina of Woody and his friends. Instead, he seems to be rejecting that generation and wresting away their music: they came with the dust but they're gone, full stop. The speaker's implication is that he will replace their obsolete Depression wanderings with, as Milton says in *Lycidas*, "fresh fields and pastures new." Whether we call this deliberate ambition or canny instinct, it is a significant reversal for a supposedly insouciant arriviste.

How to Imitate Perfect

In "Farewell, Angelina," three years (and a lyrical lifetime) after his original composition debut with "Song to Woody," Dylan wrote the following verse:

> The camouflaged parrot, he flutters from fear
> When something he doesn't know about suddenly appears
> What cannot be imitated perfect must die
> Farewell Angelina
> The sky is flooding over
> And I must go where it's dry

Joan Baez recorded "Farewell, Angelina" in 1965 without this verse. According to Clinton Heylin, "it may be that Dylan added this verse post-Carmel, but it seems more likely that Baez exercised some editorial control and clipped 'the camouflaged parrot' from her version," suggesting that the verse "adds only atmosphere to what is, in either form, a classic 'mid-period' Dylan composition."[73]

Despite apparently not considering the song for *Bringing It All Back Home*, Dylan recorded it in 1965 and included the "camouflaged parrot" verse (released on *Bootleg Series, Vol. 1–3*). The pertinence of the verse to Dylan's creative relationship with his most influential forebears makes me wonder if, perhaps, Dylan was the one who "exercised editorial control" and withheld the verse from Baez to keep for himself. The barely veiled references to bad imitation underscore Dylan's commitment to a dynamic form of imitatio. The "camouflaged parrot" refers to writing that fails the test of the apian metaphor—fails, in Senecan terms, to blend, digest, and transform the original language. A camouflaged parrot is, arguably, a mindlessly repeating squawker fitted out in war gear. This image combines with the portentous line "what cannot be imitated must die" to form the foundation of Dylan's ars poetica. To hide oneself from the past, to be secretly at war with it, while parroting the language of a bygone era, is doomed to ruin one's art. Every artist struggles with the past to emerge as unique, and in this struggle mere camouflage is a compromise. Dylan's compact image echoes Seneca's advice that, in using past authors, "we should so blend those several flavors into one delicious compound that, even though it betrays its origin, yet it nevertheless is clearly a different thing from that whence it came."[74] A different thing, not a camouflaged parrot. (In the Renaissance the corresponding negative image was usually an ape—minus the camouflage.)

To say that "what cannot be imitated must die" is another way of saying farewell. I think those few words have more resonance with Dylan's artistic transformations of past music than his signature farewell-to-folk in "Baby Blue." "Farewell, Angelina" is not as good a song as "Baby Blue"—few songs are, in or out of Dylan's canon—but in the former the young artist seems to give more thought to his relationship with past songs and past performers than he does in the biting,

accusatory imperatives of the latter. While both songs signal and effectively en-
act a separation, in "Farewell, Angelina" Dylan's speaker hints at an artistic future
based on perfect imitation. This is not so much a restless as a resigned farewell,
less caustic than so many of Dylan's goodbyes. The speaker seems to apprehend
the difference between cutting ties with the past ("Don't think twice") and as-
similating it, blending it, flower by flower, into a new compound that betrays its
origin but is clearly "a different thing from whence it came."

"Farewell, Angelina" refers to the quality of artistic interaction. The poetics of
imitation are at stake. The camouflaged parrot "flutters from fear / When some-
thing he doesn't know about suddenly appears" because, for slavish imitators,
the unfamiliar threatens identity. Imitation, by enlarging the circle of the artist-
imitator's repertoire, serves as a kind of protective cloak against unforeseen at-
tacks. It almost seems a non sequitur or a dissociative leap when Dylan sings
"What cannot be imitated perfect must die," because he shifts from the parrot
to the "something"—the something that the suddenly frightened bird is unable
to, well, *parrot*. Engagement with the past should never result in a dead—and
desiccated—present work. Dylan demonstrates this interaction with a linguistic
twist in the irony of the "die/dry" rhyme: the threat of desiccation (in death or
in the death of art) versus the safe-from-high-water-everywhere dryness when
the sky is flooding over. The two very different kinds of dryness mirror the two
kinds of response to the past, the slavishly imitative and the creatively digestive.
But the song is clear: it is not the parrot who must die (though maybe he [or she]
does too), but the things he cannot imitate because his art is bad, not sufficient.
The "die/dry" irony cuts both ways.

The speaker of "Baby Blue" offers only a damage report, an account of loss
and reversal ("The vagabond who's knocking at your door / Has taken all his blan-
kets from the floor"). The song contains no specifically artistic critique and no
promise for the offspring of the "I-was-in-the-Lincoln-Brigade" generation. Baby
Blue can only strike another match and go start anew. The metaphor is ambigu-
ous: a match flame might flare briefly and sputter out or might ignite something
to burn brightly in the future. The music discourages the latter interpretation as
the high notes of every long line tumble downward in a falling scale. The short
lines—"Yonder stands your orphan with his gun / Crying like a fire in the sun,"
and so forth in every stanza—seem to be a reprieve, maintaining a tonic equilib-
rium that Dylan tempers with the timbre and volume of his voice. But this reprieve
is canceled as Dylan's voice increases abruptly in volume and as he stretches the
pitch in the following lines ("The sky too is folding over you" . . . "The carpet too is
moving under you" . . . "Strike another match, go start anew"). The refrain—"It's
all over now, Baby Blue"—is delivered (in the recorded version) with a kind of
ruthless calm as Dylan's voice returns to the volume and timbre of the short lines.

Although too much has already been said about the scene in the D. J. Penne-
baker documentary *Don't Look Back* in which Donovan plays a song and Dylan

follows with "Baby Blue," I'd like to add a few remarks because, in my view, the scene offers a rare example of Dylan interacting with an imitator, a singer manifestly an ephebe. The supposed controversy between Dylan and Donovan is a storm in a teacup and does not stand up to closer scrutiny of Pennebaker's film. The alleged conflicts between the two are largely the result of the post hoc, ergo propter hoc fallacy, fueled by conclusions about Dylan's (and Albert Grossman's) career decisions rather than by the encounter itself. In a recent interview with Pennebaker, Clayton Dillard referred to "the altercation or interaction" with Donovan, but there's scant support for the widespread opinion that Dylan's song is meant to slam Donovan down, let alone that there was an overt altercation.[75] In other scenes, Dylan coyly refuses to speak Donovan's name, and, as Ian Bell puts it, may want to "twist the wig of Donovan" as an upstart, but in their one shared scene the two singers seem friendly and unstrained—although there is the glow of hero worship in Donovan's eye.[76]

The transcript of the film, done by Pennebaker himself and in print since 1968, cannot catch that ephebe's glow, but it serves as a useful corrective to the controversy seekers. Although, as Pennebaker says in his brief forward, it "is no substitute for the reality of the film," the transcript provides an accurate record of everyone's words—or "as accurate as the fallible human ear can make it."[77] Most important, the transcript rescues the inaudible mumbles and off-camera gestures lost in Pennebaker's "direct cinema" process.

This excerpt comes soon after the notorious incident of the glass being thrown out a window.

Donovan begins playing the guitar.

DYLAN   Hey, he plays like Jack, man.

DONOVAN *sings a verse of "To Sing for You"*

DYLAN   Hey, that's a good song, man.

DONOVAN *sings next verse. Applause.*

DYLAN   That's okay, man.

VOICE   Hey, play one, Bob, play one.

DONOVAN   I wanna hear "It's All Over Now, Baby Blue."

DYLAN   You wanna hear that song? Do you have a flat pick?

DONOVAN   I got that in a "D" tuning.

DYLAN   What key did you tune it down to?

DONOVAN   "D" tuning.

DYLAN *sings.*

> *You must leave, take what you need*
> *You think will last*
> *But whatever you wish to keep*
> *You'd better grab it fast.*
> *Yonder stands your orphan with his gun*
> *Crying like a fire in the sun*
> *. . . . .*
> *The vagabond, he's rapping at your door*
> *He's standing in the clothes*
> *That you once wore.*
> *Strike another match,*
> *Go start anew.*
> *And it's all over now, baby blue.*[78]

Just to be clear on a few things, and to counter the chronic misinterpretations of this scene: Dylan is singing *for* Donovan, not at him or against him, as if in some kind of flyting match. True, when he sings "Yonder stands your orphan with his gun," he starts to smirk. But he isn't looking at Donovan, and there's no reason to infer that his twinkling delivery is meant to undercut Donovan. He's looking at someone across the room, possibly Derroll Adams.[79] In any case, during the first refrain he's facing away from Donovan. Then the camera pans and we see first Adams, rapt, and then Donovan, also rapt, sitting still and composed (holding a cigarette). During the last refrain Dylan faces Donovan and delivers "It's all over now, Baby Blue" with the generosity of a singer fulfilling a personal request for a song. And immediately afterward, Dylan is eager to know that Donovan liked the song and asks about playing another.

What rivalry?

Supersubtle readings of the scene persist, usually bringing conflict to the fore. Yet, as the film shows and the transcript confirms, the tenor of the scene has no such conflict. Donovan has already finished his song when Dylan stands to take the guitar, and Dylan doesn't deliver his song as an arch response. On the contrary, Donovan requests "Baby Blue."

Donovan was four years younger than Dylan, and just starting out. He had a couple of hits on the British folk/pop charts, but Dylan would have been unlikely to spurn him as a fossilized element of the New York scene.[80] Dylan instead seems tickled by Donovan's song, and maybe by the imitation, especially when the young Scotsman's voice tumbles down to the refrain:

> Call out to me as I ramble by,
> To sing for you,

That's what I'm here to do,
To sing for you

What a perfect song choice as a humble recognition of his place in the hierarchy, reminiscent of Dylan himself in Woody Guthrie's hospital room. The performance is an obvious homage to Dylan and almost mawkishly enacts the song's title and refrain. Donovan the singer asks what else he can do but sing for you—that's what he is "here to do," to sing for Bob Dylan. Usually anonymous, the pronominal "you" here takes on a living identity ("Hey, Hey, Woody Guthrie"). Donovan sings his lover's plea to Dylan, more up-tempo than on the recording, raising his voice on the melody's unexpected treble notes (*as* I ramble *by*) with force enough to pierce the hubbub in the room.

Dylan has always spoken ambivalently about being an idol, but there's nothing in the Pennebaker scene indicating that he is rejecting Donovan's song—or the entire folk music milieu—by singing "Baby Blue" as if to render a harsh verdict. Donovan's unabashed tribute in and of itself established a musical genealogy, and even behind the shades Dylan was probably not unaware of the implicit bid to join the family tree.

Farewell, Angelina Revisited

In the introduction I suggested that the Joan Baez jacket notes offered a rare peek at Dylan engaging another artist and redefining the category of the artistic debate. Of course, the jacket notes manipulate and dramatize the climax of Dylan's aesthetic bildungsroman (in miniature) in a way the encounter with Donovan at the Savoy never could have (at least not in Pennebaker's direct cinema mode). But the jacket notes nevertheless confirm Dylan's attitude toward the master-ephebe model of artistic production. He not only accepts the notion of models among peers but seems satisfied—if the *Don't Look Back* scene is viewed without press hype and jaded hindsight—to play his role as a model of imitation. By 1965 this role was already familiar. In response to a question for the *Biograph* liner notes (see above), Dylan recalled that, although his technique annoyed the old guard of folksingers, "quite a few of [the younger ones] began to copy my attitude in guitar phrasing and such." He doesn't expand on this statement, yet the inference can be reasonably drawn that he was pleased—even vindicated—by the imitation of his peers. More to the point, and germane to his encounter with Donovan, Dylan never abandons the imitative process itself nor his belief in a genealogical order of precursor models.

In this regard, Dylan's willingness to perform "Baby Blue" on request has an irony all its own: the name Baby Blue (or "sobriquet," as Marqusee calls it) comes from a Gene Vincent song. The second part of the title, however, echoes Mance Lipscomb's "Sugar Babe," recorded in 1960 on his album *Texas Songster*:

Sugar Babe, I'm tired of you
It ain't your honey but the way you do
Sugar Babe, it's all over now

All I want my baby do
Make five dollars and give me two
Sugar Babe, it's all over now

Went downtown an' bought a rope
Whupped my babe till she Buzzard Lope[81]
Sugar Babe, it's all over now

Sugar Babe, what's the matter with you?
You don't treat me like you used to do
Sugar Babe, it's all over now

Went to town an' bought me a line
Whupped my babe till she changed her mind
Sugar Babe, Sugar Babe it's all over now

Sugar Babe, I'm tired of you
It ain't your honey but the way you do
Sugar Babe, it's all over now

Reports of domestic abuse were, regretfully, not uncommon in blues lyrics. But "Whupped my babe till she Buzzard Lope" and "Whupped my babe till she changed her mind" are tame in comparison to jealousy songs like "Frankie and Johnny," "Delia," or "Blood in My Eyes," which are manifestly and vindictively violent. But the violence is inescapable, as is the repellent sense of male force, despite the ludic element in the lyric and Lipscomb's upbeat bluesiness.

The speaker's ambivalence in "Sugar Babe" is mirrored by both the speaker in "Baby Blue" and Dylan's transitional status in his musical development. First Lipscomb's frustrated speaker jettisons his lover—"I'm tired of you . . . it's all over now"—just as Dylan's portentous lover calls out "You must leave now, take what you need . . . it's all over now." Lipscomb's lyric offers two opposite solutions, both the result of a beating: the speaker will beat his lover (with a rope) until she dances the Buzzard Lope, or he'll beat her (with a line) till she changes her mind. In the first instance the beating produces a minstrel show dance, in the second a change of mind (presumably in relation to her unacceptable conduct, "the way you do").

Did Dylan exploit the difference in the two beatings in composing "Baby Blue"? I don't hear that nuance in the lyric. Did he hear "Whupped my babe till she changed her mind" as he adapted Mance Lipscomb's sharecropper milieu to the urban middle-class bohemians of the "Baby Blue" cohort? Maybe he did. And, finally, was he chuckling to himself at Lipscomb's "bought a rope" as he "whupped" Donovan in the hotel room? This last possibility seems highly unlikely. Much more in evidence is that his refrain demonstrates a humility, a homage paid to the Texas bluesman—possibly ironic, given Donovan's homage to Dylan.

If there is indeed a homage to Lipscomb in "Baby Blue," then perhaps Dylan is resisting the inbuilt misogyny of so many blues lyrics. A homage removes the brutal maleness of the original song, replacing it with an attenuated version of masculinity, with the lover not as a victim but as a version of the ephebe who leaves and builds a new life out of the things she's grabbed (coincidence, crazy-patterned sheets, the moving carpet). It may further indicate a dialogue, not between Lipscomb's abusive lover and his Sugar Babe, but between the poet and himself, a reading of imitation as leaving the ephebe status behind but taking things with you where you go.

In "Baby Blue"—as others have noted—Dylan deliberately inserts himself as the transitional, and transformative, step between traditional music and the unpredictable musical future. His anonymous homodiegetic speaker may urge the pronominal lover ("*You* must leave" . . ."*Your* empty-handed painter") to leave her (or his) stepping-stones behind.[82] But it is Dylan himself—the performer/composer, not the song's speaker—who embodies those very stepping-stones. He linked himself to Mance Lipscomb's influence very early, as recorded in an entry in Izzy Young's notebook for October 20, 1961, most of which became the brief biography issued by Young's Folklore Center in connection with Dylan's 1961 Carnegie Hall concert. Young jotted down Dylan's dubious, but revealing claims: "He learned many blues songs from a Chicago street singer named Arvella Gray. He also met a singer—Mance Lipscomb—from the Brazos River country of Texas, through a grandson who sang rock and roll. He listened a lot to Lipscomb. He heard Woody Guthrie's album of Dust Bowl ballads in South Dakota."[83] In 1961 Dylan had probably not yet been to South Dakota, and the rest of Young's biographical data is riddled with similar, and even more spectacular, inventions. Yet, like all the early life stories, there's a grain of useful truth amid the flurry of fantasies. Young reports three singers mentioned by name as influences or teachers, and Lipscomb is one. While this section of the entry is in the third person, the remainder of this and other entries in the notebook quote Dylan, as Jeff Burger points out, and refer to him in the first person. The October 20 entry includes Dylan's first-person views on folk music, his favorite contemporary singers, and weird pronouncements, like "I dress the way I do because I want to dress this way and not because it is cheaper or easier." And the entry ends with a typically paradoxical, yet pertinent, Dylan remark: "No one is really influencing me now—but actually everything does. Can't think of anyone in particular now."[84]

The truth, in 1961, was closer to "actually everything" than to "no one," as is well-attested. But the prominence of the Mance Lipscomb reference as early as that year more than justifies the association of "Baby Blue" with "Sugar Babe." Dylan's Janus gaze has always been his most characteristic compositional and performance feature. Even in his oeuvre's voluminous, and variously cast, farewells to the past—farewells to women, to towns, to bad habits, to the folk music scene, and to the various arts—and even in the grip of his most associative imagery, both his musical allegiances and his allusive power glance backward. Donovan probably didn't get this double message as Dylan sang to him at the Savoy, but Dylan would have been aware of the delicate balance. And his sense of supersession would have been tempered, as it always is in his writing and singing, by an imitative reverence for his forebears.

From Woody to Woodstock

As the young songwriter of "Farewell, Angelina" already intuited, to "imitate perfect" does not mean to copy exactly but to form a dynamic, transformative relationship with the writers and songs of the past—to be more a bee than a parrot. If this is an indictment of the folkies who tried slavishly to imitate their idols and reproduce their sounds, then it is perspicacious and accurate, and much more explicitly stated than the admonitory metaphors of "Baby Blue." While the Woody Guthrie Machine certainly started out in the Village by trying to reproduce his predecessors' sounds, he soon saw the fundamental impossibility—and the dead end—of this approach. If in 1963's jacket notes to *Joan Baez in Concert, Part 2*, Dylan had named Hank Williams as his first idol (soon to be abandoned), in 1964 he names his last and most significant idol in "11 Outlined Epitaphs," the liner notes for *The Times They Are A-Changin'*:

> Woody Guthrie was my last idol
> he was the last idol
> because he was the first idol
> I'd ever met
> that taught me
> face t' face
> that men are men
> shatterin' even himself
> as an idol

Just as Guthrie shatters his own myth, Dylan's self-debunking became one of his most familiar practices. From the shock of *Another Side* to the new voice of *Nashville Skyline* to *Renaldo and Clara* to the impassioned Christian conversion to—more recently—Victoria's Secret, the Christmas album, and *Shadows in the Night*—through these and other musical (and moral) developments, Dylan has paradoxically inflated the myth of the mercurial "I-Am-Not-There" persona while attempting to "shatter even himself." The "Outlined Epitaph" continues:

> an' that men have reasons
> for what they do
> an' what they say
> an' every action can be questioned
> leavin' no command
> untouched an' took for granted
> obeyed an' bowed down to
> forgettin' your own natural instincts[85]

Shattering a musical idol is complementary to rejecting slavish imitation, an instinctual musical consciousness Dylan always understood. To shatter oneself, debunking one's own myth, leaves only a kind of protomyth, what Kermode called "the myth before the myth began."

In a slight, but surprising verse from "Guess I'm Doing Fine," written in 1964 and recorded on the Witmark Demos, Dylan sings,

> Well, I ain't a-got my childhood
> Or friends I once did know
> No, I ain't a-got my childhood
> Or friends I once did know
> But I still got my voice left
> I can take it anywhere I go
> Hey, hey, so I guess I'm doin' fine

It is impossible to do justice in writing to Dylan's singing here, the stretched emphases followed by grace notes, as in the last line. The verse has buoyancy and strong tempo, as if performative levity could counter the catastrophic loss of childhood and friends. But the song isn't a blues. There's no self-pity or stoical resignation in the tumbling lines. Instead, the singer offers an utterly stripped-down human specimen, scarcely even a socialized character, reduced to a voice alone. Yet, as Dylan recognizes, the voice redresses the imbalance of a lost past and, alone, promises the future. This voice that the singer can take anywhere, unattached to his own past or to social binding and somehow disembodied in the song, *sings* the song and creates itself as a protomyth.

Dylan is always singing that same song. Rigorously, comprehensively, and ruthlessly, he strips away his "childhood" and "friends" from his artistic persona. Left only with his voice, he becomes the embodiment of the tradition he imitates. But even early on Dylan explained himself. In what might generously be called an uneven interview with Cynthia Gooding in 1962—an interview laced

PAST THE VERNACULAR

with Dylan's colossally implausible fibs about being "with the carnival off and on six years"—the twenty-one-year-old reveals a precocious sense of imitation.

> Gooding. And this is one of the quickest rises in folk music, wouldn't you say?
>
> Dylan. Yeah, but I don't really think of myself as a folk singer, because I don't play much across the country . . . I like more than just folk music, too. And I sing more than just folk music. A lot of people, they're just folk music, folk music, folk music. I like folk music like Hobart Smith stuff and all that but I don't sing much of that, and when I do it's probably a modified version of something. Not a modified version; I don't know how to explain it. It's just there's more to it I think. Old-time jazz things. Jelly Roll Morton and stuff like that.[86]

Whether this is genuine inarticulateness or fashionable mumbling (à la Brando and Dean), the phrases "a modified version of something," followed immediately by "not a modified version," and then "old-time jazz things," reflect an attempt to explain (or conceal) the process by which a songwriter improvises a new version based on an earlier model. Hence the "jazz thing" and also the connection to imitation. Scholars such as Richard Schoeck and Peter Brown have linked the "impromptu performance" of classical rhetoricians to the improvisatory techniques of Hot Jazz musicians, suggesting that, like, say, jazz trumpeters, rhetoricians could plumb their memories for themes "held in readiness . . . by centuries of tradition" and weave them into speeches for a current audience.[87] If this technique of memory, improvisation, and performance was manifest in Hot Jazz, then Cool Jazz redoubled the complexities of the technique, and the virtuosity of such postwar phenomena as Charlie Parker, Dizzy Gillespie, Joe Pass, Miles Davis, and maybe even James Marshall (later Jimi Hendrix) made an impression on many up-and-coming musicians.

The connection to jazz would seem to make sense, not least because Dylan himself, in the Cynthia Gooding interview, refers to "old-time jazz things." His reworkings of songs in performance have always seemed to be the artistry of a fluid improviser. But in a 2020 interview with Douglas Brinkley, Dylan convincingly rejects that impression:

> Brinkley. What role does improvisation play in your music?
>
> Dylan. None at all. There's no way you can change the nature of a song once you've invented it. You can set different guitar or piano patterns upon the structural lines and go from there, but that's not improvisation. Improvisation leaves you open to good or bad performances and the idea is to stay consistent. You basically play the same thing time after time in the most perfect way you can.[88]

According to this surprising answer, Dylan eschews improvisation or any such off-the-cuff undertakings as Allen Ginsberg's "spontaneous poetry." He won't risk improvisation because that would open the door to good or bad performances and he needs to stay consistent—either because the songs *as they were written* can't be changed or because they mean so much to him in their original nature. In every performance of every song, then, as different as the songs might sound to us, Dylan delivers unchanged versions. He plays "the same thing time after time in the most perfect way."

There was a time, not so long past, when Dylan and the Beatles were the equivalent of cultural paideia: to steal a line from them would have been like stealing the club of Hercules. Dylan suffered famously from this phenomenon: whenever he altered the musical structure or lyrics of his own songs, disappointed fans objected, sometimes vigorously, to the impromptu revisions. They wanted to hear exact replicas of the recorded "originals." But Dylan's idea of replication and originality always seemed to differ from that of his most literal-minded fans. The changes he makes in performance are reminiscent of Henry James, whose celebrated revisions didn't affect the perfection of the novels—according to James's loyalists. Or Walt Whitman, who is often compared to Dylan as a vatic influence and as an American proto-Guthrie original: Whitman added many lines to *Leaves of Grass* but kept the essence of that long poem unchanged—the "Me Myself" core.

The key to understanding Dylan's idea of imitation is here: his aim from the start of his career in folk was to produce "modified" versions of songs, which were unique in every performance. They were somehow unique but still the "same thing," always perfect at the core in his imitations. This kind of ambition would eventually require an encyclopedic knowledge of American music. It would include ruthlessly borrowing and reshaping songs, clichés, and cultural icons. Dylan stands out for his electrifying ability to exploit song tradition. Even when his exploitations have been misnamed thefts or plagiarisms, his virtuosic imitations have captured listeners and, through melody and lyric alike, have become part of living cultural memory.

The *Bootleg Series* of studio outtakes and performance recordings demonstrates Dylan's virtuosity in this area, seemingly capturing in amber the revisionary and self-revisionary process of his Whitmanian rewriting. Columbia Records began releasing the *Bootleg Series* in the eighties; as of this writing, it is up to volume 16 (*Springtime in New York*, 2021). Each new release offers an invaluable trove of different versions of his songs, as well as recordings of unreleased songs and covers of others' tunes. For those who know the original album versions, the *Bootleg Series* seems to offer an archive of comparisons. It may be a boon to Dylan-industry commerce. But, above all, the *Bootleg Series* provides a permanent record of Dylan's relationship to imitation, emulation, and self-imitation.

2 | SAVAGE INNOCENCE
Dylan's Art of Appropriation

My clothes are wet, tight on my skin
Not as tight as the corner that I've painted myself in
—"Mississippi"

In the film *The Savage Innocents*, Anthony Quinn plays Inuk, an Eskimo hunter. Inuk, I would suggest, is the inspiration for Dylan's famous song, which, as Heylin reminds us, was originally called "Quinn the Eskimo" and renamed "The Mighty Quinn" by Manfred Mann.[1] Although no one seems to have cited this film as the source of the song, I have not seen an explanation anywhere as to why the "mighty" Quinn should be an Eskimo. Most critics don't even give space to the song while the few who do avoid digging too deeply and instead dismiss it with faint praise as, for example, "delightfully indecipherable" or "a half-cocked paean to impending renewal."[2] Yet with *The Savage Innocents* as background, the lyrics are possibly somewhat clearer.[3]

The film was released in 1960, directed by Nicholas Ray, who also wrote the screenplay. Ray was renowned for his 1955 picture *Rebel without a Cause*, whose star, James Dean, the matinee idol bad boy, cast a long shadow of influence on Dylan's generation.[4] Ray's directorial role might have been enough to get Dylan to the theater, and the movie, for all its flaws, might have provided grist for the Village intellectual mill, a chance to engage the theories of such popular thinkers as Ashley Montagu. But, as likely as this scenario might be, there is no evidence that Dylan saw *The Savage Innocents*. In fact, the absence of any mention of the film among Dylan's contemporaries makes it harder to argue the identification.

Nevertheless, I am confident the film is the song's source. If Quinn the Eskimo is in fact *Anthony* Quinn the Eskimo, then perhaps the film's mise-en-scène and the fate of Inuk deserve to be held up as a mirror to the "indecipherable" lyrics. Despite an earnest effort to challenge postwar pieties, the film cannot quite overcome its offensive Hollywood exoticisms, such the Eskimos' fake accents and weird use of personal pronouns (as if they can't even speak their own language fluently), not to mention the questionable practice of wife-sharing. But maybe 1960s cultural sensibilities would not have been offended and Inuk is by any yardstick a larger-than-life figure, more than merely a force of nature. He is a man with a strict moral code: regardless of how ruthless he might seem in contrast to the "white men," he remains loyal to the "law of his father." Throughout the plot, Quinn comes across convincingly as the mighty Inuk.

The film opens with a cautionary scene, as if to set the "savage" mood: even before the credits run, Ray allows the camera to discover pristine icebergs rising in a calm sea. A polar bear is swimming through the water. There's a reverse perspective on two figures fully covered in furs paddling a kayak or canoe. One of them releases a harpoon-like spear. The perspective turns again and the harpoon pierces the polar bear. Blood appears at the wound site, staining the water, and the polar bear sinks, dragging the harpoon's line under water. As the credits begin, the camera pans away from the hunting scene to a stark landscape of only ice and water. Then comes a narrator's voice: "On top of the world, nearer to the north pole than to any civilized area, there live a race of nomads. They're so proud they call themselves simply 'The Men.' We in turn call these people 'Eskimos,' meaning 'eaters of raw flesh.' And in the age of the atom bomb they still hunt with bow and arrow. They share whatever they own and they are so crude they don't know how to lie." As the narration stops, Inuk appears and parks his dog sled outside an igloo. He dives into the dwelling and hears uproarious laughter, which seems to make him laugh. The camera discovers a man and a woman naked in bed (under a sealskin), slapping at each other gaily. The conversation turns to finding a wife for Inuk, who suddenly becomes embarrassed and rushes out of the igloo. The woman urges the man to stop him. So the man catches up with Inuk just as the dog sled is pulling away. He scolds him for running off so quickly and offers the customary hospitality: "You may laugh with my wife for a while. You have permission. It does her good. Makes her eyes shine."

The shock value of this sexual sharing quickly establishes the alien a-Christian character of Eskimo culture. Inuk is a legatee of this culture and an amiable member of its far-flung community. But Inuk is also redoubtable, a towering fur-clad figure, who, as the reprehensible saying goes, "has never seen a white man." Anthony Quinn plays him as an insouciant cultural conservative, whose hunting prowess becomes an obsession once he learns that he can trade "worthless" fox furs for a gun. On his first trip to the trading post, which is run by a redhaired Canadian, he trades for the gun, but he doesn't receive any bullets and plans to hunt another few seasons to bring in the fox furs to trade for bullets. This plan upsets his wife, Asiak, who has been eating inferior fox meat for too long, and, unbeknownst to Inuk, she gives away the gun as they are hurriedly leaving the trading post after Inuk and the local, assimilated Eskimos engage in a fight. (As appeasement, Inuk offers Asiak to one of the Eskimos, foreshadowing the plot's crucial moment.)

Ray sets the trading post contretemps as a classic clash of cultures: Inuk and Asiak represent purity while the Eskimos, Canadians, and Catholics at the trading post represent a more jaded, worldly concatenation of values. In any case, Inuk and Asiak escape from the mayhem of the trading post and build themselves an igloo for the night nearby. In the morning they receive a visit from a Catholic priest who has come to save them from themselves. He accuses them of being sinners, particularly for offering to share Asiak. But Inuk and Asiak don't understand him. Nevertheless, despite the priest's earnest discomfort, they treat him with customary Eskimo hospitality: they offer their best food—which happens to be a bowl of their oldest meat crawling with fresh maggots—and then Inuk suggests that the priest "laugh with his wife." The appalled priest refuses both food and wife, which infuriates the now-insulted Inuk who bangs the priest's head against the igloo wall until he splits open his skull.

The movie scene is a kind of parody of patrimonialism and colonial blundering, with utterly tragic consequences. The film programmatically dramatizes a stalemate between "savage" and "civilized," between "primitive" and "progressive." The plot continues: Inuk and Asiak flee the trading post and after several seasons simply forget about the dead priest. But all the while, from spring to spring, two Canadian troopers are trying to track down Inuk, who, unbeknownst to himself, is now an outlaw murderer (which would be a new category of outlaw for Dylan—John Wesley Harding et al. certainly knew they were murderers). The troopers are determined to take Inuk back to be hanged. But, of course, they aren't prepared for the ice: after they capture him (without a fight) one of them carelessly steers the dog sled into the freezing water and dies, while Inuk saves the other's life. He takes him back to his igloo for the winter and in the spring decides, with Asiak's agreement, to bring the trooper back to the trading post. To his credit, the trooper makes it clear that Inuk will be his prisoner if they go back together, and that the court will likely recommend the slipknot. Nevertheless, the obtusely honest Inuk and Asiak are confident they can persuade the judge to see the law their way. When they arrive outside the settlement, the trooper makes one last attempt to convince Inuk how wrong he is. Inuk shrugs this off, unable to believe the white men won't see reason. So the trooper, obviously grateful (and necessarily patronizing), pretends to reject Inuk's friendship and stalks off on his own. The baffled Inuk and Asiak write this unexpected insult off to occult ethnoracial Otherness and return with their freedom to the ice. The symmetry of the result leaves both cultures intact, at least as long as the wilderness provides a buffer.

Maybe *this* is the geometry of innocence. Or maybe it's the moment when we should say, "To live outside the law you must be honest."

Despite the dumbed-down accents and the pop anthropology, Ray manages to stage an irremediable clash of cultures with more insight than even the most sensitive Westerns of the fifties or sixties. Asiak at one point says that one should not bring one's own laws into another country. Clifford Geertz could not have said it better.

Meet Me in the Margin

The bowl of squirming maggots Inuk and Asiak serve to the priest could have provided the source of the line "It ain't my cup of meat." And the crime, an accidental murder—Asiak suggests that the priest's head was too soft, an excellent pun—gives ample support to the idea of Quinn the Eskimo's "mightiness." But, while there are elements in *The Savage Innocents* that could be actual sources, the broader argument I'd like to make is that adding a source to "Quinn the Eskimo" makes Dylan more, not less, original.

"Pure" originality belongs in the searching-for-a-unicorn category. But without a source such as *The Savage Innocents*, much of the allusive content and the lyrical clarity of "Quinn the Eskimo" is lost. Ironically, in fact, without an original source, Dylan's true originality is also lost. In the film, there's nothing haphazard or one-size-fits-all about Inuk's return to freedom: the cruelty of the icy wilderness combined with the tragic violence acted out by both sides make it hard to imagine the "Mighty Quinn" as a savior. Even such lines as "When Quinn the Eskimo gets here / Everybody's gonna jump for joy" sound more problematic than celebratory once you've seen the film.

When Inuk and Asiak are at the trading post, the local assimilated Eskimos, including those working for the white Canadian, play a jukebox: everybody dances and Asiak and Inuk join in, although their dance is the "primitive" one they danced with their friends in the igloo. They, rather than the locals, seem to jump for joy, grinning and moving gaily in time to the music. Everyone else dances in a Western fashion. After the dancing, everyone goes to bed in the same room—as in the lyric, "But when Quinn the Eskimo gets here / Everybody's gonna want to doze."

We can make of this what we will hermeneutically. But, regardless, the originality of the song is augmented by thinking of *The Savage Innocents* as a prominent source. This is not imitation so much as allusion or referential framework. The juxtaposition of the film and the song helps define Dylan's perennial (sometimes controversial) relationship to originality. Unfortunately, the line between legitimate borrowing and criminal theft—and between collage, allusion, imitation, and plagiarism—seems to be determined by how obvious the reference, how easy to catch the allusion, or how superficial the field of reference. It's as if legitimizing allusive content were delimited by ignorance rather than challenged by knowledge—at least where Bob Dylan is concerned.

In his 2020 review of *Rough and Rowdy Ways*, Hartman characterizes the problem well: "Though the Nobel may have removed the racy thrill from debates about 'the folk tradition,' appropriation, and so on, it's still a tempting sensation to drag out for a review. In fact, we know perfectly well how to tell homage from plagiarism: if the writer wants us not to recognize the source, it's cheating. If, instead, Dylan means us to hear the original through his recontextualization, the echo always signifies something: at least a tribute that he may hope will lead us back to the source ([Junichi] Saga's sales soared), and perhaps a transformation of the transplanted material. This distinction is simple enough, but applying it can get complicated. It depends on how probable the author's guess is about the audience's knowledge."[5] It has become increasingly difficult to guess an audience's knowledge or to gauge the ignorance of culturally parochial listeners.

Although, for a rock 'n' roll songwriter, Dylan's lyrical associations and allusions range widely and even deeply, his field of references remains relatively modest. There is little point in comparing his lyrics to Dante's "polysemous" verse or Spenser's allegorical epic or Milton's encyclopedic theodicy. Even Dylan's most skilled intertextual weaving pales before the intertextuality of Ovid's *Metamorphoses*. But none of these authors, for all their complexity, were able to combine a musical context as a referential field or as a countervailing allusion (unless we consider the use of "common meter" derived from Sternhold and Hopkins). It may be that, as Horace Engdahl put it in his Nobel presentation speech, "In a distant past, all poetry was sung or tunefully recited, poets were rhapsodes, bards, troubadours." But we've lost the music they "tunefully recited": we only have the lyrics now.

At the same time, Dylan's songs continue to be sung, continue to draw on musical or "rhapsodic" history. Even as his lyrics have become increasingly allusive—"The Cuckoo is a pretty bird, she warbles as she flies / I'm preachin' the Word of God / I'm puttin' out your eyes" ("High Water")—many of his underlying references have continued to be musical, as they were in his Greenwich Village period. Back then, his audience would have heard, without the necessity of footnotes, not only simple references like "Lord Randall" in "Hard Rain," but also "Nottamun Town" in "Masters of War," "No More Auction Block" in "Blowin' in the Wind," and maybe even Paul Clayton's "appropriation" of the folk song "Who Gon' Bring You Chickens" for his "Who's Gonna Buy Your Ribbons (When I'm Gone)," which provided the melody Dylan adapted for "Don't Think Twice."[6] (It might be added that Clayton's title echoes Woody Guthrie's "Who's gonna shoe your pretty little foot / Who's gonna glove your hand?"— lines Woody adapted from Lead Belly's take on traditional ballads.) Dave Van Ronk would have heard and processed the allusion to "Nottamun Town" as part of his understanding of "Masters of War." Because he and the others in Dylan's first coffeehouse audiences easily detected the melodies' origins, the songs became more, not less: listeners layered the meaning of "Masters of War" with its original musical context.

Even later in his recording career, when he was no longer playing to an informed coffeehouse audience, Dylan transformed familiar songs. "I Dreamed I Saw St. Augustine" is a deliberate (and somewhat defiant) imitation of the organizing song "I Dreamed I Saw Joe Hill Last Night," a favorite among folkies. The title and first line are perfect metrical copies of the original. Dylan, the traditional music scholar, might have known that Earl Robinson wrote the union ballad, but it is doubtful he would have known that the song was an adaptation of Alfred Hayes's poem. There is what might be called "secondary imitation" at work here: the layers of imitation become complex when we must separate primary and secondary allusion, and when we are unable to determine if, as in this case, Dylan was aware that he was imitating a literary source as well as a musical precursor.[7]

Detecting topical or musical references in this way demonstrates a form of erudition—combinatory erudition, aural and verbal—even if the *eruditi* are sitting around nursing their coffee in the Gaslight. Later listeners and critics invariably depend on explication.[8] There's nothing wrong with this, if the same listeners don't then, *because of* their ignorance, accuse Dylan of stealing a melody for his secret use, rather than recognizing that he transfigures an appropriation to enhance his composition. No one, to my knowledge, complained about Dylan's "theft" of "I Dreamed I Saw Joe Hill," because the song was so familiar: the transparency of the musical allusion made it possible for almost every listener to try to connect Dylan's demoralizing lyrics to that old organizing ballad.

But erudition can go beyond the casual recognition of similarities and involve deep learning. For example, it would be misleading to say Richard Thomas, a classical scholar, hears Virgil where we hear Dylan (as at least one reviewer observed). Not only does this do Thomas a disservice, but, more significantly, such statements do a disservice to all forms of erudition. Thomas hears Dylan *and* hears Virgil in Dylan: he chooses to write about Virgil or Ovid because he has expertise in this while most of the rest of us don't. His writing about Virgil does not obfuscate what the rest of us hear when we listen to Dylan. The function of erudition is not to suppress the text or supplant it but to enhance and augment it.

As time passes and initiated core groups dissipate—"it's for myself and my friends my stories are sung" ("Restless Farewell")—references lose topicality or familiarity and become increasingly obscure. As in poetry, so in songwriting. In a perfect world, stealing from past songs would be like stealing the club of Hercules—in other words, an impossible feat.[9] If contemporary listeners recognized traditional lyrics and references the way Greek (and later, Hellenistic) audiences would have recognized lines borrowed from Homer—that is, if poetry and song were our paideia, the basis of our education—then there would be no question of theft. On the contrary, songs would gain allusive authority.

Ironically, in the sixties and seventies, stealing a line from Dylan would have been like stealing Hercules's club. No aspiring songwriter could have composed a song containing a Dylan line without being caught out, just as Dylan had no intention of stealing the club of Child in composing "Hard Rain." There are now many examples of where it is necessary to annotate Dylan's songs, just as we need the annotations of Dryden's "Absalom and Achitofel" or Keats's "On First Looking into Chapman's Homer"—where *is* that "peak in Darien" and what was Keats's historical blunder? Footnotes and marginal commentary in poetry from earlier centuries fill in the blanks for us on topical references, forgotten names, historical and literary allusions, and even physical gaps in the material text. Contemporary poetry, on the other hand, shouldn't need the same volume of explanation and historicizing in the margins (Eliot's notes to *The Waste Land* notwithstanding). And popular songs should require a scholarly apparatus least of all. Or so one would think. Yet, even now, only fifty years later, how many first-time listeners would catch the acronym LSD in "Lucy in the Sky with Diamonds"? How many would get the glaring reference to Martha and the Vandellas's "Dancing in the Street" in Bruce Springsteen's transfigured New Jersey hymn, "Racing in the Street"? And these songs are within living memory. It's a dead certainty that most young listeners would miss the improvisatory revision, not to mention the joke, in Frank Sinatra's recording of this verse from Cole Porter's "You're the Top":

> You're the purple light
> Of a summer night in Spain,
> You're the National Gallery
> You're Crosby's salary,
> You're cellophane.

Here's the original version:

> You're the purple light
> Of a summer night in Spain,
> You're the National Gallery
> You're Garbo's salary,
> You're cellophane.

Not just an update, of course, Crosby for Garbo, but something more. The competition between the pioneering crooner Bing Crosby and the "upstart" Sinatra dominated popular music PR in the forties and early fifties (culminating in the film they made together, along with Louis Armstrong and Grace Kelly, *High Society*). Sinatra's revision alludes, playfully, to his famous rival's success and wealth. But think of the footnote needed to explicate this throwaway change: (1) give Porter's original line; (2) briefly explain who Garbo was, and why the Garbo-Crosby parallel works; (3) outline the Crosby-Sinatra rivalry; and (4) (for specialists) note that Sinatra expertly uses a trochee to keep the meter of the line.

So, should Cole Porter CD collections be issued with a scholarly apparatus, like Library of America editions of Longfellow and Melville?

Similarly, and perhaps closer to the kind of "theft" Dylan is often accused of, should the lyricist Johnny Mercer have somehow cited Alexander Pope for stealing his line "Fools Rush In (Where Angels Fear to Tread)"? Should Tommy Dorsey, Frank Sinatra, and Billy Eckstein have prefaced every performance with an acknowledgement to Pope? This would have been unheard of and nonsensical in the context, not only because Pope is in the public domain but because sheet music and musical performances do not *by accepted convention* include explanatory notes. Finally, how many audience members would have known that the source of the title was Pope's *An Essay on Criticism*? None, probably, unless a professor of eighteenth-century literature was on hand.[10] Does it matter? Or—more reasonably—is it incumbent on listeners (like readers and museum visitors) to know the traditions, the artists, and the genealogy of the works they encounter?

Many of Dylan's listeners, and not a few of his learned critics, do not seem to feel this incumbency. Coming belatedly to the songs, uninitiated in the allusive field, they "discover" what they term a theft of melody or even language. Yet this is merely an example of how passing time effaces context. Dylan, however, is not a pedant even if he is profoundly erudite in his chosen field of traditional music: song, lyrics, narratives, recordings, and artists. As recently as 2012, in the *Rolling Stone* interview with Mikal Gilmore, he linked tragedy, tradition, and his role as a songwriter. Gilmore asked him about the last three songs on *Tempest*:

> Gilmore. There's a fair amount of mortality, certainly in the last three songs—"Tin Angel," "Tempest" and "Roll On John." People come to hard endings.
>
> Dylan. The people in "Frankie and Johnny," "Stagger Lee," and "El Paso" have come to hard endings, too, and definitely it's that way in one of my favorite songs, "Delia." I can name you a hundred songs where everything ends in tragedy. It's called tradition, and that's what I deal in. Traditional, with a capital T.

Another way of putting this is that, as I said above, it is the listener's (or reader's) responsibility to hear and recognize the allusions—drawn from the Traditional with a capital T—even if they seem to be "stolen." Appropriation is a weave whose warp and weft contain references and cross-references. The problem with allegations of theft and plagiarism in the context of aesthetic appropriation is that they are often subliterary and submusical. They flourish among litigious men that quarrels move. Better a well-wrought urn, I think.

Originality Is Suicide

In the introduction I referred to the difference between originality and imitation as pre-Romantic concepts. I tried to distinguish between strictly derivative works of art and innovative imitation. "Often," as David Goldstein reminds us in his useful article on "Originality" in the *Princeton Encyclopedia of Poetry and Poetics*, "the strongest declarations of originality are themselves imitations or translations." He adds that "after the romantics, ideas of originality found their strongest focus in three contrasting dicta," citing Pound's widely applied "make it new" and Eliot's observation in "Tradition and the Individual Talent" that the most "individual" parts of a poet's work "may be those in which the dead poets, his ancestors, assert their immortality most vigorously." The third dictum, according to Goldstein, was Gertrude Stein's "I am inclined to believe there is no such thing as repetition." This leads to the paradoxical conclusion that "if there is no repetition—i.e., if every repetition is actually in some sense a new creation—then there can also be no originality because every new instance of language is as original as every other. The use of repetition," Goldstein's article goes on, "has since been explored most pointedly in visual art, from Marcel Duchamp's *Fountain* to Andy Warhol's Campbell's Soup experiments to Sherrie Levine's 'Appropriation Art.'"[11] The contention that repetition and originality are in conflict is at the heart of Stein's so-called dictum. But the history and practice of imitation make it clear that forms of repetition *define* originality.

Ironically, critics have long accused Duchamp of theft in the production of *Fountain*. The claim, on little or no evidence, is that he stole the idea for the work, and maybe the concept of conceptual art, from Elsa von Freytag-Loringhoven.[12] And so we beat on.

In "Self-Reliance," Emerson says "imitation is suicide." But this is misguided: Emerson believed the myth (in his case transcendentalist) of a divine spark in humans. His magical thinking permitted him to entertain a notion that there is a pure artistic "intuition" while all else is "tuition." But understanding imitatio reduces the need for magical thinking—which is not to deny the various beliefs in the supernatural that every poet from Seneca to Sidney held. A better way to understand Emerson's statement is to recognize he means *slavish imitation is suicide*. If, as Dylan says, "everything that can't be imitated perfect must die," then imitation would have to be key to life, above all aesthetic life. To imitate would be part of the cycle of creation: one creates through imitatio to be "imitated perfect" and to live.

Significantly, Emerson's notion that "imitation is suicide" refers not to poetry but to education and growth, the *Bildung* of the (predominantly male) American: "There is a time in every man's education when he arrives at the conviction that envy is ignorance; that imitation is suicide; that he must take himself for better for worse as his portion; that though the wide universe is full of good, no kernel of nourishing corn can come to him but through his toil bestowed on that plot of ground which is given to him to till."[13] Even putting aside the superstitious element here—"given to him," presumably referring to a deity—Emerson has chosen an odd metaphor to represent self-reliance. The tilling of a plot of ground requires *seeds* if it is to produce a "kernel of nourishing corn." If it is Emerson's point that both seeds and labor originate from the same source, and that the aim is "every man's education," then there is an uncomfortably autotelic quality to his American ideal. And there is also a suggestion of self-creation. After all, as Emerson would have known well, Milton's Satan fell from Heaven precisely as a result of this mistaken reasoning, because he refused to acknowledge his own creation. In his pre-battle speech he asks the rebel angels:

who saw
Thy making, while the Maker gave thee being?
We know no time when we were not as now;

> Know none before us, self-begot, self-raised
> By our own quick'ning power. ”[14]

The parallel between Satan's "self-begot, self-raised" and Emerson's idea of the seedless self-origin of tilth has probably not escaped critics. But then Satan's exhortations, for all their wrongheaded hubris in the poem, often ring true to the democratic ear.[15]

Emerson's drive to reverse convention and create an American cult of originality afflicts the analysis of all contemporary imitation, muddying the pool by confusing syncretism with oppression. In *Nature* he writes, "Our age is retrospective. It builds the sepulchers of the fathers. It writes biographies, histories, and criticism. The foregoing generations beheld God and nature face to face; we, through their eyes. Why should not we also enjoy an original relation to the universe?"[16] This "complaint of retrospection," according to Anthony Kemp, "can only originate within a culture that senses itself cut off from the past and yet still enslaved to it, a culture whose model of time is one of epistemological supersession, of new forms of knowledge superseding and making irrelevant the old."[17] Kemp's point seems to be that Emerson, and his likeminded idealists of originality, are denying the indissoluble bond to the past—a bond expressed in poetry and songwriting by the practice of imitatio. Emerson demands, "Why should we not have a poetry and philosophy of insight and not of tradition, and a religion by revelation to us, and not the history of theirs?" Maybe the Mormons are an answer to the latter question, if the revelations of Joseph Smith measure up to the Emersonian standard. And Kemp may be correct that in order to conceive of such an originality Emerson would have had to conceive of time in terms of supersession. But there can be no such thing as poetry (or even philosophy) that rejects tradition utterly; nor would Emerson have been likely to endorse such an idea of poetry. As Christoph Irmscher pointed out to me, the operative terms in Emerson's question are "insight" and "revelation." Emerson is not advocating wholesale newness. As a poet, he used traditional forms of versification, including rhyme and meter. But he also argued for a new conception of rhyme, one that would open the reader's eyes to the pairings found in nature. He advocated for writing motivated by insight rather than by knowledge of tradition, of the past, and of historical revelation.

Present-day ideas of "pure" originality, which have become the bugbears of Dylan's most vociferous (and ill-informed) critics, might seem to lead back in American genealogy to Emerson's exuberant "complaint of retrospection." But this would be inaccurate: that Emerson rejects pure imitation doesn't mean he advocates pure originality. In contrast, an absolute standard of "pure originality" became the hallmark of the European artistic avant-garde in the twentieth century. The Futurists were probably the first, the wackiest, and the most ominous group to connect self-creation to originality, and originality to power.

The buttoned-up Emerson could not have foreseen this connection. Rosalind Krauss, in a well-known essay, recounts the famous Futurist origin myth: "[Filippo] Marinetti, thrown from his automobile one evening in 1909 into a factory ditch filled with water, emerges as if from amniotic fluid to be born—without ancestors—a futurist. This parable of absolute self-creation that begins the first *Futurist Manifesto* functions as a model for what is meant by originality among the early twentieth-century avant-garde. For originality becomes an organicist metaphor referring not so much to formal invention as to sources of life. The self as origin is safe from contamination by tradition because it possesses a kind of originary naiveté."[18] As his Futurist manifestos and other writings attest, Marinetti came boisterously to life supporting energy, speed, struggle, war ("the world's only hygiene"), poetic spontaneity, and a wholesale rejection of the past. Militarism aside, a good deal of Marinetti's hyperbole seems to underlie the modern concepts of originality that contravene notions of supersession and imitation of the past. "Why should we look back, when what we want is to break down the mysterious doors of the Impossible?" (from the first *Manifesto of Futurism*, #8). At other times, Marinetti, desperate to shed Italian literary and artistic history, seems to pave a long and winding road to Dylan's door: "Museums: cemeteries! . . . Identical, surely, in the sinister promiscuity of so many bodies unknown to one another. Museums: public dormitories where one lies forever beside hated or unknown beings. Museums: absurd abattoirs of painters and sculptors ferociously slaughtering each other with colour-blows and line-blows, the length of the fought-over walls!"[19] Marinetti is as exercised as the jaded narrator of "Visions of Johanna," who sees the "jelly-faced women" in the museums where "infinity goes up on trial." And those "absurd abattoirs of painters and sculptors" trapped on the walls recall the desperate speaker "stuck inside a painting" in "Don't Fall Apart on Me Tonight."

It may be that at one time the arrogant young Dylan thought "colleges are like old folks' homes" and rejected the petrified cultural landscape in terms resembling Marinetti's: "Daily visits to museums, libraries, and academies (cemeteries of empty exertion, Calvaries of crucified dreams, registries of aborted beginnings!) are, for artists, as damaging as prolonged supervision by parents of certain young people drunk with their talent and their ambitious wills. When the future is barred to them, the admirable past may be a solace for the ills of the moribund, the sickly, the prisoner."[20] The facile polarization of past and present, ambitious will and moribundity, might almost—but not quite—describe the immature political aesthetic of the sixties. The great Futurist claimed, for example, "The oldest of us is thirty: so we have at least a decade for finishing our work. When we are forty, other younger and stronger men will probably throw us in the wastebasket like useless manuscripts—we want it to happen!"[21] Subtract ten years and the assertion sounds too familiar: "Don't trust anyone over thirty." But this political propaganda was rarely voiced by musicians, and never by Dylan. It would have been nonsensical for him to deem the past moribund when his art was (and is) dedicated to tradition: its origins are consummately the mark of its identity and the proof of the songwriter/artist's transformative originality.

For Dylan—the Dylan of "Hard Rain" (1963) and *Bringing It All Back Home* (1965)—the present is moribund. It would be a mistake to align Dylan's contempt for museums in "Visions of Johanna" (1966) with a bid to be avant-garde. He might reject nostalgic uses of the past, but his sixties' contempt for museums—now revised, presumably, since he has become a museum exhibitor—never quite encompassed a contempt for infinity. It was rather a supercilious reaction to the idea that "infinity" or permanence could be given substance, collected in a museum, and placed before unworthy jelly-faced judges. The arrogance of this posture has been well-attested in the myriad analyses of that famous fourth stanza from "Johanna." But, while Dylan's arrogance might be misplaced in the song, neither his speaker nor the song itself challenges the past as a complement to originality. Krauss quotes Kazimir Malevich's dictum that "Only he is alive who rejects his convictions of yesterday," and she summarizes: "The self as origin is the way an absolute distinction can be made between a present experienced *de novo* and a tradition-laden past. The claims of the avant-garde are precisely these claims to originality." Yet, despite appearances to the contrary, Dylan has never been (nor aspired to be) a member of an avant-garde.

The controversy surrounding Andy Warhol's *Silver Elvis* painting, which Dylan supposedly pushed Warhol into giving him and then traded for his manager Albert Grossman's couch, would seem to support an impatience with the self-styled avant-gardism of Warhol's "Factory," if that is the right word for Warhol's Pop-Art originality.[22] In any case, Dylan's sixties posturing was apparently at odds with Warhol's. Gerard Malanga, a Factory denizen, recalled it this way in an interview with John Bauldie: "I don't know if Dylan was interested in Andy's work that much. I think he kind of frowned upon it to tell you the truth. Dylan represented a certain milieu that was almost the antithesis of Andy's milieu in the sense of you had the heterosexual grouping and you had the so-called homosexual grouping. . . . And Dylan's group obviously didn't take Andy that seriously, you know. They were out to walk all over Andy and walk away with something. And they did. Dylan walked away with a very expensive Elvis Presley painting."[23]

Even a cursory understanding of American traditional music reveals an ingrained belief in a preservationist commitment to past expression, especially when contemporary transformations embrace supersession and radical departures.

Where does Dylan fit? To repeat Krauss's observation: "Originality becomes an organicist metaphor referring not so much to formal invention as to sources of life. The self as origin is safe from contamination by tradition because it possesses a kind of originary naiveté." The "organicist metaphor" lives on and has spread, mostly among Dylan critics and bloggers who insist on looking for "originality" as a function of the self rather than as a product of syncretic imitation. It may be that at times and in certain media (prose and painting especially), Dylan's method of collage and imitation plays a kind of brinkmanship game with compositional ethics. But brinkmanship in art, as Robert Polito observed (and I quoted above), should not lead us to treat Dylan's work like a term paper. Marinetti's cry of "No ancestors"—incidentally echoing Satan's "self-begot, self-raised"—is like a false note heard in the background when Dylan's detractors accuse him of plagiarism or theft. They are the current purveyors of the organicist metaphor. Ironically, that metaphor is itself a hardy survivor of the past, descended from ancestors as diverse as Leonardo da Vinci, Wordsworth, Emerson, and Marinetti. But it makes no sense to think of rock 'n' roll in terms of organicist originality, nor to see rock artists and songwriters as self-created. Virtually by definition, rock 'n' roll contains what Krauss calls "contamination by tradition" and could never therefore be considered an avant-garde movement. Rock 'n' roll embraces its debts to the past, embodying them in musical forms in spite of, or concomitantly with, the most radical stylizing. As an ambition, "originary naivete" is meaningless for the wide-flung imitators of the twelve-bar blues. Happily, there are no Futurists in the Rock and Roll Hall of Fame.

Walking Antique

Allegations of plagiarism or "unoriginality" simply refashion the old illusion of the artist who "don't look back," an illusion Dylan demolished early on with "She Belongs to Me." The supposedly forward-focused artist of that song enthralls the speaker with a heady combination of exoticism, fetishism, nostalgia, and theft. Her "originality" in the song derives expressly from an arbitrary concatenation of art objects and cultural exploitation, rather than from an inner Emersonian self-reliance. Like much of 1965's *Bringing It All Back Home*, "She Belongs to Me" frames a confrontational relationship between past and present. And, as if to call attention to this confrontational stance, the song comes as an aural relief after the raucousness and the vatic telegraphing—what Hinchey calls "alternating gnomic and plain-spoken tips"—of "Subterranean Homesick Blues," the album's opener. That song may be an American musical landmark but its placement as the first cut has a shock value meant, no doubt, to bring it all back home all at once.

With its slower tempo, the gentle percussion, and the harmonious treble notes of the electric guitar, the album's second cut, "She Belongs to Me," seems to offer a moment of reflection, even expansion, on the project of recapturing the past—both the recent past of British borrowing ("theft") of American blues tradition and the longer past of the American folk revival. The opening stanza presents the first in a series of misleading oppositions:

> She's got everything she needs
> She's an artist, she don't look back
> She's got everything she needs

She's an artist, she don't look back
She can take the dark out of the nighttime
And paint the daytime black

The irony is thick here: the stanzaic form imitates the blues, two repeating lines followed by an answering line. Significantly, the stanza's focus is on a painter, who, refusing to look back, has the artistic power to replace night with day and day with darkness. In a typically coy revision during the studio rehearsals for the Rolling Thunder Revue, Dylan sings, "She can take the dark out of the nighttime / And make the daytime crack."[24] The explicit mention of a painter disappears and the artist suddenly wields a Zeus-like power to shatter the sky (and maybe bring on darkness): there's something very deft about the image of the "daytime" cracking on a tour called Rolling Thunder. Granted, Dylan is only singing a casual rehearsal line and it would be ill-advised to read too much into it. Yet the augmentation of the artist's role, from painter to natural/supernatural force, is provocative.

Unlike the song's artist, the song itself "look[s] back," as do the songwriter and the singer, artists both—even if the unidentified narrator thinks otherwise. Tim Riley speaks of the "blues skeletons" of "She Belongs to Me" and "It Takes a Lot to Laugh, It Takes a Train to Cry."[25] Similarly, if less colorfully, Timothy Hampton observes that "the verse form evokes the blues" and goes on to point out how Dylan's musical arrangement differs from typical blues: "Musically, the traditional form of the blues requires three chords: the tonic chord, for the first line, the subdominant chord, for the second line, and a third line divided between the dominant chord and the subdominant, resolving to the tonic. Here [in 'She Belongs to Me'], however, the musical harmony pushes against the traditional blues form. For the third line, Dylan uses an unconventional chord sequence. Instead of going to the expected dominant or V chord, he turns to a major chord on the second degree of the scale, thereby introducing a note of tension."[26] Hampton is astute to notice the "unconventional chord sequence." He adds that Dylan's chord progression is "pushing against the expectations of the blues, lending the blues a pop inflection." Many pop songs, especially early rock, capitalize on the I, IV, V chord progression without necessarily "pushing against expectations"—or at least not consciously. Hampton brilliantly identifies Dylan's expressive realignment of musical convention and his capacity to merge, and transfigure, generic expectations.

In terms of imitation, I think there might be a further realignment. In "She Belongs to Me," Dylan seems deliberately to invoke the tension between blues and modern popular music by exploiting the conflict between the traditional blues verse structure and the lyrics themselves, with the chords having an almost secondary effect. "She's an artist, she don't look back" clashes with the backward-looking verse structure, belying the obvious indebtedness to tradition and traditional form. But this is the song's lyrical (and consummately Dylan-esque) innovation: the false contradiction between—or the hidden combination of—a backward-looking verse form and an artist who doesn't look back is reminiscent of the denial-cum-absorption of poetic imitatio.

But the song also confirms the interdependent relationship of appropriation to transformation. There is no question here of Dylan's denying the Delta blues origins of the musical structure or enacting a hegemonic white colonization of Black precursors. On the contrary, the parallel balance of lyrics and verse form openly shares the cultural authority. Aidan Day refers to the song as "another of Dylan's lyrics [like 'Desolation Row'] to examine the imaginative principle informing artistic creation."[27] And from "artistic creation" we can infer imitatio because only through that process can the "imaginative principle" find expression, with the manifest debt to the blues forming a consummate homage as Dylan "brings it all back home."

There is more than homage, however, in Dylan's imitative process. He demonstrates how art has the capacity to embody an interdependent but also a *revisionary* relationship between the present and the past by describing a woman artist who appears to have everything she needs without looking back, or, more suggestively, *because* she doesn't look back. But there's a conundrum here. The "she" in Dylan's song can only be an artist, if she is an artist and not a fraud, precisely because she looks back—that is, precisely because she revises and redeploys the cultural jumble of the past. There is of course a warning built into the impossible ideal of pure artistic self-reliance. The most famous artist to look back, disastrously, is Orpheus. As the type of the poet-vates in classical literature and legend, the catastrophe of his backward glance resonates throughout the canon. But what does it mean? Is the loss of Eurydice as the pair emerge from underworld a sign of the poet's weakness, of his lack of faith in the divine command, or of his rebelliousness against Hades's authority? Or is it a metaphor for the impotence of art? In ancient literature, no human escapes death through art. Only the sheer strength of the demigod Hercules can rescue Alcestis.

Stephen Scobie sees the "she" of the song as a classical deity herself, a Muse, whose "Egyptian red ring" is "a symbol of eternity . . . associated with ancient goddesses of wisdom and fertility such as Isis, who was worshipped by the Egyptians as 'thou lady of the red apparel.'"[28] He connects the "red ring" of performed versions to the goddess Isis (*and* to the song "Isis" [1975])—the word "red" does not appear in the printed or online versions of the lyrics—and hearing future echoes seems far-fetched in terms of Dylan's symbolic lexicon. Still, the notion of an inscrutable Egyptian deity provides a useful foil for determining the attitude of the song's quasi-narratorial "you" and the valence between art and worship.

The lyrics have more to do with originality than worship, or even with Orphic continuity. By giving the artist an Egyptian ring, Dylan seems to allude, at once, to Pharaonic oppression and artistic imaginative range, as if the latter could supersede or neutralize the former. If, supposedly, the artist doesn't look back, her accoutrements certainly do. Rings have many meanings, such as fidelity, possession, or even bondage. But this magical ring has special quasi-prophetic properties: it "sparkles before she speaks." One can only wonder if Dylan's artist controls the sparkling. Or, alternatively, does the ring itself retain mystical Egyptian properties that anticipate the modern artist's speech? Is this a symbiotic relationship or a kind of Pavlovian ventriloquism? Answering these questions touches on a broader historical debate about whether the artist refashions the past by means of human intelligence and labor, or whether she is a vessel through which inspiration flows, "as through trumpets." Milton puts it this way in describing his relationship to Urania, his "Celestial Patroness,"

> who deigns
> Her nightly visitation unimplored,
> And dictates to me slumbr'ing, or inspires
> Easy my unpremeditated verse.[29]

Dylan has several times said he doesn't know where his early songs came from, as if a muse or deity made a "visitation unimplored" and dictated "unpremeditated verse" to him. Yet, if the ambivalences of "She Belongs to Me" have any resonance with the songwriter's experience, there might be another way to look at supernatural inspiration.

Traditionally, in the eras when imitatio prevailed, this kind of unpremeditated composition was called furor poeticus, the "madness" of the poet. Imitatio and furor poeticus conflict, however, with the former indicating a poet's agency in choosing precursor models and the latter removing all agency, as if the poet, maddened by creativity, would cede control of compositional authority to a higher "inspirational" power. As popular as this notion of inspiration was, however, poets resisted the neglect of human effort and studious craft in the production of poetry.

Dylan's speaker in "She Belongs to Me" sketches out this ambivalence, always in the disembodied second person, as if warning the next generation or the next suitor or the muse's next invocateur (or invocateuse):

> You will start out standing
> Proud to steal her anything she sees
> You will start out standing
> Proud to steal her anything she sees
> But you will wind up peeking through a keyhole
> Down upon your knees

The introduction of exclusion and jealousy eroticizes the speaker's relationship to the muse. In the classical pantheon, all the Muses were female, which is not to say that postclassical women poets as early as Celestine, Mary Wroth, or Katherine Philips didn't invoke them. Rather, it highlights the traditional aspect of the "you"/"she" dynamic in the song. As in so many of Dylan's songs (and scores of critics have remarked on this), the pronouns tend to be interchangeable. Dylan told John Elderfield, "A song is a prismatic thing, nonlinear."[30] Critics celebrate "Tangled Up in Blue" as Dylan's most brilliant evidence of this nonlinearity. But the pronoun alternations in "She Belongs to Me" can also serve as examples. They appear as refractions seen through a prism, with the "artist" and the "you" sometimes divided, sometimes joined. *You* are the artist, and *I* am you. The pride in "stealing her anything she sees" aligns the lover, who is simultaneously the poet in the refracted glass, with one of Dylan's favorite pariah images: the thief.

Theft of Fire

In the opening section of the edition of Rimbaud's *Illuminations* that Dylan read in the early sixties, there is an 1871 letter to Paul Demeny: "The poet makes himself a *visionary* through a long, a prodigious and rational disordering of *all* the senses. Every form of love, of suffering, of madness; he searches himself, he consumes all the poisons in him, keeping only their quintessences. Ineffable torture in which he will need all his faith and superhuman strength, the great criminal, the great sickman, the accursed,—and the supreme Savant! . . . So then, the poet is truly a thief of fire."[31] The notion of the poet's Promethean responsibility fits well with Dylan's transformative artistry in the mid-sixties, his sense—or is it our sense?—that he has brought a new form of energy to the American lyrical imagination. His originality is rooted in this transformative element.

Hampton uses phrases from the passage I quoted above as section headings in the chapter he devotes to Dylan's "visionary song" and its indebtedness to Rimbaud.[32] I discuss Hampton's take on Rimbaud's importance in the next chapter on vatic poetry. But here I would like to focus on the parallel Rimbaud draws between the visionary poet and the "great criminal." This is a pairing woven throughout Dylan's songs, even after the manifestly "visionary" period of the mid-sixties. Significantly, listeners have often associated Dylan himself with that Promethean figure, a reluctant thief of fire:

> No, I do not feel that good
> When I see the heartbreaks you embrace
> If I was a master thief
> Perhaps I'd rob them
> ("Positively 4th Street")

Or, as an unanswerable question:

Tears of rage, tears of grief
Why must I always be the thief?
Come to me now, you know
We're so alone
And life is brief

The thieves in these verses balance somewhere between the anointed outlaw-criminal charisma of Pretty Boy Floyd et al. and Rimbaud's Promethean poet.

Unsurprisingly, much theft in Dylan songs owes its self-righteousness to folk tradition: disenfranchised men turn to crime to survive, and, at the same time, to strike back at the soulless bourgeois authority that wronged them. Even the worst of Dylan's outlaws, like Joey Gallo, has a patina of this self-righteous rebellion against social norms (despite being a gangster).

In the song "Joey," Dylan inverts reality and makes Gallo a sympathetic victim. This is an ethical step beyond the glorification of such lyrics as:

John Wesley Harding
Was a friend to the poor
He traveled with a gun in every hand
All along this countryside
He opened many a door
But he was never known
To hurt an honest man

This sentiment is, in effect, a self-consciously updated version of Woody Guthrie's "Pretty Boy Floyd," a song about a farmer-turned-bank-robber who nevertheless leaves thousand-dollar bills under the napkins when sympathetic families feed him. Of course, the bills are stolen, but in the Dust Bowl scenario the banks "rob you with a fountain pen" (Woody's words), so Pretty Boy Floyd is simply returning the money to the wronged parties.

In contrast, Joey Gallo's criminality and violence are unjustifiable: as Lester Bangs points out in an excoriating review of *Desire*, "Joey" is essentially the glorification of a gangland psychopath "which paints a picture of Joey Gallo as alienated antihero reminiscent of *West Side Story*'s 'Gee, Officer Krupke' lyrics."[33] Time and obscurity bury the worst details about historical criminals. And some of Dylan's real-life thieves, like John Wesley Harding, have a dash of integrity to leaven their criminality. No doubt their integrity is just as romantic and just as misplaced as Joey Gallo's supposed gentleness with children. But Bangs is bent on unmasking everything hypocritical and fraudulent in Dylan's apparent return to protest singing with the two long songs on *Desire*.[34] Even granting the veracity of the newspaper reports he cites and Gallo's biographer, on whom he depends, Bangs nevertheless pays little serious attention to the poetics of romanticizing outlaws and Dylan's appropriation—and imitation—of this venerable musical tradition.

For Dylan, as for other artists, the process of imitation depends on the appropriation of other works and models, or of extant myths and traditions. But only the practitioners of this methodology who eschew mere copying for genuine imitation successfully combine appropriation with transformation and repurposing. This is the only way to reach true originality.

Jonathan Lethem recognizes the functional poetics of appropriating and subsequently imitating the romantic outlaw tradition. In a *Harper's Magazine* article titled "The Ecstasy of Influence: A Plagiarism," with a nod to Harold Bloom's "anxiety of influence," Lethem invokes the well-known connection between one of Dylan's most famous lines, "To live outside the law, you must be honest" ("Absolutely Sweet Marie" [1966]), and Don Siegel's 1958 film *The Lineup*, which was written by Stirling Silliphant. Lethem focuses on the "worth" of the line to Siegel, Silliphant, and their audiences as opposed to its cultural worth now, "after Bob Dylan cleaned it up a little."[35] The movie line is "When you live outside the law, you have to eliminate dishonesty," a bit of dialogue that, according to Hinchey, "says the same thing as Dylan's reworking, but . . . lacks its resonant force and barbed panache. Dylan turns a poetic thought into poetry."[36] Recognizing the value of a "reworking," Hinchey is right about the "poetic thought." But it is hardly an original thought in *The Lineup*. The sentiment is hackneyed and, of course, manifestly untrue—more an instance of poetic license. The adage "There's honor among thieves" (which also could be a source of Dylan's line) is as absurd as the notion that outlaws are honest with each other or that they maintain a special code of integrity. We even have a word for the dishonesty among crooks: the double-cross. Criminals cheat each other, turn each other in for rewards, and lie pathologically for gain. Virtually every noir film ever made includes a double-cross.

Loyal and honest outlaws are poetic fantasies, as Dylan realized. Therefore, if the line from "Absolutely Sweet Marie" is a revision of Silliphant's dialogue, then we should be looking not for theft but for irony and transformation. Riley speaks of "the knowing befuddlement" of "Absolutely Sweet Marie," a song he aligns with "Temporarily Like Achilles" and "Obviously Five Believers" as "a string of backhanded arguments about the manipulative tactics of art, the limits of song craft, rock credulity, and message-bound sentiment."[37] The notion of "manipulative tactics of art" implies a much more self-conscious act of composition than merely borrowing a line and plugging it into a song, even after cleaning it up a bit. In fact, Dylan's verse brings together an ambivalent collage of different traditions and media. The brash originality of the stanza is born precisely of unexpected tropes and repurposed allusions.

> Well, six white horses that you did promise
> Were fin'lly delivered down to the penitentiary

But to live outside the law, you must be honest
I know you always say that you agree
But where are you tonight, sweet Marie?

The speaker, notionally serving time in a penitentiary (a Lead Belly/Guthrie styling for "prison"), has "six white horses" delivered, purpose undetermined. Hinchey maintains that these are gifts from Marie and that "six white horses" call to mind "an image that in blues tradition is usually associated with death and funerals," which is true. Recall, for example, the "two white horses following me" in "See That My Grave Is Kept Clean." But Hinchey isn't satisfied with this obvious reference. "Here," he contends, "I think they are the same 'six white horses' that will bring her 'comin' round the mountain' in the nursery rhyme, a song Dylan recorded with the Band during the Basement Tapes sessions." The nursery rhyme makes for a collocation of images particularly apt for *Blonde on Blonde*: "They are," suggests Hinchey, "emblems of the promise of sex, so that their funereal connotations are not, especially on *this* album, out of place after all." The juxtaposition of sex and death is germane not only to *Blonde and Blonde*, but, unsurprisingly, to *The Lineup* and the noir genre. The medium-bending accommodates Dylan's tropes. Hinchey concludes that "the horses symbolize the promise of sex, but in fact, here they represent the betrayal of those promises."[38]

The speaker's querulous response to the delivery of six ambiguous white horses is "But to live outside the law, you must be honest / I know you always say that you agree." But evidently Marie doesn't agree. She seems to have double-crossed him. Dylan might have had an old Bill Monroe song in mind. In Monroe's "6 White Horses," the horses refer to a comparable betrayal:

Oh, that six white horses, going two-by-two,
Oh, that six white horses, going two-by-two,
Some other woman has took my love from you.

A woman is the speaker in Monroe's song: she too has been betrayed, however, and the white horses represent not escape but the double-cross. It seems as likely that Dylan would have known this Monroe tune as that he would have seen *The Lineup*, and the combination of the two references should underscore his originality in combining referential material. Further, while it is just as likely that Dylan saw *The Lineup* as that he based "Quinn the Eskimo" on *The Savage Innocents*, his reshaping of the language into a metrical line is more significant than the unoriginality of the subject matter. To call this theft or inappropriate borrowing would be a colossally reductive misunderstanding of Dylan's imitative technique.

While we can't assert that the speaker in the penitentiary is a thief, it would not be too far-fetched a conclusion, given the coincidence of the famous line "To live outside the law . . ." and the faux wisdom "There's honor among thieves."

But this vagueness is par for the course: ambiguous and ironic identities are rife among Dylan's many thieves. Few have Gallo's or Reuben Carter's public record on the police blotter. Most of them are much more difficult to categorize. They inhabit a liminal moral landscape, something like the Kierkegaardian hinterland of the unnamed thief of "All Along the Watchtower" who says to the joker, in the face of impending doom, "No reason to get excited." This figure seems closer to Rimbaud's visionary poet, uttering gnomic advice like the "supreme Savant," than he does to a Texas outlaw.[39] Even so, however, a clear link between Dylan's romanticized, aestheticized, American thieves and Rimbaud's poet rarely emerges—unless lethal charm counts as a form of poetics, as with the Jack of Hearts. Yet the prismatic pronouns of "She Belongs to Me" suggest just such a connection, with thefts in the balance—thefts of cultures, affections, convictions, and works of art. It may be, as Dylan's speaker says, that "*you* start out standing / Proud to steal her anything she sees," but that means *she*, the artist of the first verse, "starts out" as a receiver of stolen goods (or a fence, if she sells them on). Not to belabor the metaphor, the propinquity of art and theft is nonetheless provocative. In the coded diction of the song, stealing, a career-long sore point for Dylan, seems to represent the artistic process: what you steal for your Muse, *or* for the artist inside you, you steal from the past and from other works of art. These are the models that "she"— again, Muse alone or Muse-and-artist in mystical symbiosis—will imitate.

"She Belongs to Me" forms a kind of tableau of the present and past in art— which, not coincidentally, also reflects the relationship of British rock to American musical roots. With past and present, blues and pop interwoven, the song's title is a ferociously possessive declaration of where the musical present belongs. It belongs to us.

Appropriation Engineer

After connecting the Siegel film and "Absolutely Sweet Marie," Lethem goes on to say in his *Harper's* article, "Appropriation has always played a key role in Dylan's music." Citing a few of the usual suspects beyond *The Lineup*, such as Saga's *Confessions of a Yakuza*, Lott's *Love and Theft*, Henry Timrod, and so forth, Lethem concludes that "Dylan's originality and his appropriation are as one."[40]

Another way to say that originality and appropriation "are as one" is to define the combination of the two as a single process: imitatio. This clarifies Dylan's originality and helps spell out why his use of appropriation differs from that of others who more clumsily steal or try to fuse others' works into their own. When does something stolen become one's own? What does imitation really look like? In Dylan's case, it begins with the kinds of coincidences or chance borrowings alluded to in "It's All Over Now, Baby Blue." It then proceeds via appropriation, which includes a balance (or absorption) of collage, fusion, translation, transformation, and repurposing. These stages of imitation—from appropriation to transformation—embody true originality. For Dylan, originality is the culmination of all the stages of imitation and its transformative character is inseparable from his compositional methodology.

In a valuable discussion of "fair or transformative use" Robert Shore cites the "legal tergiversations in the case of Cariou v. Prince." Here, he refers to a 2008 exhibition at the Gagosian Gallery in New York—where, notably, Dylan has also exhibited his work—and to the catalog published by Rizzoli. The exhibition showcased a series of artworks by Richard Prince—deemed an "appropriation pioneer" by Shore—titled *Canal Zone*. The photographer Patrick Cariou took Prince to court, however, alleging that he had copied the images of Cariou's book *Yes, Rasta* without attribution Perhaps surprisingly, Prince did not deny that he had used Cariou's photographs but claimed fair use. The court at first disagreed with this justification and "found the works to be infringing and nontransformative." Then, on appeal, a second court in April 2013 reversed the initial decision: "It declared that the first court's claim that Prince's work was required to be a commentary on Cariou's was faulty; to qualify as transformative, it was sufficient for his work to present a fundamentally different aesthetic, although the court also cautioned that cosmetic change of format would not automatically qualify a secondary work as fair use."[41]

The question of plagiarism is more appropriately a question of fair use, a notoriously slippery component of Section 107 of the Copyright Act. According to *Campbell v. Acuff-Rose Music* (1994), "a court will look to whether the new work you've created is 'transformative' and adds a new meaning or message. To be transformative, a use must add to the original 'with a further purpose or different character, altering the first with new expression, meaning, or message' (Campbell, 510 U. S. at 579). Although transformative use is not absolutely necessary, the more transformative your use is, the less you will have to show on the remaining three factors." Fair use is usually thought to be limited to "criticism, comment, news reporting, teaching (including multiple copies for classroom use), scholarship, or research"—none of which is an infringement of copyright. But it is "a common misconception . . . that any for-profit use of someone else's work is not fair use and that any not-for-profit use is fair. In actuality, some for-profit uses are fair and some not-for-profit uses are not; the result depends on the circumstances. . . . Although courts still consider the commercial nature of the use as part of their analysis, they will not brand a transformative use unfair simply because it makes a profit."[42]

Transformative use fits well with the idea of translation in works of visual art, which, in turn, reflects the practice of poetic imitation. Dylan's painting, like his songwriting, embodies what Christina Oberstebrink, discussing John Dryden, calls "imitation as the form of translating that also incorporated invention." She explains that Dryden, whose theories of imitation had profound influence on eighteenth-century "modern" art, differentiated between "a common, lowly form of imitation and an idealizing one."[43] This distinction Dryden no doubt found in myriad sixteenth-century poetic treatises that eschew slavish imitation. But Dryden's metaphor is painterly, providing fresh license to apply theories of imitation and translation to visual art. Oberstebrink quotes Dryden's *Preface to Sylvae*: "'Tis one thing to draw the outlines true, the features like, the proportions exact, the colouring itself perhaps tolerable; and another thing to make all these graceful, by the posture, the shadowings, and chiefly, by the spirit which animates the whole."[44]

Dryden's description of "the spirit which animates the whole" as the distinguishing marker between a simple copy and a transformed work of art adumbrates the much later Walter Benjamin's notion of the "aura" of a work of art. But Benjamin was worried that mechanical reproducibility would destroy the uniqueness of individual works of art: his specific bugbear was film and its abuse by authoritarian regimes. That said, the animating spirit of a work of imitation has nothing to do with mechanical reproducibility, but, instead, is associated with the transformation of a model or models—regardless of the amount of transformation. "Imitation as the premoderns saw it," Ackerman reminds us, "operated forward: while the student was expected to *copy* one or more canonical masters of the past, the mature artist moved ahead from this experience into new and individualized expression. The curriculum . . . based on drawing from ancient and classical models, was seen as the necessary preparation for emulation, the step forward into creative self-realization, as if in competition with one's antecedents."[45]

Ackerman is contrasting imitation with influence, which he claims characterizes modern interpretations of art, and which, he notes, can only be assessed after a work is finished. Imitation has more to do with the transformative process of past models leading to a potentially competitive and creative "self-realization." Also important is that artists are as collaborative with the past as they seem competitive with it. But, most significantly, it is necessary to read Romanticism in reverse in understanding Dylan's compositional method: "For the ancients," as Ackerman concludes, "imitation provided . . . the structure for articulating the history of an art or technique; imitation was what kept an art or technique moving on." Can we hear the strains of "Song to Woody" in this description? Or, more convincingly, in this celebrated (and contested) transformation:

Original:

> In fair Nottamun Town, not a soul would look up
> Not a soul would look up, not a soul would look down
> Not a soul would look up, not a soul would look down
> To show me the way to fair Nottamun Town
> I rode a grey horse, a mule roany mare
> Grey mane and grey tail, green striped on his back
> Grey mane and grey tail, green striped on his back
> There weren't a hair on her but what was coal black

Transformation:

> Come you masters of war
> You that build all the guns
> You that build the death planes
> You that build the big bombs
> You that hide behind walls
> You that hide behind desks
> I just want you to know
> I can see through your masks

The melody is required to recognize the borrowing, and, while this was an extant American folk song when Dylan wrote "Masters of War," Jean Ritchie's (copyrighted) recording of "Nottamun Town" was already available. Few critics would dispute the young Dylan's "transformative use" of the original melody, although not everyone would agree—even at this late date—that the transformation is coterminous with Dylan's originality.

But a reworked song is not the same kind of appropriation as those that get critics so exercised, such as Dylan's paintings, his Timrodiana, and his borrowings in *Chronicles*. Yet even in this context early modern practice offers a germane comparison. As Ackerman explains, "Some postmodern artists have introduced, by appropriation, objects that re-present preceding works of art, dissolving the authority in authorship; and deconstructive criticism has proposed an 'intertextual' relationship of the maker to his or her forebears in which the similarly dissolved 'author' serves as a vehicle for the processing of all prior and present verbal acts." Dylan as a "dissolved 'author'" is hard to see until Ackerman explains that "this view of making [i.e., appropriation] bears a greater affinity to imitation than to influence, because both propose a community of past and present and give the maker a pursuit beyond the expression of his or her individual identity."[46]

Seeing the affinity between early modern practices of appropriation and contemporary ones is crucial: it allows us to acknowledge that proposing a community of past and present gives the contemporary artist a competitive reason to pursue individualized creative realization. But there's a difference among kinds of appropriations. Whereas, for example, in the twenty-first-century art world, Richard Prince might be an "appropriation pioneer," to use Shore's phrase, it would be more accurate to call Dylan an "appropriation engineer." If by no means the first, he is probably the best-known and most reviled artist of our time deliberately to radicalize the past in the present by appropriating and transforming others' works.

Images and Distorted Facts

Two of Dylan's recent art exhibitions flaunt appropriation, as if saying, "when gravity fails and negativity won't pull you through," sheer transparency might do the trick. If, for example, Dylan's *Revisionist Art* exhibition proves anything at all, it is that Dylan has a keen, playful awareness of the use, abuse, distortion, and artistic value of appropriation. The exhibition was on display from November 28, 2012, to January 12, 2013, at the Gagosian Gallery in New York. As the accompanying glossy catalog demonstrates—and as the large-type, interleaved introduction by Luc Sante attempts to explain—the exhibition reverts to the same sort of pairing that Dylan started to use in his lyrics as far back as *Bringing It All Back Home*— forty-seven years earlier. Something about the confrontational revisionism and quirky satirical symbolism is reminiscent of Dylan's sixties' style, although the grotesqueness of many of the silkscreens seems to degrade even the satire.

Still, the comparison with Dylan's compositional method is not such a stretch. More than any other of Dylan's exhibitions, and more than his drawings, *Revisionist Art* satirizes the pretenses of artistic syncretism while, at the same time, practicing its own ludic, syncretic art. The Gagosian's website blurb ingenuously puts it this way: "Dylan has long been a willful contextualizer of his own source material. All personas are interchangeable. His diverse musical output spans a wealth of genres. His Revisionist art provides a glimpse of an artistic process that is equally maverick and elusive . . . [his] visual art is marked by the same constant drive for renewal that characterizes his legendary music." A contextualizer, yes, and an artist whose work reflects "a constant drive for renewal." But there's no need to mystify Dylan's artistic process as "maverick" and "elusive." On the contrary, his process, especially with music, is manifestly transparent. Dylan expects his best listeners to recognize the musical innovations, the revisions and imitations, the sophisticated lyrical digestion of prior works.

And he presumably expects the same of the audience viewing the garish silkscreens of the *Revisionist Art* show. In terms of visual art, however, a significant example of Dylan's engagement with tradition, and with deliberately selected artists, is his controversial 2011 *Asia Series* exhibition, also at the Gagosian. The show drew a crowd, doubtless made up largely of Dylan aficionados less critical of the art than appreciative of a new way to experience the man. At least that was how it seemed to me as I processed with other visitors in a slow queue from room to room. The gallery lights were low, and Dylan's canvases hung in heavy frames, dramatically spotlighted. As later became clear, the paintings were in fact imitated from postcards and photographs depicting scenes redolent of colonial-era East Asia, or as Douglas Heselgrave put it in a review, "the dusty postcards you can still buy on Hong Kong's Hollywood Road of Chinese histories that never existed."[47]

In short order, stories in the press brought out the best, and predictably, the worst of Dylan criticism. Tony Norman summarized it well in the *Pittsburgh Post-Gazette*: "This week, a variation of the 'Dylan is a plagiarist' meme erupted for the umpteenth time in the mainstream media. 'The Asia Series,' 18 colorful paintings inspired by Mr. Dylan's recent tour of China, Japan, South Korea and

Vietnam, are on display at Manhattan's prestigious Gagosian Gallery." Norman adds the rub: "'The Asia Series' was originally billed by the gallery as 'firsthand depictions of people, street scenes, architecture and landscape.' From this description, one would assume that as long as Mr. Dylan avoided getting arrested in Seoul the way he got picked up for vagrancy [in New Jersey], the scenes he sketched or photographed while rambling around Asia provided the basis for his paintings."[48] The original blurb was obviously not Dylan's doing. In fact, the Gagosian quickly replaced the first version, when, as David Itzkoff reported for the *New York Times* ArtsBeat, their press representative admitted that "while the composition of some of Bob Dylan's paintings is based on a variety of sources, including archival, historic[al] images, the paintings' vibrancy and freshness come from the colors and textures found in everyday scenes he observed during his travels."[49]

The chief objections surrounded Dylan's alleged "copying" (in paint) of photographs by Henri Cartier-Bresson, Léon Busy, and Dmitri Kessel (figures 2–4).[50] Although reactions to Dylan's painted copies of photographs varied, we should make no mistake: this technique of copying is a consummate form of imitatio. Scott Warmuth suggested at the time that the "*Asia Series* could be a subversive act created with thoughts of Duchamp. If the intent was to cause controversy then the installation at the Gagosian Gallery is wildly successful." And, citing Milton Glaser's "iconic portrait," he adds that "Dylan as Duchamp is not a new idea."[51]

On the negative side, there was everything from disappointment to public allegations of plagiarism. National Public Radio's Robert Siegel even hosted

Figure 2. Léon Busy, *Woman Smoking Opium*, Vietnam, 1915. Collection Archives de la Planète - Musée Albert-Kahn/Département des Hauts-de-Seine (collections.albert-kahn.hauts-de-seine.fr). Flickr: https://www.flickr.com.

Figure 3. Henri Cartier-Bresson, *China*, Beijing, 1948 / Magnum Photos.

Figure 4. Dmitri Kessel, *Boys Playing Siamese Chess in front of the Trocadero Hotel*, Thailand, *LIFE* Magazine, April 15, 1950; Copyright © Time Inc.

a show on the topic, combining interviews with NPR reporter Joel Rose, Rob Oechsle, and Michael Gray.

> Joel Rose. It was attentive fans on the Bob Dylancentric website, Expecting Rain, who first noticed something odd about his show at the Gagosian Gallery. A painting of two Chinese men is a full color reproduction of a famous black-and-white photograph by Henri Cartier-Bresson. Six other paintings in the show look a great deal like more obscure historical photos of China and Japan.
>
> Rob Oechsle. I said, Wow, that's my stuff. Those are pictures from my archive. Look at that.
>
> Rose. Rob Oechsle is an American photographer who's lived in Japan for much of the last forty years. He runs a Flickr blog called Okinawa Soba, where he posts historical photos from his substantial archive. It is perfectly legal to copy images like these, which are in the public domain. Still, Oechsle wishes Dylan had given some credit to his sources.
>
> Oechsle. It's plagiarism, plain and simple, to take something that's beautiful that someone else composed and just trace over it. Get out your little paintbrushes and bottle of poster paints, paint over the lines, put that up and say: This is my experience. This is my composition. That is what I saw. This is what I did.[52]

Rose dubs Dylan's imitation of the Cartier-Bresson photograph a "reproduction," obviously a misnomer and evidence of the kind of art-historical blind spot the exhibition encountered. Oechsle, meanwhile, seems to have two gripes: first, that Dylan didn't credit his (Oechsle's) Flickr archive, and, secondly, that he took "something that's beautiful that someone else composed and just trace[d] over it." But is the Flickr archive a protected source? I don't see why Dylan, as a painter, would be expected to cite his model (and where? I've never seen a painting with a scholarly apparatus attached.) Oechsle's second objection is meaningless, since Dylan didn't "just trace over" any of the photographs: he demonstrably created new works in a different medium, some significantly less faithful to their models than others.

Siegel introduced Gray as "a blogger and author of the 'Bob Dylan Encyclopedia,'" failing to acknowledge *Song and Dance Man*. "My own feeling is one essentially of disappointment," Gray said, "not that it's from a photograph, that's okay. Lots of people paint from photographs. But that the entire composition, the exact composition of a painting Dylan has copied that. That just seems to me to betray a lack of ideas, a lack of originality about the whole thing."[53]

Gray is right about the paintings' compositions. Still, while the originality of a painting depends partly on its composition, there still is a world of originality to experience in the *Asia Series* beyond composition. In fact—without special pleading—we might even contemplate the possibility that the true *exercise* of these paintings is to express originality *without* original composition.

Better-informed critics, especially those with less investment in Dylan, showed little patience with the "copycat" accusations. Norman links the *Asia Series* reworkings to Dylan's earliest imitations of Woody Guthrie: "Could it be," he asks, "that Mr. Dylan's 'borrowing' of other artist's images is a continuation of this folk-inspired tradition in another medium? Those interested in emulating the masters can be found in museums all over the world doing the same thing. They're called copyists. They're part of a tradition stretching back to the Renaissance."[54] The tradition goes back to antiquity, but Norman is quite right to identify the Renaissance as the battleground between slavish imitation (or copying) and invention.

The scare quotes around "borrowing" are not necessary. As I indicated in the introduction, borrowing from past models is the foundation of successful imitation in all premodern art, including painting. In fact, Norman's reference to "emulating the masters" has its origins in the Renaissance, in the concept of em-ulatio, a term coined in the sixteenth century as a kind of back-formation meant to complement the Roman imitatio. Initially, imitatio and its Greek counterpart, *mimesis*, a word Aristotle introduced in the *Poetics*, were developed to describe poetry and poetic method. Although no ancient treatises on the plastic arts have survived, it seems likely that ancient painters and sculptors also practiced mimesis and imitatio. If Horace's dictum, *ut pictura poesis* ("as in painting, so in poetry"), has genuine resonance, then we might assume that the art of painting included a mimetic tradition comparable to that of poetry. It was in the Renaissance, rather than in antiquity, however, that treatises on painting began to appear and imitatio was adapted to the other arts in a way we would recognize today.

Having said that, however, I would argue that Dylan's *Asia Series* paintings represent a less conventional form of imitation. His work produces what we might call a *translation* of photographs and painted postcards from one medium (or mixed medium) to another. Christina Oberstebrink, discussing Joshua Reynolds and neoclassical art of the eighteenth century, notes that the term imitation encompassed "originality, genius and inspiration" as well as "a certain method of contemporaneous translation."[55] The identification of imitation with translation suggests a provocative way to understand Dylan's painterly methods. Oberstebrink continues: "[Reynolds] was under great pressure to defend his views against the critique of plagiarism and also to uphold the assertion that originality was possible only by the imitation of preceding art."[56] Sound familiar? Dylan himself never seems to be "under great pressure to defend his views against the critique of plagiarism," but plenty of his loyalists have taken up the standard. Jim Linderman, for example, wrote an acute post on the Dylan fan website Expecting Rain. He called the post "Bob Dylan Paints Just Like a Painter," with a wink to Dylan's "Just Like a Woman" (1966), a song that itself has caused some controversy: "Now there is a big hoo-dada over questions that Dylan's paintings at

Gagosian are copied from old masters . . . or less old and lesser masters anyway. . . . If we were to list the painters who used photographs or other source material for their paintings, we would never get out of the room. Much ado about nothing, and that the questions are being raised by folks who do not paint is obvious. . . . In fact, sometimes paintings are literally painted OVER existing images. How many great paintings in museum collections even actually have a photograph under them? A question art scholars do not often pursue and museums do not want to know. So called 'crayon portraits' were common in the years before color photography."[57]

Heselgrave was even more emphatic about "the controversy surrounding the images": "Respectfully," he begins, "those writers who ballyhoo about this as proof that the painter is a no talent fake obviously know nothing about visual art and its history. Artists—like musicians—have always taken from life and worked with existing source material as a template to communicate their ideas and emotions."[58] A remark by Dave Van Ronk comes to mind: "No musician's yet been born who hasn't had his hand in someone else's pocket." Robert Morgan echoes both Heselgrave and Van Ronk, if with more bite: "As for the commercial media's charge of 'plagiarism' as related to Dylan's paintings from The Asia Series, I would suggest that the commercial news media is out of touch with issues of 'quotation' and 'appropriation' in contemporary art—as, for example, made explicit with Pop Art in the '60s—and that Dylan has done this with 'folk songs' since the outset of his career. His paintings are simply what they are, and his deployment of photographs is not a criterion for negative judgment. It is a media problem that unfortunately reveals how uninformed they are in relation to this widely-accepted practice in art today, including John Baldessari's exhibition at the Metropolitan Museum in New York (2010) and Gerhard Richter's exhibition earlier at MoMA in 2002."[59] Morgan lays the blame for the needless uproar on the first press release by the Gagosian Gallery, which, as David Itzkoff reported, the gallery amended almost immediately in a statement.[60]

Although this second statement should have solved the nomenclature problem, even the keener art critics hedged their bets. After defending Dylan's so-called copying, Norman concludes, with a kind of resignation, "Still, we'll never be able to listen to his classic song 'When I Paint My Masterpiece' the same way again."

Well, let's hope not. Let's hope the *Asia Series* exercise provides some grounding in the relationship of artists to masters and therefore of art production to masterpieces.

Unique Copy

Case in point: Heselgrave is right to point out that most of Dylan's images in the *Asia Series* probably come from postcards, although they are not only drawn from those "you can still buy on Hong Kong's Hollywood Road of Chinese histories that never existed."[61] For instance, Dylan's painting *Idol* is modeled on copies of Japanese Buddhist figures from Tōdai-ji, which was renowned as the

"Great Eastern Temple"—despite Dylan's (and his critics') mistaken impression that the "histories" are Chinese.[62]

Similarly, as Miwako Tesuka pointed out to me, Dylan's *Mae Ling*, who has a Chinese name, is dressed in a ceremonial costume of the Ainu, an indigenous Japanese people.[63] We could call this a case of Einstein dressed as Robin Hood, if we believed Dylan knew the intricacies of indigenous Japanese costume.

Like most of the paintings in the *Asia Series* exhibition, *Mae Ling* is a copy of a photograph. This is hardly revelatory or unique in art history, despite the hair-pulling and denunciations of the Dylan-watchers. Degas, Gauguin, Toulouse-Lautrec, and Van Gogh, among others, produced paintings from photographs (without being condemned for it).[64] The best way to ignore the din of "unoriginality" that accompanied—and, thanks to the eternal internet blogs, continues to accompany—the *Asia Series* is to recognize that copying photographs constitutes a specialized imitative technique. The originality is in the translation.

There is a further layer to Dylan's art in the *Asia Series*. Tesuka notes that, mainly toward the end of the nineteenth century, hand-colored photographs were produced for tourists. The painted photograph in figure 5, for example, demonstrates both the studio element of the pose and the hand-coloring. Compare the frame on figure 5 to Dylan's *Scribe* (whose robe suggests samurai

Figure 5. Japanese Meiji-era (1868–1912)
hand-colored photograph. Pinterest.com.

costume). This kind of frame was a common prop found in studio photographs in which models appeared dressed in costumes.

The painterly act in most of the examples from the *Asia Series* involves a more layered aesthetic approach than mere copying because Dylan's paintings are new creations of *painted* artifacts. His brushwork, light effects, color selection, and draftsmanship constitute, in the aggregate, a reimagining of an original model. The process of imitation thereby gains a nuanced character not unlike, to give one example among many possible ones, the album title *Love and Theft*. To accuse Dylan of plagiarism for painting an existing *painting*, even a painted photograph, is a prime case of the critical arrow missing its mark.

Significantly, the *Asia Series* marks a maturity in the painter and a step forward in imitative technique. Rather than merely "copying" from Cartier-Bresson, Léon Busy, Dmitri Kessel, and myriad postcards—or rather than only copying—Dylan is practicing the techniques of such artists as Warhol and Perec, for whom the relationships of "original" to "copy" to "mutation" remain at play.[65] It is a category error to allege that Dylan plagiarizes the photographs. He is in fact imitating a quantifiable artistic practice, one that resembles the technique of imitation and transformation he has practiced all along with his songwriting.

Because the *Asia Series* is a nexus of imitation, translation, and transformation, not to mention celebrity, the media storm surrounding the exhibition could almost have been predicted. A head-on clash of Dylan-watchers and art historians was inevitable.[66] And, as it turned out, the Gagosian Gallery included an essay by Richard Prince (Shore's "appropriation pioneer") in the exhibition catalog, possibly a preemptive challenge to the allegation-hurlers. I am not sure when the gallery decided to include the Prince essay as a kind of envoi to the catalog, and I doubt they would admit that it was post hoc in reaction to the knee-jerk accusations of plagiarism. But, whenever his remarks were added, Prince's presence begs the question of copying. Prince is best known, or most infamous, for his "rephotographs" of Marlboro cigarette advertisements—the landmark *Cariou v. Prince* fair use court case that I discussed earlier served to cement his controversial status. His essay, "There Goes My Hero," starts out by reflecting on a first meeting with Dylan on the tour bus and continues with a description of Prince's visit to a mysterious location in Los Angeles: "Dylan's studio. I think it was Dylan's studio. It didn't look like any artist's studio I'd ever been in. . . . Except for the art supplies, there wasn't a single thing in this room that would tell someone, 'Art made here.' It was kind of astounding. It was like Dylan was painting in a witness protection program."[67]

Prince doesn't pay attention to the "plagiarism meme" and is unconcerned about the origins or models for the paintings. He focuses instead on the allusive quality of such works as *LeBelle Cascade*. Ungrammatical French title notwithstanding, this painting has identifiable Japanese stylistic features, but Prince prefers to "read" it in terms of its Western resonances, perhaps because he thinks a

Western genealogy better reflects Dylan's compositional imagination: "I liked a painting called La Belle Cascade [*sic*] because it looked to me like one of Cézanne's Bathers. And Cézanne's Bathers are some of my favorite works of art: The paint is nice and thin, like it's been applied directly on the wall of a Roman emperor's home. I'm not sure of the time they're set in—it could be any time. And the geometry is interesting. It's real. The lines break up the space as if he was anticipating Cubism . . . Most of what Dylan paints is straightforward. There's nothing really to be interpreted or guessed at, and the rendering seems to say, 'I don't want excitement, and I don't want to be exciting.' If I were to describe the painting in musical terms, I would say they're more acoustic than electric."[68] The impulse to compare painting and guitar-playing reflects a common thread among viewers of Dylan's art. Critics and reviewers inevitably try to tease out connections between Dylan's art and his songs. This can have a positive effect on critical appreciation of the art. Critics not distracted by misguided plagiarist allegations, for example, are better able to notice the invention in Dylan's paintings and to link his painterly technique to his songwriting, in the way Prince imagined *LeBelle Cascade* as "more acoustic than electric."

Ingrid Mössinger, in her introduction to the German *Face Value* catalog, sees it from the other side: "It was the lyrics and video clip of his song *Subterranean Homesick Blues* that motivated me to mount the Bob Dylan exhibition *The Drawn Blank Series* in 2007. The flow of the words and images in that clip are reminiscent of 20th-century art trends such as Dada, Futurism, Beatnik, concrete and visual poetry that merged the visual and the acoustic in word-image combinations and in sound-images."[69] This is a translation from Mössinger's German, where such compounds as "word-image-combinations" (*Wort-Bild-Kombinationen*) and "sound-images" (*Klangbilder*) are less awkward. But the importance of Mössinger's remarks is that she perceives the persistence of twentieth-century art movements in that famous video of Ginsberg, Dylan, and the cue cards. Yet, since Dada, Futurism, Beatnik, and the other movements Mössinger cites occurred long before *Subterranean Homesick Blues*, it makes more sense to say that Dylan's music imitates those art movements. Recognizing elements of those movements, specifically of their radical attempts to distort meaning and reality, is to acknowledge the *imitative* process at work in the composition and performance of the song.

Robert Morgan, too, sees a connection with the music, though more methodological than art historical. He suggests that "Dylan paints as if to unravel the consequences of what he observes through poetic insight. What appears insignificant therefore becomes significant. . . . Dylan paints in a manner that is parallel to his songs: he visualizes allegories of a sleight-of-hand destiny, filled with irony and the necessity of compassion."[70] While it may be difficult to find the "poetic insight" in *any* painting, including Dylan's, the need to see a parallel between Dylan's painterly expression and his songs is irresistible. At times, this effort by critics undermines the isotropic value of the painting or sculpture, as if the artwork only justifies itself in conjunction with the unimpeachable achieve-ment of the songbook. I don't think this is always the intention of the writers who strive for parallels, but the implication lingers.

As with all Dylanalia, there is material that stretches hermeneutic limits, even when it's meant to be playful. For instance, in the *Drawn Blank Series* catalog, Alessandro Allemandi Miró tells a story about arranging a private tour of the Re-ina Sofía museum for Dylan and his entourage, which he says "went off perfectly":

> More than anything we were able to contemplate Picasso's "Guernica" in ab-solute silence. A true delight. All Bob Dylan's entourage took part with great enthusiasm. Everybody but Dylan himself. We were not sure he was going to come, but then at a certain point Tony Garnier, his bass player and musical right-hand man, received a call and had to leave early. Dylan was waiting for him . . . Tony Garnier had to break off his contemplation of "Guernica" and rush to the ring of a gym in Madrid, for he had been called by Dylan, a keen boxer, to act as a sparring partner. The following day, Tony turned up at the concert in the Alcalá de Henares with a black eye—yet another way of being struck by Bob Dylan and his colours.[71]

Evidently Miró was appalled that Dylan had so little respect for high art that he would deprive his bass player of his "contemplation of 'Guernica'" in favor of a sparring match. (Perhaps he hadn't heard the story about Andy Warhol's *Silver Elvis* painting and Albert Goldman's couch.) But Miró doesn't let what he im-plies is Dylan's Philistinism obstruct his art criticism. I don't know if his famous surname reflects a genealogical connection to the great Joan—who was Catalan and had only a daughter—but there's certainly something surreal about his spec-ulations on "being struck by Bob Dylan and his colours."

John Elderfield is more direct. He begins his introductory essay in Dylan's *Brazil Series* catalog with "Songs are journeys that may tell of journeys, and in Bob Dylan's songbook there are miles of journeys told in lines."[72] The double meaning of "lines," simultaneously referring to music and painting (or drafts-manship), indicates Elderfield's canniness as an art critic, especially since the word "lines" also suggests the line he himself is drawing between the two media.

Even in his paintings, Dylan is apt to confuse the critics, precisely because there is no paradigm set for them to read the art. Just as influence doesn't seem to work unproblematically as a critical category in Dylan's songwriting and per-formance, self-allusion and self-quotation don't work conventionally when ap-plied to Dylan's productions in different media. In fact, self-allusion and self-quotation are yet another area where Dylan might echo the ragged clown from "Mr. Tambourine Man" and say, "I have no one to meet"—a line that itself might be an allusion to Eliot's "The Love Song of J. Alfred Prufrock."

3 | SELF-PORTRAIT IN A BROKEN GLASS
Dylan Imitates Dylan

I asked Fat Nancy for somethin' to eat, she said, "Take it off the shelf—
As great as you are a man
You'll never be greater than yourself"
—"High Water (For Charley Patton)"

The Canvas Mirror

Despite the many attempts to interpret Dylan's paintings through the lens of "Bob Dylan's songbook," Dylan himself for the most part avoids making a link. The metalwork guitar and the two clefs in his Halcyon Gallery exhibition *Mood Swings* might be an exception, but there's little convincing reference going in the direction from the paintings to the poet or songwriter (as opposed to the opposite direction). No Gypsy Gals or Tambourine Men or Streets of Rubble haunt Dylan's canvases. In the *Drawn Blank Series*, there are four paintings of railroad tracks disappearing into a perspectival vanishing point, qualifying perhaps as Elderfield's "journey's told in lines."[1] The tracks inevitably recall the ubiquitous railroad imagery in Dylan's (and everyone else's) songs. And the emptiness of the scenes has a palpable companionability with all those lonesome traveling songs. The four paintings, called *Train Tracks*, are basically identical, with slight variations on the edges and utterly different color schemes governing the whole of each. Generic as *Train Tracks* is, it's difficult not to see an allusion to such songs as "It Takes a Lot to Laugh, It Takes a Train to Cry" (1966) or even individual lines like "While riding on a train going west / I fell asleep for to take my rest" ("Bob Dylan's Dream" 1963).

There is a more tempting link to the songs, however, in a painting from the *Brazil Series* called *Politician*.[2] The painting depicts, in broad brushstrokes, a nearly topless dancer in pasties and a G-string holding a small tambourine in one hand and a drumstick in the other. The urge to imagine Dylan mixing "Mr. Tambourine Man" (1964) with "Tangled Up in Blue" (1974) on the same palette is irresistible. But, somehow, the fleshy figure of the woman sidling up to the politician doesn't bring to mind the topless woman of "Tangled Up in Blue"—if in fact she was topless and wasn't just a waitress or bartender "workin'" in a topless place." Nor, if we believe Dylan's assertion that Bruce Langhorne's enormous tambourine (in actuality, a Turkish drum frame) inspired the song, does the topless tambourine woman's shrunken tambour have much resonance. Nevertheless—could this be an unprecedented instance of self-allusion or self-quotation in Dylan's painting?

Doubtful, but *Piano Player*, from the same series, contains the merest whisper of an autobiographical allusion. In his catalog commentary, Kaspar Monrad remarks that "a painting such as *Piano Player* can . . . be regarded as a portrait of the artist." Citing "a conversation with the artist," Monrad adds that "Dylan originally intended to depict the piano player in a dance hall where the background offered views of a few dancing couples and people waiting to find someone to dance with. He had second thoughts, however, and ended up just focusing on the musician." Oddly, Monrad refers to the piano player as a male when in fact the figure is obviously female. Notwithstanding this oversight, Monrad's discussion of the painting as a kind of narrative is accurate: "We are not told with whom he [*sic*] has eye contact, but we are given a clear sense that the piano player is adapting his [*sic*] playing to one or more persons. By using this device, Dylan makes the narrative of the painting depend on something that takes place outside of the image."[3] True, but hardly original. *Piano Player* is not *Las Meninas*. The most provocative aspect of the painting is the autobiographical adaptation of Dylan as a rock 'n' roll piano player to the female club singer at her upright piano—notionally, Dylan in Judy Garland drag. Her expression—what Monrad says gives "a clear sense that the piano player is adapting his [*sic*] playing"— seems to rule out a narrative of performer's isolation. This piano player, at least, sees more than just dark eyes in her audience.

Dylan, too, sees more than dark eyes as he composes and performs. Often he seems to be able to penetrate the darkness with his lyrics, a trait so familiar in his songs as almost to be expected. At other times, he seems to reverse perspective entirely and turn his compositional imagination inward, as if with a looking-glass introspection. In fact, it is sometimes difficult to avoid seeing forms of distorted self-portraiture in Dylan's lyrics.

For example, there is the revealing stanza from "Up to Me," which was an outtake from *Blood on the Tracks* (1974):

> We heard the Sermon on the Mount
> And I knew it was too complex
> It didn't amount to anything more
> Than what the broken glass reflects
> When you bite off more than you can chew
> You pay the penalty
> Somebody's got to tell the tale
> I guess it must be up to me
> ("Up to Me")

According to Bell, this stanza offers "still more evidence, before the bolt from the blue, of a movement toward religious belief"—the bolt from the blue being Dylan's late seventies conversion to evangelical Christianity. On the surface,

Dylan is referring to the glass stomped on and broken by the groom at a Jewish wedding ceremony. The "broken glass" in this Jewish tradition is a symbol of fear and trembling: that is, there can be no raucous nuptial joy without the memory of suffering (such as the destruction of the Second Temple).[4]

But Bell sees a different nuance: "This *seems* to say that Christ's sermon ('too complex') simply describes what a man sees in his broken mirror."[5] Reading self-reflection into the line is a superb insight, since Dylan's Jewishness inevitably draws us to imagine him seeing himself or his tradition in a parallel relationship with the Christian tradition, metaphorically the kind of fractured, "broken" image one would see in a shattered mirror.

This chapter explores just such ambiguous self-representation in Dylan's art. Deliberate inflections of self-portrait, self-reflection, and, ultimately, self-imitation resonate throughout the songs and drawings, as in the 2018 *Mondo Scripto* exhibition at the Halcyon Gallery in London. In fact, beginning with multiple self-portraits and *Self Portrait(s)*, forms of self-imitation have increasingly punctuated Dylan's career.[6] As his canon of songs has grown, so too, along with (digestive or absorptive) self-imitation, have appeared unmistakable self-reference, and—never far off—self-parody. Examples are legion: from the Halloween "Bob Dylan mask" at Town Hall in 1963 to the masquerades and masque performances of *Rolling Thunder*; from *Renaldo and Clara* to *Masked and Anonymous*; from "In comes Romeo, he's moaning / 'You belong to me I believe,'" which is probably a reference to Dylan's own song, "She Belongs to Me"; from his first *Self Portrait* album, both the cover art and the contents; to *Another Self Portrait, the Bootleg Series, Vol. 10*, with slightly different cover art and utterly different content recorded in 1969–71 (but not released until 2013).

The increase in self-imitation and self-reference is partly a function of the exponential growth in the volume of his songs as the decades passed and partly a result of Dylan's more sophisticated use of allusion and imitation in his writing. If the technique of imitatio best describes Dylan's compositional methodology, then self-imitation contributes to the overall definition of his poetics. It, too, qualifies as a technē, not separate but complementary and augmentative in his traditional imitation of other poetic models. Though occasionally acknowledged in critical analyses, this technique of self-imitation has for the most part flown under the radar or, as in Terry Kelly's view, produced a form of forgery. Paraphrasing W. H. Auden's definition of a poet's self-imitative later work as forgeries of his or her earlier, stronger work, Kelly sets out to be provocative (his essay ends with the phrase "J'accuse, anyone?"). He hears a "stilted literariness" in "Dark Eyes," for instance, and "obvious self-imitation, undermining the power of the much stronger lover songs" on *Empire Burlesque*.[7] But, for Kelly, self-imitation can only be negative, a sign of decay. Neither he, nor Auden for that matter, refers to imitation as a process or technique. They define imitation as copying, mirroring, aping—without the singularly important digestive element that distinguishes imitatio as a compositional technique.

This is not meant as an unambiguous apology, however. Certainly, there are later lyrics that compare unfavorably to earlier ones. As in earlier chapters, my attention is drawn to Dylan's technical poetics and to imitatio in as value-free sense as possible. That is, the method is the message. And, in this regard, Dylan's self-quotation has not received much attention, despite the hermeneutic possibilities of an artist cherry-picking his own words. The remarkable lyrics of the *Blonde on Blonde* era were often labeled Surrealist, although they might better be described as metonymic, associative poetic technique. Aidan Day hears in Dylan's lyrics "a difficulty and opacity, a dislocation of common sense."[8] And dislocation rings true for the lyrics of *Blonde on Blonde*. Referring to the earlier "Lay Down Your Weary Tune," Gray suggests Baudelaire's *correspondances* as models for Dylan's method of constructing his images.[9] This too is a persuasive characterization, and the Baudelairean methodology never really disappears from Dylan's technique: that is, he is more inclined to use a contiguity of associations, or correspondences, rather than the deliberate *dis-contiguity* of Surrealistic imagery. As Kermode perceptively concluded, "What he offers is mystery, not just opacity, a geometry of innocence . . . His poems have to be open, empty, inviting collusion."[10]

To invite collusion through a song's mystery is tantamount to producing a listening experience that seems to pique the critical imagination, a rare enough phenomenon in rock and roll. But Dylan's irascible lyrical persona, especially in his mid-1960s hipster posture, tends to reject collusion as a weaker form of imitation. As even his homages are tinged with supersession, his most collusive lyrics expressly and disdainfully challenge his audience *not* to act as critics. He expects us instead to listen as artists ourselves and to see the songs as imaginative exemplars that demonstrate how a musical-interpretive experience can become a creative (rather than collusive) opportunity.

The interpretive creativity Dylan's songs foster mirrors his own practice of productivity through absorptive imitatio. From the beginning of his career, this singer-listener dynamic has been manifest, as has Dylan's courage as an artist. Despite the off-putting snarl and the snide vituperations in some songs, Dylan's unmasking of collusion has required self-exposure on his part, a kind of linguistic sharing and intimate dependency on his audience. Maybe this is the "geometry of innocence."

His Craft and Sullen Art

An unexpected form of self-exposure appeared in 1973. Dylan published *Writings and Drawings*, a collection that included lyrics, album-cover poems, and drawings (all for $6.95).[11] In the *New Republic*, Karl Shapiro, after a unique discussion of the book's colophon and end papers, expressed his amazement: "Perhaps the most interesting feature of the book is the price. Literary economics, as every poet knows, is a mysterious business. Even a medium-sized novel nowadays may cost $10; but here is a quarto of more than 300 pages, illustrated and sturdily bound, for only $6.95! One can only commend the publisher for this extraordinary display of confidence in poetry. And with the word 'poems' so wisely in small italics."[12] A poet himself, Shapiro reads *Writings and Drawings* as a book of poetry.[13] His remark about the word "poems" in "small italics" probably refers to the typeface in the lists of album contents, although it's difficult not to read the sentence as damning Dylan with faint praise. In any case, Knopf presumably priced the book with the expectation that Dylan's audience base at the time would not want to (or be able to) spend large sums.

The strategy was only marginally successful. Appearing in the era of pirated bootlegs, the book should probably have received more fanfare, as John Wisniewski suggested at the time in the *Syracuse Post-Standard*. He marvels, "No advance notice. No hints in the rock press. Not even rumors preceded this latest Dylan venture. Here it is, nonetheless. A collection of lyrics to nearly every song Dylan has written, interspersed with line drawings a la Thurber or Lennon. And a complete set of self-penned album liner notes too." Although Wisniewski doesn't dwell on the liner notes, he heralds the value in *Writings and Drawings* of "numerous Dylan numbers never recorded by the man himself or anyone else for that matter."[14] The printed lyrics included all of the released songs on the albums from *Bob Dylan* through *New Morning*. The lyrics to unreleased songs, printed with different albums, were probably unknown at the time, although many have since appeared in the *Bootleg Series*.

Beyond—or alongside—the lyrics, *Writings and Drawings* showcases both Dylan's already published jacket-cover verse and his unpublished poems. Although Dylan occasionally published his poetry, as with the *Joan Baez in Concert 2* jacket notes, his visibility as a poet-of-the-page was minimal. He confined himself to small journals, despite the power of his name. Before *Writings and Drawings*, Dylan had not ventured onto the more popular literary scene, except with his genre-bending *Tarantula*. Yet he had earned a wide (if not universally accepted) reputation as a poet, probably more so even than Leonard Cohen, his nearest rival as a poet with an uppercase P among recording artists.[15] An endearing example of this reputation is a letter Dylan received from Hibbing State Junior College:

June 6, 1969
Dear Robert,
    A copy of poetry written by students in Miss McVay's creative writing class is enclosed.
        We at the college are proud of it. Any comments from an authority?
                Sincerely
                [Signed]
                B. J. Rolfzen[16]

Written on stationery from the junior college in Dylan's Minnesota hometown, the address "Robert" ironically seems more intimate than the public name "Bob," returning Dylan to his Zimmerman roots. The letter was accompanied by a small chapbook of poems by members of the class, mostly free verse but none in the associative style of Dylan's album-cover poems. The tribute to Dylan's poetic authority is significant: the letter and the chapbook skirt the typical fan's attitude and paradoxically create the very authority Rolfzen wishes to tap.

Writings and Drawings seems to want to claim that authority in the medium Dylan had largely avoided during the sixties. "Rather than a book of lyrics, really, this is a book of poetry," said Michael Barrett in the *Montreal Gazette*.[17] But not a few critics disagreed. After admiring how "prolific and various" Dylan had been in the sixties, Edward Grossman brings down his gavel: "On closer reading this impression must be modified and added to. Without the music, lacking the powerfully distracting sound of Dylan's voice, his harmonica and guitar, the mass of his words on paper conclusively prove that, contrary to reputation and claims, he is no poet."[18] As negative and definitive as this sounds, however, Grossman turns out to be a more sensitive reader than many. Although he claims that Dylan's "rhyming is crude, the lines do not scan, signify or move (in either sense), and many of the images are arbitrary, if not impossible," he also notes that "what is missing in this book is Dylan's essence, which can only be apprehended by listening to him sing."[19] And he concludes that "if Dylan's collected words prove he isn't a poet, the entire body of his songs so far, listened to patiently in a long sitting, suggest [*sic*] that, from the beginning, he had a calling foremost as a musician, and even when he sang with bitter, cruel, or cynical words, in a willfully 'ugly' voice, he expressed a swinging joy distantly removed from the dry, perhaps equally necessary, duties of the political life."[20]

The poetry in the "large, pink book," as one reviewer calls it—another says "magenta" and another "cerise"—is printed in a light gray typeface to set it apart graphically from the lyrics. This visual distinction has two effects: on one hand, the lighter shade seems to give less emphasis, less value, to the poetry. On the other hand, however, the inclusion of the poetry and lyrics side by side implies parity between the songwriter and the poet-of-the page. The complete list of the nine poems designated as such follows a generally chronological line:

1. "Advice for Geraldine on Her Miscellaneous Birthday" (copyright 1964, printed along with *The Times They Are A-Changin'*)
2. *Bringing It All Back Home*, jacket notes
3. "11 Outlined Epitaphs," jacket notes for *The Times They Are A-Changin'*
4. *Highway 61*, jacket notes
5. *Joan Baez in Concert, Part 2*, jacket notes
6. "Last Thoughts on Woody Guthrie" (copyright 1972) released on

The Bootleg Series, Vol. 1–3 (1991) [The copyright is puzzling, since Dylan performed this song in the sixties.][21]

7. "My Life in a Stolen Moment" (copyright 1962, printed just before "Last Thoughts on Woody Guthrie" in the volume)

8. "Some Other Kinds of Songs, poems by Bob Dylan," jacket notes for *Another Side*

9. "Three Kings," jacket notes for *John Wesley Harding*[22]

Curiously, in addition to the poems above, "Talkin' John Birch Society Paranoid Blues," "I Shall Be Free, no. 10," and "Talkin' WW III Blues" are printed in light gray typeface and linked visually to the poems. These are the only song lyrics to be given this status, which encourages such questions as: Is Dylan equating these songs somehow with the theme or style of his poetry? Is he offering an aesthetic valuation (or validation) by pairing these talking songs with the poetry (and, if so, why omit "Talkin' New York" from the group)? And, finally, did Dylan make the choice at all or was it an anonymous editor or printer who made the decision to include these three talking songs among the poems? We might ask this same question about the choice of lighter typeface: who made the decision to mark off the poems by giving them a faded look that unavoidably seems secondary to the bolder-faced lyrics? Of the various and uneven reviews of *Writings and Drawings*, no reviewer seems to have asked this question about choice of typeface. Yet the problematic that underlies this disparity between typefaces, or looms over it, is Dylan's relationship to his own imaginative writing, and perhaps by extension in a book of drawings, to Dylan's view of himself as the Artist as a Young Man.

Writings and Drawings contains sixteen simple line drawings spread over 299 pages, always on a recto page. They tend to kindle an en face electricity, obliquely illustrating the song on the facing verso page, but with a puzzle or a pun in the image. The cover of the first edition has a quasi-Cubist drawing of a guitar, certainly apt, as is the sketch of a dog with the head of a man on the page facing "If Dogs Run Free."[23] Playfully, for "Walkin' Down the Line," Dylan prints a drawing of an enormous telephone with a stick figure walking across the receiver—notionally, walking down the telephone line.[24] Except for the *Planet Waves* cover, his drawings did not see the light of day until *Writings and Drawings*. Yet Dylan's notebooks for the last fifty years are chock-a-block with all manner of drawings in ink and pencil, including marginal doodles, full-page geometric designs, and small figure sketches. The publication in 1973 of the drawings alongside the lyrics seems to indicate Dylan's wish to adduce a complementary and *competing* medium to his writing.

This added medium might have been richer ground for an analysis of self-imitation if the music had been part of the package. Significantly, however, *Writings and Drawings* does not print the music for the songs, as if all the lyrics—not merely the designated poems like "11 Outlined Epitaphs" or "Last Thoughts on

Woody Guthrie"—were "poems-for-the-page." Dylan has always insisted, and rightly so I think, that his art is in the delivery of the songs: performance versus page. His extreme version of this is the offhand "I'm just a guitar player," a familiar answer to interviewers. Which makes the absence of musical notation, or even chords, potentially more interesting in *Writings and Drawings*. It is as if Dylan's sense of himself as a model of imitation has shifted slightly, or expanded.

Twelve years after *Writings and Drawings*, Dylan released *Lyrics 1962–1985*, with the subtitle "Includes all of *Writings and Drawings* plus 120 new writings." The new writings are almost exclusively song lyrics. Only three new poems appear: two are slotted into the text before *New Morning* (the last album contained in *Writings & Drawings*) and the third is the brief *Desire* liner notes—which, inexplicably, are not printed in lighter gray. Whether this is an oversight or a meaningful material statement remains unrevealed. Yet someone—editor or publisher or Dylan himself—made the effort to reorder the contents of *Writings and Drawings* in compiling this later volume. Not only have the editors integrated the new poems "Off the Top of My Head" and "Alternatives to College," but the addition of *The Basement Tapes* allowed them to gather in one section song lyrics that had been scattered in *Writings and Drawings*. The effect of this reorganization is that the chronology of composition and first recordings is sacrificed on the altar of exactly the kind of portmanteau album clarity that the *Bootleg Series* eventually dispelled.

This is not to diminish the importance of *Writings and Drawings* and the later *Lyrics 1962–1985*. Both reveal Dylan's precocious impulse to hypostasize himself, to let his works face off against each other, and to show his capacity to imagine himself imitating himself. It might be said that a traditional competition (*paragone*) of painting and poetry plays out in Dylan's facing-page contests between his line drawings and his lyrics. To those of us who have heard the songs, the contest is won before we even open *Writings and Drawings*. Yet there also seems to be a challenge to view the lyrics as poems, like the one Karl Shapiro offers. The nonmusical presentation at once lowers the status of the songs and creates a temporary parity between the poetry-on-the-page and the line drawings. A provisional threshold is manifest, as if Dylan deliberately suppressed the authority of his voice, and, in the silence, went walkin' down the line drawing. The resistance to self-imitation is almost palpable even as Dylan augments the lyrics with drawings and seems to be illustrating himself.

En Face Value

Self-illustration creates what Dante called a polysemous text in his *Epistola X* (to Can Grande) and what recent commentators have labeled Dylan's polyvocality, although the stress on voice (*vox* > vocal > vocality) in the latter begs the question of parity between page and performance.[25] Self-illustration is at once a form of self-imitation and a form of self-portrait. At times, in fact, it has been difficult to separate the two in Dylan's work, and it seems that Dylan is playfully conscious of this overlap. Perhaps the most interesting silkscreen in Dylan's *Revisionist Art* exhibition was the *Life* magazine cover of the simultaneous Sinatras. A superimposed caption reads "Frank Sinatra and Joey Bishop Have a Laugh at a Fundraiser for Presidential Hopeful Rudy Giuliani."

But the photograph belies the caption, adding a dimension of imitation and self-imitation at the same time. Joey Bishop does not appear on the magazine cover—both pictures are of Sinatra, one smiling in middle age (the Capitol years?) and the other in full voice as a youthful crooner. Dylan has layered this silkscreen with the image of self-imitation, and inevitable self-comparison, that attaches to an artist who lasts half a century. And he has further complicated the notion of imitation by introducing Joey Bishop's name in the caption: Bishop was part of the infamous Rat Pack, all of whom were Sinatra imitators, wannabes, or ephebes (except maybe Sammy Davis Jr.).

In the *Revisionist Art* silkscreen Dylan translates musical self-imitation into visual representation. This kind of artistic syncretism reflects his own painting and sculpture perhaps, but more strikingly underlines the quandary and the value of a face-to-face encounter with the past. The *Life* magazine cover suggests a simultaneity in the paired Sinatras, rather than a progressive development. The inference is that the imitation of the self, the former and latter performers that audiences react to, are parallel manifestations—just as the two Sinatras are compositionally equal in the cover art.

Dylan enacts a similar artistic syncretism, redefining the value of self-imitation, on the album *Another Self Portrait, the Bootleg Series, Vol. 10*. Released in 2013, forty years after the recordings in 1969–71, Dylan sings a version of the traditional English ballad "Pretty Saro." According to Philippe Margotin and Jean-Michel Guesdon, "Bob Dylan added a literary dimension" to the song:[26]

> If I were a poet and could write a find hand
> I'd write her a letter that she'd understand

But Margotin and Guesdon might have missed the Doc Watson version. Although several artists recorded the song in the fifties and early sixties, including Ed McCurdy, Peggy Seeger, and Judy Collins, no poet had appeared in the verses. Instead, they sang "I wish[t] I was a *merchant* and could write a fine hand." Doc Watson, however, followed a different hand-me-down tradition, and sang, a cappella, a verse almost exactly anticipating Dylan's cover, poet and all.[27] The implication of the former, presumably, is that a merchant would have enough schooling or practical experience with written documents to have mastered a good copperplate. In the latter case, our inference might be mixed: would a poet "write a fine hand" because he had an education or simply because, to be a poet, it is necessary to write? Or are poetic faculties and penmanship separate, and is the singer wishing he were not only a poet but also a poet who wrote a fine hand? A merchant might have good handwriting, but he's unlikely to be a poet—thus the content of the letter and the graphic representation are unrelated. For the poet, however, the content and the "fine hand" could be interdependent.

In any case, Dylan does not add the "literary dimension" since Doc Watson had already sung the same line. It was already part of the song's tradition. Still, he chooses to sing the Doc Watson version over the other recordings. We probably shouldn't make a mountain out of this choice, and, of course, it's impossible to determine his motive, but whether intended as restoration or homage, his imitation of "Pretty Saro" transfigures the song. Covering the Doc Watson version introduces the irony of a poet (Dylan) wishing he were a poet.

The lyric contains a striking reference to visual art. I would like to believe Dylan noticed the reference, and maybe even kept the Doc Watson verse for this reason (but maybe that's just wishful thinking). In the lines "If I were a poet and could write a fine hand / I'd write her a letter that she'd understand," the would-be letter-writer yearns for a poetic faculty analogous in value to having a "freehold" and gold to win his beloved. There's a haunting lyrical grace in Dylan's voice when he sings this verse, and, peeking through the romantic surface is, surprisingly, the hint of a syncretic artistic sensibility. The conceit that a poet must write "a fine hand," which seems so right in context, reveals a conundrum that speaks volumes to our ability to hear but not listen, to feel the poetic image without necessarily parsing its logic.

Yet the image offers a trenchant example of syncretic imagination, whether the author (and traditional singers) "intended" the syncretism or simply felt the aptness of the image in the context of the speaker's inadequacies. The lines imply an interdependent relationship between poetry and calligraphy, the latter being a graphic art. The word "letter" in context almost certainly refers to correspondence, a billet-doux, although we might stretch a point and allow the word to indicate, inaccurately, a single calligraphic character.

This is not to argue for a deliberate misinterpretation, but because, as Dylan probably knows, the contiguous relationship between poetic meaning and graphic representation is a concept instrumental in the formation of Chinese, Japanese, and Islamic aesthetics. But the concept is pragmatically alien to Western manuscript and print culture. In calligraphic poetics the link between "a fine hand" and the meaning of the represented language and even the ethics of the writer is indissoluble. As Adriana Proser explains regarding developments in aesthetic factors affecting early Han Dynasty calligraphy, "The first of these [factors] is a new interest in the quality of brushwork, in particular the brush itself, and the second is the use of the brush as an expressive instrument which can embody morality and character. This second factor, wielding the brush in such a way as to convey moral qualities . . . led to the production of writing that formally evokes the general thematic content and context of the text."[28] In consequence of this traditional relationship between written form and content, readers of calligraphy have always been able to say, for example, as does a commentator on Yan Zhenqing's "Eulogy for a Nephew," "The calligraphy flows with the passion of grief, and is a powerful embodiment of the horrible turn of events it laments"; or, with equal certainty about an anonymous Tang Dynasty "Epitaph Inscription for Princess Yongtai," "The calligrapher's name is not mentioned, but the severe and graceful block script is well suited indeed to the tragic Princess's story."[29] Indeed—the affective association of block script with tragedy fully captures the interrelation of the graphic and the thematic.

In the West, on the contrary, critical interpretation takes for granted a separation between writing and meaning—except in the case of concrete poetry or something like Charles Olson's eccentrically printed *Maximus* poems.[30] Authors are notorious for their snarled scrawls, while their illegible manuscripts have provided a livelihood for generations of scholars and professors. In fact, where more antique hands are concerned, we even have a discrete field of study: paleography. The scribes who copied manuscripts, including those who produced illuminations, usually remain anonymous, and, in any case, would never be associated with the content of the manuscript. For instance, the illuminations of *Le Roman de la rose*, a popular fourteenth-century French allegory, are neither credited to, nor do they garner credit from, the authors of the tale, Guillaume de Lorris and Jean de Meun. This fact of scribal life is more obvious where biblical illumination is concerned but holds true as an axiom of all manuscript, incunabula, and printed book culture.

In contrast, in calligraphic cultures, poetry and "writing" (brush, brushwork, cursive or block script) are usually indivisible. It is incumbent on a calligrapher, whether composing poetry, copying a classic, or, significantly, writing private correspondence, to "write a fine hand" because the graphic art coexists and suffuses the inked character's concept. It is a small measure of traditional lyric's poetic genius that the image in the penultimate couplet of "Pretty Saro" has an emotional force and intelligibility despite its illogical sense in a Western context. This is more than only a "literary dimension," and, however casual or inadvertent, Dylan's inclusion of the verse contains the syncretic hint linking Eastern-style calligraphy with what seems to be a romantically primitive Western literacy. Nuanced, but not buried, is a provocative reference to a combination of painting and drawing, penmanship and poetry.

Although, to some extent, this combination reflects Dylan's self-illustrations in *Writings and Drawings*, his first exhibition after receiving the Nobel Prize, *Mondo Scripto*, displayed the facing-page confrontation of penmanship and poetry.[31] In 2017 the Halcyon Gallery opened a show comprised of sixty songs that Dylan had handwritten—or, more accurately, *re*-handwritten, since autograph drafts and revisions from decades ago are extant at the Bob Dylan Archive and the Morgan Library. The rewritten songs, which are done in "a fine hand," are illustrated with new facing-page line drawings.

As with the typeface in *Writings and Drawings*, the text of the songs has a voice of its own. In fact, Dylan engages in some of his signature Emersonian or Whitmanian revision. While it wouldn't be amiss to expect "fair copy" of the exhibited songs, some of them include surprising crossings-out and overruns into the margins. Odd, really—why not recopy the song before putting it on display? But maybe this lack of slickness is what David Sexton felt in reviewing the exhibition: "Dylan himself may have said in his Nobel acceptance speech that songs are meant to be sung, not read, but reading them here, in his own recent hand, they come alive, lifting off the page, sounding themselves out, the rhythms and rhymes moving you all over again."[32] Dylan said songs are meant to be sung not only in his Nobel speech (and in interviews for most of his career) but even in the *Mondo Scripto* catalog. In the interview introducing the volume, an anonymous questioner asks, "Did you ever find the illustrations changed the meaning of the song for you?" And Dylan replies, "The meaning of the song is in the hearing of it." This seems definitive yet unsatisfying in the context of a set of documentary representations. The interview continues:

> Interviewer. Did you ever consider doing paintings for each of the songs instead of drawings?
>
> Dylan. There wasn't time for that really. Not only that, it's just not practical. A song is really a form of storytelling that changes from minute to minute, and adapts itself to different circumstances. A painting is a fixed scene, where something is nailed down and made permanent. You can't leave holes in the center. With songs you can do that. I wouldn't mix the two to try to force them together.

It seems fair to ask how line drawings differ from paintings in terms of the "fixed scene." How are paintings, such as Dylan's *Face Value*, *Brazil Series*, or even the repainted postcards of the *Asia Series* somehow more fixed than the line drawings accompanying the calligraphic versions of the songs?

The adaptability of songs comes as no revelation, at least in Dylan's lexicon, nor do the "holes in the center." But the *Mondo Scripto* catalog extends that adaptability and makes it a graphic reality by printing two versions of "Knockin' on Heaven's Door." Not only is there a single image accompanying the first appearance of the song but the catalog ends with the "Knockin' on Heaven's Door Series," a kind of comic strip (or graphic narrative) in which the verses, all in caps, are written across the line drawings. But Dylan is clever here: his line drawings imitate his own revisionist stance. If, as he says, songs are a form of storytelling that "[change] from minute to minute, and [adapt] . . . to different circumstances," then his illustrations for "Knockin' on Heaven's Door" are a form of self-imitation because he draws as many different images as there are repetitions of "knockin' on heaven's door" in the refrain. It's as if the mood and audience and "circumstances" change with every new drawing, and the singer-draftsman adapts:

I FEEL LIKE I'M KNOCKIN ON HEAVEN'S DOOR
[A man with a garden rake is in the act of striking an elaborate, arched, double set of doors.]

KNOCK KNOCK KNOCKIN ON HEAVEN'S DOOR
[A man with a baseball bat is about to batter a different set of double doors.]

KNOCK KNOCK KNOCKIN ON HEAVEN'S DOOR
[A man with an iron bar is trying to break the hinge on a wooden door.]

KNOCK KNOCK KNOCKIN ON HEAVEN'S DOOR
[A man with a jackhammer is trying to break through the bottom of the same wooden door.]

KNOCK KNOCK KNOCKIN ON HEAVEN'S DOOR
[A hand holding a cross is knocking on the wooden door.]

The changing cast of (all-male) knockers on heaven's door, coupled with their different implements, reinforces Dylan's description of storytelling. The implements are all hopelessly pathetic against the closed doors: banging a garden rake against a steel portal, using a jackhammer to crack the foundation of the threshold, even the wishful thinking of outside hinges on heaven's door. And, while the cross seems to negate any chance of an ecumenical resonance in the word "heaven," following five pointless implements, it offers only ambiguity: is it another inadequate human tool or is it the silver bullet?

Each of these vignettes reflects a revision of the previous one. Each demonstrates the changing circumstances and changing audience Dylan describes as part of the performance of the song—all types of "the changing of the guard," perhaps. They are graphic translations of self-imitation. In every alternative version Dylan's imaginative and performative choices are implicit. In addition, because the graphic possibilities mirror the artist's selection process, they offer audience and observers a kind of agency, graphically representing a collusive opportunity recast as part of the creative process. Dylan's more obvious revisions to the song texts in *Mondo Scripto* have countless precedents in live performances.

It is as if Dylan wanted to hammer home the unfixable nature of a song—"The meaning of the song is in the hearing of it." *Mondo Scripto* is the visual equivalent of this principle.

In the 2019 release of *Rolling Thunder Revue: The 1975 Live Recordings*, for instance, he replaces the immemorial first verse of "If You See Her, Say Hello" with what seem impromptu lines:

> If you see her say hello
> She might be in Babylon
> She left here last early spring
> Took a while to know that she was gone
> Say for me that I'm all right
> Things are kind of in a mess
> She might wonder where I am by now
> If she don't know let her guess

This recording of an almost entirely reimagined lyric is rare as an official release, but old hat to concertgoers and bootleg traders. The ostensible rarity isn't as interesting as the lyrics' proof of Dylan's self-imitation. To transform one's own song into a model from which to select parts (melody and language) and thereby to produce a new song is exactly the sort of transfiguration Alessandro Carrera describes as the culmination of the process beginning with appropriation.[33] It is a playful exercise in self-imitation.

Even if, as is probably the case here, the "She might be in Babylon" version isn't as strong, either lyrically or metrically, as the "She might be in Tangiers" version, the changes Dylan rings on the original utterly refocus and hypostasize *Blood on the Tracks*. In the *Rolling Thunder* version, the delicate balance between guilt and bitterness seems to have swung toward the latter. This version maintains, miraculously, the wistful sting of the breakup, but seems to have an edgier, steeled resignation than the album cut. Ambivalence has given way to a rawness, even anger, it would seem. As if the Tangier of the recorded version were not exotic enough, Dylan here consigns "her" to Babylon, the Ur-nation of Middle Eastern civilization and Nebuchadnezzar's capital during the exile of the Jews. We can do with that what we will (is "she" in Babylonian exile from the speaker, or does she simply represent an Ur time and place?). But compare the excruciatingly intimate lines of the original,

> Say for me that I'm all right though things get kind of slow
> She might think that I've forgotten her, don't tell her it isn't so,

with the parallel lines in the impromptu stanza:

> Say for me that I'm all right
> Things are kind of in a mess
> She might wonder where I am by now
> If she don't know let her guess.

There is little comparison in terms of subtlety. But maybe the point of the transfiguration is to refit the lyrics to a new audience and circumstances. This *Rolling Thunder* recording was made during what the CD calls "Studio Instrument Rentals Rehearsals" (October 21, 1975). The audience would have been Dylan's fellow musicians and his pre-Revue cohort. We can speculate that his freedom to imitate himself, even to perform a kind of self-parody, might have depended on how familiar the people in the studio were with the state of Dylan's marriage and the relation of this new persona to the touring carnival in the works. Maybe, to the initiated, the impromptu studio lyrics herald a climacteric, a message Dylan telegraphs through recognizable self-imitation of his song.

Similarly, it could be that *Mondo Scripto* indicates yet another climacteric, again discoverable through Dylan's self-imitation. One of the most telling changes in the exhibition is Dylan's rewriting of "You're Gonna Make Me Lonesome When You Go." Tom Piazza supplied the critical blurbs in the exhibition catalog and his full paragraph preceding this song is germane: "In their original recorded incarnation, the lyrics to this song are luminous with the sensuality of new love, intoxicated with its immediacy and worried that it won't last. In this almost wholly reimagined version, the poet is looking back at a distance from that love, with an older eye and a cagier relation to love's ups and downs. Dylan even throws in references to English poet John Milton, country music legends the Carter Family, and in the words 'footprints in the snow,' throws a wink to bluegrass music patriarch Bill Monroe for good measure."[34] (Not to mention an allusion to Bob Seger's "fire down below.") Sexton echoes Piazza, making a comparable observation about unexpected references in his review: "Many [of the songs] have been extensively re-written," he observed, "including five great songs from *Blood on the Tracks*. 'You're Gonna Make Me Lonesome When You Go' has changed completely, in words and mood: Rimbaud and Verlaine are gone and instead Dylan writes: 'I see things inside my mind—things Milton saw after he went blind.'"[35]

The unexpected allusion to Milton, replacing the usual French suspects, shifts the emphasis of the lines from Verlaine's twisted obsession with Rimbaud to Dylan's identification with a visionary poet—the most celebrated religious visionary poet in English, William Blake notwithstanding. The lines describing an inward-looking vates appear in the invocation to book 3 of *Paradise Lost*:

> But cloud instead, and ever-during dark
> Surrounds me, from the cheerful ways of men
> Cut off
> . . . . . .
> *So much the rather thou celestial light*
> *Shine inward, and the mind through all her powers*
> *Irradiate, there plant eyes, all mist from thence*

Purge and disperse, that I may see and tell
Of things invisible to mortal sight.[36]

Whether Dylan had read this passage or was simply describing his romantic idea of a blind prophet only matters if we're looking for intertextual connections. Milton's pun of a "universal blank" to a blind man who sees only "ever-during dark" and his plea that the "celestial light / shine inward" would appeal to Dylan's metaphysical (and metaphorical) imagination, but there isn't enough detail in Dylan's allusion to prove that Dylan knew the invocation to book 3.

Somehow that seems less important than the substitution of Milton for Rimbaud and Verlaine. This switch indicates a frank genealogical bid linking Dylan not only to a pinnacle of high-culture literature but also, significantly, to the most salient vatic literary descent in the language (not to mention that the "fire down below" takes on a special meaning in a Miltonic context). Coming fast on the heels of his Nobel, this deliberate identification with Milton's "introverted" vision reflects how close to the surface Dylan's literary ambitions are, despite his self-deprecating denials to the contrary.

Dylan seems to encourage his *Mondo Scripto* viewers to recognize the sea-change of poets from the French Symbolists to the newly adopted John Milton when looking at the exhibited text of "You're Gonna Make Me Lonesome." What Piazza calls "the almost wholly reimagined version" conveys Dylan's lyrical changes through a material instability. There are crossings-out in four verses, giving the sheets an impermanent, temporary feel. Dylan inexplicably provided his viewers with what could be a notebook page (but isn't), as if to heighten the process of composition and throw the notion of a pure original into doubt.

In contrast, while the written lyrics indicate fluidity and self-imitation, the line drawing set beside them is static: a shaded country road running through tall trees. The crossing-out and the "correction" distort an irreducibly familiar text "forged" in the memories of Dylan fans and Halcyon Gallery customers. Not unlike his *Asia Series* experiments, Dylan's crossed out lines and new verses represent a unique challenge to his viewers: the changes he makes revise the unrevisable, transforming a permanent song-icon from *Blood on the Tracks* into a model of imitation. Viewers are asked, then, to hold both texts in mind, as one would in reading any imitation of a past work. Dylan's revised verses are, in effect, "Things unattempted yet in prose or rhyme"—except of course they have been attempted, by Dylan himself and in an earlier (supposedly completed) version of the same song. Problematically, the handwritten song hanging on the wall or published in the catalog seems just as permanent, and more up to date, than the "original" from *Blood on the Tracks*.[37]

At this point, perhaps, the calligraphic question should fill our heads and fall to the floor: why does the speaker in "Pretty Saro" say "If I were a poet and could write a fine hand," when the Nobel laureate of *Mondo Scripto* scribbles and crosses out his verses? It's fair to wonder what the material connection might be between the handwritten characters and meaning—not necessarily the meaning of the verses themselves but of the process of transcribing and transfiguring. Does the deliberately included corrected text reflect a change in Dylan's attitude to his literary and musical forebears, or are the corrections the message? If *Mondo Scripto* refers (in Petrarchan Italian) to the "Written World," then what does it mean if the calligraphy has blotches and revisions? The artist's choice is equally strong on both sides of the facing pages.

A tentative answer to these questions might lie in an allusion in the Halcyon catalog version of the song, a reference entirely absent from recordings both live and in the takes of *More Blood, More Tracks*. Dylan builds a "play-within-the-song" into the exhibition's "You're Gonna Make Me Lonesome":

> The play was over 'fore I knew it—my part was easy, I walked right
>   through it
> There are things I never knew but now I know

This is from the third verse and contains what might be another reference to Bob Seger: in his song "Against the Wind," Seger sings "I wish I didn't know now what I didn't know then." But more than Seger, the introduction of a play-within-the-song, and a short play at that, irresistibly recalls *Hamlet*, especially when Dylan returns to it in the last verse:

> I don't talk and I don't ask—I wear the magic actor's mask
> I'm all covered up from head to toe

Much could be said of these lines: the "magic actor's mask" is a Dylan perennial. A "masked and anonymous" figure appears as the speaker "covered up from head to toe," and it is tempting to place him behind the arras *after* the revelations of the play-within-the-song. In any case, the changes to the original model—which I have termed versions of self-imitation—clearly bring a new aesthetic to the song, and to the idea of lonesomeness and loss. The future tense of "you're gonna" is telescoped by self-imitation into a reformulated present moment. Just as all imitatio transfigures the past by reimagining it as part of the cultural present, Dylan performs the process of imitation on the page. The surprise of the digestive process he reveals is that he is plucking the nectar from his own fifty-year-old song and transforming it into the honey of a new medium.

Mythoclastes

Yet Dylan's commitment to self-imitation in new media does not seem to extend to self-portraiture. There's a "drawn blank" element about all the faces he paints, as is clear from the twelve portraits in his *Face Value* exhibition (and catalog). His choice of a limited palette of browns and grays, sapped of color and background, is reminiscent of the two self-portraits on the albums of the same name. In his introduction to the *Face Value* catalog, Elderfield sows a seed of doubt about these portraits: "Since the cover of *Self Portrait* bore no title and comprised only a reproduction of this painting [catalog fig. 1, referring to the cover art], it was inevitably taken to be a self-portrait."[38] Had anyone before Elderfield asked this question? Who said the cover art had to be a self-portrait of Bob Dylan?

Even if it seemed reasonable to take the portrait on an album called *Self Portrait* as a self-portrait, the surprise content of Dylan's covers of other artists might have been a hint that the cover wasn't strictly what it seemed. The aggregation of other artists' songs might have been paired with the album art. Both contained a map of imitations. The same might be said for *Another Self Portrait, the Bootleg Series, Vol. 10.* Although it is not clear if the album art is from the same period in Dylan's painting career, the songs on the albums were recorded within a few years of each other. The 2013 release date on *Another Self Portrait* is therefore misleading. Indeed, as Fantuzzi has now established, and as the sketching in notebooks at the Bob Dylan Archive attests, Dylan was more than a casual hobbyist when he painted his self-portraits for the album covers.

Yet, it may be that the most interesting feature of Dylan's self-portraits on the two *Self Portrait* albums is that they so closely resemble each other while neither looks like Bob Dylan. We could account for this by citing Dylan's limited skills as a draftsman. But how limited is he? His drawings range from stick figures, as in *Writings and Drawings*, to the more sophisticated line drawing of *Mondo Scripto*. His painting, as I've noted already, can be expressive and self-conscious. According to Dylan, even the gray portraits of the *Face Value* exhibition are meant to resemble live models, although he is cagey about how much fiction he mixed (self-consciously) with reality:

> Elderfield. You have said that you work from sitters, from images, and from your imagination; were these sketches made from only one or more of these sources?
>
> Dylan. The sketches were done on the run, mostly from inspiration and luck with transportable setups. The source material is all real with a bit of fiction thrown in.
>
> The process changes anyway from minute to minute.[39]

"All real with a bit of fiction thrown in"? This is about as helpful as Dylan's quip, "This song comes from the newspaper. Nothin's been changed, except the words." But Dylan qualifies this vagueness about source material tellingly: "The subject always contributes to the result in some kind of way. A person can appear with a variety of expressions. We see people who know how to put on a smiling face or a sad one or an angry one, but it's only a front. An actor can fake just about any emotion, but that's not who they are in real life. You can tell only so much by looking at a person's face. Body language is way more important."[40]

These last sentences might be written in the margins as commentary beside Dylan's own album face-portraits, which, regardless of whether we take them to be *self*-portraits, evidently "only tell so much." Dylan obviously doesn't seem to see much "face value" in his self-portraits. The impasto flatness and the studied lack of resemblance seem defiantly to beg the question of identity. For instance, Scobie observes about *Self Portrait* that "this painting, with its overstated *unlike*-ness to any previous images of Dylan, challenges the process of identification implicit in any notion of the 'portrait' of a celebrity."[41] Where are the famous profile, the wild curls, the lips that blew a thousand harps? And why, if he really wanted to paint himself "to the life," didn't he work by copying photographs, as he eventually does (to cries of plagiarism and "*dilettantismo*") in the *Asia Series*? His self-portraits could have been painted versions of, say, Daniel Kramer photographs, or illuminated copies of any one of a hundred familiar Dylan images.

Yet neither of the two *Self Portrait* album covers captures the recognizable "face value" we would expect—which, if we take Dylan's statement from the interview with Elderfield seriously, means we should be looking for his "body language" in those albums. If "an actor can fake just about any emotion," then the un-Dylan-like faces on the *Self Portrait* albums should steer us away from assigning face value to something untethered to either the public image or the Bob Dylan Halloween mask. Maybe we should be looking *past the vernacular* for the "body language" of the *Self Portrait* albums, the vernacular being, paradoxically in the context of a Dylan album, Dylan's own compositions.

Getting past the Bob Dylan vernacular requires mythoclasm—a return to the myth before the myth began. No figure in rock-and-roll culture needed mythoclastic change more than Bob Dylan in 1970. In the wake of his sixties fans' stubborn refusal to accept shapeshifting itself as intrinsic to the Dylan myth (they insisted instead on a superseded, petrified version of Dylan), the artist's survival depended on remythicizing his musical image. The *Self Portrait* album provided an unexpected, and largely missed, heuristic opportunity. In it, Dylan augmented the vocal and lyrical remythicization that *John Wesley Harding* and *Nashville Skyline* should have accomplished by providing a mirror up to mimesis. *Self Portrait*, warts and all, did (and continues to do) what no other Dylan album since *Bob Dylan* had done: it focused on process over product. The irony is that while the dazzling albums of the previous decade seem to reflect and *identify* the artist, a truer portrait of the artist is the broken looking-glass with shards of traditional music, folk appropriations, Gordon Lightfoot, Paul Simon, and an orchestrated choral opener. Without falling into an Escher staircase of new Dylan masks leading to old leading back to new, it seems clear that *Self Portrait* breaks with the past.

How conscious Dylan was of himself as a mythoclast is open to question.

But the album's title, unless it's just coyness, indicates at least some effort to step out from behind the curtain. Graham Reid, for instance, notes that Dylan's "myth-destroying *Self-Portrait* double album of 1970 is one of those oddities you can return to and find the oddball rubbing shoulders with the truly awful and the occasional sublime song."[42] Reid's notion of "myth-destroying" describes the album and its effect well—again, regardless of how tactically Dylan thought about it. Reid also calls attention to something other critics alleged, namely that Dylan took credit for composing songs he'd only arranged.[43]

Why Bob Dylan, the most celebrated American songwriter in history (given the press and fanaticism he generated before he was thirty), would need to claim composing credit for, say, "Alberta," no one seems to have asked—especially since that particular song had a storied public history of recordings by, among others, Lead Belly, Mary Wheeler, Bob Gibson, Burl Ives, and Odetta. Any other artist might be forgiven for expecting his supposedly informed audience to know a bit more about the folk tradition. In other words, if the lack of "arranged by" set beside a Lead Belly song suggests theft (rather than emulation/appropriation), then the onus is on the listeners to shed their ignorance and get past petty moralizing. Directing the controversy in a more productive direction, Hampton compares the album to Joni Mitchell's "self-dramatizing and romantic re-creations of her own adventures" and concludes that Dylan, "by contrast, offered an album called *Self Portrait* that consisted of songs by other people. Quite unlike both [Leonard] Cohen and Mitchell, Dylan radiates outward in his work, and his interest lies in absorbing into his singing persona all of the material of the culture around him."[44] Dylan's capacity to "radiate outward" produces a less introverted version of self-portraiture, and, arguably, underscores his commitment to imitation, testifying to a combination of emulation and the digestive process of composition.

Ultimately, however, discussions of the motivation behind *Self Portrait* come down, at best, to informed speculation. That Dylan's audience misjudged him, both overestimating his commitment to the sixties' Dylan myth and underestimating his ruthless self-reflection, is now common knowledge. A curious example of this has recently come to light. One of the more hostile critics of *Writings and Drawings* objected indignantly in the *Hartford Courant* that "it's a joke, right? A put-on? I mean—a coffee table book by Bob Dylan? Better you should buy Abbie Hoffman's etiquette book, or 'How to Make a Killing in the Stock Market' by Karl Marx."[45]

Ironically, the idea of a Bob Dylan coffee table book was not so bizarre. Long before *Writings and Drawings*, in 1964, Dylan "wrote a suite of twenty-three poems inspired by [Barry] Feinstein's photographs of Hollywood." Never completed, the book is now available, with the somewhat misleading title *Hollywood Foto-Rhetoric: The Lost Manuscript*. "Not that the poems were ever truly 'lost,'" Luc Sante explains in his foreword, "'in the way that mittens and some of the theorems of Pythagoras are lost; rather, they were just set aside and forgotten until the photographer came across a manila envelope one day, opened it up, then picked up the phone and called Bob Dylan with a good idea for a book."[46] So was it a book project in the sixties or wasn't it? The vagueness of Sante's conclusion leaves us wondering what format Dylan thought he was writing for. Yet books of photographs are generally glossy, large-format publications—meant, if not for coffee tables alone, then for the art-market consumers. In the now-published volume, Feinstein's photographs of old Hollywood appear with Dylan's poetry facing them. While apparently there never was a print-ready manuscript in the sixties, Dylan wrote his poems as complements to specific photographs. This would indicate that he expected them to be published in a glossy, large-format book, which might have puzzled his fans (and definitely would have surprised the *Hartford Courant* reviewer).

The poems are written in Dylan's telegraphic sixties' style, all lowercase with short lines and dramatic line ends and enjambments. As always with Dylan, powerful, even affecting passages nestle against banality and autobiographical ambiguity. But the book repays study in that Dylan clearly responds to the photographs and to the passing of the Hollywood of his childhood. According to Sante, "Dylan carried Hollywood within him, maybe even more so than the average citizen of his generation."[47] And he suggests that the book reflects a parallel between "the collapsing feudal system of old Hollywood and Dylan's eventual disillusionment with the world of celebrity."[48] Without doubt, Dylan became disillusioned with celebrity early on. Yet his poem accompanying two photographs of Marilyn Monroe's house on the day of her death seems to herald her supersession of death:

> death silenced her pool
> the day she died
> hovered over
> her little toy dogs
> but left no trace
> of itself
> at her
> funeral[49]

The poem may pale before Frank O'Hara's "The Day Lady Died," his immemorial tribute to Billie Holiday, but the resonance of loss mirrors the stillness and emptiness of the black-and-white photograph. And, as a kind of bonus, Dylan adds a vatic element, refuting the silence of death with death's absence at the funeral.

One of the most astonishing poems, however, comes at the end of *Hollywood Foto-Rhetoric*. Facing five pages of photographs, from the last in a series depicting scenes from Gary Cooper's funeral (1961) to a series of close-ups on hands and gleaming statues during the 1960 Academy Awards, these lines appear:

lookin at life
watchin it being lowered into the ground
unable t-change a thing
you too
yes
have committed
some wicked sins
receiving this award once
from whom i presumed
kind givers of good wishes
thinkin that they
knew what they were doin
i at least thought
t some degree
acceptin this then
i stood on the
platform an said
"i see something of
myself in the killer
of the president"
some givers booed
screwed their faces up
sneered terribly
i could've stopped
an asked
"is there one person
out there who does
not believe he could
say the same thing?"[50]

It's a lucky thing he didn't stop and ask. He is referring to the disastrous occasion on which he received the Tom Paine Award. There were quite a few people "out there" among the awards-dinner audience who didn't believe *they* could say such a thing and were justifiably appalled. It's hard to imagine how else the audience could have responded to the Oswald reference only a few weeks after the assassination.

The speaker of the poem continues in the tone of misunderstood youth:

ah mama but it's so hard
for i'm livin in the movement
not stopping an categorizing
the movement

an so
i could not explain to them
about what i was doin

One wonders if "mama" is the "Ma" from "It's Alright, Ma (I'm Only Bleeding)" or "Mama, You Been on My Mind": that is, does the vocative formulation infantilize the speaker or sexualize him? A further question arises from the typographical ambiguity. Dylan says he is "livin in the movement" but it seems unlikely in the narrative that he could mean the political Movement with a capital M. Rather, he seems to be casting himself as the young rebel living the revolution who is made to stop living it and face a roomful of staid and obsolete liberal hypocrites. (Or does he mean "movement" in a more metaphorical, not to say metaphysical, sense?)

i could not explain t them
about what i was doin
instead i finished
my thoughts
without compromise
(a course
of course
for none
but one)

Inside the parentheses Dylan manages a deft bit of diction, the two "courses" resolving first in the cancellation of two in "none" and then in the emergence of "one," which rhymes with "none." But the speaker finishes "without compromise," which fits with the discomfiting arrogance and misplaced self-congratulation of the overall poem. Still, a generous reading might recall Dylan's early "Eternal Circle," in which the performer in the song *sings of* an uncompromising need to finish the verses—"But the song it was long / And it had to get done." The artistic compulsion not to compromise costs him the chance to meet the girl in the shadows.

Yet half the shock of this poem is its appearance in a glossy coffee table book. The juxtaposition with the Academy Award figurines captures the underlying ridicule in the poem, while the narrow, magnified focus of the photographs implies an intimacy plausibly reflected in the verses. Imagine if these lines, unmistakably referring to the Tom Paine Award, had appeared in the mid-sixties. The mere fact that Dylan meditates on the ceremony in a poem, in such a public forum, would have brought out the piranhas. His self-justifications probably would have condemned him. There's no evidence of apology or confession in the poem, and, for the most part, lacerating judgments seem to complicate the peek-a-boo self-laceration. But the point, certainly, is not that (yet once more) we pin Dylan to the specimen board. Once again, as early as the mid-sixties, Dylan breaks through his own myth, offering a different kind of self-portrait in an ostensibly alien generic format. He demonstrates his capacity not only to "radiate outward" but also to embrace an unlikely syncretism of the arts.

Stuck Inside a Painting

As Dylan's associative lyrics gave way to the less pyrotechnically spectacular, but no less impressive, lyric precision of *John Wesley Harding, New Morning, Planet Waves*, and—first among equals—*Blood on the Tracks*, his capacity for self-imitation increased. Unlike any other rock artist, and indeed unlike most other poets, he has managed deftly to detach himself from his earlier songs and turn to them as if to poetic predecessors. The effect of this is twofold: on one hand, he elevates his songs to the imitative status of the American blues and English ballads he has always transformed in his best work, raising himself in tandem with Charley Patton, Woody Guthrie, Son House, and so forth. On the other hand, he doesn't look to these songs for influence (which would open an existential abyss) but rather treats them as a trove of imitative material: flowers for the bee to visit. This imitation and "digestive" transformation of his own songs can act as reproof, a kind of self-correction to what seems fixed and immutable in recordings. But it is here, in lyrical transformations, that the revisionary character of Dylan's performances merges with the imitative technique of his songwriting.

Art, however, presents Dylan with a dilemma, or so his songs allow us to infer. After the publication of *Chronicles, Volume One*, an interviewer asked Dylan when we could expect the second volume. In response, Dylan prevaricated and finally demurred, "When I'm writing, I'm not living." Flip perhaps, but also a map of Dylan's ongoing Jacob-like struggle with art and with the artist's necessary detachment. It may be that, at first, only the artist can evade the bourgeois trap of "Maggie's Farm." In the end, however, that evasive strategy—like Aeneas's departure from Carthage—comes at the cost of irreparable detachment.

For example, in "Don't Fall Apart on Me Tonight" (*Infidels*), Dylan characterizes painting as a form of imprisonment or paresis:

> I ain't too good at conversation, girl
> So you might not know exactly how I feel
> But if I could, I'd bring you to the mountaintop, girl
> And build you a house made out of stainless steel
> But it's like I'm stuck inside a painting
> That's a-hanging in the Louvre
> My throat starts to tickle and my nose itches
> But I know that I can't move.

It's as if the speaker were buried alive in a painting hanging in the most famous museum in the world—the same museum, not coincidentally, that houses the

Mona Lisa and her highway blues smile. Evidently trapped by the art as much as by the picture frame, the frustrated speaker can feel a tickling throat and itching nose. The allusion is obvious. For anyone who knows the Dylan catalog, the speaker's anguish as he hangs suspended in the Louvre would recall what Hinchey refers to as "the celebrated fourth verse" of "Visions of Johanna":

> Inside the museums, Infinity goes up on trial
> Voices echo this is what salvation must be like after a while
> But Mona Lisa musta had the highway blues
> You can tell by the way she smiles
> See the primitive wallflower freeze
> When the jelly-faced women all sneeze . . .

When the speaker's "throat starts to tickle and [his] nose itches" in "Don't Fall Apart on Me Tonight," the notorious putdown of "the jelly-faced women" in the earlier song comes forcibly to mind. Now it is the speaker (stuck inside a painting in the Louvre) who is about to sneeze. But this is more than simply self-reference or personal allusion. Although, as listeners, we can't be sure if the speaker is trapped inside his own self-portrait or inside the singer's (Dylan's) most famous allusion to the Louvre—"*Mona Lisa* musta had the highway blues"—we can recognize that both conceits are present in the lyric, and that they aren't mutually exclusive. This is sophisticated self-imitation, a redeveloped image that shows borrowing from his own earlier metaphor.

Things have changed inside the museum. The speaker, stuck in the painting, is now *facing* the jelly-faced women and has become the object of their (perfunctory?) visit to the gallery. Discussing "Visions of Johanna," Scobie says, "Even the ideal state [salvation] becomes a prison. The paintings in the museum long for change, for movement, for anything." And, he adds, "Almost twenty years later, in 'Don't Fall Apart on Me Tonight,' Dylan returned to the same image, the same setting."[51] In "Don't Fall Apart," Dylan reverses perspectives, undermining or resensitizing the speaker of "Visions of Johanna."

"Jelly-faced" certainly suggests a vituperative, insulting correlation between overweight, perhaps aging women and artistic philistinism. This is an absurd correlation, of course, revealing nothing about women with loose facial skin and quite a bit about the young songwriter's callowness: it is reminiscent of Dylan's insulting remark about bald men in the Tom Paine Award speech and is incongruous in a song whose speaker is characterized by nuanced, enigmatic perspectives.

In fact, there's an odd parallel between the Tom Paine Award and the "Louvre" stanza in "Don't Fall Apart on Me Tonight." In December 1963, the National Emergency Civil Liberties Committee "marked Bill of Rights Day" by giving the twenty-two-year-old Dylan an award in the Americana Hotel in New York before an audience of what Robert Shelton calls "about fifteen hundred Old

Left burghers in new middle-class security and mellowed radicalism," a group that Ian Bell refers to as "the liberal great and good, with the writer James Baldwin in attendance."[52] Dylan himself, according to an interview with Nat Hentoff about ten months later, recognized the audience as "people who'd been involved with the left in the thirties, and now they were supporting civil-rights drives."[53] Before his speech Dylan got drunk. He was probably ill at ease about accepting the award, too, if only from the perspective of achievement (Bertrand Russell had been the previous recipient). His speech was, by turns, straightforward, insulting, and weird, culminating with an inarticulate attempt to empathize with Lee Harvey Oswald—but "not to go that far and shoot."[54]

Forty-nine years later, Dylan seems to allude to this bizarre reference in one of his works from *Revisionist Art* at the Gagosian Gallery in New York, an exhibition that ran from November 2012 to January 2013. As the catalog shows, the exhibition consisted of doctored reproductions of slick magazine covers, including *Life*, *Philosophy Today*, *Playboy*, and *TV Guide*. The photos and copy on the magazine covers spoof, mock, and parody contemporary culture—for example, a provocative soft-porn image of a woman standing in an elegant hallway on the cover of *Architectural Digest* and a ballet troupe incongruously pictured on the front of the "Soul Train" issue of *TV Guide*. All the covers attempt to shock or discomfit. "They are a little threatening," Luc Sante observes in his introduction to the catalog, adding, "They exist in a peculiar temporal continuum; the past fifty years have been cut, shuffled, and redealt." Among these slightly threatening silkscreen canvases is a *Life* magazine cover of Lee Harvey Oswald with the feature title, "The Secret Life of Outlaw Assassin Lee Oswald." The cover also has a tease promising to reveal "Oswald's Hidden Treasure."

Here again, as in the Tom Paine Award speech, Dylan seems to be expressing a vague sympathy with Oswald by interpolating him into the time-honored category of "outlaw assassins" that he has sung about throughout his career: Pretty Boy Floyd, John Wesley Harding, and Joey Gallo might not have been assassins of the same stripe either as Oswald or as each other, but in the end they were all killers. The difference in the *Revisionist Art* representation of Oswald, in contrast to the award speech blundering, is the patently parodic intent of the silkscreen, especially as it is surrounded by other canvases equally excessive as cultural spoofs.

But most interesting about it in terms of self-imitation is its reappearance as part of what Sante calls a "peculiar temporal continuum."[55] The cutting, shuffling, and redealing of the Oswald reference resembles the apian method of imitatio latterly applied to Dylan's own earlier reference and transformed from sermonizing to art, and from unfocused adolescent hostility to simultaneously self-revision and cultural critique, as he had done in *Hollywood Foto-Rhetoric*, supposedly to be published in the sixties but remaining "lost" until 2008. There is something discomfiting, but instructive, about seeing Dylan revise himself: his original lack of eloquence is transformed, in the alternative media of poetry and silkscreen, into new works of art. This is consummate self-imitation, in which the models for the new works are Dylan's own earlier performance.

But let's return briefly to 1963. In the course of his farrago, Dylan managed an ad hominem attack on the older men in the audience: "It's took me a long time to get young and now I consider myself young. And I'm proud of it. I'm proud that I'm young. And I only wish that all you people who are sitting out here today or tonight weren't here and I could see all kinds of faces with hair on their head and everything like that, everything leading to youngness, celebrating the anniversary when we overthrew the House Un-American Activities just yesterday—because you people should be at the beach. You should be . . . swimming and . . . just relaxing in the time you have to relax. [Laughter] It is not an old people's world. It has nothing to do with old people. Old people when their hair grows out, *they* should go out."[56] Shades of the famous conceit of "My Back Pages"—"I was so much older then, I'm younger than that now"—seem to appear in the statement that "it took me a long time to get young." But the song, which was written and recorded seven months later in June 1964, displays a modicum of humility, as well as a nascent maturity absent from the speech.[57] Whereas in "My Back Pages" the speaker expresses doubt about his uncompromisingly self-righteous positions and seems to acknowledge that "getting young" is part of his moral and intellectual bildungsroman, the Bob Dylan of the award speech has no such insights. Egregious and even vituperative (to lift Scobie's word from another context), Dylan's rejection of balding old men—who seem to be a synecdoche for all old people—adumbrates his sneering dismissal of the "jelly-faced" women sneezing in front of great paintings in museums. They are the flabby relics who put infinity on trial, ignorant of their own complicity in turning salvation into a stagnant old people's home.

In the award speech Dylan peevishly observed from the podium, "I look down to see the people that are governing me and making my rules—and they haven't got any hair on their head—I get very uptight about it."[58] But, however true that might have seemed in the moment, he told Nat Hentoff six months later that he had ignored his own credo: "I just can't have people sit around and make rules for me . . . I fell into a trap . . . when I agreed to accept the Tom Paine Award."[59] And this statement echoes the famously cryptic opening of "My Back Pages," the same song Dylan seemed to be edging toward in the speech:

> Crimson flames tied through my ears
> Rolling high and mighty traps

The "crimson flames" presumably represent the fiery left-wing rhetoric that engulfed Dylan in his "finger-pointing" period, while the "high and mighty traps" could be the same trap Dylan described to Hentoff, the trap of having other people make the rules. The turnabout from politics and the failure of "using ideas as [his] maps" enraged the true-blue folk crowd at the time—with the *Judas!* moment still a year away.

Dylan's escape from the trap of politics is significant because he escaped into Art with a capital A. And if this is not precisely art for art's sake, then it is at least art for the artist's sake. His public rejection of the "spokesman" role remains one of the benchmarks of his career, comparable only to his "going electric," the motorcycle accident, the divorce, and the Christian albums (and now maybe the Nobel Prize era). He was twenty-three years old and very deliberately refused a leadership role and its perquisites of fame and followers—not just fans, but a ready-made, charisma-hungry audience. This is quite a fierce decision for a man so young.[60]

As it turned out, Dylan's fame only grew after *Bringing It All Back Home*, despite the loss of some of his original fan base. Nevertheless, it would be preposterous, not to say anachronistic, to suppose that he could have expected the sixties—or even that he could have known in advance how instrumental he would be in fashioning the new zeitgeist. In *Chronicles* Dylan remarks that "if anything, I wanted to understand things and then be free of them."[61] Like much of the memoir, the author is vague about when he felt this way. But the vagueness somehow makes his remark more credible than hyperprecise versions of Dylan's decision making.

Inside the Museums Redux

The decaying women and the wallflower of "Visions of Johanna" are, for different reasons, frozen out from the paintings. The working title of this song was "Seems Like a Freeze Out." Scobie offers a brilliant reading of the *Mona Lisa* stanza: "But *freeze*," he argues, "can also be spelled *f-r-i-e-z-e*, in which case it means a horizontal band of painting or decoration on a wall. This sense works much better in the museum setting and provides a possible application for 'primitive.'" Although it would be difficult for Dylan to inflect the verb "freeze" to indicate the homonym, there's no denying its aptness in the stanza and the field of associations it opens up.

The phrase "Voices echo this is what salvation must be like after a while" also opens a field of associations. It recalls Prufock's "In the room the women come and go / Talking of Michelangelo" and links the older, "jelly-faced" women to Prufrock's anxiety about his age: "a bald spot in the middle of my hair." Significantly, the line focuses on a verb that derives from a proper noun, the name of a doomed Greco-Roman nymph. Echo, as every Hibbing High Latin Club member would know, was cursed by Juno to repeat the last thing she heard, which robbed the nymph of what we'd now call rhetorical "agency." In Ovid's version—the gold standard of the legend—Echo falls in love with Narcissus and tries to embrace and cling to him. He rejects her, not least because she can't speak for herself and declare her love: all he hears is the last thing he said to Echo. When Narcissus wastes away and dies trying vainly to satisfy his passion for his own reflection, Echo is there. She cries "Alas" when Narcissus cries "Alas," and "Farewell, dear boy" after Narcissus utters those words to his fading image. Whether Dylan was thinking of this legend when he wrote "Voices echo" is less important than the certainty that an "echo" is, classically, a frustrated inability to speak your mind—a curse that imprisons Echo in the language of other people. For Dylan, whose voice was his freedom, Echo's plight would have had particularly shocking resonance.

Add to the classical underpinnings the fact that Bobby Zimmerman's high school girlfriend was Echo Helstrom. Famed already as the putative Girl from the North Country, Echo's place in Dylan's Hibbing past is—and already was at the time of *Blonde on Blonde*—the stuff of origin myths and romantic legends. If there is an allusion to Echo Helstrom in "Voices echo this is what salvation must be like after a while," perhaps there is also a background reference to the permanent bourgeois imprisonment of Hibbing melded to the hopelessness of the Ovidian legend.

In "Visions of Johanna" Dylan (through his speaker) still seems to hold art as a reserved space, a space of freedom from the trap of bourgeois values, old age, lack of passion, and conformity. *The Bootleg Series, Vol. 12* (titled *The Best of the Cutting Edge*) helps confirm this. Take 5 of "Johanna" reflects the resistance to the trap. On this version the tempo is upbeat, with the band more loudly mixed than on the final pressing. Dylan delivers the lyrics in his familiar mid-sixties drawl, less contemptuous than impatient, and the voice leaves little to the imagination regarding the speaker's feelings about Louise, the rain, museums, salvation, the fish truck, and the other metaphorical loci of the song. The song seems less hallucinatory in this version, and maybe less magical too. But the oppositions between art and the other choices are clear.

In contrast, by the time *Infidels* and "Don't Fall Apart on Me Tonight" appear, the trap of art, or art-and-celebrity, is as paralyzing as the trap of politics, despite the condescending speaker's confidence *inside the museums*. (What happened to the humility of "Good and bad I defined those terms / Quite clear no doubt somehow / Ah but I was so much older then / I'm younger than that now"?) The speaker's predicament in "Don't Fall Apart on Me Tonight" may not be a comeuppance for the sarcastic sneer about jelly-faces and wallflowers, or hostile remarks directed at a roomful of "Old Left burghers." But it is clearly an unhappy reversal.

In terms of self-reference, being "stuck inside a painting" and being "stuck inside of Mobile with the Memphis blues" are comparable. Both lines describe frustration of the desire to escape. Both indict art—painting and the blues—as the agents of physical limitations, converted, at least metaphorically, into metaphysical despair. Dylan sings, "Oh, Mama, can this really be the end / To be stuck inside of Mobile with the Memphis blues again?" "Mobile," the city, also doubles (in lowercase) as the word for movement. The song's ironic pun is that it refers to someone immobilized. The pun—a rare rhetorical device in Dylan's lyrical arsenal—seems to encapsulate the frustration inherent in being hemmed in by the arts, particularly by merging literary and musical forebears:

> Well, Shakespeare, he's in the alley
> With his pointed shoes and his bells
> Talking to a French girl
> Who says she knows me well
> And I would send a message
> To find out if she's talked
> But the post office has been stolen
> And the mailbox is locked.

In this stanza, the French girl acts as a link between Shakespeare and the speaker, but her presence also proves the speaker is one remove from the canonical literary icon, just as he is trapped in Mobile, one remove from Memphis, home of W. C. Handy and Elvis Presley, and birthplace of the Memphis Blues. The speaker wonders if the French girl has talked, tempting the listener to question what Dylan's speaker might be worried about—that is, what damaging or embarrassing information could the girl give to Shakespeare. If nothing else, the literary timeline is inverted: Shakespeare should be informing the French girl, who would then pass on the information (or influence) to the speaker. The language also implies indiscretion ("to find out if she's talked"), along with a mildly offensive sort of intimacy where the speaker doesn't even remember if he knows the French girl. There is a sense of ambivalence, of distance nearly bridged. And there is a unique reciprocity in that the speaker's secrets might be passed on to a humanized Shakespeare, whose name alone brings along the baggage of the whole traditional canon. Even if we infer a parallel between rock lyricism and literature, however, nothing in the song promises escape from Mobile, or immobility.

Yet it could be that being stuck inside of Mobile causes the same desperate enervation as being stuck inside a painting in a grand museum. Culturally assured permanence in painting—despite, or because of, a tradition of esteem—seems tantamount to petrifying stasis for Dylan, a deprivation of agency analogous to that of a lover unable to fulfill his hyperbolic ambition of building his girl "a house made out of stainless steel" on a mountaintop. Stainless steel represents the modern technological equivalent of permanence, the Philistine "flesh-colored-Christ" solution to decay. Two utterly opposing forms of preservation face off in the stanza, and we might be cheered to see the Philistine approach lose out to the venerable idealization of artistic permanence. But caveat emptor: if we celebrate the victory of art over stainless steel, we too will fall into the frame-trap that holds the speaker, a totally unexpected result in the pursuit of artistic freedom. Being "stuck inside a painting" has no redeeming or enduring cultural value in this song. Institutional preservation of creative achievement and artistic expression buries the artist alive, enforcing immobility and a living lover's desperate frustration.

Callin' Out That He's Been Framed

Self-reflection and self-critique are the counterparts of self-imitation. Dylan's speaker in "Don't Fall Apart on Me Tonight" is in effect "calling out that he's been framed"—both literally and metaphorically—as if alluding to the isolated martyr figure of "I Shall Be Released":

> Down here next to me in this lonely crowd
> There's a man who swears he's not to blame
> All day long I hear him cry so loud
> Callin' out that he's been framed[62]

The word "framed" in the last line means, in the dated vernacular of Hollywood films, to be unjustly accused of or held for a crime, often with rigged evidence. Effaced from the term is its origin, which, serendipitously, refers to a picture frame. Purportedly, the innocent man is forced into the space determined by the borders of the frame—in the lingo this is known as a "frame-up" (or in British slang, being "put in the frame" for something).

While there isn't an overt suggestion of a picture frame in Dylan's line, the background metaphor lingers and even carries over to the image of a speaker "stuck inside a painting" in "Don't Fall Apart on Me Tonight." More importantly, this notion of being unjustly held for a crime resonates with the ubiquitous Dylan problematic of blame and exculpation: Whose fault is it that the speaker is trapped inside a painting? Is the speaker "framed" or self-immolated? In "Up to Me," one of the outtakes from *Blood on the Tracks*, Dylan sings "Someone had to reach for the risin' star / I guess it was up to me." But that "risin' star" of fame seems to have lost its luster by the time of *Infidels*. Perhaps, tentatively, the imprisoning painting is fame itself, what Milton calls "the last Infirmity of noble mind." If so, the song's speaker (Dylan?) is probably also the painter, the one responsible for the frame-up in this scenario. After half a lifetime of creating and recreating himself, the singer-icon now has only a hypostasized identity that prevents him from moving and cuts him off from human touch, despite the tickling and itching he feels. Maybe the line from "Dirge" a decade earlier on *Planet Waves* should come to mind: "I paid the price of solitude, but at least I'm out of debt." This solitude adumbrates the frozen desperation of the lines in "Don't Fall Apart on Me." In the later song, the image is more explicit, and Dylan's plaintive voice more acutely reflects the failure of art to bridge the emotional gap.

"Don't Fall Apart on Me Tonight" may be an uncharacteristic album-closer in the company of "Baby Blue" or "Desolation Row" or even "Buckets of Rain." But the song worthily plumbs the album's uncanny metaphysical anxieties, from the shape-shifting of "Jokerman" to the paranoid vatic inversions of "Man of Peace" and even the stunning biblical crises of "I and I." The song's conceit is familiar enough, a minor variation on the ubiquitous folk blues pleas of "don't leave me" or "please come back (baby)." Dylan adds a harrowing edge of stress to "Don't Fall Apart on Me Tonight," however: the usual pleading is complicated by a notion that the speaker and the lover are stuck with each other tonight, just as the speaker ("little boy lost"?) is stuck with Louise in "Visions of Johanna." This complication, this lyrical interstice, creates the song's powerful dialectic.

Religion, science, art, moral idealism, beauty, and finally even Yahwistic creation fail to resolve the distance between yesterday and tomorrow, between memory and disappointment. From the first stanza the cavalcade of failures multiplies:

> You know the streets are filled with vipers
> Who've lost all ray of hope
> You know, it ain't even safe no more
> In the palace of the Pope

Historically the highest holy authority on earth (Vicar of Christ), the Pope now has no power to protect the world from desperate vipers (serpents) in the streets.[63] But if hierarchical religion has failed, the speaker ruminates, then maybe science can provide an answer for the future:

> I wish I'd have been a doctor
> Maybe I'd have saved some life that had been lost
> Maybe I'd have done some good in the world
> 'Stead of burning every bridge I crossed

Except that, as the next stanza laments, the speaker chose art instead and ended up trapped in a painting. Heylin speaks of "the bridges he burned nightly in May 1966, to the beat of Mickey Jones's pugilistic drums," and Dylan could be alluding to those scorching years of rising fame, and to his "don't look back" aesthetics ("She's an artist, she don't look back").[64]

But there are bridges and then there are bridges. Perhaps we should detect a sly reference to the musical and stanzaic bridges in song composition: it's tempting to imagine the songwriter burning the musical bridges in his own songs, while at the same time turning a new facet on a tired cliché. And, in fact, the bridge in "Don't Fall Apart on Me Tonight" brings together, or bridges, sibling arts. Clark Gable meets Cab Calloway on St. James Street, and celluloid immortality comes face-to-face with the deadly St. James Infirmary.

Who are these people who are walking towards you?
Do you know them or will there be a fight?
With their humorless smiles so easy to see through
Can they tell you what's wrong from what's right?
Do you remember St. James Street
Where you blew Jackie P.'s mind?
You were so fine, Clark Gable would have fell at your feet
And laid his life on the line

The entire bridge is a series of questions meant as aide-mémoire. There's a light-ning connection between recognition and primitive hostility: "Who are these people" ... "Do you know them or will there be a fight?" But the primitive quickly evolves into a moral challenge: can these people, if you know them, tell you right from wrong? The refrains in the song might offer an oracular view of yesterday and tomorrow, memory and empty predictions for the "supposed" future. In the song's (burning?) bridge, however, the present comes to life as a nameless, hu-morless, morally cryptic, and possibly hostile group of Others.

"Would have fell" is an arresting solecism, a metrical necessity that seems to condemn the poet's lack of ingenuity as assuredly as the line in "New Pony," "I'm sure it hurt me more than it hurted her." But no critic would call Dylan a lazy pro-sodist or doubt his ingenuity. Something is clearly afoot (pun intended) when he calls our attention to words by using totally unidiomatic solecisms. This is a distinct category, separate from such pseudo-idiomatic solecisms as "That light I never knowed" in "Don't Think Twice." In a song pleading "Don't Fall Apart" the word "fell" stands out. In fact, it stands out more than if Dylan had used fallen. The "fell" removes the conditional element implied by "would have 'fell'" and makes it a past fact: he fell.

And it means something utterly different: it is a protomyth in the making. Dylan mixes, or syncretizes, the arts by bringing Clark Gable to St. James Street. The avatar of manly Hollywood glamour mixes it up with the locals inside an allusion to one of the most famous sites of the blues, the St. James Infirmary. American film glory and American blues history comingle in a narrative cluster. Clark Gable, according to Dylan's speaker, would have *fell at your feet* to sacri-fice himself to the "girl's" beauty or glamour or erotic power. But the girl herself might *fall apart*, not as a physical being, but as a psychic presence. Dylan's use of the solecism underscores the difference, and though "would have fell" is tempo-rally conditional, Gable's (voluntary) prostration seems to be an unconditional obeisance. He has the capacity *not* to fall at the girl's feet, which makes his sac-rifice worth something, everything. In the same way, the girl has the capacity *not* to fall (apart). Despite the neurasthenic overtones, the girl's choice has an Edenic force in the song vis-à-vis the speaker's salvation for a night.

Undermining the urgency of the speaker's plea, and of the title itself, the wistfulness of the "Do you remember" refrain frames a prior epoch of worldly success and spiritual delusion. This rhymed quatrain, the second half of an eight-line stanza, stretches from death to life to Hollywood, from beauty to stardom to (human) sacrifice. There's an unexpected circularity in the lines: "St. James Infirmary," a wrenching blues standard in which a man catches sight of his lover dead in a winding sheet and, anticipating his own death, requests, variously according to the cover version, chorus girls to sing at the funeral, a jazz band on his wagon, rubber-tired taxis for the mourners, and a silver dollar on his watch chain to show them on the other side that he died "standin' pat." (Dylan's "Blind Willie McTell" also alludes to "St. James Infirmary" with the lines "I'm gazing out the window / Of the St. James Hotel.")

The last stanza of "Don't Fall Apart on Me Tonight" unhinges the speaker from his failed fixes. It is replete with promises of apocalyptic salvation:

> Let's try to get beneath the surface waste, girl
> No more booby traps and bombs
> No more decadence and charm
> No more affection that's misplaced, girl
> No more mudcake creatures lying in your arms

"Mudcake creatures" stunningly punctuates the list of promised eliminations. The image refers to Genesis 2:5–7. Here are two translations, the Authorized Version, also known as the King James Version (KJV), followed by William Tyndale's translation:

> the Lord God had not caused it to rain upon the earth, and there was not a man to till the ground. But there went up a mist from the earth, and watered the whole face of the ground. And the Lord God formed man of the dust of the ground, and breathed into his nostrils the breath of life; and man became a living soul (KJV).

> The Lord God had yet sent no rain upon the earth, neither was there yet a man to till the earth. But there arose a mist out of the ground and watered all the face of the earth: Then the Lord God shope man, even of the mould of the earth and breathed into his face the breath of life. So man was made a living soul. (Tyndale)[65]

Both versions underscore the earthiness of the process in this creation, the mixing of dust or "mould" with rain to make clay. The anthropomorphism of Yahweh has always been problematic for Christian revisionists. And, as if to make matters worse, there's no mention of heaven. Robert Alter explains: "In this more vividly anthropomorphic account, God, now called YHWH *'Elohim* instead of *'Elohim* as in [Genesis 1], does not summon things into being from a lofty distance through the mere agency of divine speech, but works as a craftsman, fashioning (*yatsar* instead of *bara'*, 'create'), blowing life-breath into nostrils, building a woman from a rib."[66] Water rises in springs or mists from the earth rather than falling from the sky. The biblical J-Writer, whom scholars identify as the poet of this chapter, casts Yahweh as a primitive sculptor and his hand-fashioned being as born from and bound to the earth. Harold Bloom has pointed out that, unlike the Egyptian or Mesopotamian "maker-gods," Yahweh has no potter's wheel. Instead, according to Bloom's description in his popular *The Book of J*, "Yahweh molds the clay, not as the potter does, but in the manner of a child making mud pies, freestyle with his own hands."[67] Hence, perhaps, Dylan's "mudcake creatures," and the gnawing possibility offered in Genesis 2 that the hand-molded first human (Hebrew *'adam*) had no connection to the divine face of the cosmos as described in Genesis 1:26: "And God said, Let us make man in our own image, after our likeness" (KJV).

The speaker in "Don't Fall Apart on Me Tonight" renounces mudcake formation and affirms his vow to lie in the girl's arms, not any longer as a mere creature of the clay but as a man newly connected (or converted) to the deity. This renunciation complements the earlier rejection of painting, film, and literature as fixes—but on a vaster scale. The speaker hints at breaking the primitive mold, of changing his form. And Dylan obliges by changing the stanzaic form: instead of two quatrains separated by different end rhymes, the final is divided into a five-three structure. Just after the "mudcake creatures" line, which is the one that distorts the form because it rhymes imperfectly with "charm" in the third line, a cryptic reminiscence shifts the temporal mode of the song:

> What about that millionaire with the drumsticks in his pants?
> He looked so baffled and so bewildered
> When he played and we didn't dance

Once again in these lines, the speaker rejects an art form, or forms: music and dance. This is particularly ironic since the medium of rejection is a rock song, replete with drumsticks. And the drumsticks, being "in his pants," have obscene overtones. The inclusion of dance complicates and completes the song's moral reversal. Is the millionaire drummer expecting them to dance to a corrupted musical ideal, or is it a ritual dance they avoid participating in? The signal complication of these last lines is temporal: the scene of rejection seems to have already taken place sometime in the past.

At first, the last three lines seem unrelated to the rejection of mudcake existence. But in fact there may be a biblical thread to follow. Speculatively, the last three lines might refer to 1 Corinthians 15:45, the Pauline revision of creation history: "And so it is written, The first man Adam was made a living soul; the last

Adam was made a quickening spirit." The distinction is between monism and dualism: as Bloom puts it, "when Yahweh blows the *nishmat hayyim* ('breath of life') into the nostrils of the clay figurine, he creates a monistic 'living being' rather than an animated carcass."[68] In the Hebrew Bible, this "living being" was not a separate soul and body as it later becomes in the Christian myth. In Eden and afterward the covenanted monistic beings danced to the ancient Yahwistic rhythm. Obedience offered no promise of salvation until the advent of the "last Adam," Christ. As William Orr and James Walther explain in their Anchor Bible commentary on 1 Corinthians: "The most humble material was employed to produce the first humanity; the second creation has its origin from heaven, whence came Christ to bring a new nature to humanity. By natural generation human beings after *the first person Adam* participate in the same *earthy* material. Those who by spiritual generation are given a new nature by *the last Adam* participate in his heavenly being. As the first Adam had successors, *earthy people*, so Christ has successors, *heavenly people*; and the contrast of the successors is based upon the contrast of the two Adams."[69] This absolute division between the "earthy" and the "heavenly" might help explain the disdainful turnabout in Dylan's stanza and the apparently unconnected question, "What about that millionaire with the drumsticks in his pants?" Maybe the millionaire's bewilderment is brought on by the rejection of his *earthy* rhythm once the mudcake creatures are no more—once they are saved as Christ's successors with the promise of spiritual generation. The curious time element of the speaker's question—everything in the last tercet has already occurred—confirms the encircling temporality of the Christian or salvationistic experience. The deity's foreknowledge preempts time and those who "participate in [Christ's] heavenly being" are always already dualistic beings, body and soul.

But Dylan is no pedant, fortunately, and it is unlikely he used an exegetical trot while writing "Don't Fall Apart on Me Tonight." Nevertheless, the lessons of 1 Corinthians permeate American Protestantism and Dylan has clearly absorbed them. As a poet raised in the Hebrew tradition, however, theological ambivalence prevails over dogma even during his Christian evangelical phase, and certainly in its immediate wake. The ghost of Pauline doctrine might howl in the bones of Dylan's post-seventies work, but a palimpsest of orthodoxy and monism can be detected just below the surface of many lyrics. It comes as no surprise to find this theological ambivalence imprinted on an album called *Infidels*.

Dylan usually spells the word "God" with the letters G-d. Notebooks and draft copies of songs spanning Dylan's career from the sixties to *Tempest* reveal his systematic use of the Orthodox spelling of the deity's name: he writes and types "G-d" in virtually all the papers collected in the Bob Dylan Archive.[70] Even as late as *Tempest* Dylan continued to use this spelling in his drafts, as seen on a piece of notepaper from the Steigenberger Hotel in Linz (figure 6).

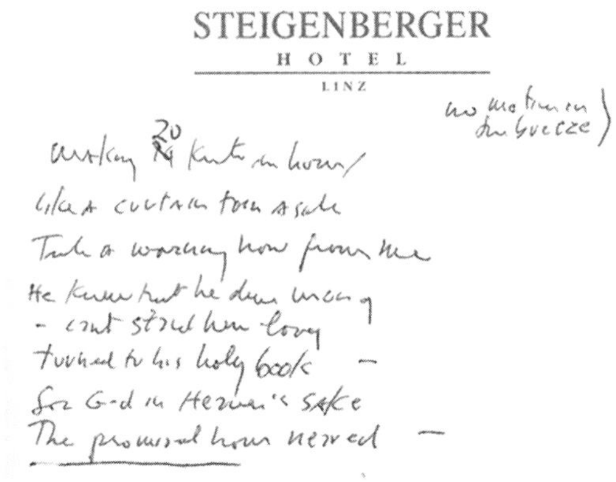

Figure 6. *Tempest.* Courtesy of the Bob Dylan Archive®
Collections, Tulsa, OK.

Much could be made of this practice, no doubt, in terms of the tetragram-
maton and such lines as "One says to the other, no man sees my face and lives"
("I and I"). But it may just be the way Dylan spells the word. He uses the Ortho-
dox spelling even when the god in question clearly isn't the fiercely jealous Yah-
weh of Hebrew myth. In a typed but unfinished lyric from circa 1982, for exam-
ple, Dylan speaks of a very different kind of figure:

> HE WHO BROUGHT ME THIS FAR WILL BRING ME THE
>   REST OF THE WAY
>
> like he brings the river down to the sea
>   personal public
> in every kind of confusion & personal illusion
> g-d will take care of me[71]

These few lines describe a deity protecting the speaker not only from external
"confusion" but also from internal "illusion." Perhaps this is the Yahweh who
protects the tribes of Israel and brings them "down the river" with a promise of
redemption. But the internal element, guidance through "personal illusion" is
quasi-Christian, possibly a sign of the New Testament in the lyric ("If we say that
we have no sin, we deceive ourselves, and the truth is not in us" [1 John 1:8]).
The Orthodox spelling of "G-d" is the palimpsest of Hebrew practice, just as
the manuscript's insertions above the line could represent alternations between
modes of curative experience.

Apropos of this liminal pattern is an interview Allen Ginsberg gave to Wes
Stace in 1985. According to Ginsberg it was to be expected that Dylan would

"evolve out of [born-again Christianity] as something closer to his natural Judaism . . . People still think he is [a born-again Christian] but five years ago he changed." Ginsberg elaborates: "In the conversation we had a couple of weeks ago there was a great deal of judgmental Jehovaic or Nobodaddy—'nobody daddy up in heaven,' a figure of judgmental hyper-rationality. There's this judgmental Jehovaic theism in his recent work, and he said: 'Allen, do you have a quarrel with God?' And I said: 'I've never met the man.' And he said: 'Then you have a quarrel with God.' And I said: 'Well, I didn't start anything!'" This element of "Jehovaic theism" is precisely what the Orthodox spelling "G-d" indicates. Ginsberg concludes in the interview that Dylan "still has a fixed notion of divinity, and I think that's a mistake, as a non-theistic Buddhist: that any solidification of the ideal God like the ancient Jews warned against—naming the name of God—is a mistake. It's a psychological error on a simple point."

"Don't Fall Apart" is certainly not as strong as its predecessors of the same ilk in the Dylan canon. But, like many songs in the second half of Dylan's career, it represents an ideal of self-imitation—the digestion and transformation of a model that is the songwriter/poet's own. The result—lyrically if not vocally—is yet one more lesson in the poetics of self-portrait. The song dangles an imaginary space, a haven between memory and expectation. This space is itself a kind of self-portrait and seems to exist between two poles.

On one hand, the lyrics lead us through the human experiences of losing auspicious protection, choosing the wrong profession, burning all one's bridges (metaphorical as well as musical), and trapping oneself in the detachment of art. On the other, there is the oracular or vatic echo of the chorus: "Yesterday's just a memory / Tomorrow's never what it's supposed to be." Dylan saves this chorus from being hackneyed with the second line, where, speaking of past tomorrows, he scrambles time and imperfect pessimism—imperfect because it can be undone by romance. This curious admixture of the quotidian and the grandiose resolves itself generically, in an alteration on the stereotypical blues plaint, "I need you." To this grizzled posture, which is both a plea *and* an admission of weakness, Dylan adds the psychological puzzler, "Don't Fall Apart on Me tonight," as if the nameless girl is extrafragile and prone to breaking down. But it isn't only the girl whose fragility causes concern: the needy speaker pleads from the brink of something, evidently losing his grip. And, of course, "falling," as in "Don't Fall Apart," brings the song back to mudcake Eden.

The circularity of these different aspects of falling mirror the self-imitation Dylan develops as his career becomes more complex and he gets older. Falling can suggest the traditional felix culpa—or "fortunate fall"—that precedes redemption for Christians. But it also implies that Dylan can find his own originality by returning to himself as a source.

4 THE WIZARD'S CURSE
The American Singer as *Vates*

The crystal ball up on the wall hasn't shown me nothing yet.
—"Dirge," *Planet Waves*

Young Prospero

Arguably, Dylan has always been a Prospero figure in popular culture. That is, he has always been poised between a unique authority and wishing, as Shakespeare's Prospero said he would, to "drown [my] book." His liminal status as a reluctant but overwhelmingly successful vates of the twentieth century, coupled with his polarizing effect on critics and listeners, has blurred the line between influence and imitation—as does his own performance. The historicization of Dylan has been the project of a half-century, detailed in biographies and codified in hermeneutic analyses. Yet historicizations tend to focus less on method than on results, just as influence studies subordinate imitative practice to textual psychology.

From early on, Dylan has asserted he doesn't want to be a spokesman for anyone. But ultimately that claim comes into conflict with his vatic ambitions. While the phrase "the wizard's curse" in "Tempest" probably refers to Prospero, it might also be attributed—ambiguously—to Dylan himself. He is simultaneously the magician casting a curse as he does in "The Times They Are A-Changin'" *and* "just a guitar player" cursed with being heard as a wizard. This latter predicament follows from the first, and Dylan's infusion of vatic language in so many of his songs paradoxically seals his own (Jack) fate. It may be that the "crystal ball up on the wall hasn't shown [him] nothing yet." But he persists in imitating the biblical poetic language that implies, if not clairvoyance, then "vague traces" of otherworldly authority. Even in his 2020 release, *Rough and Rowdy Ways*, there are lyrics that call attention to their vatic resonances. But any claim to prophecy calls up the specter of the false prophet, the charlatan, the mountebank—or perhaps suggests there's merely a human being behind the mask.

"False Prophet," for example, a tantalizingly titled song, begins with Dylan challenging his own vatic stature. "Another day without end," he sings, "another ship going out." Inevitably, the phrase "another ship going out" brings to mind one of the young Dylan's most famous angry generation songs, "When the Ship Comes In" (1963). The refrain of that song marked Dylan as a voice speaking for all the disenfranchised. The song was rousing—even when sung by Peter, Paul, and Mary, who named an album after one of its lines. But above all "When the Ship Comes In" turns the old adage "when my ship comes in" into a vengeful prophecy. Released on *The Times They Are A-Changin'*, the last lines promise a comeuppance of biblical proportions (and contain one of Dylan's most renowned solecisms):

> . . . we'll shout from the bow your days are numbered
> And like Pharaoh's tribe
> They'll be drownded in the tide
> And like Goliath, they'll be conquered

This is one of Dylan's most pronounced jeremiads, and he delivers his stinging prophecy with all the vatic authority he can, drawing out the notes of "conquered" and suspending the word until he's sure that they're dead.

Dylan does not personally "shout from the bow your days are numbered," the notorious motel employee slight notwithstanding. Nor, surprisingly, do those words belong exclusively to the song's fictional speaker. The true vatic authority derives from the famed writing on the wall in the book of Daniel. The transformation of the biblical source, however, is pure, unmediated Dylan. The language in the KJV is "MENE; God hath numbered thy kingdom, and finished it. TEKEL; Thou art weighed in the balances and found wanting" (Daniel 5:26–27). Dylan's homodiegetic figure may speak the words in the song, shouting from the bow, but Dylan's voice gives life to the speaker's words, edging them with anger over the unrelenting strumming of the guitar. Performance breeds portent as much as do the lyrics.

Dylan's allusion adds an unexpected resonance to this anthem. The speaker's crowing admonition recalls the biblical scene in which King Belshazzar summons Daniel to decipher the disembodied hand's writing on the wall. Daniel, one of the "children of the captivity of Judah," is brought in with the hope that, with his "light and understanding and excellent wisdom," he'll be able to interpret what the "wise men, the astrologers" have failed to decode. He succeeds, of course, proving that covenantal Hebrew magic supersedes the blind efforts of the older, uninitiated soothsayers. Daniel's visionary skills hover as a model behind "When the Ship Comes In." The stern warning is there, but even more than that is the message of Daniel's triumph over the failed or "false prophets." The song's lyrics reveal Dylan's seminal competitiveness, his budding *agonistic relationship*, with prior vatic authority. Just as Daniel supersedes the wise men and soothsayers, a young Dylan (along with the new-generation ships' passengers) will overcome the "foes," and in the bargain surpass the atrophied vatic authority of the past.

The first line of "False Prophet" sends that conquering ship out, however, and with it goes the prophetic authority the young singer had arrogated to himself. But rather than erasing the prophetic authority of Dylan's new song, this obvious self-imitation and reversal only complicates the speaker's vatic posture.

The lyrics contain clear references to otherworldly inspiration—"My fleet footed guides from the underworld / No stars in the sky shine brighter than you / You girls mean business and I do too." Not only is the speaker guided by a species of underworld Muses, but he "means business" just as they do. The implication of otherworldly vengeance is clear, what Thomas refers to as "the ominous and threatening tone [of 'Pay in Blood'] brought back to life in 'False Prophet.'"[1] The vengeance of "False Prophet" might not boast the Yahwistic authority that drowned Pharaoh or guided David's stone against Goliath, but the new voice contains equal parts of contempt, exculpation ("I ain't no false prophet—I just said what I said / I'm here to bring vengeance on somebody's head"), and opacity. But the prevalence of the speaker's "ghostly appearance," of the Holy Grail, the garden with the fountain, and the City of God create a prophetic burden in the lyrics. Does the double negative "I ain't no false prophet" equal "I am a prophet"?

Most indicative of all, perhaps, is the image that Dylan chose to accompany the release of the single. It is a full-color drawing of a skeleton in formal attire—white tie, top hat, felt-collar coat—holding in one hand a long flowerbox and in the other an oversized syringe. This is as terrifying an image of the Candy Man as one could wish, but to make things worse, behind the image is the shadow of a hanged man. Much could be taken from this ominous iconography on its own. But regarding "False Prophet," the image points to Dylan's traditional musical influences. "Candy Man" was a staple among the folkies of the sixties: Mississippi John Hurt's is the definitive version but others, including Van Ronk, recorded it. Whether we take the false prophet to be the Candy Man himself or the contents of the "Candy Man's stick," Dylan's *visual* reference to the song honors his models of imitation while forcefully transforming and expanding the song's original admonitions.

Imitation pervades *Rough and Rowdy Ways*, not only in the imagery on the singles but also in the cascading verbal and musical allusions. Dylan is at pains to make fine distinctions among early influences and imitative models, as if to define his place on the genealogical family tree. A complexly woven text of musical/lyrical identity emerges from *Rough and Rowdy Ways*, with the range and associative brilliance of the imagery impinging on every song. But at the heart of the album is a portentous voice. "Murder Most Foul," the longest song Dylan ever recorded, was released first: it appeared during the height of the COVID-19 pandemic accompanied by a few words of encouragement from Dylan. The song itself, possibly an outtake from *Tempest*, is ostensibly about the Kennedy assassination, although the lyrics reach far and deep into American culture. The song, and the album itself, mark the reemergence of America's foremost vatic poet.

He Contains Multitudes

Dylan's scrambled signals about the source of his lyrical authority have always confused his relationship to imitatio. In "I Contain Multitudes" (*Rough and*

Rowdy Ways), he alludes to literary figures from Edgar Allan Poe to Anne Frank: "Gotta tell tale heart like Mr. Poe," the speaker sings, "Got skeletons in the walls of people you know." So the ominous "The Tell-Tale Heart" and "The Cask of Amontillado" lead the references. But others pile on:

> I'm just like Anne Frank—like Indiana Jones
> And them British bad boys the Rolling Stones

This is a strange combination of similes—like the victim in the Poe story, Anne Frank was also walled up. But the links to Indiana Jones and the Rolling Stones are less obvious and seem more about "multitudinous" breadth. The song includes a reference to Blake—"I sing the songs of experience like William Blake / I have no apologies to make"—literally citing the *Songs of Innocence and Experience* but not the later visionary works. It's as if Dylan had cached his own vatic impulses, with purposeful misdirection, in a song named for the renowned Whitmanian line "I contain multitudes" from "Song of Myself."

But this misdirection is not unexpected. While Dylan has often claimed to be a conduit for divine expression, he has repeatedly referred to his influences, his practical musical concerns, and the meter of his lines. He has rejected political responsibility, yet acknowledged his charismatic endowment. He has denied having prophetic authority and emphatically separated his songs, germane as they might seem, from worldly applications.

In contrast, Dylan's fans have heaped laurels on him and virtually scooped the sand from his footsteps, as the farmers did when St. Anthony walked in exile through the desert. (The story goes that the farmers poured the sand on their crops to make them grow.) The analogy isn't as eccentric as it sounds. Dylan's fans have used his songs as a universal balm, a unique kind of wisdom literature, vatic in its authority, but also avant-garde, a combination of poetic inspiration and prophetic vision. So many of Dylan's fans, especially in the sixties, cast him as their hip Jeremiah, their snide Elijah. And, whether he admits it or not, Dylan encouraged these possibilities in many of his pounding, accusatory lyrics: "I'll stand over your grave till I'm sure that you're dead," he snarls to the nameless arms manufacturers in "Masters of War." That single line, sung over Dylan's droning strumming, comes across as so angry, so admonitory and final in the same breath, that the posture of prophecy is difficult to ignore.

According to Howard Sounes, "Dylan has always felt he is a channel for divine inspiration, and has said that the words stream through him. The ability to create brilliant work over a long period of time, without straining for ideas is the signal characteristic of his genius."[2] Dylan himself, in Scorsese's *No Direction Home*, seems to refute Sounes's assumption, observing that while the earlier songs just came to him, now he works much harder for them. Yet, even at this late date, his signals are mixed. For example, he belatedly confirms an early impression of supernatural endowment when explaining the origins of "Like a Rolling Stone" to Robert Hilburn in 2004: "It's like a ghost is writing a song like that. It gives you the song and it goes away, it goes away. You don't know what it means. Except the ghost picked me to write the song."[3] This statement describes what ancient and Renaissance literary theorists called the furor poeticus, a state of madness in which the poet becomes a conduit for the Muses, or for divine utterance. Furor poeticus is a charismatic state, a definable moment when a human being is seen as one of the "bearers of specific gifts of body and mind that were considered 'supernatural' (in the sense that not everybody could have access to them)," and the Dylan of the sixties often seemed to achieve this exalted quasi-supernatural status as a vatic voice.[4] John Milton says of the muse Urania, his "Celestial Patroness," that she "deigns / her nightly visitation unimplored, / And dictates to me slumbering, or inspires / Easy my unpremeditated verse."[5] It would be difficult to find two poets more different than Dylan and Milton, yet, like Milton, Dylan credits a ghostly visitation, his furor poeticus, for the "unpremeditated" "Like a Rolling Stone." In this instance at least, he cedes authority to a voice or mind other than his own.

Ironically, while he attaches himself to this tradition, he seeks at the same time to overturn it. Because his speakers' voices and his performative presence have so often been conflated with his public persona in an attempt, by fans and press and critics, to fashion a unified hero figure, Dylan has balked. He has forcefully and repeatedly rejected the idea of linking his songs to a sociopolitical mission, of being the "voice-of-a-generation," a cultural icon, or a leader of any kind. At the ascendency of his polarizing fame in 1966, Dylan gave an interview to Nat Hentoff for *Playboy*:

> Playboy. Still, thousands of young people look up to you as a kind of folk hero. Do you feel some sense of responsibility toward them?
>
> Dylan. I don't feel I have any responsibility, no. Whoever it is that listens to my songs owes *me* nothing. How could I possibly have any responsibility to any kind of thousands? What could possibly make me think that I owe anybody anything who just happens to be there? . . . I really don't know what the people who are at the receiving end of these songs think of me, anyway. It's horrible. I'll bet Tony Bennett doesn't have to go through this kind of thing. I wonder what Billy the Kid would have answered to such a question.[6]

During a 1984 *Rolling Stone* interview, Dylan reflected on his late-sixties attitude. He was less petulant but still firm about the relationship of social authority to music—without any references to outlaw notoriety: "I'd also seen I was representing all these things that I didn't know anything *about*. Like I was supposed to be on acid. It was all storm-the-embassy kind of stuff—Abbie

Hoffman in the streets—and they sorta figured me as the kingpin of all that. I said, 'Wait a minute, I'm just a *musician*. So my songs are about this and that. So *what*?' But people need a leader. People need a leader more than a leader needs people, really. I mean, anybody can step up and be a leader, if he's got the people there that want one. I didn't want that, though."[7] Both passages are about leadership. Dylan's rejection of the prophet's mantle is justified, especially from a poetic perspective. To express oneself with vatic authority—"Everything Is Broken" or "Highlands," "False Prophet" or "Murder Most Foul"—is not by any means to make a bid for actual followers. In fact, as both interviews above show, Dylan denies the existence of a bond with fans who think they have a social relationship with him—a relationship that constitutes something more than the typical (and typically deluded) sense that a person on stage is singing directly to each audience member. Despite the enthusiasms and excesses of fans from the Bobbysoxers through Beatlemania, rarely if ever in American song has there been a performer whose compositions encouraged listeners to see him or her as a public figure, a political leader, and a counterculture icon with responsibilities *beyond the stage*.[8]

Bob Marley might be an exception, but, because of his untimely death, his enduring political value has been posthumous. In sixties culture, not even the Beatles, for all their astonishing influence, rose to the status of revolutionary leaders (Ringo at the barricades?). The crazy prophecies and secret messages dug out by zealots from *Sgt. Pepper*, *Abbey Road*, and *The White Album* tended to be autotelic. Rock and roll, and the counterculture as a whole, gradually abandoned genuinely political singers like Pete Seeger, along with Phil Ochs and similar younger-generation political stalwarts—not without good reason, perhaps, as many of them were hobbled by topical didacticism or stuck in the Big Muddy of pseudo-folk music and the Old Left. There were songs such as Buffalo Springfield's "For What It's Worth," Country Joe MacDonald's Vietnam song, and Arlo Guthrie's "Alice's Restaurant" that pointedly addressed topical issues and stayed popular. But nothing and no one replaced the informed politics of Old-Left figures like Lee Hayes. At the same time, none of the more socially conscious bands of the sixties, such as Jefferson Airplane and The Who, produced songs to rival Dylan's in sheer vatic authority.

Visionary Technology

The vatic element in Dylan's poetry is consummately a literary phenomenon born of imitation. It is aesthetic prophecy. Ultimately, Dylan's most fascinating lyrical reconfigurations result in his intuitive recasting of American blues as vatic or visionary expression: "Don't say I never warned you if your train gets lost," as the portentous speaker of "It Takes a Lot to Laugh, It Takes a Train to Cry" howls in a crawling twelve-bar blues. Christophe Lebold has remarked on "how the singer-songwriter oscillates between two postures (fake bluesman and authentic guardian of the tradition), just as he wavers between a nostalgia for vitality and the vitality of nostalgia."[9] Dylan perfects this wavering, or supersedes it, with a vatic voice which is neither all bluesman nor all nostalgia.

As long ago as 1970, Sandy Perlman, in a brilliant (and brilliantly cryptic) article, captured Dylan's transformational achievement: "From the beginning, Bob Dylan's songs were about nostalgia ('Song to Woody'). But Bob was such a dilettante. He'd mix 'n' match all the nostalgic technologies . . . Although Bob's titles were *Bringing It All Back Home* (Columbia CS-9128) and *Highway 61 Revisited* (Columbia CS-3189), only a few sharp ones recognized this visionary and mythic Muzak as a *method* to induce nostalgia in the public, in other words, a nostalgic technology." Perlman deliberately uses the derogatory term Muzak as a kind of trope, not because he wants to diminish Dylan's musical achievement but rather to prove his genius:

> Bob's Muzak music technology made for unprecedented cumulative effects, for Muzak's spirit's nothing less than the inevitable total occupation and organization of all available sonic space, i.e., silence denial. By inevitable, I'd mean, every Muzak sound is absolutely predictable. The music lacks surprise to a supernatural extent. Such inevitability spells perfection on a visionary scale. ("Visions of Johanna" is visionary accumulation.) Into this repetitious field Bob introduced an apparent principle of contradiction, a visionary technique, *the unknown tongue*. Unknown tongues are musical forms with unpredictable inevitability or inevitable unpredictability or something like that . . . visionary music technology par excellence.[10]

Perlman hits on several valuable interpretations. When he says, for example, that "Bob introduced an apparent principle of contradiction, a visionary technique, *the unknown tongue*," he might well be describing Dylan's conscious aim to go "past the vernacular." Perlman also speaks of a "visionary technique," but the technique behind that technique is the Senecan imitative process. Dylan's originality is wrapped up in his vatic stylings, which are in turn tied to his bid for artistic supersession.

Hampton, as I mentioned in the last chapter, invokes Rimbaud's *Illuminations* as proof that Rimbaud was the most important branch on Dylan's visionary family tree. "To think about the process of visionary self-creation in the modern age," he suggests, "we must . . . turn, not to Ginsberg, nor to Ginsberg's idol William Blake, but to the French Symbolist poet Arthur Rimbaud (1854–1891). It was Rimbaud who had first given voice to the brand of visionary modernism that Dylan would embrace."[11] Hampton's adds that "For mid-sixties Dylan, the visionary is the modern."[12]

Rimbaud in fact appears amid a mostly narcissistic cavalcade of images in a video made for "Series of Dreams": many known influences, such as Kerouac and Ginsberg, appear side by side with would-be influences in footage of Dylan performing, riding a horse, painting his face, and so forth. Among the still images there is a flash of the famous Rimbaud portrait, whose edges suddenly melt and reform (eighties digital art). Rimbaud only appears once as opposed to the multiple appearance of the others, but there's no denying his fleeting parity with them.

Heylin includes "Series of Dreams"—which is a song Dylan omitted from *Oh Mercy* but released on the *Bootleg Series, Vol. 1–3* eighteen months later—in a short list of songs from Dylan's "erratic decade" (the 1980s), "which no other songwriter could have conjured."[13] The word "conjured" is serendipitous in regard to the video, whose images suggest a conjurer's collage of undifferentiated experiences and memories—and, indeed, words appear scrawled across the screen, sometimes repeating the verses and sometimes seeming unattached to the song.

The flash of Rimbaud's portrait in the collage only emphasizes that he was, if not the solitary seed of inspiration, clearly a contributor to Dylan's visionary inspiration. According to Hampton, "The visionary mode involves a break with the brute phenomena of everyday experience, as it recombines or transforms elements from the sensorium into some new artifact. For Dylan, the leap into hallucinatory abstraction required a studied break with the earlier tradition of political protest music that had made him famous."[14]

As is well known, this "studied break" occurred with *Another Side of Bob Dylan*: the album title might not have been Dylan's own, but the songs clearly broke with his previous topical songs and, in the case of "My Back Pages," virtually renounced old attitudes.

This kind of renunciation and reversal describes the basic conditions of charismatic authority required to stake a visionary claim. As Max Weber explains: "All *extraordinary* needs, i.e., those which *transcend* the sphere of everyday economic routines, have always been satisfied in an entirely heterogeneous manner: on a *charismatic* basis."[15] Bearers of charismatic authority, by definition, overturn tradition and break with the past. "In a revolutionary and sovereign manner," according to Weber, "charismatic domination transforms all values and breaks all traditional and rational norms."[16] Granted, Dylan's charismatic appeal did not rise to "domination." But the basic Weberian concept holds. And, in the context of charisma, Perlman's idea of a "music technology"—a kind of Muzak that accomplishes "nothing less than the inevitable total occupation and organization of all available sonic space"—is less hyperbolic than it seems. Hampton seems to suggest something similar: "As the 1960s rolled on, Dylan's singing would begin to hover above the musical accompaniment, as if he were singing, not a melody, but some abstracted version of a melody that the listener could seek to reconstruct through the interplay of instrument and voice."[17] Hampton's "hovering above" and Perlman's "total occupation and organization of all available sonic space" are not far apart, and Hampton's suggestion that Dylan set it up for listeners to "reconstruct" an "abstracted version of a melody" points to the active agency of charismatic management.

The charismatic figure fosters that kind of totalizing group experience and creates the myth of comprehensive sharing. As Donald McIntosh observed some time ago, "charisma is not so much a quality as an experience. The charismatic object or person is *experienced* as possessed by and transmitting an uncanny and compelling force."[18] But the charismatic experience, like the charismatic leader, can only survive in a symbiotic atmosphere.

The visionary elements of, say, Dylan's *Blonde on Blonde* era were an extension of his charismatic authority. Dylan had always had a charisma-hungry audience. As he moved into his electric phase, he was forced to manage his charisma more closely than he had in the early years—the protest movement often supplied ready-made followers. The remythicization of Dylan's charismatic persona required a heightened sense of sharing between him and his audience. The shift to more abstract lyrics, the hyper-aestheticization of his mid-sixties' songs, was as much a *response* to his charismatic followers as pure, individualized innovation.

Too much has been made of Dylan's Newport performance and his "going electric." But that shift provides an excellent example of how a charismatic leader creates mild chaos among followers so that he or she can reorganize and manage that chaos. According to Thomas Spence Smith, charismatic groups depend, not on order, but on disorder to survive. Leaders who introduce and *manage* these destabilizing conditions ensure both the survival of the group and, concomitantly, their own continued leadership authority.[19] And, while Smith is referring to more delimited social groups like religious sects or even street gangs, the principle of entropy-management applies as well to the charisma-hungry fans of a rock poet.

Dylan has always had the capacity to destabilize his own myth, to create mild chaos among followers, and then to resolve the chaos and reorganize his charismatic group or fan base. All of Dylan's so-called masks stem from this phenomenon—that is, from his (often instinctive) destabilization of a current image, only to take possession of and manage the new mask or remythicization. Most charismatic figures do this same thing, at least the ones who survive the first burst of popularity. Dylan seems to have a special facility with the protean reorganizations—hence descriptions of his mercurial character. Dylan may very well be mercurial in character, but he uses or manipulates his charismatic myth by managing his mercurial changes. Difficult to see which is the cart and which the horse.

In any case, instinctual conflation of entropy generation and chaos resolution is Dylan's abiding vatic strength: to embody prophecy and portentousness in his songs while managing a shared charismatic balance with his listeners. In contrast, pure visionaries—from Isaiah to Laocoön to Blake—tend to cry out in isolation and are often defined by their lonely (if righteous) martyrdom.

It may be that Dylan's vatic voice goes underground in later sixties albums, but the portentous timbre of lyric and performance is always, if subtly, manifest. Dylan makes no obvious effort to echo his vatic predecessors or steal their verses (better the negligible stick of Henry Timrod than the club of Hercules). The peripatetic speaker of "Tangled Up in Blue" (1974) might describe a book "from the thirteenth century"—probably Dante, from the fourteenth century (unless Dylan was reading Guido Cavalcanti or Chrétien de Troyes, unlikely candidates for "words" that "glowed like burnin' coals / Pourin' off of every page / Like it was written in my soul from me to you"). But direct allusion to canonical poetic lines is rarer in Dylan's earlier work, especially in comparison to his frequent quotation and revision of lines from folk songs and blues. But, as Thomas and others have shown with intertextual connections, in later lyrics he often interpolates Homer, Virgil, or Ovid.[20]

Prophecy and Imitation

For all the apocalyptic rock-and-roll pyrotechnics of the 1960s, Dylan emerged as the singularly vatic figure of the era. His songs became anthems and his unexpected voice cut through the record industry and Tin Pan Alley with the clarion call of a new *auctoritas*. What the Beatles had in popularity, Dylan redoubled in vatic superiority. And, in the final analysis, prophetic poetry is the art Dylan is most readily associated with. While no one could object to calling poetry an art, classifying prophecy as an art might raise eyebrows. But the combination of poetry and prophecy in the figure of the vates, as I've already noted, is at least as old as Virgil. Other forms of prophecy, specifically that associated with the Hebrew Bible, are also properly *artes* because prophecy is a rhetorical exercise. And rhetoric—historically, the *ars eloquendi* or *ars dicendi*—furnishes the tools of the vatic style. Individual vatic styles among modern poets derive not only from the imitation of prior poets but also, particularly in the case of post-Renaissance Judeo-Christian poets, the imitation of *translations* of the biblical prophets. Even if you accept the fiction that Isaiah, Virgil, Dante, Milton, Whitman, Ginsberg, and Dylan are vessels through which their various (wildly diverse) deities issued "unpremeditated verse," as if through trumpets, the prophetic strain in poetry nevertheless contains an element of human art.

Ironically, Dylan's gospel period is the low point of his vatic authority. Harold Bloom observed, astutely I think, that belief is the death of poetry. He was referring to the Hebrew Bible, specifically the J-Writer, and the redaction of the poetry of the Solomonic court to a "sacred" text for worship. On a less apocalyptic scale, Dylan's gospel sermonizing (often from the stage) canceled out the art of his vatic poetry. Except for such songs as "Slow Train," in which the vatic artist is again a haunting voice, the self-righteous believer replaced the apprehensive figure on the watchtower and—thirty years later—the ambiguous watchman of "Tempest."

In 1978, after the release of *Renaldo and Clara*, Allen Ginsberg interviewed Dylan. The topic of the "conscious artist" came up:

> Dylan. I don't think you're a conscious artist, Allen. I don't think you know what you're doing. Anybody can be an unconscious artist—I am a conscious artist.
>
> . . . .
>
> Ginsberg. What do you mean, I'm not a conscious artist? Are you a conscious artist?
>
> Dylan. Yes, because I had a teacher who was a conscious artist and he drilled it into me to be a conscious artist, so I became a conscious artist.
>
> Ginsberg. A painting teacher?
>
> Dylan. Yeah.
>
> Ginsberg. And what does a conscious artist practice?
>
> Dylan. Actuality. You can't improve on Actuality. Let's say this is what God gives you—he gives you a flower. [*Dylan offers a flower.*] Let's see you improve on it. [*Ginsberg, confused, tries flower arrangement. Dylan says he means "improve" it by photographing it or singing it.*]

The naivete of this last remark might be touching if it weren't delivered so confrontationally, with Dylan's arrogant identification of himself as a conscious artist in contrast to Ginsberg. It seems an odd posture to strike with the man who wrote

> I saw the best minds of my generation destroyed by madness,
>   starving hysterical naked,
> dragging themselves through the negro streets at dawn looking for an
>   angry fix.[21]

Inexplicably, Dylan seems to want to provoke Ginsberg in this interview. He is determined to see his own oeuvre in terms of preconscious and postconscious periods of production, and at the same time to dismiss Ginsberg, who was an undeniable poetic influence.

Ginsberg's attitude is also a bit of a puzzle. He seems piqued by Dylan's remark that "I don't think you're a conscious artist, Allen. I don't think you know what you're doing." Maybe it was Dylan's tone, but it is difficult to see why Ginsberg would object. He had spent his poetic lifetime praising Kerouac's "spontaneous prose" and had in at least one interview declared, "Primary fact of my writing is that I don't have any craft and don't know what I'm doing."[22]

"Conscious" or not, didn't Ginsberg anticipate Dylan as the poet of Actuality? Isn't "Actuality" itself already a flower arrangement (as Wallace Stevens knew)?[23] More to the point, as *Howl* and *Kaddish* flagrantly demonstrate, Ginsberg very consciously complicates the Romantic or Emersonian ideals of reality, truth, and Nature with a Whitmanian vatic strain. Ginsberg, whom Lionel Trilling called his most brilliant student, might well have suspected that Dylan's poetics of Actuality leads, not so surprisingly, back to Wordsworth's *Preface to the Lyrical Ballads*: "[the Poet] will feel that there is no necessity to trick out or to elevate nature: and, the more industriously he applies this principle, the deeper will be his faith that no words, which *his* fancy or imagination can suggest, will be to be compared with those which are the emanations of reality and truth." Or, in Dylan's version, Let's see you improve on the flower.

Paradoxically, despite his challenge to Ginsberg, Dylan does not fit the Wordsworthian mold, nor does he recognize the sovereignty of Nature with a capital N or Actuality with a capital A. It may be that Dylan's idea of Actuality harks back to the "thin, wild mercury sound" of *Blonde on Blonde* and the "sound from the street" he wished to attain. In any case, it comprises, architectonically, a kind of Bob-Dylan-aesthetic, as crucial to understanding his work as, say, magic realism would be to understanding Gabriel García Márquez or allegory to understanding the *Commedia*. Dylan in effect *performs* Actuality from his earliest perfection of the Iron Range Dust Bowl persona. In his lexicon, performance provides him with his unimprovable flower. But if he were truly as conscious as he claims in this interview with Ginsberg, Dylan would recognize that much of his own music shatters Actuality with the same transcendent lyrical ambition as Ginsberg's poetry, and that—not to put too fine a point on it—he had affixed himself to an American vatic genealogy in which Ginsberg, more than Woody, was his most immediate predecessor.

Although he seemed definite when he claimed to be an artist of Actuality, Dylan effectively contradicts himself in response to Jonathan Cott in 1978, less than a year later. Cott offered an apropos, and erudite, biographical introduction: "For years he has been worshiped—and deservedly so. His songs are miracles, his ways mysterious and unfathomable. In words and music, he has reawakened, and thereby altered, our experience of the world. In statement . . . and in image . . . he has kept alive the idea of the poet and artist as *vates*—the visionary eye of the body politic—while keeping himself open to a conception of art that embraces and respects equally Charles Baudelaire and Charley Patton, Arthur Rimbaud and Smokey Robinson."[24] The interview concludes with this exchange:

> Cott. But you seem sure of yourself.
> Dylan. I'm sure of my dream self. I live in my dreams, I don't really live in the actual world.[25]

So much for Actuality. As Cott recognized, Dylan, like Ginsberg, is a vatic poet. This is evident even in his most apparently Romantic (and romantic) love lyrics. In a performance of "Tomorrow Is a Long Time," caught on the Witmark demos (1962–64), Dylan sings:

> There's beauty in the silver singin' river
> There's beauty in the sunrise in the sky
> But none of these and nothin' else can match the beauty
> That I remember in my true love's eyes

The river, the sunrise, and the sky are details of the natural landscape, surpassed—in the singer's eyes—only by the beauty in the beloved's eyes. Her or his eyes—the lines could be sung by a woman, as in the Joan Baez and Odetta versions—would contain, reflect, and surpass the beauties of the natural world. This is the Wordsworthian poet's supreme praise, that the beloved's beauty is greater than all other earthly beauty. Dylan's performance underscores the song's Wordsworthian bona fides: his quiet, unemphatic vocal, accompanied by an almost too-simple fingerpicking, confirm that the singer feels, with Wordsworth, "that there is no necessity to trick out or to elevate nature." Here again Walter Jackson Bate's notion of the poet's bringing "nature" to art comes to mind: the acoustic, rough-voiced Dylan returns love to its "natural" setting, rescuing it from the slickness and aridity and "tricked-out" language of Tin Pan Alley.[26]

All well and good, if Romanticism is your goal. But in another performance of the song, at New York's Town Hall in April 1963, Dylan sang:

> There's beauty in the silver singin' river
> There's beauty in the *rainbow* in the sky
> But none of these and nothin' else can touch the beauty
> That I remember in my true love's eyes[27]

The rainbow's the rub, arguably complicating a transparent genealogical descent from the *Lyrical Ballads*. The difference between a sunrise and a rainbow brilliantly and ambiguously realigns the song. The true love's beauty no longer merely surpasses natural manifestations. The rainbow—especially in Dylan's repertoire—inevitably calls to mind the biblical covenant. And, because the beauty of the true love's eyes transcends even that extraordinary *supernatural* bond, the singer's voice necessarily engages and resonates with the vatic poets of the Hebrew Bible.

Dylan's vatic language is everywhere, woven like a motif in album after album, in ballads and love lyrics and protest songs, from performances as early as Town Hall in 1963 to recordings such as "No Time to Think" on *Street-Legal*, supposedly just after he became a "conscious artist":

> Memory, ecstasy, tyranny, hypocrisy
> Betrayed by a kiss on a cool night of bliss
> In the valley of the missing link
> And you have no time to think

The first line is like a table of contents, and the joining of the central New Testament crisis with the legendary anthropological crises in the following two lines defines the language of visionary poetry. But this kind of language is manifest, not only in this song (which is a vatic grab bag) but in all of Dylan's work. Open the *Lyrics* and throw a coin and you will surely hit a vatic phrase, line, axiom, borrowed expression, or directive. Dylan's diction is replete with obscure inflexions drawn from the King James Bible and its shadowy traces in the Christianity of his most revered influences. The prevalence of curses, weeping, loyal servants, Egyptians, morning dews and evening suns, Satan, chiming bells, venal judges, exiles, towers, and flooding river banks—these and scores of other words and phrases lead back to their biblical echoes in the country music young Bob Zimmerman listened to on the radio in high school, and afterwards to Lead Belly, Robert Johnson, Ma Rainey, Charley Patton, Blind Lemon Jefferson, W. C. Handy, the Carter Family, Big Joe Turner, and the other blues artists he sought out and absorbed.

As Michael Gilmour says, "much of the folk and blues music that proved to be so formative was infused with biblical imagery."[28] The implication of Gilmour's statement is valuable: if Dylan's music takes its form, at least in part, from the influence of "folk and blues . . . infused with biblical imagery," then Dylan is responding to religious *art*. Despite the posture of direct engagement with a deity—of possessing a divine afflatus—and despite implications of being merely a conduit for the songs, Dylan absorbs and rewrites the language, printed and sung, of a supposedly holy text. Yet, this language is consummately the product of human art because virtually every literary legatee of the Western tradition alludes to, quotes, or borrows from the infinite variety of biblical texts.

Full recognition of this mediated relationship of imitatio is crucial in analyzing Dylan's poetics. Dylan simultaneously responds to the embedded biblical diction of the blues and to an "always already" aestheticized version of a text accepted as sacred. More to the point, the biblical diction heard in blues standards and folk movement anthems echoes not only the linguistic traits of the Delta or Washington Square but also, unmistakably, the powerful translations of early modern prose stylists. Dylan long ago attached himself to the train of anglophone vatic poets from Wigglesworth to Walcott who appropriate the portentous archaisms of the Bible and assimilate anachronistic dictional resonances to augment the authority of their modern verse (or songs). And, with Dylan as with most of the others, the neglected or suppressed fact is always the same. Poets who imitate biblical diction tend to do so with the calculated pretense—or, maybe, poetic posture—of echoing sacred utterance Itself. But this is not what's strictly happening in terms of biblical imitation. The inescapable *literary* reality is that these vatic poets are in fact echoing and imitating sixteenth- and seventeenth-century English translators.

Therefore—that is, in light of this often-overlooked textual relationship—the definition of the American vates should be revised a bit, mainly to subordinate the poet-theologian (*poeta theologus*) to intertextuality. This revision leads to an unexpected, or unexplored, conclusion. Because of the ubiquitous and fruitful dependence on biblical diction among anglophone poets, William Tyndale emerges as the most influential author in the English language. This might sound like hyperbole, but as Andrew Muir has noted, discussing the influence of the Bible's translations and adaptations, "William Tyndale's extraordinarily adept and memorable phraseology, and pithy quotes are often misattributed to Shakespeare."[29] Tyndale's translations of the New Testament (1526; 1534) and of the Pentateuch (1530), which were declared heretical and cost Tyndale his life, had, in Muir's words, "a pervasive influence on the 1560 *Geneva Bible*," which was significant for Shakespeare (and therefore for everyone else following Shakespeare). More important, perhaps, is that Tyndale's Bible translations provided about 80 percent of the 1611 Authorized Version (the KJV). This disproportionately large contribution to the fundamental linguistic source of the English poetic tradition inarguably makes Tyndale more influential than any other author, Shakespeare included. To object that Tyndale and the other translators did not actually write the words in the KJV, but only transmitted them, is to misunderstand the nature of intertextuality. Most anglophone authors do not read the original biblical languages—John Milton and Allen Ginsberg notwithstanding—but instead respond to the literal diction of the text.

A book on Bob Dylan might seem an unusual locus for calling attention to Tyndale as the most influential writer in English. Yet nothing could be more appropriate, given Dylan's unmatched status as the preeminent vatic poet of our time and his continual response to biblical verse as a songwriter. Dylan probably would not have read Tyndale or even have heard his name. Few people beside scholars know his place in literary history. Yet Dylan's patently biblical diction engages Tyndale as a poetic predecessor and enforces the aesthetic dimension of Dylan's vatic authority. No author's language strikes such familiar echoes throughout literary history, in virtually every poem, play, novel, and folk song.[30]

Tyndale's diction, his brilliant phrasing, and his (sometimes erroneous) translations have permeated speech and poetry with such rooted patterning as to be almost inseparable from the English idiom itself. Not only High Church priests, evangelical preachers, and snake-handling charismatics draw on Tyndale. The linguistic legatees of Tyndale's translations are legion, numbering every writer and poet from the seventeenth century to the present, particularly those with vatic ambitions, those whose words strive for portent. This long literary genealogy stems from Tyndale's linguistic authority, inextricably woven into the supposed sacred nature of the words he translated.

Yet, as Yeats slyly asks in "Among School Children," "Are you the leaf, the blossom or the bole? / O body swayed to music, O brightening glance, / How can we know the dancer from the dance?" Although the valence between sacred content and living diction might be indeterminable, this much can be said. Like so many of his poetic predecessors, Dylan responds just as much to Tyndale's diction as to a nameless, cosmic, evangelical Word. Bert Cartwright has noted that "at some points Dylan is clearly basing his allusion upon a specific translation of the Bible; at others it does not seem to matter." He adds, "contrary to some critical analysts . . . Dylan was not bound to use of the King James Version."[31] True, but for Dylan, as for Ginsberg, imitation of biblical language usually echoes the archaic language of the seventeenth-century translations.

These echoes indicate Dylan's characteristic preference for imitation over influence. Lines in songs like "Hard Rain" or "All Along the Watchtower" or "High Water" only scratch the surface of a palpably textual and literary relationship—a relationship characterized by vatic imitation, emulation, and even outright rivalry. Tyndale's inimitable voice becomes Dylan's linguistic Other, and Dylan's vatic authority emerges both in conflict and collusion with that Other—again, primarily as an aesthetic phenomenon. Biblical diction, framed usually in Tyndale's voice, is central to Dylan's engagement with the apocalyptic. As Mike Marqusee perceptively observes, "What grabbed the young Dylan about the Bible was what grabbed him about folk and blues: its archaic and resonant language, the metaphorical power that enabled it to speak to a deeper experience, a more abiding mystery, than the language of newspapers and magazines."[32] He adds that "a visitor to Woodstock found two books on Dylan's table: a Bible and a volume of Hank Williams's lyrics."[33] But there is a significant difference between those two books on Dylan's table. On one hand, Hank Williams's lyrics remain a stable textual source, specific, petrified in print and in recordings. On the other hand, the "Bible" is notoriously unstable as a textual source, not least because it exists in multiple translations, reflecting normative interpretations, and, most important, using different vocabulary.

Dylan's relationship to the art of biblical poetry is consummately a relationship to the art of biblical translation. Dylan has always found (and continues to find) the "archaic and resonant language" that he reworks in his lyrics for the most part in the diction of the KJV. The specificity of this translation cannot be overemphasized. When a poet, any poet, engages a precursor—when Milton echoes and rewrites Virgil, or Ariosto Boiardo, or Derek Walcott Homer—the prior text is treated as a relatively stable entity (like Hank Williams's book of lyrics). To say Dylan is "grabbed" by biblical language, then, is fully meaningful, at least in a poetic sense, only if we know which version of the Bible is doing the grabbing.

Dylan's biblical references, along with his portentous echoes of "sacred" texts, have received significant critical attention. So much of Dylan's lyrical expression has a vatic quality—Perlman's "visionary music technology par excellence"—that it has become almost required to describe his originality as the result of a

Jacob-like struggle with the prophets of the Hebrew and Christian Bibles. True as this might be in imaginative terms, the more accurate material reality is that Dylan engages the biblical J-Writer, the Nevi'im, and the Evangelists through the poetic authority of the writers and translators of the Authorized Version (the KJV). Critics have not emphasized this patently textual connection, which is unfortunate, because as a result Dylan's vatic language has been judged against an amorphous power of religious portent. Yet, just as Thomas shows with Peter Green's translation of Ovid's *Tristia*, Robert Fagles's of *The Odyssey*, and Allen Mandelbaum's translation of Virgil, Dylan's vatic authority owes as much to his aesthetic engagement with—and imitations of—the hidden translators of the Bible as it does to the mystical content of Judeo-Christian myth.[34]

It bears scrutiny that Dylan's portentous voicings and prophetic status are echoes, not of some numinous divinity but of translators writing in English. Just as it is the translators' art in transforming the classical authors, it is the biblical translators' art, not Holy Writ, that preoccupies Dylan. Lacing his lyrics with biblical references, Dylan sometimes assumes—or is afforded, against his will—a prophetic mantle. "I hear rumors of war / and of wars that have been," sang the draft-age Bob Dylan in "Let Me Die in My Footsteps," echoing the KJV's Matthew 24:5–6. For the biblically savvy, the lines link the singer/speaker to Jesus himself, who prophesies, "Many shall come in my name, saying, I am Christ; and shall deceive many. And ye shall hear of wars and rumors of wars: see that ye be not troubled: for all these things must come to pass, but the end is not yet." The singer's quotation of the biblical phrase, implying recognition that the "end is not yet" though perhaps imminent, cements his precocious vatic role.[35] And, more than half a century after these lyrics, and many others such as "And like Pharaoh's tribe / You'll be drownded in the tide / The hour when the ship comes in," journalists and critics continue to brand Dylan's songs as "oracular."

Dylan's reactions to the authority of the central text of Western literary culture are unpredictable: he variously satirizes, honors, imitates, embraces it as a species of truth, and faces it as a poetic precursor. Yet, throughout, the contest is an aesthetic one. Dylan tangles with the powerful, resonant verse of the Hebrew and Christian Bibles as it is manifest in the historically specific—that is, "archaic"—poetic diction of Tyndale and the seventeenth-century translators.

Dylan Vates

Although Dylan's biblical diction alone doesn't make him a vatic poet, his language signals and solidifies his status. A vates is not a poet who simply makes pronouncements, but one who does so with lasting impact. A vatic utterance has an all-inclusive quality, pertaining to substance, tone, and effect.

Virgil is the consummate vates, or poet-prophet. His towering status has lasted through millennia, despite wildly different receptions of his work. In ancient Rome, during his lifetime, he was the official voice of the *pax Augustana*.

In the Middle Ages he was often seen as a magus, his magisterial *Aeneid* used to cast superstitious Sortes Vergilianae (according to some legends, the Emperor Constantine sometimes resorted to this method to make military decisions). In the Renaissance, Virgil provided the perfect model of a poetic career with what was called the Virgilian wheel (rota): pastoral poetry to begin, then Georgic, followed by the impossible challenge, epic. Even long after the Renaissance, Virgil's vatic authority continued to carry weight. The American motto "e pluribus unum" comes from the *Moretum*, a poem mistakenly thought to be Virgil's. The poem is a recipe for garlic spread, hardly a lofty topic, but evidently the authority of the pseudo-author and the linguistic link to Rome inspired the Founding Fathers to decontextualize the line for propaganda purposes.[36]

For some, comparing Dylan to Virgil might beggar credulity. Yet the tie between Virgil and the American experiment is provocative. It shows the lasting transcultural power of ancient vatic authority even in relation to a new nation frantically disassociating itself from Old World constraints. After all, Virgil is the founding voice and pattern of Eliotian tradition and the Poetic Establishment. Dylan, on the contrary, remains a marginal figure whose enigmatic poetic authority challenges, scorns, and sometimes, willy-nilly, embraces that tradition. Even after a Nobel Prize in Literature, Dylan's performative artistry, which is inextricably linked to the lyrical and literary content of the songs, resists classification (and sparks fractiousness among the classifiers). Yet Dylan and Virgil share a poetic heritage. Like Dylan and Milton, Dylan and Whitman, or Dylan and Ginsberg, they meet on the American plane of vatic expression. An undeniable portentousness—replete with both divine and political resonances—pervades their verse just as it has pervaded the verse of all aspiring vatic poets since Aeneas crossed from Troy to tell his tale to Queen Dido of Carthage.

Virgil is only part of the intricate story of vatic influence. The awkward merging of Greco-Roman tradition with Christian poetry is a long and complicated tale, and this is not the place to review it. Suffice it to say that as much purging as merging occurred, and that the somewhat emptied-out language of the ancients served as an invaluable transcultural vessel, a kind of poetic amphora to be filled with the portentousness of the Hebrew Bible and the Christian New Testament. The final product, now so familiar that we don't even notice its hybrid qualities, was a poetic language unique in its vatic potential. From Dante to Petrarch (in the *Africa*), Ariosto to Tasso, the vatic hybrid echoed. Anglo-American inheritors of this linguistic legacy include, among others, Spenser, Milton, Michael Wigglesworth maybe, then Blake, Keats, Whitman, Jeffers, Sandburg, Plath, H.D., Ginsberg (and other Beats as well, though not with equal skill), Anne Carson, and Walcott.

Several of these poets form a lineage to which Dylan attached himself early on—and almost immediately sought to supersede. For example, "My age it ain't nothin' / My name it means less," the opening words of "With God on Our Side," are patently untrue for Dylan the poet, although their irony inhabits the tone of the song. The song's first line is one of Dylan's most memorable, not only for the words but for his unmistakable vocal delivery when he reaches from the tonic on "ain't" all the way up to the fifth on the first syllable of "nothin"—"nuuuuu-thin.'" But the extraordinary emphasis undercuts the meaning of the words. The speaker's age and name might be unimportant to the revelations of hypocrisy that follow. Standing behind the work, however (paring his fingernails, as Stephen Dedalus would say), is the poet whose age means nothing because the vatic voice is ageless, and whose name, like the silent presence of the tetragrammaton itself, need not (and cannot) be uttered to command authority. As for Aeneas at Carthage, so for Dylan's young speaker: the depredations of nationalism and war should speak for themselves, but, because "You never ask questions / When God's on your side," it takes a vatic emissary to deliver the news:

> Oh the history books tell it
> They tell it so well
> The cavalries charged
> The Indians fell
> The cavalries charged
> The Indians died
> Oh the country was young
> With God on Its Side

The country was young and vicious. Young and racist, young and gruesomely expansionist. The singer too is young, and the parallel between his voice and the youth of the country is inevitable. The putative heroes of Manifest Destiny destroyed a culture with the same combination of ignorance, entitlement, and divine sanction that brought Columbus, Cortés, and the conquistadors to claim ownership of the Americas. Yet, for all its underlying anger, the song is not ultimately polemical. Instead, through a nameless, ageless speaker, the stanzas resound with the insouciant puzzlement of a latter-day wanderer through history when he (or she) is confronted with the sublime irony of divine sanction.

I use the word "sanction" advisedly here because it is what Freud referred to as a "primal word." That is, "sanction" has two opposite meanings (like the word "cleave" in English or *sacer* in Latin [sacred or accursed]): a sanction can be both a censure and a permission. Dylan balances his verses on just such an ambiguity, hinting at ambivalence. The speaker's tone is never sarcastic, but never quite persuaded either. The sanction of having acted "with God on [Y]our Side" balances on a razor's edge between justification and horrified condemnation. This irresolvable ambiguity captures the portentous authority of Dylan's vatic aims, simultaneously divided from and entangled with the voice that performs the song.

Every vatic moment is a departure blessed by some form of divine auspices. The locus classicus of this kind of departure, in Western culture, is the Sibyl's acceptance of the Golden Bough from Aeneas as he descends into the underworld. Few symbolic moments have resonated as comprehensively in the literary-cultural imagination. Not all vatic journeys are descents, nor do all lead claustrophobically to shades of the dead. Yet, like Aeneas, who gleans a vision of the future from those shades in Hades, the vates fulfills the promise of poetic portent. This pattern imprints itself on virtually all vatic poetry, even in the absence of a literal epic journey. Dante travels through three supernatural constructions in the *Commedia*, simultaneously experiencing a change within himself and (according to contemporary Florentine legend) being physically returned from Inferno, Purgatorio, and Paradiso. This last point is vital to understanding Dante's vatic status: not only was he an unrivalled poet-prophet, but he was also known as "the man who had been to Hell."

The reality of this conceit in fourteenth-century Florence, absurd as it sounds today, offers a useful if unexpected parallel to Dylan's predicament as "first-person" narrator in his songs. For Dante, the personal and the poetic intertwined, though he himself explained that the poem should (or could) be read on four separate allegorical levels. Dylan never had anything so complex in mind. When he says, for instance, "Now as I'm leavin' I'm weary as hell," he is not speaking as Bob Dylan per se. He is relying on a homodiegetic, or first-person, speaker. Nevertheless, he also isn't completely distinct from the passion and prophetic quality of his verse. While Dylan might justifiably disavow the political motives imputed to him, his vatic charisma inheres in the musical arrangements and diction of his songs.

Sibyl-ing Rivalry

Somewhere in virtually every Dylan song, cached even in the most unexpected lines, portentousness is manifest ("there's high water everywhere"). In this respect, critics who continue to hear oracular language in Dylan's work are right. It is tempting to consign Dylan's most trenchant vatic diction to the short anthem period, implying that his later work abandoned any such posture in favor of *other* "other sides." As such work as "False Prophet" and "Murder Most Foul" clearly show, Dylan's diction never loses its vatic resonance, even when the overt visionary howl of "With God on Our Side," "The Times They Are A-Changin'," and "When the Ship Comes In" disappears. As he developed into a more sophisticated songwriter—composer and lyricist both—Dylan's engagement with prophetic authority became equally complex, sometimes imitative and other times fiercely agonistic. In all his recordings, even the most recent ones, Dylan deliberately enhances the numinously cryptic power of his verses. While "Hard Rain" demonstrates an extraordinary command of vatic expression very early on, Dylan's later songs from "All Along the Watchtower" to "Dirge" to "I and

I" to "Mississippi," "High Water," "Not Dark Yet," and "Highlands" exhibit an ongoing and profound commitment to that same mode of writing and performance. Even the knotty, cryptic, accusing verses of such experimental standards as "Gates of Eden" and "It's Alright, Ma (I'm Only Bleeding)," while eschewing the anthemic voice of the pabulum years, resonate with visionary challenges.

Through this kind of engagement with biblical verse, Dylan fashions a customized vatic authority. Philippe Margotin and Jean-Michel Guesdon, discussing the song "Arthur McBride" from *Good as I Been to You*, say that "for a good cause, Dylan picks up his pilgrim's staff. From the first notes on his guitar, he takes us back some thirty years to the mood of *The Times They Are A-Changin'* and *Another Side of Bob Dylan*. His voice is less sententious than in the past, probably because of the weight of experience. But Dylan has amazing charisma, and he definitely holds the attention of his listeners, even if the intonation of his voice is more nasal than before."[37] The pairing of *The Times They Are A-Changin'* and *Another Side of Bob Dylan*, a connection the album titles belie, points not only to a similarity of "mood" but also to a welling, sustained vatic authority carried from "The Times They Are A-Changin'" (1963) to "Chimes of Freedom" (1964) to the unlikely "Arthur McBride" (1992). Like Mellers, who speaks of Dylan's "extraordinary, instantly recognizable voice," Margotin and Guesdon identify an "amazing charisma" in Dylan's voice even at this much later stage, a power that draws in and enthralls listeners just as that amazing voice did in the early sixties. They instinctively recognize that there can be no charismatic figure without followers—in this case listeners: there can be no charisma without an interdependent relationship with an audience. Dylan's charisma combines vocal with lyrical authority, and he has continued to effect this combination brilliantly. His voice might have become "more nasal" and lost some of its "sententious" baritone force by the time he recorded *Good as I Been to You*. But his music grew more complex even as he pressed the blues into service, matching his voice to new imitations. And, above all, his lyrics delved—and still delve—into a well of biblical diction.

An exhaustive list of Dylan's more vatic songs is impossible because lines and stanzas echoing biblical, Whitmanian, or Ginsbergian diction (to name prominent models) appear in virtually all his recordings. Most familiar from the sixties are the frankly sociopolitical songs of *The Times They Are A-Changin'* and *Freewheelin'*, with the addition of, for example, "Chimes of Freedom" from *Another Side*. But the more understated expression of the vatic posture deserves notice as well. Among unreleased songs that fit the bill are the Guthrie-esque "Let Me Die in My Footsteps" and the deservedly celebrated "Percy's Song" (the former released in the 1991 *Bootleg Series, Vol. 1–3* and the latter on *Biograph*).

The former pits the individualistic Great Historical Traveler against the politics of death and destruction, while "Percy's Song" quietly invokes the harsh natural elements as metaphors for the burden of systemic injustice.

A crash on the highway flew a car into a field
Turn, turn, turn, turn again
Four people dead and your friend was at the wheel
Turn to face the rain and the wind

"Percy's Song" comes from the period in which Dylan and other acoustic guitar players were making diligent efforts to produce instant artifacts, that is, original compositions (sometimes with borrowed, slightly altered melodies) that sounded like authentic songs drawn from the traditional canon. This now sounds like a pretentious and hopeless project, but many of the songs managed to imitate the traditional folk style expertly, with pleasant and lasting effect. Dylan was probably the best imitator among this group, or simply the best songwriter, with his "Don't Think Twice" leading the pack.[38] Many other mock-traditional gems came out of this era, too: a tendentiously cherrypicked list might include Tom Paxton's "Ramblin' Boy" and "The Last Thing on My Mind," Ian and Sylvia Tyson's "Four Strong Winds," Patrick Sky's "Many a Mile," Buffy Sainte-Marie's "Cod'ine," Donovan's "Yellow is the Color of My True Love's Hair," Eric Andersen's "Thirsty Boots," and so on.[39] Apart from the more ambitious topical songs, however, songwriters rarely managed or even tried to infuse a vatic presence into their lyrical imitations.

While few would challenge Dylan's vatic authority in the topical context— "The answer, my friend, is a-blowin' in the wind"—his ability to carry that authority across to lyrical songs was what distinguished the force of his writing from that of his equally ambitious peers. "Percy's Song" is an exercise in this kind of genre-straddling. "Turn, turn, turn again . . . Turn to face the rain and the wind," sings the friend of the disenfranchised driver sentenced to ninety-nine years in prison ("two sixes upside down," as Woody Guthrie sang). The verse structure of "Percy's Song," in which the refrain is interpolated between the lines and remains constant as the narrative progresses, highlights the most ancient conflict of them all: worldly lives unfold and injustice prevails in the face of an implacable Nature (or god). The underlying voice in "Percy's Song" is disenchanted yet resigned. There's a fine parallel between Dylan's articulate, unaccompanied fingerpicking, his resonant voice, and the song's mood of broken innocence and nascent mordancy.

Even without investigating judicial sentencing guidelines, it seems plausible to conclude that the sentence mentioned in "Percy's Song" is excessive. But how excessive is another question. The narrator admits,

It may be he's got a sentence to serve
Turn, turn, turn, turn again

And quickly qualifies this:

But ninety-nine years he just don't deserve
Turn to face the rain and the wind

The automatic, unchanging circularity of the *Turn, turn, turn* refrain adumbrates the deadly repetition of ninety-nine years in Joliet prison. The words echo Shakespeare, Ecclesiastes (and Pete Seeger), and especially the traditional ballad "The Wind and the Rain" sung by Paul Clayton. Dylan claims to have borrowed the melody from his friend's version of the ballad, but, regardless, the combination of melody and imitation lends unimpeachable poetic authority to the lines that come between the refrain. The first-person narrative continues because of, or despite, the circularity of the refrain. And the incommensurateness of the sentence to be served, at least in the speaker's eyes, is hammered home by the dual extremes: the unrelenting repetitive verses in contrast to the unraveling narrative, and the maximum-security Joliet versus the delicate creature who "wouldn't hurt a life that belonged to someone else." The extremes, however, provide the justification for Dylan's vatic breath.

Dylan polarizes himself, and always has, in the personae of his songs. He deliberately *destabilizes* his charismatic presence, introducing an entropy situation that the vatic voice resolves. Often, to achieve this destabilized site, he casts his narrative voice as either outsider or interloper, thief or victim, spurned Petrarchan lover ("Mama, You Been on my Mind" [1964], "Simple Twist of Fate" [1974]) or untamable wanderer: "Goodbye is too good a word, gal / So I'll just say fare thee well" ("Don't Think Twice, It's All Right" [1963]). His aliases appear, variously, as solemn visionaries—"I have stood on the side of twelve misty mountains"—or impish rebels—contemptuous, scathing, superior—or brilliant combinations of these extremes. But, inevitably, the vatic promise comes through, braced by portentous hearing or seeing:

> I have heard the turning of the key
> I've been deceived by the clown inside of me
> I thought that he was righteous but he's vain
> Something's tellin' me I'll wear the ball and chain'
> . . . .
> Send out for Saint John the Evangelist
> All my friends are drunk they can be dismissed
> My head says that it's time to make a change
> But my heart is telling me I love ya but you're strange.
> ("Abandoned Love," Bitter End Version)[40]

The song opens with the portentous "I hear the turning of the key." The appearance of a patron saint and an Evangelist (only in the "Bitter End" version) suggests the possibility of St. Peter's famous golden key. But the final stanza is clearly in a normal room, and the key could well be opening or locking an ordinary door. In any case, the vatic portentousness is supported by the motif of change and disorientation. The narrator announces his departure (or departures) throughout the song. About "to make a change," he calls for Saint John the Evangelist, author of Revelation, apparently for a viaticum. Eclectic image groups fill the song: "righteous" clown, patron saint, and Spanish moon, Saint John and drunken friends. Dylan's voice at the Bitter End seems to mirror this eclecticism. He draws out extra-long notes, which is not unusual, but he also mixes in surprising stopped beats like spondees in the last line of the stanzas—"my/heart/is/ tel-/ling/ me"—followed by a fast resolution that threatens, and even dares to violate, the song's meter (e.g., "Won't you let me in your room one time before I disappear?").

Quoted lines will not suitably reflect Dylan's vocal command during the Bitter End performance: he managed that night not only to enchant his audience but even to get a few laughs with the crowd-pleasing contradiction of "I love ya but you're strange." With superb comic timing, Dylan intentionally polarizes the effect of the song. He inverts the Petrarchan theme, ambivalently spurning his lover, and merges that persona with the departing vates, the visionary seeker abandoned by his divine protector: "My patron saint is fighting with a ghost / He's always off somewhere when I need him most."

Blue-Eyed Son (or Lord Robert A.)

For narrative inspiration, Dylan sat at the feet of Woody Guthrie and the American balladeers. He was a quick study and the ephebe soon surpassed the masters, his achievements in narrative song culminating in the superbly revisionist "Lily, Rosemary and the Jack of Hearts" (1974) and the stunning "Tangled Up in Blue" (1974) (not to mention the much later "Highlands" [1997], a song inimitable in its narrative plasticity). Dylan didn't look far beyond the American tradition for instruction in storytelling. Among his contemporaries, he singles out for surprising praise Kris Kristofferson's "Sunday Morning Comin' Down," a song saturated in nostalgia with a meanderingly evocative narrative.

While American narrative song seems to have provided Dylan with ample space for imitation (and emulation), the broader Western canon supplied him with models for imagery and for the rhythms of a new vatic voice. The combination of Rimbaud and Mallarmé on one hand, with Whitman, Ginsberg, and the biblical translators on the other, helped him forge the riveting diction that characterizes his work at every stage.[41]

As many critics and Dylan-watchers have noted, the first, most revolutionary manifestation of Dylan's ability to combine and supersede his influences is "A Hard Rain's A-Gonna Fall." This song represents more than the sum of its parts: it is arguably an utter reinvention of the lyric possibility of folk or traditional song. According to Dave Van Ronk, "Hard Rain" was the song that changed it all for him and his contemporaries: "Within a couple of years, Bobby changed the whole direction of the folk movement. The big breakthrough was when he wrote 'A Hard Rain's A-Gonna Fall,' because in that song he fused folk music with modernist poetry. The tune was borrowed from an old English ballad called 'Lord Randall,' and it was in the same question-and-response form, but the imagery was right out of the symbolist school. . . . I heard him sing it for the first time during one of the hoot nights at the Gaslight, and I could not even talk about it; I just had to leave the club and walk around for a while. It was unlike anything that had come before it, and it was clearly the beginning of a revolution."[42] Van Ronk's stupefaction almost certainly refers to a musical and, above all, a lyrical revolution. The overturning of the traditional was a consummately charismatic gesture. Dylan's language destabilized the audience's expectations and his bold displacement of the traditional words reorganized the mild chaos of substitution with a new vernacular.

This charismatic revolution, however, was also a resuscitation of the American vatic voice. Dylan's great Other on the folk scene might have been Pete Seeger, the revivalist stanchion, but his vatic Other was Woody Guthrie. "Hard Rain" challenged Woody's voice. And, by the sheer force of his lyrical talent and virtuosic performance (at the Gaslight and on *Freewheelin'*), Dylan sealed the promise he had made in "Song to Woody," in effect to turn in a new, different direction and to revise the past.

In "Hard Rain," the speaker's claims resonate with a vatic tenor:

> And I'll tell it and think it and speak it and breathe it
> And reflect from the mountain so all souls can see it
> Then I'll stand on the ocean until I start sinkin'
> But I'll know my song well before I start singin'
> ("Hard Rain")

"I'll stand on the ocean / Until I start sinkin' / But I'll know my song well / Before I start singin.'" This isn't Dylan exactly, but the reimagined, socially conscious voice of the Child ballad's Lord Randall in American guise. The source of this passage is unmistakable, even if the "singer's" posture isn't easily glossed. In four lines Dylan manages a brilliant conflation of Matthew 14: 22–31 as it appears in the KJV. After the miracle of the loaves and fishes, and the feeding of the five thousand, Jesus sends his disciples away: "And straightway Jesus constrained his disciples to get into a ship, and to go before him unto the other side, while he sent the multitudes away. And when he had sent the multitudes away he went into a mountain apart to pray: and when the evening was come, he was there alone. But the ship was now in the midst of the sea, tossed with waves: for the wind was contrary. And in the fourth watch of the night Jesus went unto them, walking on the sea" (Matthew 14: 22–25). In this celebrated passage, the King James

Version copies nearly verbatim William Tyndale's 1538 translation of the New Testament.

The Lord Randall of the traditional song is doomed, in some versions poisoned by a meal of bad eels served by his lover.[43] The hapless boy singer, Lord Randall, bemoans his betrayal to his mother in a private dialogue. In contrast, the public, vatic ambition of Dylan's Lord Randall avatar couldn't be clearer: the speaker will harken back to the aquatic miracle of salvationistic Christianity for his authority. But that authority is immediately tempered by the singer who will "stand on the ocean / Until I start sinkin'." Sinking is the inescapable mortal destiny. The speaker knows the finite nature of his humanity will compromise the portentous force of his voice. And that compromise too is built into the allusion. An audience as astute as Dylan's young voice in the song might well identify the narrator, not as Jesus walking on the Sea of Galilee but as Peter, first walking on the water and then sinking for lack of faith.

> And when the disciples saw him walking on the sea, they were troubled, saying, It is a spirit; and they cried out for fear. But straightway Jesus spake unto them, saying Be of good cheer; it is I; be not afraid.
>
> And Peter answered and said, Lord if it be thou, bid me come unto thee on the water. And he said, Come. And when Peter was come down out of the ship, he walked on the water, to go to Jesus. But when he saw the wind boisterous, he was afraid, and beginning to sink, he cried, saying, Lord, save me. And immediately Jesus stretched forth *his* hand, and caught him, and said unto him O thou of little faith, wherefore didst thou doubt?[44]

It is Peter, after all, who founds the Church—"on this rock," and so forth—just as Dylan's narrator sets forth on his evangelical mission to sing about change and freedom and a new American conscience.

Dylan laces his lines with evangelical portent but redirects the expected hermeneutic: Peter for Jesus, human agency (and sociopolitical action) for divine faith.

Matthew 13:57, coming just before the water-walking chapter, has an equally famous coinage, and it is tempting to wonder if the young Dylan had this in mind too: "A prophet is not without honour, save in his own house." The Tyndale Bible, slightly different, is more familiar: "a prophet is not without honour, save in his own country, and among his own kin." (This version appears in the KJV Luke.) Perhaps we should hear a doubt, a built-in sense of resignation when the speaker says, "I'll know my song well before I start singing." Perhaps Dylan, if not the speaker, recognizes the likelihood that the vatic voice will echo without honor in its own country.

Of course, that wasn't how it went. No wonder Dylan was stunned when "in his own country, and among his own kin," people thought he was an actual prophet.

Don't Say I Never Warned You

A case in point: critics often categorize the haunting and magical "All Along the Watchtower" from *John Wesley Harding* as later, postvatic Dylan, citing the generally accepted motorcycle accident climacteric. Yet "Watchtower" might be seen to hold a Janus-like position among the sixties songs, facing both ways from the parapet:

> "There must be some way out of here," said the joker to the thief
> "There's too much confusion, I can't get no relief
> Businessmen, they drink my wine, plowmen dig my earth
> None of them along the line know what any of it is worth"
> ("All Along the Watchtower")

The music begins with the guitar's methodical strumming of higher strings. Then Dylan's plaintive harmonica comes in, shortly after which a "muffled" but fulsome bass drives the song.[45] The first two stanzas are a dialogue between two characteristically marginal, aleatory, carnivalesque figures, a joker and a thief—this time less a Robin Hood or underdog hero than a kind of value-free thief. Opening, as Marqusee notes, in medias res, the song allows us to overhear a vaguely desperate conversation between an anthropomorphized playing card figure—the Joker—and a thief, who would be real enough except that he is stripped of criminality and romanticized as sympathetic, kind, and even philosophically perceptive.[46] The contrast between the Joker's desperate cultural claustrophobia and the thief's calming wisdom mirrors the Janus-like position of the "watchman" on the tower.

"All Along the Watchtower" represents an emergence from the experimental lyrics of the *Blonde on Blonde* era. The song's allusive structure reveals a kind of subterranean vatic strain. Dylan's watchtower is a virtual copy of Isaiah's and the Joker-Thief dynamic recapitulates—somewhat impishly—Isaiah's "grievous vision" and his interaction with the "the Lord of Hosts, the God of Israel" (Isaiah 21: 2–10). The entire divine encounter is a justification for Isaiah's oracular pronouncements, which, even by biblical standards, are at least as coded and hermetic as Dylan's lyric, but without the haunting musical accompaniment.

Most significantly for imitation, "Watchtower" offers a unique example of how imitation is sometimes a process of layering and how this layering locks Dylan's vatic language to the translators' art. There is more than one reference to watchmen in Isaiah, in addition to the appearance of watchmen in Jeremiah and Psalms. In some measure all these different references underlie Dylan's allusive creations on the watchtower. The most obvious basic source is probably Isaiah 21:

> Prepare the table, watch in the **watchtower**, eat, drink: arise, ye princes, *and* anoint the shield. For thus hath the Lord said unto me, Go, set a **watchman**, let him declare what he seeth. And he saw a chariot *with* a couple of

horsemen, a chariot of asses, *and* a chariot of camels; and he hearkened dil-
igently, with much heed: and he cried, A lion: My lord, I stand continually
upon the **watchtower** in the daytime, and I am set in my ward whole nights:
and, behold, here cometh a chariot of men, *with* a couple of horse men. And
he answered and said, Babylon is fallen, is fallen; an all the graven images of
her gods he hath broken unto the ground.[47]

The watchman here, in direct communication with the deity, is standing on a
watchtower. As I discuss below, Dylan returns to the watchman "set in his ward"
sixty years later in the apocalyptic "Tempest." But before reckoning with that
other, belated watchman, it is crucial to unpack the allusive architecture built
into "All Along the Watchtower." To that end—in addition to Isaiah 21, there is
Isaiah 52: "Thy **watchman** shall lift up the voice; with the voice together shall
they sing: for they shall see eye to eye, when the Lord shall bring again Zion"
(Isaiah 52: 8). This oracular remit of Isaiah includes the injunction to "lift up the
voice," which means, effectively, that the watchman enacts his charismatic role
with a vatic song.

But there are also blind watchmen in Isaiah: "they are all ignorant, they *are*
all dumb dogs, they cannot bark, sleeping, lying down, loving to slumber . . .
Come ye, *say they*, I will fetch strong wine, and we will fill ourselves with strong
drink" (Isaiah 56: 10; 12). A hint of Dylan's "businessmen they drink my wine"
emerges from this passage. But the blindness of the watchmen is the key to the
warning: asleep on watch, they fail to alert their people to the Lord's message.

The watchman in the Tanakh (except perhaps for Isaiah 56) is the vatic
voice, the oracle who leads the congregation to recognize the coming of Jerusa-
lem. Usually, as in Jeremiah, the Lord's pronouncement is amply clear: "Also I set
watchmen over you, *saying*, Hearken to the sound of the trumpet. But they said,
We will not hearken. Therefore hear, ye nations, and know, congregation, what *is*
among them. Hear, O earth: behold, I will bring evil upon this people, *even* the
fruit of their thoughts, because they have not hearkened unto my words, nor to
my law, but rejected it" (Jeremiah 6:17–19). In this case, the watchmen, despite
their efforts, were unable to get the "nations" and the congregation to hear the
divine trumpet. The results of this deafness or rejection are dire: the Lord "will
bring evil upon this people, *even* the fruit of their thoughts." This too, of course,
has prophetic force in the mouth of Jeremiah. The recounting of the past is al-
ways also an admonition for the future, a Janus-like position characteristic of all
vatic utterances.

And, in fact, the watchman of Israel, at least according to Ezekiel, has ex-
tended duties:

> But if the **watchman** see the sword come, and blow not the trumpet, and the
> people be not warned; if the sword come, and take *any* person from among

them, he is taken away in his iniquity; *but his blood will I require at the watchman's hand.*

So thou, O son of man, I have set thee a **watchman** unto the house of Israel; therefore thou shalt hear the word at my mouth, and warn them from me.[48]

Ezekiel's watchman is also an executioner in the Lord's name—a very tricky position to be in regarding the same congregation that is supposed to trust you.

I could multiply references to watchmen, as Dylan himself might have done had he availed himself of a *Strong's Exhaustive Concordance of the Bible* or with a KJV with a concordance in the back. But the overwhelming message—one might even say the repeated message—of the numerous watchman references is one of urgency. "Two riders are approaching" right enough, but is the city awake to recognize them and take the proper steps? As the Psalmist says,

> Except the Lord build the house,
> they labor in vain that build it:
> except the Lord keep the city,
> the **watchman** waketh *but* in vain.[49]

All along the watchtower, princes might keep the view. But if "except the Lord keep the city," the princes, barefoot women, Joker, and thief watch in vain.

Clearly "Watchtower" plumbs the vatic resonance of the biblical prophets, primarily Isaiah. But the multiple references throughout the Nevi'im to virtually the same watchman found in Isaiah and the impinging admonition to "hearken to" the divine trumpet (also repeated regularly) also infuse Dylan's lyrics. It is reasonable to ask, therefore, whether Dylan knew and imitated, for example, the later references in Isaiah, or the one in Psalm 127, or Jeremiah, or Ezekiel. Did he realize he was invoking all these different biblical watchmen and watchtowers?

But ultimately those questions miss the point. What matters most is that the *translators* of the Bible knew the allusions. While secondary allusion (which is inadvertent) occurs in much poetic composition, in the biblical translations the allusions to prior verses would have been deliberate. The translators would have been echoing and repeating their own diction in Psalms, Isaiah, and Ezekiel. Although Dylan might not have known specific passages beyond Isaiah, the reference to Psalms was already built into the translation via the tone of the language, which was influenced by the translators' direct allusions and by their sense of the emotional weight of the passage. Consequently, the heavy diction of Dylan's "Watchtower" does not only reflect Isaiah 21:5–9 and later chapters in the same book (Isa. 53, 56, 62). The language of the song also cannot evade built-in allusions, most prominently to Psalm 127, Jeremiah 6, and Ezekiel 3. Dylan cannily manipulates the prophets' (and the Psalmist's) apocalyptic, monitory tone.

Apart from the title, the final stanza has the only mention of a watchtower, the only indication of where the joker and thief might be holding their talk. The song opens with the joker's speech, a full quatrain in a twelve-line song. His plaint, so aptly anticipated by Dylan's harmonica, begins with a personal plea, a need to escape (the walls?). But the thief's reply is evidently meant to assuage the joker's panic. And a kind of tautology develops when he says, "'There are many here among us who feel that life is but a joke / But you and I, we've been through that, and this is not our fate.'" To learn that the joker knows that his fate is *not* to feel life is "but a joke" seems to close the circle on the dialogue. As is the case with all tautologies, there is no escape from this one, so that even the thief's reassurances reflect the culture trapped inside the walls, where "there's too much confusion." Two couplets follow the dialogue between the joker and the thief. Within the song's fiction, these couplets are spoken by a narrator or, perhaps, a watchman "set" on the watchtower. We infer that this figure is standing above or away from the joker and thief. Rather than looking inside the walls, however, this unidentified narrative voice looks outward, "outside in the distance." What he (or she) sees has a disjointed visionary quality. In place of literalness, the narrator seems to pick out signs, symbolic features of the landscape appearing at that moment. The signs are open-ended, potentially negative, and, admittedly, only barely intelligible. But, of course, intelligibility is the subject of those last lines, as it is with all visionary expression. The vates does not provide translations or a crossword key.

The enveloping bass thrum and the unwavering melodic line do little to alleviate the dark ambiguity of the narrator's observations. Landscape details are scarce in the lyric and the words "growl" and "howl" break into the abstractions of the joker-thief dialogue. Dylan emphasizes this irruption of reality (from the Watchtower) into the abstract plane by pairing the linguistic descriptors and the rhyme, as if revealing a live aural connection to the parapet experience. Between the rhymed lines, Dylan's narrator observes, "Two riders were approaching," and leaves it at that. This unembellished observation nestled between two ominous signs—the growling wildcat and howling wind (Isaiah's whirlwind?)—falls with ambiguous Sibylline portent. It's as if the narrator himself has become the Watchtower, simultaneously facing that confusing abstract culture within the walls and an ominous, indeterminate future beyond them.

Imitating the Hexagrams

Dylan's vatic authority, on full display in "Watchtower," evolved from the anthemic chimes of his earlier compositions to a more restrained, if still portentous, diction. Dylan once gave a hint of his evolution. Bristling from Nat Hentoff's reworking of the already moldering question—"Do you feel that acquiring a combo and switching from folk to folk-rock has improved you as a performer?"—Dylan delivered a compact tour de force in response. First, he ticked off his views on performing ("I'm not interested in myself as a performer") and witheringly dismissed folk-rock. Then he expostulated on folk and traditional music: "Folk music is a word I can't use. Folk music is a bunch of fat people. I have to think of all this as traditional music. Traditional music is based on hexagrams. It comes about from legends, Bibles, plagues, and it revolves around vegetables and death. There's nobody that's going to kill traditional music. All these songs about roses growing out of people's brains and lovers who are really geese and swans that turn into angels—they're not going to die."[50] Defensive and offensive, a bit cryptic, telegraphic, and apparently tossed off, this description of the force and mystery of traditional music nevertheless captures the conceptual incomprehensibility of the traditional canon. For Dylan, the hexagrams are trenchantly important because, as he has always intuited, a knot of unintelligibility lies at the core of the music he responds to. With a specific cadre in mind, he says, "I mean, you'd think that the traditional-music people could gather from their songs that mystery— just plain simple mystery—is a fact, a traditional fact."[51] Presumably, the mystery comes through in diction, semantics, imagery, and metaphor, in addition to the traditional crazy subjects of "roses growing out of people's brains and lovers who are really geese." Dylan is referring to "Lord Randall" and "Polly Von." One could compare these weird tales of biosynthesis with tales, for example, of superhuman strength ("John Henry," who "beat that steam-drill down") and puzzling eternal chastity ("Silver Dagger"), of shocking punishment ("Buffalo Skinners") and equally shocking crime ("Omie Wise," "Tom Dooley"), of mothers abandoning infants ("Gypsy Davy," "House Carpenter"), of cold-blooded murderers ("Stagger Lee"), natural disasters, vigilante massacres, and venereal disease. The language of these songs might be more straightforward than, say, "Absolutely Sweet Marie," but the concatenation of sex, murder, violent jealousy, union battles, cowboy ethics, and firearms abuse is no more intelligible to a middle-class audience than the language of "All Along the Watchtower."

Dylan recognized this fact very early in his career. His imaginative revolution began when he made a swap between unintelligible categories, shifting from subject to language. Ironically, that switch brought it all back home: Rimbaud's "dérangement des senses," while altering the musical horizon, also had an unexpectedly sympathetic appeal to educated listeners. In a way, it was less pretentious to be interpreting Dylan's symbolic forays than to be posing as folklorist Allan Lomax clones in every club and college and coffee house from East Orange to Bleeker Street to Cambridge.

The *Playboy* interview continues: "I listen to the old ballads; but I wouldn't go to a *party* and listen to the old ballads. I could give you descriptive detail of what they do to me, but some people would probably think my imagination had gone mad. It strikes me funny that people actually have the gall to think that I have some kind of fantastic imagination. It gets very lonesome."[52] The implication in these last sentences is that traditional music already contains the wildness and mystery that people want to ascribe to Dylan's post-acoustic songwriting. Dylan's contempt for this misattribution serves as a kind of warning: the roots and branches of his increasingly suprarealistic imagery spring primarily from the very same American strain that inspired his earliest songs, but with the added difference of Dylan's contemporizing genius, a kind of Cubist reformation of the figurative revolution he himself began with "Hard Rain." Brecht and the Symbolist poets certainly exerted influence on his style, and maybe even on his sense of the poète maudit.[53] But Dylan remains unwavering in emphasizing his imaginative debt to American traditional music. "Like anything else in great demand," he tells Hentoff, "people try to own [traditional music]. It has to do with a purity thing. I think its meaninglessness is holy. Everybody knows I'm not a folk singer."[54]

Though apparently non sequiturs, these last sentences have a portentous effect. Whether they are verbatim transcripts of a conversation (with proper punctuation added) or simply Nat Hentoff's reconstruction of the twenty-four-year-old Dylan's telegraphic style, the leaps and gaps give the impression of clipped oracular declarations (and perhaps gave a similar impression to the interviewer).

The interview, which was published long before the release of the *Basement Tapes*, confirms that Dylan's indebtedness to traditional music was there from the beginning. Even as his imagery grew more associative and (at times) surrealistic, Dylan held onto one stem of his vatic voice, the "legends, Bibles, plagues," the "death and vegetables" of traditional music. This music is inextricably intertwined with another vocal stem, Tyndale's KJV diction. These are Dylan's rose and briar, and in convergence they form his vatic voice.

Age of Fiberglass

The full stanza from which this chapter's epigraph comes imparts a sense of mission:

> There are those who worship loneliness, I'm not one of them,
> In this age of fiberglass I'm searching for a gem.
> The crystal ball up on the wall hasn't shown me nothing yet,
> I've paid the price of solitude, but at least I'm out of debt.

The lines of the stanza are linked and not linked, displaying that kind of logical gap reminiscent of biblical verse. Each line stands alone and generates meanings. But the lines also have a provocative adjacency: the speaker is in solitude (though he is not one of those who "worship loneliness"), yet he continues on his mission to find a "gem" in "this age of fiberglass." The clash between "gem" and "fiberglass"—calling to mind, perhaps, the stainless-steel house in "Don't Fall Apart on Me Tonight"—could represent natural purity against manufactured dross but seems to imply that the gem itself could be *made*: that is, finer art versus commercial art. So—is the crystal ball made from fiberglass rather than genuine (magical) crystal? The historical, or fairy-tale, implement of clairvoyance has, in any case, let the speaker down. His mission to find a gem, undertaken without the map of clairvoyance, marks a new departure *on behalf of the ideal*.

This gesture is that of the pure charismatic. Weber gives the example of Jesus who says, in Matthew 5:17, "Think not that I am come to destroy the law, or the prophets; I am not come to destroy, but to fulfil" (KJV). The inference of this stanza from "Dirge" is the same: the speaker does not reject the prophetic mantle. On the contrary, it has gotten him out of debt, despite having left him alone ("on top of twelve misty mountains"?). He comes to fulfill the mission or "call" to search for a gem in a fiberglass age. Dylan sings the song as a lament, a consummate dirge, and the plaintiveness in his voice translates irresistibly to the rejection of present superficialities and past methods. This is the voice of vatic reversal, the new mission to find a gem retrenching the original direction toward truth or purity or artistic genuineness.

Dylan effects a similar contest with biblical, as opposed to secular, prophetic language in "Blind Willie McTell" (1983), a song, as Heylin says, that is "immersed in the Apocalypse."[55] Unreleased when recorded, the song appears on the *Bootleg Series, Vol. 1–3* in 1991. Once again, the *Bootleg Series* helps trace Dylan's development in terms of imitatio: rather than having abandoned imitation of old models as he progressed, Dylan kept his models close to his work but realigned himself. His transformations of "digested" material attained new perspectives. For example, regarding "Blind Willie McTell," David Yaffe made the perceptive observation that "'nobody could sing the blues like Blind Willie McTell,' [Dylan] sang, but nobody sang about not being able to sing those blues like Dylan, which in turn made for compelling blues in its own way."[56] Yaffe has added that "Robert Zimmerman spent . . . all of his adult life, off and on, in a reckoning with blackness."[57] This imitation on Dylan's part led to a kind of "racial transference" allowing him to reconcile his (and everyone else's) white appropriation of Black musical culture. But Dylan's imitations and transformations were never done in bad faith. His aim was not to suppress his sources but to bridge the discontinuities, and, in Arthur Kinney's words, allow "the audience [to] see the residual traces of the original, which has been the initial impulse or model."[58]

The "racial transference" Yaffe identifies is significant. Dylan transforms efforts at "sounding Black," which was one of the sore points of blues exploitation. Instead, he sang *about* not being able to sing the blues like Willie McTell: he reimagined Delta musical culture in lyrical terms. He honored the blues sound with vocal approximations—not imitations precisely, but gestures toward emulation. In "Blind Willie McTell" he instinctively positions himself as an observer of the exploitative aping of Black blues voices even as he acknowledges his own exploitation of the blues.

The song imitates the irrational force of the blues lyric and by doing that transforms it into what might be called vatic lament, a lament in conscious, agonistic relationship with the authority of biblical poetry:

> Seen the arrow on the doorpost
> Saying "This land is condemned
> All the way from New Orleans
> To Jerusalem"
> I traveled through East Texas
> Where many martyrs fell
> And I know no one can sing the blues
> Like Blind Willie McTell.

Dylan's first line echoes the portentous voice of Deuteronomy 6 and 11, the passages rolled into the parchment of the mezuzah affixed to the doorframes of Jewish homes in accordance with the relevant Torah portion: "And thou shalt write [these words] on the doorposts of thy house, and on thy gates" (Deut. 6:9). In Deuteronomy 6 Moses gives "the Instruction—the laws and rules—the Lord your God has commanded [me] to impart to you." Dylan might have been reading the Tanakh version: "Take to heart these instructions," Moses says, "Bind them as a sign on your hand and let them serve as a symbol on your forehead; inscribe them on the doorposts of your house and on your gates" (6:6; 6:8–9).[59] But the KJV is also a possibility: "And thou shalt write them on your doorposts of thine house, and upon thy gates: that your days may be multiplied, and the days of your children, in the land which the Lord sware unto your fathers to give them, as the days of heaven upon the earth" (Deut. 11:20–21.) Common to both versions is the sense of hope, of liberation from slavery, of a future guaranteed by covenant.

But Dylan transforms the mezuzah to the "arrow on the doorpost," disrupting the protective element of the covenantal sign. The song is in e-flat minor, and the piano chords are sustained. Dylan's voice and the instruments work to the same effect, moving from an initial impression of carelessness to a sense of oracular and vatic celebration.[60] As the stanzas build up in intensity, however, the accompaniment rises in volume and Dylan begins to enunciate with precision, raising his voice to a level of oracular celebration: "See them big plantations burning / Hear the crackin' of the whips" . . . "God is in his heaven / And we all want what's his / But power and greed and corruptible seed / Seem to be all that there is." The lyrics have the stunning enigmatic force of biblical verse, but, unlike the rolled parchment on the doorpost, they indicate no homage to a deity, no promise beyond bleak fatalism—"corruptible seed" and the ghost of the St. James Infirmary—nothing for future generations. That arrow "says"—speaking in a voice at once Mosaic and Christian—that *this* land is condemned.

Dylan has a signal advantage over Moses. His voice is live, a performative experience, while Moses exists only in translations twice or three times removed from his original language and towering presence. The diction of "Blind Willie McTell" grandiosely exploits this vocal advantage, while at the same time demurring to Blind Willie as an earthly power of expression beyond its own. As Dylan would have known, Moses, a stutterer, used his brother Aaron as a mouthpiece, whereas Dylan, in contrast, has full control of what Ricks calls a voice "that cannot be ignored, and ignores nothing, though it spurns a lot."[61] Moses was ignored (as was the more commanding Author of the Instructions), to disastrous effect for the Israelites. But Dylan's refrain makes it amply clear that in his confrontation with Deuteronomy and the mezuzah, with historical captivity, enslavement, and sin, he has no ambition to reframe prophecies. He deliberately engages with art over oracle, lament over law. Blind Willie McTell's blues provide the modern vatic counterpart, not to suffering itself but to the linguistic authority of biblical poetry.

Dylan's voice seems to surge out of the bleakness of the lyrics: "All the way from New Orleans / To Jerusalem . . . and I know no one can sing the blues like Blind Willie McTell." In the acoustic version on the *Bootleg* album, Dylan never pauses as he sings the lines, driving headlong as he enjambs the lines from verse to verse, while the music remains steadily ominous, almost as if it were holding back the inevitable doom of the lyrics. Heylin remarks that in the live version that Dylan began performing onstage in 1997, he changed "Jerusalem" to "New Jerusalem," and he adds that this change "made the message of the song marginally more explicit."[62] Yet in terms of generic engagement and authorial genealogy the change complicates rather than clarifies, and even adds to the portentousness of the lyrics. Throughout the song, Dylan seems intent on emphasizing the repetitiveness of the chord changes and the ghost of a blues progression—like a guilty conscience behind the façade—"where many martyrs fell"—while he demolishes the linguistic and conceptual boundaries of his models. Like John Milton confronting his Greek and Roman predecessors, Dylan deliberately supersedes the Mosaic voice of Deuteronomy with the Christian voice of Saint Peter.

You Need the Blood on Your Door

Yet Dylan never abandons the Mosaic voice as a viable vatic alternative. Significantly, however, Moses represents not a unique charismatic figure but an ordinary person for Dylan, a kind of anti-vatic prophet. He makes this point emphatically in a rapping introduction to the song "God Uses Ordinary People"[63] on his gospel tour (December 5, 1979): "Mona Lisa's gonna come and sing a song called, 'God Uses Ordinary People.' You know he does use ordinary people. He doesn't use big superheroes or strange mystical people, he uses ordinary people. That's right. Moses was an ordinary person."[64]

He continues with a potted version of Yahweh commanding Moses to approach Pharoah, Moses's speech impediment ("Now Moses couldn't talk so well"), the demand to "let the people go," Pharoah's refusal—"He had a rebellious spirit"—and then a summary of the hail and "all kinds of plagues." Dylan assures the audience, "You can read about it yourself, if you want to." He then concludes with a vernacular tour de force: "Anyway, Pharoah still did not want to let those people go. He would not let them go because they were working for him. They were what you call slaves. Anyway, the last time, God told Moses, 'You go tell Pharoah that all the first-born sons in Egypt are going to die tonight.' God does that, you know, God will just use his judgement, however he sees fit. Anyway, Moses said to God, 'Well how will this destroying angel know the Hebrew children?' And he said, 'Well, if you go kill a lamb and you put the sign of the blood on every door.' And that's what Moses did. And the blood was on every door. And you know you need the blood on your door."[65] "Anyway . . . Anyway . . . Anyway . . ."; "Well . . . Well . . ."; "And . . . And . . . And . . .": using the rhetorical figure anaphora, working toward a crescendo through repetitions, is a proven way to build momentum in a rousing speech. For example, "*This* royal throne of kings, *this* scepter'd isle, / *This* earth of majesty, *this* seat of Mars, / *This* other Eden, demi-paradise, / *This* fortress built by Nature for herself" (*Richard II*, 2.1.40–43; emphasis added).

Dylan was no stranger to anaphora, as the openings to the stanzas in "The Times They Are A-Changin'" prove: "Come gather 'round people"; "Come writers and critics"; "Come senators, congressmen"; "Come mothers and fathers." And anaphora is a familiar rhetorical figure in evangelically inspired public speeches, including the most famous one of all:

> I have a dream that one day on the red hills of Georgia . . .
> I have a dream that one day even the state of Mississippi . . .
> I have a dream that my four little children will one day . . .
> I have a dream that one day down in Alabama . . .
> I have a dream that one day every valley shall be exalted, every hill
> and mountain shall be made low.[66]

Dylan was there to hear that speech and, along with Joan Baez, played a song for the massive crowd in front of the Washington Monument.[67] Yet it seems to matter less whether Dylan consciously imitated that preacherly style, constructing his intro raps to resonate with momentum-building repetitions like King's. What matters, or mattered, to his audience was that it was *Bob Dylan* delivering these heated religious admonitions between songs. Famed for his reticence during a set, not given to lengthy introductions, Dylan must have seemed freakishly off kilter by the sheer prolixity of his raps. Did he, after two decades of denial, start believing his own press, and, in a turnabout, accept the quasi-Messianic role thrust upon him by his sixties fans? His exhortations from the stage during the gospel tour show him in the awkward role of an explicit prophet of the End of Times.

Dylan has always come across more as a vates when shrugging off the mantle of the prophet. Weird warnings like "You need the blood on your door," unexpected and inappropriate at a rock concert, even on a tour for *Slow Train Coming,* seem, paradoxically, to undermine his vatic authority. He's too exercised, too unsubtle. His enigmatic posture cannot survive the evangelical hammer effect of the intros.

Dylan's performances, on albums and on stage, had always thrived on what might be called deniable listener-response messianism—deniable as messianism by Dylan but construed as a vatic-charismatic bond that he shared (or was complicit in). Charisma is not merely an individual attribute. It is, instead, a patently *inter*dependent group experience, and prophetic charisma is no exception. The interdependence of the vatic Dylan and his audience broke down, however, when Dylan divided himself from his charismatic group and started preaching. As good as some of his gospel-inspired songs are, the lyrics tend to exclude the audience. The speakers (or Dylan himself if we can make a connection with his stage raps) define themselves in terms of righteous isolation, as in "Ain't gonna go to hell for nobody" or "When you gonna wake up?" (which implies the speaker is already awake). This sense of isolation is not surprising in the context of Christian evangelism. Although Alexis de Tocqueville first used the word *individualism* when describing nineteenth-century America, the word "individual" in fact came into use in the context of Reformation Protestantism. The idea of the *individuation* of humans to the Christian God—that is, a spiritual condition undivided from the deity and unmediated by bishops (or the pope)—has deep ties to early evangelical movements, such as Quakers and Seventh Day Adventists. The Vineyard Discipleship, not to mention Hal Lindsey's prophecies, are inevitably linked to these early movements.

For Dylan, however, the Christian blend of individual righteousness and communal salvation was an awkward, even impossible, match for his delicately balanced charismatic authority. His sudden individuation and identification as a born-again Christian, not surprisingly, shredded the unspoken interdependence that characterized his unique bond with his audience. As many of his lyrics from the gospel period suggest, and as his sermonizing from stage highlights, Dylan and his audience no longer needed each other. By his own declaration, *they* needed *him*: that's what the End Times warnings were all about. For the first time in his career, he seemed to accept the role of Isaiah. There is an irony in this, of course: Dylan's audience had always wanted to see him as a crypto-Isaiah figure. But not many of the audience, and virtually none of the music critics at the time, were comfortable with Dylan's self-anointment.

In Albuquerque, on December 5, 1979, Dylan performed "When He Returns":

> Truth is an arrow and the gate is narrow that it passes through
> He unleashed His power at an unknown hour that no one knew

How long can I listen to the lies of prejudice?
How long can I stay drunk on fear out in the wilderness?

The delivery was especially plaintive and slow that night. The last line deliberately calls to mind Matthew 4: 1–11, the story of Jesus in the desert, and Dylan's skillful association as a kind of humanized Messiah ("drunk on fear") is reminiscent of some of his memorable vatic self-identifications: "She walked up to me so gracefully and took my crown of thorns / 'Come in,' she said, 'I'll give you shelter from the storm'" ("Shelter from the Storm," *Blood on the Tracks*). But it is difficult to reconcile the messianic reference with the speaker's frustrated questions "How long can I listen to the lies of prejudice?" in the light of Dylan's spoken intros during the tour. For one among numerous examples, before a performance of "Are You Ready" on April 28, 1980, Dylan proclaimed from stage, "Remember the girl earlier, who told you about Jesus? Remember that name now! Don't matter what your friends say, it won't be some eastern religion you never heard of before [that'll save you]. Okay? He who is free is free indeed."[68] Dylan's apparent intolerance is a bit jarring. Blatantly anti-Buddhist and anti-Hindu—and probably anti-Muslim too—Dylan's rap seems to manifest the worst side of reactionary evangelicalism. The song "Precious Angel" reinforces the same religious prejudice:

> You were telling him about Buddha, you were telling him about
> Mohammed
> in the same breath
> You never mentioned one time the Man who came and died a criminal's
> death
> (*Slow Train Coming*)

Andrew McCarron suggests that Dylan's "post-conversion zeal hardened into righteousness as the '79 tour made its way across the United States and Canada."[69] He quotes what he calls one of Dylan's "mini-sermons" from a show in San Francisco: "I think it's either one-third or two-thirds of the population that are homosexuals in San Francisco . . . I guess they're working up to a hundred percent. I don't know. But anyway, it's a growing place for homosexuals, and I read they have homosexual politics, and it's a political party. . . . All right, you know what I'm talking about? Anyway, I would just think, well, I guess the iniquity's not yet full. And I don't wanna be around when it is!"[70] Distasteful as Dylan's religious bigotry is, this homophobic screed seems even worse. Seth Rogovoy maintains that, in his preachy stage raps, Dylan "was very much parroting" Hal Lindsey's "obsessively eschatological brand of Christianity" in *The Late Great Planet Earth* and *Satan Is Alive and Well on Planet Earth*.[71]

Stephen Webb defends the religious exclusivity and even the intolerance (though not the homophobia) as necessary functions of monotheism and "the recognition and rejection of false gods."[72] From what proof we have, Dylan has always been a monotheist: otherwise, why write G-d in his manuscripts? But he never sang about monotheism until the gospel albums, and until then his deism (if that's the word for it), expressed vaguely in interviews, tended to refer to his inspiration for the songs—his furor poeticus, or divinely inspired poetic madness—and did not appear in his lyrics. The first verse of "Highway 61"—"God said to Abraham / Kill me a son"—hardly paints a pretty picture of a monotheistic G-d, while the young voice of "With God on Our Side" (*Highway 61 Revisited*) conveys a biting, mordant skepticism about the deity's power (or existence): "The words fill my head / And fall to the floor / If God's on our side / He'll stop the next war" (*The Times They Are A-Changin'*).

The born-again Dylan caused justified concern about what seemed an overtly prejudiced perspective: Heylin notes, for example, that Dylan's anti-Muslim lyrics "prompted howls of protest from liberal-minded reviewers."[73] He's referring to such songs as "Slow Train":

> All that foreign oil controlling American soil
> Look around you, it's just bound to make you embarrassed
> Sheiks walkin' around like kings
> Wearing fancy jewels and nose rings
> Deciding America's future from Amsterdam and to Paris
> And there's a slow, slow train comin' up around the bend
> (*Slow Train Coming*)

Williams calls this stanza "jingoistic."[74] Indeed, Dylan's evangelical fervor sometimes has an unexpected, and unwelcome, chauvinistic character, and his salvific imperative can seem distinctly American. Even without howls of protest from "liberal-minded reviewers," such decidedly anti-Muslim caricatures as "Sheiks walkin' around like kings / Wearing fancy jewels and nose rings" would be offensive—"disgraceful," according to Williams.[75] And, inevitably, those lines cast a shadow on such hallowed images as the Sad-Eyed Lady's "Arabian drums" (*Blonde on Blonde*) and the famed "Egyptian (or Egyptian-red) ring . . . that sparkles before she speaks" in "She Belongs to Me" (*Bringing It All Back Home*).

Webb argues that "Prophets cannot be tolerant," a truism perhaps, but not the sort of description Dylan's audience wanted to believe (except where the intolerance was directed against entrenched traditions, such as the binding of Isaac).[76] Dylan's vatic stance had garnered much of its momentum in the sixties from association with explicit calls for tolerance and restraint like those issued by the Civil Rights movement and heard in antinuclear protests. The voice of "The Times They Are A-Changin'" might be intolerant of the older generation's intractability, and the roused-up speaker of "When the Ship Comes In" might want to see his foes, "like Pharoah's tribe . . . drownded in the tide." But this is not the same kind of Christian exclusivity or evangelical intolerance as the songs of *Slow Train Coming*, and, less markedly, *Saved* and *Shot of Love*. It might be unfair to compare the exclusionary language of Dylan's Christian proselytizing and his overt attack on ecumenicalism to lyrics he wrote twenty years before. But the temptation is irresistible when remembering, for instance, the speaker in "Chimes of Freedom," who assures us that the bells are tolling "for every hung-up person in the whole wide universe," while the resigned lover of "One Too Many Mornings" observes, immemorably:

> ev'rything I'm a-sayin'
> You can say it just as good.
> You're right from your side
> I'm right from mine.

These sentiments reveal an equable tolerance no longer acceptable to the evangelical monotheist.

Most of Dylan's audience would never have heard his stage sermons, which were not collected and published until 1991.[77] And there are no introductions to the songs on Dylan's release of the gospel concert tour, *Trouble No More, the Bootleg Series, Vol. 13 1979–1981* (2017). Williams reports on seeing the first concerts on the tour, but while he charts the awkwardness of Dylan's first-night performances of the Christian songs, he doesn't mention the intros. The only preachiness he identifies refers to the songs themselves on *Slow Train Coming*, and he contrasts those earlier Christian songs to what he sees as the more devotional songs of *Saved* and *Shot of Love*. Williams, who calls himself "a stone Bob Dylan fan," admits that "it's a lot to swallow" that Dylan wrote and performed as a born-again Christian. Yet his impressions of the concerts (from one of the most experienced Dylan-watchers on the planet) suggest how difficult it is to dismiss the gospel albums as anomalous: "The fifth night (still the same songs, same order) was the equal of any concert Dylan has ever done. It was fabulous. The seventh was as good or better. Dylan sang, and his band played, with gut-wrenching conviction; and his new songs were unmistakably revealed as among the best he's ever written."[78] Williams frankly admires Dylan's born-again conviction (despite not sharing it at all) and his performative brilliance on the tour.

As in the performances on the tour, in his gospel-inspired songs on the albums, Dylan's creative dynamism prevails. He manages to transform the dogmatic elements of the evangelical message through a sophisticated imitative process. "Every Grain of Sand" is a case in point. The interweaving of New Testament language—"every sparrow falling"[79]—and the riveting, hymnlike performance reconceive rock music as a form of devotional lyricism. The song is a focused, heartfelt prayer, both as performed with piano and light instrumentation on the *Bootleg* version (*Bootleg Series, Vol. 1–3*) (with dog barking) and in the slow rock version on *Trouble No More* (disc 4, no. 15, labeled a rehearsal).

Credible or not to diehard followers, Dylan's sense of awe about "the Master's hand" ("Every Grain of Sand") and the End Times was redoubled by his repurposing of rock and blues in devotional, gospel, and spiritual modes. Gayle Wald has observed that critics often use the term *gospel* "as shorthand for the 'Christian' Dylan" and warns that "approaches that focus on the written text overlook the performativity of gospel."[80] But the release of *Trouble No More* is a reminder of how daring Dylan can be in refiguring lyrical and musical forms in performance as well as on the page. His sense of transformative imitation buoys the performances on the live album. We can hear a deep investment of heart in his voice, an earnestness unleavened by Dylan's usual sense of amusement—except for "Man Gave Names to All the Animals," perhaps. *Trouble No More* tracks the concerts chronologically, and as the tour progresses, the band gathers behind him joyously and with a rocking synchronization to the moods of his voice. Because the CDs do not contain the intros, there's no dogma framing the songs. Instead, we're treated to Dylan's sometimes plaintive, sometimes admonitory voice totally inhabiting the music. He is not singing alone, however: the songs swell and echo with the soaring voices of his all-Black, all-female backup group. Wald calls attention to these backup singers as emblematic of "Dylan's rich and complex relation to gospel as an African American musical practice" and insightfully underscores "the centrality of black women as creative agents who facilitate Dylan's engagements with gospel."[81] This performative interdependence fostered the most compelling aspects of the Christian-era music. According to Wald, "Dylan's backup singers not only supported him sonically in this era through their arresting vocal arrangements and skillful percussive accompaniment, but also pushed him to be a better—that is, more spirit-infused—singer."[82]

The power of Dylan's rock reimagining of gospel music and spirituals transforms conventional evangelism and reconnects it to the roots of rock and roll—bringing us all back home. The hybridization of African American gospel, blues format, rock and roll tempos, and New Testament language woven into the lyrics is further testimony to Dylan's imitative genius. Jeffrey Lamp argues that, at least in part, Dylan owed his repurposing of religious emotion to Lindsey's books, which provided "the newly converted Dylan with a specifically Christian source of imagery to direct [his] long-established appropriation of prophetic biblical language in his new gospel way."[83] It is impossible to measure the full extent of Lindsey's influence, however, especially when factoring in the importance of the backup vocalists as bearers of a performative fund of spiritual vocabulary. But Dylan was evidently conscientious about doing his Christian Bible school homework. As figure 7 shows, he even prepared an alphabetical concordance of New Testament verses corresponding to an idiosyncratic list of virtues, vices, emotions, and character traits. The autograph sheet of yellow

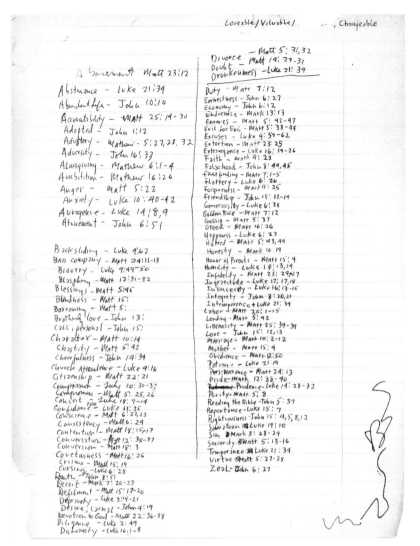

Figure 7. Concordance of Dylan's categories aligned with New Testament verses on yellow paper. Notes, writings, and unfinished lyrics from *Shot of Love*, ca. 1981. Courtesy of the Bob Dylan Archive® Collections, Tulsa, OK.

paper is collected in a box labeled "Notes, Writings, and Unfinished Lyrics from *Shot of Love*, ca. 1981."

Some of the correspondences in the list require a stretch, as in "Church attendence [*sic*]—Luke 9:16."[84] The verse in the KJV is "Then he took the five loaves and the two fishes, and looking up to heaven, he blessed them, and brake, and gave to the disciples to set before the multitude." It isn't clear how this celebrated tale of miracles conveys the idea of "church attendance," or whether

Dylan—possibly with the help of the Vineyard Discipleship—took Luke 9:16 more as inspiration to believe. But in his entry for "Devotion to God—Matt 22:36–38" the correspondence is crystal clear.[85] The cited verses include the dialogue, "Master, which *is* the great commandment in the law? Jesus said unto him, Thou shalt love the Lord thy God with all thy heart, and with all thy soul, and with all thy mind." Unlike the command to obey issued by the ruthless cartoon-image Yahweh of Dylan's "Highway 61," this "Lord thy God" requires instead a commitment of love (Christian caritas).

The entry for Perseverance is Matthew 24:13: "But he that shall endure unto the end, the same shall be saved." This verse anticipates the verses later in the same chapter that refer to the End of Days: "But of that day and that hour knoweth no *man*, no, not the angels of heaven, but my Father only. But as the days of Noah *were*, so shall also the coming of the Son of man be. For as in the days that were before the flood they were eating and drinking, marrying and giving in marriage, until the day that Noah entered into the ark" (Matt. 24: 36–39). In "Gonna Change My Way of Thinking," from *Slow Train Coming*, Dylan repurposes these verses:

> Jesus said, "Be ready
> For you know not the hour in which I come"
> Jesus said, "Be ready
> For you know not the hour in which I come"
> He said, "He who is not for Me is against Me"
> Just so you know where He's coming from
> ("Gonna Change My Way of Thinking")[86]

This is an excellent example of Dylan's compositional method. The song translates the verses into a lyrical format whose repetitive phrasing invokes the blues, transforming plaintiveness or victimhood into a not-so-veiled warning. The direct quotation from Matthew 12:30, words spoken by Jesus—"He that is not with me is against me"—challenges and polarizes Dylan's listeners. But Dylan complicates the challenge by closing the stanza with a summary idiom—"Just so you know where He's coming from." The idiomatic nature of the phrase makes it ambiguous, and because the ambiguity applies to Jesus, there is a merging of the different meanings. To say, "you know where He's coming from" can mean, idiomatically, "to know what he means," and literally "to know the place from which he started out." The brilliance of this ambiguity indicates how Dylan transforms his models of imitation: the phrase merges place and meaning because, in Jesus, heaven (place) and salvation (meaning) are one concept. Moreover, the vernacular (or profane) dissolves into the divine, and the worldly is superseded by the otherworldly: the stanza's last line embodies Dylan's lyrical (and musical) reimagining of eschatological awe.

In *Paradise Lost*, ambiguity comes into the world after the fall of Adam and Eve. In Dylan's song, ambiguity disappears at "the hour in which I come." This kind of lyrical brilliance suffuses the gospel albums. In hindsight it might be easy to dismiss the songs because Dylan's conversion didn't stick, regardless of how sincere he sounds on *Trouble No More*. If the born-again state was transient, the reasoning seems to be, then the emotion behind the songs and performances must have been superficial, even insincere. Webb asks, "Was it luck, good business sense, or Providence that brought Dylan to the gospel just as gospel music was beginning to rock?"[87] But there is little doubt about the sincerity of Dylan's conversion, which, though a brief episode, is well-attested. The live double album, more so perhaps than the studio albums from 1979–81, demonstrates Dylan's commitment.

Slow Train Coming, Saved, and *Shot of Love* are less a turn or about-face, or creative nadir, than a vatic reimagining. Despite the surprise Christian Evangelism, there is a continuity, not of ideology, but of method in these albums. In his music and lyrics, Dylan elevates the weak copycatting of his stage intros. His imitations of blues and gospel combine appropriation with transformation and repurposing. In his best religious songs, he improves the forms he imitates. For example, his religious lyrics sometimes use self-imitation, a transformative repurposing of one of his own most effective lyrical practices.

It is patently "Dylanesque" to build a song's mood on the second-person pronoun: "When *you're* lost in Juarez . . . when negativity don't pull *you* through" ("Just Like Tom Thumb's Blues"). Kevin Dettmar observes that "texts that use second-person address always hail us, always seem to be speaking to us."[88] Many of Dylan's second-person songs not only speak to us but confront us sharply, as in "Positively 4th Street" and "Like a Rolling Stone." Think of the raw contempt leveled at the anonymous second-person addressees: "*You've* got a lot of nerve"; "I wish that for just one time *you* could stand inside my shoes, / *You'd* see what a drag it is to see *you*" ("Positively 4th Street"); or, more spectacularly,

> *You* used to laugh about
> Everybody that was hangin' out
> Now *you* don't talk so loud
> Now *you* don't seem so proud
> About having to be scrounging for *your* next meal.
> ("Like a Rolling Stone"; my emphasis)

Tracing Dylan's surgical use of "you" from scornful rejection to urgent prophecy offers an unexpected epiphany of interpretation. What once was derision Dylan transforms in the gospel songs to salvific admonition. Note the use of the second person "you" in lines like "You gotta serve somebody." Strange as such servility might sound coming from the rebel Dylan, this preacherly use of the second person has continuity with Dylan's earlier writing. Therefore, rather than reject the gospel period as an aberration, it might make more sense to follow the line backward from the urgent, apocalyptic "you" of the gospel albums to that same "you" in the mouth of the snarling hipster who mercilessly cuts through the pretenses of the Fourth Street hypocrite and reduces the proud "doll" to "scrounging" humiliation.

Dylan was evidently conscious of making a connection to his earlier work. In the album version of "When He Returns" (*Slow Train Coming*) and even more so in the tour's live performances of the song, he seemed to reach for a link and simultaneously signal a transformation. For instance, in Albuquerque, on December 5, 1979 (*Trouble No More*, Disc 1, no. 5), he sang:

> How long can you falsify and deny what is real?
> How long can you hate yourself for the weakness you *conceee-aal*?
> Of every earthly plan that be known to man, He is unconcerned
> He's got plans of His own to set up His throne
> When He returns[89]

His extraordinary prolonging of the word "conceal" would make any Dylan enthusiast sit up and take notice—both in listening to the album and in hearing the live version. Dylan holds the notes exactly as his does with the same word in "Like a Rolling Stone" on the *Highway 61* album: "You're invisible now, you got no secrets to *conceee-aal*" (my emphasis).

So, inevitably, we must ask, "When *who* returns?"—because it seems that with this remarkable self-imitation, Bob Dylan, vates, returns to musical and lyrical authority.

Forty years after the gospel tour, Dylan released *Rough and Rowdy Ways*, which includes a song called "False Prophet." The title could be a self-indictment or an indictment of critics and listeners who have created a false prophet from his songs. It could be a New Testament reference to the "false prophet," who, along with the second beast, is cast alive "into a lake of fire burning with brimstone" in Revelation (19:20 and 20:10). Or it could be Hal Lindsey himself, whose prophecies in *The Late Great Planet Earth*, a book Dylan apparently embraced in his born-again period, turned out to be misguided and false. But ultimately the song turns back on the speaker and contains key elements of self-imitation:

> I ain't no false prophet - I just know what I know
> I go where only the lonely can go
>
> I'm first among equals - second to none
> I'm last of the best - you can bury the rest
> ("False Prophet")

The phrase "only the lonely" resonates. It is the title of a Frank Sinatra "concept" album, his favorite among all his recordings, and of a song written by Sammy Cahn and Jimmy Van Heusen. Although Dylan did not record "Only the Lonely" on *Shadows in the Night* (2015), the reference in "False Prophet" is unmistakable. "Only the lonely" also recalls Dylan at his most contemptuous, most dismissive: "You've gone to the finest school all right, Miss Lonely / But you know you only used to get juiced in it" ("Like a Rolling Stone"). *Miss Lonely* gets no sympathy from the street-smart speaker. The next two lines in "False Prophet" carry a modicum of that same attitude. "First among equals" translates the phrase primus inter pares, a motto once used (inaccurately in terms of equality) by Roman emperors—that is, the "Early Roman Kings" Dylan sings about on *Tempest*. But, in the context of false or true prophets, "first among equals" seems to refer to a defiant survivor, "the last of the best," an enduring vatic authority.

The Kind of Language He Used

Dylan's prophetic strain is demonstrably aesthetic in nature: the craft (*ars*)— rather than divine intervention—of biblical authority underlies his writing. *Pace* the ghost (who wrote "Rolling Stone" and disappeared), Dylan's vatic art is an art of imitation. He has at times made amply clear his recognition of this linguistic fact, as in the stunning final verse of "Red River Shore" (1997 [unreleased], *Tell Tale Signs: The Bootleg Series, Vol. 8*):

> Now, I heard of a guy who lived a long time ago
> A man full of sorrow and strife
> That if someone around him died and was dead
> He knew how to bring 'em on back to life
> Well, I don't know what kind of language he used
> Or if they do that kinda thing anymore
> Sometimes I think nobody ever saw me here at all
> 'Cept the girl from the Red River Shore.

The irony of the stanza is that the speaker, in identifying language as the means of bringing the dead back to life, plumbs *and* creates his own vatic language. The speaker's ambition doesn't run to reviving modern-day Lazaruses, however, but, we infer, simply to bringing himself back to the land of the visible. Regardless of the magical-nostalgic-pastoral-romantic idealization of "the girl from the Red River Shore," the speaker's invocation of the "man full of sorrow and strife" aligns the song's lyric with the portentous language of resurrection. If that isn't a vatic speech act, nothing is.

At the heart of that speech act is imitatio. The lyrics imitate and transform the original language of "Lazarushian" resurrection into rhyme, meter, metaphor, and imagery—none of which, vatic authority notwithstanding, can repair invisibility and longing. That really *would be* divine language (not even Virgil's Sibyl succeeds in doing that). But Dylan's art sidesteps the question of divinity by responding to the authority of supposedly divine language—he can't duplicate the original divine speech act, but he can invoke it in vatic imagery. He knows two things: the divine act is now probably obsolete—"I don't know . . . if they do that kinda thing anymore"—and linguistic imitation connects the singer to the biblical authority of the (legendary) past.

From his earliest compositions, Dylan challenged, absorbed, and sometimes superseded the diction of the Bible. It's a commonplace that weighty biblical diction was built into the folk, blues, and gospel traditions, which were themselves "immersed in the Apocalypse" as much as any other aspect of secular American culture. In consequence, there is an element of secondary imitation in Dylan's absorption of the biblical speech of the traditional canon. But there's more to it than the passive inculcation of a superseded vernacular. Dylan's imitation, digestion, and transformative reproduction of these influences, combined with his own readings—or strong *misreadings*—of biblical language, provide the weave and weft of his vatic technique.

Shipwrecks Everywhere

Perhaps Dylan consciously struggled to find his vatic voice after sacrificing his authority to the kind of didacticism and dogma he had always eschewed. But, as seen with "Blind Willie McTell" and songs such as "Dark Eyes," Dylan's vatic gifts underwent a sea change in the eighties. He transformed himself as a vates and his songs in hindsight constitute a transitional stage in the development of Dylan's vatic authority. In effect, his models of imitation changed and, whether consciously or instinctually, he moved away from dense, portentously laden lyric verse toward dramatic monologue.

This development ranks among Dylan's most astounding vatic innovations. Nothing could ever surpass the brilliance of "Hard Rain" for innovative force and pure poetic transfiguration. A musical world changed with that one vatic song. But "Hard Rain" aside, Dylan's reinvention of his vatic authority through dramatic monologue is a supreme poetic achievement. Not only does he switch his models of imitation, but he also daringly reconfigures his lyrics and his performance in accordance with two different genres. No other contemporary songwriter or performer could have done this.

Two songs demonstrate this transfiguration: "Highlands" (1997), an apprentice attempt, and the incomparably accomplished "Tempest" (2012). Both, in different ways, recast, or forge anew, the vatic voice. Significantly, at the heart of Dylan's innovative recasting of his vatic voice is the practice of imitatio. By turning to unexpected models of imitation, Dylan's performance in these songs categorically rejects any pretense of recreating his earlier lyrical authority.

The songs succeed precisely because he interweaves self-quotation and self-imitation, while, at the same time, trusting his imitation of new generic models. He seems to find his new voice by shedding all the old models and by mixing narrative and vernacular apocalypticism in an utterly new way. Speaking of "I and I," from *Infidels* (in a comparison to "Shooting Star"), Gibbens describes "a balance—or collision, perhaps—of the quotidian and the apocalyptic."[90] A similar collision—or balanced collision—occurs in "Highlands" and then, with colossal skill, in "Tempest." Dylan not only rewrites his American precursors in the Whitman/Guthrie/Ginsberg line but also performs a sort of literary dance first, and less successfully, with a kind of Burns/Browning hybrid, and then, brilliantly, with Shakespeare. He converts the greatest dramatic poet in history to his narrative aims and, in doing that, revolutionizes narrative as definitively as he did in "Tangled Up in Blue" by entrenching a new vatic signature.

"Tempest" displays Dylan's new vatic technique at its most complex, combining recognizable self-reference with a sleek cross-pollination of Shakespeare and film. Regarding the latter, Thomas calls attention to the difference between the printed lyrics and the album: whereas Jim Dandy gives up his seat to the "little crippled child" in the printed version, "on the album it was Jim Backus, the actor who played Thurston Howell III on the 1960s TV series of a different shipwreck story, *Gilligan's Island*, another lost land."[91] This allusion is probably there, but perhaps more as a shocking contrast than a similarity: *The Minnow*, in name alone, is the opposite of the *Titanic*, and, although Jim Backus is a watery victim, everyone on that pleasure boat survives. But Jim Backus might mean more to Dylan's generation than his late-career role as Thurston Howell III. Not only was he the voice of Mr. Magoo, but Jim Backus played James Dean's ineffectual, pathetic father in *Rebel without a Cause*, a film that purportedly made a strong impression on young Bobby Zimmerman (and one which, like *The Savage Innocents*, was directed by Nicholas Ray).

This cinematic multiplication, further complicated by the Cameron *Titanic* and Leonardo di Caprio, proves how skillfully Dylan manages associative contiguities in "Tempest." The lyric captures the paradox of a vatic retelling of a past event: the unidentified speaker sings of the *Titanic* "Sailing into tomorrow / To a golden age foretold." The layers of time strangle up the mind here—a century before the 2012 release of *Tempest*, on April 14, 1912, a ship sailed into a (long past) tomorrow which had been foretold to be a golden age. There are echoes of Ovid's or Homer's Golden Age, certainly, with the ominous feeling that the speaker is retelling a foretelling from the perspective of a fallen Iron Age.[92]

The song reflects Dylan's method of imitation par excellence. While he might incorporate traditional music as his acknowledged imitative model—in this case the Carter Family's "The Titanic"—his transformation of the source produces an allusive weave that supersedes it in every way. As in the Carter Family song, the "pale moon" narrates the story of disaster in Dylan's "Tempest," or rather of multiple disasters, mixing the sinking of the *Titanic* into an allusive Charybdis of historical events and personal tragedies. There are slant allusions, such as the cryptic reference to Wellington: is this the same Duke (whose "valiant heart was beating") that triumphed over Napoleon at—yes—*Water*loo? The sources for "Tempest" reveal how Dylan revises his predecessors by complicating the linear narrative with a scrambled temporal perspective. Further, he substitutes portent and prophecy for grief and mournful lament. Grief is backward-looking. Dylan's disembodied speaker in "Tempest" gazes Jeremiah-like into the future.

The Carter Family's "The Titanic" (1952/56) opens with this stanza:

> The pale moon rose in its glory
> She's drifting from golden west
> She told a sad, sad story
> Six hundred had gone to rest

Dylan begins with an echo of those lines:

> The pale moon rose in its glory
> Out on the western town
> She told a sad, sad story
> Of the great ship that went down

The Carters sing of six hundred casualties, one thousand fewer than the actual figure, which is correctly given in the fourth to last stanza of Dylan's song. Dylan skips over the Carters' error. But his opening stanza duplicates the original with the near-precision of a jazz musician playing a standard: the opening bars stay close to the original so that listeners recognize the tune. The variations begin later, usually in the second playthrough. In "Tempest," they begin in the fourth line, which hints at Woody Guthrie's *Titanic* song, "When That Great Ship Went Down":

> It was sad when that great ship went down
> It was sad when that great ship went down
> Cold ocean floor will now be your home
> It was sad when that great ship went down . . .
> ("When That Great Ship Went Down")

Dylan echoes other *Titanic* songs in "Tempest," but to open with a reference to Woody sets up a genealogical terminus a quo. If the Carter Family song situates the lyrics and melody in a traditional setting, the presence of Woody's song complicates the map with the introduction of an American vatic original.

Still, other songs use that same phrase, and Dylan's imitations of those lyrics seem ludic, or maybe impish imitation. Like many contemporary chroniclers of the *Titanic* disaster, Dylan's lyric *seems* to ascribe the disaster to divine judgment. But this too he "nixed" in his Gilmore interview:

> Gilmore. In some "Titanic" songs, there were those who saw the event as a judgment on modern times, on mankind for assuming that it could be unsinkable. Is there some of that in your song?
> Dylan. No, no, I try to stay away from all that stuff. I don't imply any of it. I'm not interested in it. I'm just interested in showing you what happened, on the level that it happened on. That's all. The meaning of it is beyond me.

Yet, here Dylan strikes me as disingenuous. Although he successfully sublimates his vatic howl and resists either the doomsaying or didactic preaching of his evangelical songs, he certainly directs the "meaning" of his *Titanic* ballad. The song is neither an anthem nor a lament per se. But Dylan allows the nameless, time-bending narrator to recount the events episodically, and with arbitrary selection.[93] It may be that, for Dylan, the ship does not go down as the result of a Yahwistic judgment—"I don't imply any of it. I'm not interested in it"—even if his typescript of "Tempest" includes the Orthodox Jewish orthography of "G-d" (as seen in his notepaper from the Steigenberger Hotel, Linz).[94] Nevertheless, despite Dylan's graphic deference to the tetragrammaton and "the name that cannot be spoken," the song "Tempest" indicates a much more ecumenical attitude toward divine retribution.

Woody's line, "When the great ship went down," seems to avoid divine judgment, which is effaced or attenuated in his simplified, repetitive lyric. But there is the likelihood that Woody knew other *Titanic* songs and borrowed his line from them. And Dylan might have known earlier versions of *Titanic* songs too, songs in which the disaster appears as divine retribution. Pink Anderson, for instance, recorded one of the contemporary ballads ("The Titanic," *Ballad and Folksinger*, vol. 3, 1963):

> When Captain Workfield was a-building, he said what he would do
> He would build a ship, water couldn't break through
> God with power in his hand showed the world it could not stand
> Wasn't it sad when the great ship went down
>
> Wasn't it sad when the great ship went down?
> Wasn't it sad when the great ship went down?
> Husbands and their wives, children lost their life
> Wasn't it sad when the great ship went down?
>
> When old Paul was out a-sailin,' had mens all around
> God spoke and told him, not a one should be drowned

> "If you trust me and obey, I will save yo all the way"
> Wasn't it sad when the great ship went down?

Anderson's cover invokes the familiar scene of Peter and Jesus on the Sea of Galilee—a scene captured inimitably in "Hard Rain," where the speaker identifies with the sinking Peter. The old ballad seems to do something similar, heightening the desperate disparity between the two sailings and strongly suggesting that the *Titanic* carried a shipload of "ye of little faith"—which led inexorably to a mass sinking. In any case, the biblical threat resonates throughout all the versions of the "night that great ship went down."

The complexity of Dylan's references and transmutations defines precisely the kind of imitation he practices. What is different and more impressive about "Tempest" is that Dylan seems to be challenging the associative contiguities. Almost more than any other song, "Tempest" reveals the "conscious artist" Dylan claims to have become forty years earlier. Until *Rough and Rowdy Ways*, the range and authority of "Tempest"'s allusive structure has few, if any, peers in Dylan's oeuvre.

For example, the watchman of the Carter Family version leads Dylan in several directions:

> The watchman was a dreaming
> Yes dreaming a sad, sad dream
> He dreamed the Titanic was sinking
> Out on the deep blue sea

Instead of one stanza from the watchman's dream state, Dylan inserts four stanzas at different points in the song. They are not bridges in the musical sense: the key and rhythmic structure (as well as Dylan's delivery) remain the same as other verses. Nevertheless, these watchman stanzas seem to be outside the narrative structure. The watchman stanzas are at once arbitrary and prophetic: they defy time, as does Dylan's vatic retelling of a time already foretold. The watchman himself is both there and not-there, a victim and an observer. But above all he is the prophet of the disaster. Dylan begins his watchman stanzas with a direct imitation. Then the variations begin:

> The watchman he lay dreaming
> As the ballroom dancers twirled
> He dreamed the Titanic was sinking
> Into the underworld

Between the two Carter Family lines, Dylan inserts rhyming lines that bookend the contrast between the gaiety on board *before* the disaster and the permanent doom to follow. The word "underworld" might conjure Woody Guthrie's "The Sinking of the Reuben James" and "her grave on the bottom of the sea" or "that dark watery grave." Possibly, too, Dylan could have recalled "House Carpenter," a traditional song he recorded in the early sixties (*Bootleg Series, Vol. 1–3*):

> Oh what are those hills yonder, my love
> They look as dark as night
> Those are the hills of hell-fire my love
> Where you and I will unite
>
> Oh twice around went the gallant ship
> I'm sure it was not three
> When the ship all of a sudden, it sprung a leak
> And it drifted to the bottom of the sea

The "hills of hell-fire" seem to be at the bottom of the sea, in the underworld, and they are burning presumably with the same divine perversion of the laws of physics that keeps the fire burning without light in Milton's Hell.

In any case, the word "underworld" also brings the lyric back to the classics: unlike the Christian Hell, the Greco-Roman Hades is known as the underworld, a place to which all epic heroes venture on their quest. Aeneas receives the Golden Bough from the Sibyl as a viaticum on his descent into Hades. Further— and this is a wonderful bonus—Dylan's rhyme of "twirled" and "-world" reminds us that the world twirls on its axis. But the association of a twirling world with the ballroom dancers twirling in innocent ignorance of the disaster about to befall them underscores the vatic authority of the voice telling the tale. Hidden in the rhyme is the unknown fate of all on board. And the twirling might recall the full lyric of "House Carpenter" (not the Dylan version):

> One time around spun our gallant ship
> Two times around spun she
> Three times around spun our gallant ship
> And sank to the bottom of the sea

The twirling, then, has a link to Dylan's traditional model, but has been transformed *poetically*, through the rhyme, into a Sibylline warning.

Anne Margaret Daniel has suggested that the song's (irregular) refrain, "The watchman lay dreamin'," might recall the "watchman with his flashlight" from "Visions of Johanna." Alluding to his own song might allow Dylan to link two distinct kinds of visionary experience, from two different epochs of his art and two different "dream" landscapes. Given the overt otherworldly heft of the shipwreck in Dylan's lyric, a more resonant link might be back to the multiple watchmen of the Nevi'im. And reference to Isaiah and Jeremiah invokes "All Along the Watchtower" and the ominous howl of that wildcat in the last line, connecting Isaiah's prophetic warning with the lunar narrative in "Tempest," the "sad, sad story" that results in the incomprehensible, but divinely ordained, destruction of the vessel.

The twinned album and song titles seem to be bold references to Shakespeare's late play. Even if the album *Tempest* weren't meant to mirror the title *The Tempest*, a cursory analysis of the title song "Tempest" reveals unmistakable parallels.[95] Not only is a shipwreck the central theme (as an apparent shipwreck starts the action in Shakespeare), but allusions to a wizard recall Prospero and make it impossible not to associate the song with the play and the songwriter with the playwright.

In terms of imitation, it may be that Dylan identifies not with Shakespeare but with Ariel. Ariel is a male figure, not originally a nymph, commanded by Prospero to change shape (and mask his sex):

> Go make thyself like a nymph o' the sea: be subject
> To no sight but thine and mine, invisible
> To every eyeball else. Go take this shape
> And hither come in't: go, hence with diligence![96]

It was all a disguise. Ariel disguises himself as a sea nymph, remaining invisible to everyone but Prospero and himself. The aptness of this behavior is obvious in connection with *Tempest*. Not only would invisibility and shapeshifting seem to fit the mercurial Dylan (of myriad interviews), but masquerade is itself a thematic of the various narrations on *Tempest*. Like the diligent Ariel, the "*The*" is invisible from Dylan's album title.

This album and particularly the song "Tempest" represent Dylan's bid for freedom from the models to which he has been "enslaved"—and from the masquerade into which he has been forced. "Tempest" is an exercise in separation: Dylan doesn't so much drown his book (which he has done so many times before) as fly free of his precursors so that he can return a vatic vitality to his voice.

Tempest co-opts song to drama and drama to song. But its main objective, in terms of a poetic signature, is to distinguish Dylan from Shakespeare. Shakespeare may be a wizard and a poet without peer. But, unlike Shakespeare who was not a Bard in the prophetic sense, Dylan is consummately a vatic singer. Dylan sings: "Petals fell from flowers / Till all of them were gone / In the long and dreadful hours / The wizard's curse played on." This last line contains a revealing metaphor: curses might remain in force until they are lifted or resolved (such as the curse on the House of Atreus). But music "plays on." The wizard's curse that plays on in "Tempest" is the recurring narrative of the golden future foretold. It is, in effect, Dylan's reinvented, "repurposed," imitation.

Two performance arts—and, by implication, two aging performance artists—are set together in interdisciplinary confrontation. Whether meant as challenge or homage, Dylan's title reveals a concerted effort to be *not-Shakespeare*. In Shakespeare's romance, Prospero's magic formula—activated by the imprisoned Ariel—produces a raging tempest that blows a ship off course and causes another of the ubiquitous early modern shipwrecks: there were shipwrecks everywhere.[97] As a result of Ariel's storm, the hapless survivors land on Prospero's unnamed island and undergo a series of humiliations and diminishing realizations. Even Miranda's astonishment at seeing a young man is a parody of revelation: the quotidian mistaken for the divine.

To this difference might be added the sometimes-overlooked fact that there is no shipwreck in Shakespeare's play. Muir points out that there's no tempest in "Tempest," yet we should probably see the parallel absence in *The Tempest*. Rather than a storm that wrecks the King's ship, there is only Ariel's tempestuous threat of shipwreck. In fact, the ship is safely hidden away and the whole "shipwreck" is a hoax or illusion:

> Prospero.   Hast thou, spirit,
> Performed to point the tempest that I bade thee?
> Ariel.   To every article.
> I boarded the King's ship. Now on the beak,
> Now in the waist, the deck in every cabin,
> I flamed amazement. Sometime I'd divide
> And burn in many places; on the topmast,
> The yards, and bowsprit would I flame distinctly,
> Then meet and join. Jove's lightning, the precursors
> O'th' dreadful thunderclaps, more momentary
> And sight-outrunning were not. The fire and cracks
> Of sulfurous roaring the most mighty Neptune
> Seem to besiege and make his bold waves tremble,
> Yea, his dread trident shake.[98]

But note that this is all seeming and appearance (Ariel created the illusion that "Neptune / Seem to besiege"). In truth, as Prospero is quick to establish, there is no shipwreck, even though the noble entourage jumped ship thinking there would be a disaster:

> Prospero. Of the King's ship,
> The mariners, say how thou hast disposed,
> And all the rest o' the fleet.
> Ariel.   Safely in harbor
> Is the King's ship . . .

The mariners all under hatches stowed . . .
And for the rest o'th' fleet,
Which I dispersed, they all have met again
And are upon the Mediterranean float
Bound sadly home for Naples,
Supposing that they saw the King's ship wrecked
And his great person perish.[99]

The fleet "supposed" they witnessed a shipwreck and returned home, sadly believing the King was dead. Meanwhile, the ship itself is safely hidden in a harbor with all hands stowed "under hatches." The rest of the action, therefore, is predicated on the illusion of a shipwreck brought about not by Neptune, Jove, or any other divinity but by Prospero's commands and Ariel's magic. And, while Prospero is undeniably a wizard, he doesn't issue a curse in *The Tempest*.[100]

In contrast, in Dylan's title song "Tempest," divinity suffuses the action. The "wizard's curse" might play on, but superseding that curse are the book of Revelation and the acknowledgment that "there is no understanding / On the judgment of God's hand." This might remind us that, according to Blind Willie Johnson's *Titanic* song, "God Moves on the Water" (recorded 1929): "God moves, moves ah know ah / An' the people had to run and pray." According to the Carter version, news of the deity's movement and the ship's destruction made it all the way across the water:

The sad news reached the city
The Titanic had gone down
There's many poor widows and orphans
A walking all over the town

But in Dylan's "Tempest" that news never arrives:

They waited at the landing
And they tried to understand
But there is no understanding
Of the judgment of God's hand

The open-endedness, the implacable mystery of the divine act, creates a gap of faith and dread distinct from the Carter Family news report. The passage itself echoes Proverbs 12:30, "There is no wisdom nor understanding nor counsel against the LORD." But the message is lyrical, not biblical: the repeated rhymes on "a-n-d" in *landing, understand, understanding*, and *hand* enforce the continuity of divine disaster, and the conjunction "and" at the center of the rhyme suggests interconnectedness of earthly events. Even in this micronarrative, there is a simultaneous conjoining of those waiting on the landing and those going down with the ship. The two groups, though conjoined in time, are ignorant of each other—just as, presumably, human beings can provide "no wisdom nor understanding nor counsel against the Lord" and "the Lord's" plan.

And Dylan's *Titanic* shipwreck, as opposed to Shakespeare's nonexistent shipwreck, has vatic authority. Referring to Hesiod's Muses who know both truth and untruth, but when they choose "know . . . how to sing the truth," Thomas concludes that "this is the culmination of [Dylan's] songwriting."[101] The watery disaster of Dylan's song, unlike Shakespeare's play, isn't caused by a storm at sea, nor is it the result merely of internecine domestic betrayal and court intrigue (which would be bad enough). Dylan sets his sights, as so often, on a much broader horizon, speaking with self-conscious vatic authority. The internecine havoc of "Tempest"—"Brother rose up against brother / In every circumstance / They fought and slaughtered each other / In a deadly dance"—interpolates Cain and Abel and the Civil War: biblical origins, slavery, Emancipation, and the permanent American rift.[102] Thomas speaks of how "Dylan took the melody" from the Carter song and "repurposed" the words to construe "the folk song components of his fictional epic."[103] And, while he doesn't use the word imitation, the compositional method he describes aptly recalls the digestive metaphor: "Dylan's song is the richer for our hearing the old song in his new song. But the new song is something else, something that through Dylan's genius as a songwriter, singer, verbal painter, has transcended the folk tradition in which it is rooted; it has become both epic and cinematic, a wholly new genre."[104] Epic, cinematic, and *vatic*: that's the new genre we hear. This is the meaning of the missing "The" in both titles and of Dylan's posture of "not-Shakespeare." He can only reforge his vatic credentials in "Tempest" by reinventing, or perfecting, the narrative experiment he began, back in 1997, in "Highlands."

AFTERWORD
Every Conceivable Point of View

I wish I didn't know now what I didn't know then.
—Bob Seger, "Against the Wind"

In a key scene from *Renaldo and Clara* (1978), Allen Ginsberg, who plays the role of the Father in the film and was a member of the 1975 tour known as the Rolling Thunder Revue, shows Renaldo (played by Dylan) at Jack Kerouac's grave. The camera fixes on the two men sitting cross-legged facing the headstone as Ginsberg intones the final line from John Keats's epitaph, "Here lies one whose fame was writ in water." Jack Kroll, commenting on this scene in his *Newsweek* review of the film, pointed out that Ginsberg garbles the Keats quotation, a stumble that he felt was symbolic of the entire project: "The right word is 'name,' not 'fame,' but the slip is significant. Fame is indeed the spur in this ego-trip disguised as deep-dish art."[1] But is the slip truly a slip? Ginsberg's misquotation was probably a deliberate, unscripted variation. There is no reaction from Renaldo/Dylan, but Ginsberg's impromptu revision of Keats strikes to the heart of the carnivalesque atmosphere of imitation that pervades *Renaldo and Clara*. And, as this small scene shows, imitation begets transformation. The word "fame" refers simultaneously to Kerouac and Dylan, giving Ginsberg a histrionically appropriate opportunity to pass on the torch from one colossally famous road poet to another, from Kerouac's *On the Road* to Dylan/Renaldo on the road. (How many roads, indeed?) Ginsberg's revisionary epitaph can serve as an epigraph for the Rolling Thunder Revue or, rather, its aestheticized representation in *Renaldo and Clara*.

The first song performed in *Renaldo and Clara*, struck like the film's I chord, is "When I Paint My Masterpiece." Dave Marsh reflected in *Rolling Stone* that "'When I Paint My Masterpiece' is one of the best songs Bob Dylan has written in the Seventies" and adds, "*Renaldo and Clara*, Dylan's first attempt at directing a feature length film, opens with Dylan and Bob Neuwirth singing the song as well as it has been sung, which is appropriate. Those verses about an artist who misunderstands the nature of art are the perfect metaphor for the film's almost total failure."[2] But "When I Paint My Masterpiece" isn't about art at all. Painting is more of an analogy than a prophecy. The song is, in Tim Riley's description, a "hilarious parable about the disorienting comedy of rock touring."[3] The parallel of painting and rock touring implies both a syncretic relationship between the two and a ludic sort of interdependence—something like Ginsberg's linking of the two kinds of road poets. Pairing a rock tour and a painting, whether in the 1968 *Basement Tapes* version or in the 1971 production of the song by Leon Russell, would seem like an outrageous concept, especially given the lyrics' general air of wry contempt and dismissal, not to mention Dylan's long gaps between public appearances. But today, in retrospect, in view of Dylan's so-called Never Ending Tour (which is not Dylan's choice of name) and after twenty years on the road and scores of gigs a year, rock touring as a painted masterpiece makes much more sense. And, as the argument of this book has shown, this ongoing tour finds Dylan engaged in a form of self-imitation, or maybe vatic self-fulfillment, as he acts out the masterpiece he anticipated decades ago.

But does Dylan even believe in masterpieces? Or would a masterpiece be what Robert Kelly, quoted in the introduction of this book, called an "unthinged" thing inside a museum? Are masterpieces too stable, staid, detached—fodder for the "self-appointed professor's tongue" of "My Back Pages" (1964)—to serve as metaphor for the work of someone so mercurial, so fluid as Bob Dylan?

Consider, for a moment, fellow musician and Rolling Thunder participant David Blue's appearance in *Renaldo and Clara*. In a key scene from Dylan's film, we see him standing at a pinball machine, working the flippers while providing an endearingly disjointed memoir of the early Greenwich Village days when he met Dylan and other Gaslight denizens, as if to spin out what Frank Kermode (via Wallace Stevens) called "the myth before the myth began."[4] Blue's reminiscences are intercut with scenes where the central figure of the plot, Renaldo aka Dylan, appears onstage singing Dylan songs. Blue's early version of Dylan overlaps and merges with Renaldo, as if the ephebe and the master stepped through the looking glass together. The imitative model and the imitation seem to coexist, made indistinguishable from each other by the film's cinéma verité style.

Behind this fragmented narrative, Dylan directs a consummate experiment in the poetics of imitation. *Renaldo and Clara* constantly interrogates Dylan's authority, raising questions about his vatic status, thus ultimately—as I have argued in this book—confirming it. Autobiographical realities become tangled up in fictive relationships. Dylan's ex-wife Sara plays Clara, while his ex-lover Joan Baez plays the cryptic Woman in White. "Bob Dylan" is a famous but unattainable presence in the plot: for example, a man at a delicatessen announces he has tickets to see Bob Dylan, and Bob Neuwirth, a well-known member of Dylan's offscreen entourage, appears onscreen wearing a mask saying, "I'm not Bob Dylan, I'm the Masked Tortilla." Other references to a real-life Dylan, juxtaposed with the imitative Renaldo character, seem simultaneously to mock and hypostasize vatic authority. Throughout the film, characters try to find and identify Dylan among the musicians and hangers-on, while Dylan himself meanders in and out playing a rock star with a different name who looks and performs just like Bob Dylan. The temptation to untangle the identities can be irresistible.

But wanting to track down and identify the real Dylan is a mistake, according to actor and playwright Sam Shepard, who traveled along with the original Rolling Thunder Revue troupe and kept a journal of his impressions. In what he called his *Rolling Thunder Logbook*, he wrote an entry titled "The Inventor":

Dylan has invented himself. He's made himself up from scratch. That is, from the things he had around him and inside him. Dylan is an invention of his own mind. The point isn't to figure him out but to take him in. He gets into you anyway, so why not just take him in? He's not the first one to have invented himself, but he's the first one to have invented Dylan. No one invented him before him or after. What happens when someone invents something outside himself like an airplane or a freight train? The thing is seen for what it is. It's seen as something incredible because it's never been seen before, but it's taken in by the people and changes their lives in the process. They don't stand around trying to figure out what it isn't, forever. They use it as a means to adventure.[5]

To say Dylan "invented himself" is a commonplace of Dylan criticism, and there are books (*Alias Bob Dylan*) and movies (*I'm Not There, Masked and Anonymous*) that seem to discover and rediscover that same fact repeatedly in different media. But no one has quite put it the way Shepard does when he says that Dylan is "not the first one to have invented himself, but he's the first one to have invented Dylan," qualifying that statement with "No one invented him before him or after." He might have added *not for lack of trying*, since Dylan became one of the most-mimicked and most-copied artists of his time.

But Shepard's signal message is that we—fans, audiences, players, and critics alike—should take the invention of Dylan as it is without "trying to figure out what it isn't." Perhaps this is what Ginsberg was getting at with his misquotation of Keats's epitaph, "Here lies one whose *fame* was writ in water": the slipperiness of Dylan's persona, both famous and ungraspable, is a kind of liquid masterpiece, the only kind of masterpiece Dylan would want to write or paint. Dylan, therefore, could never *paint* a masterpiece because, for him, a masterwork doesn't pin down the master. The metaphors remain in flux. The analogy is with the process, not with the product. So when Dylan says, in "When I Paint My Masterpiece," that the tour is like a masterpiece, the comparison also changes the vehicle: we think differently about the tour and we think differently about painting.

Imitation is the core of Dylan's invention of himself and of the process he used to invent a new art form. His transformations of the past were never seen before and they changed lives. Maybe Shepard is right and we shouldn't try to figure out what those transformations are not, but instead use them, like other kinds of inventions, as means to imaginative adventures: after all, everyone knows it takes a train to cry.

––––

Frank Zappa reputedly said, "Writing about music is like dancing about architecture." Those words, spoken with ingenious finality by a formidable authority, are enough to make any writer quiver. And, in fact, I've often felt while in the throes of this book, that I was contorting myself in a cryptic dance about an alien subject.

But, like other critics, I have wanted to dance beneath the diamond sky. And, in a sense, I've been dancing about architecture all along—the architecture, or architectonics, of Dylan's songwriting. Or I'd like to think of it that way. Zappa, of course, might call this special pleading and remind me that the critic's face, like the executioner's, should stay well-hidden (especially when he starts using words like "architectonics"). And, granted, to see a critic dancing around with one hand waving free is like watching a painter join a human head to a horse's neck, in Horace's phrase. My only justification—a modest offering at the altar of the Mother—is that imitation is not music. Nor is it lyrics or performance. Imitation is technique, the technique of Dylan's originality, the technique before the music begins—the technique that takes us to the myth before the myths began.

NOTES

INTRODUCTION

1. Just for the record, Dylan didn't mention, for example, Brecht or Ginsberg in his Nobel speech, though exposure to their work probably helped to sophisticate his lyrics. The literature of his adult years seems to fall into a different category of influence.

2. Christopher Ricks, *Dylan's Visions of Sin* (New York: HarperCollins, 2004), 15.

3. *Bob Dylan: Mondo Scripto*, exhibition at the Halcyon Gallery, London, October 9–December 23, 2018, https://www.halcyongallery.com. Exhibition catalog, Carlotta Cooper, 2018. See chapter 3 for a discussion of this exhibition.

4. Bob Dylan Archive, box 94, folder 5 (hereafter referred to as BDA). Dylan later typed some of these comments, but not as extensively. The brief typescript is in the same box and folder.

5. BDA, box 85, folder 7.2. I have made the editorial insertion "a shooting star tonight and I thought of you." Dylan didn't complete the line in the manuscript but, for those who don't know the song, it might be helpful to hear the rhyme.

6. And, rightly so, copyright remains copyright: inserting instantly accessible recordings might threaten artistic ownership and complicate permissions.

7. See Tom Moon, "Trickster Treat: Bob Dylan's New Song Sounds Awfully Old . . . and Familiar," NPR, May 12, 2020, https://www.npr.org.

8. See J. H. Matthews, ed., *An Anthology of French Surrealist Poetry* (London: University of London Press, 1966), 35.

9. Frank Kermode, "Bob Dylan: The Metaphor at the End of the Funnel: But Is It Art?" *Esquire Magazine*, May 1972, 188. *Esquire* printed this Kermode essay and an identically named Stephen Spender article side by side, as if to provide typographical parity.

10. Wallace Stevens, *The Palm at the End of the Mind: Selected Poems and a Play*, ed. Holly Stevens (New York: Vintage Books, 1972), 210.

11. Benjamin Filene, *Romancing the Folk: Public Memory and American Roots Music* (Chapel Hill: University of North Carolina Press, 2000), 187.

12. Karl Hagstrom Miller, *Segregating Sound: Inventing Folk and Pop Music in the Age of Jim Crow* (Durham, NC: Duke University Press, 2010), 5.

13. Miller, *Segregating Sound*, 5–6.

14. Miller, 6.

15. Miller, 8.

16. Eric Lott, *Black Mirror: The Cultural Contradictions of American Racism* (Cambridge, MA: Harvard University Press, 2017), 195. Lott does not cite the interview that he paraphrases.

17. Lott, *Black Mirror*, 195. Lott's sour mash metaphor has an amusing and pertinent real-life resonance: in 2015 Dylan went into the bourbon business and became a partner in Heaven's Door Whiskey. The name comes from the famous song and the labels from Dylan's plastic art. See Heaven's Door Whiskey website, "Iron," accessed October 31, 2021, https://www.heavensdoor.com: "The iron gates depicted on bottles of Heaven's Door Whiskey were created by Bob Dylan at his metalworking shop, Black Buffalo Ironworks, and are comprised of found objects collected from farms and scrap yards across America."

18. Filene, 189.

19. Timothy Hampton, *Bob Dylan's Poetics: How the Songs Work* (New York: Zone Books, 2019), 46.

20. Greil Marcus, *The Old, Weird America: The World of Bob Dylan's Basement Tapes* (New York: 2011), 20.

21. Hampton, *Bob Dylan's Poetics*, 46.

22. William Shakespeare, *The Winter's Tale*, ed. Stephen Orgel (Oxford: Oxford University Press, 1996), 4.4.95–97.

23. See Filene, *Romancing the Folk*, 183: "The focal point of Seeger's pride and hopes was Dylan. The twenty-two-year- old sensation seemed to meld a political conscience with a performance style, persona, and repertoire firmly rooted in American folk traditions, and he was demonstrating conclusively that this combination could be commercially powerful."

24. Marcus, *The Old, Weird America*.

25. James S. Ackerman, *Origins, Imitation, Conventions: Representation in the Visual Arts* (Cambridge, MA: MIT Press, 2002), 137. The male pronoun "his" is Ackerman's but it isn't inappropriate in the context of imitation. Although many women poets practiced imitatio— in England alone, for example, Mary Wroth, Aemelia Lanyer, Elizabeth Cary (a playwright), and Queen Elizabeth herself (in English and Latin)—they invariably call attention to their imitation of prior male authors. More significantly, the genealogies generated in the poetic treatises on imitation usually do not include any women poets (with the occasional exception of Sappho). The gendered bias of imitatio, from the Greek ephebe to the Senecan apian metaphor (the bees are males), is on prominent display throughout poetic history. Women imitators consciously call attention to themselves imitating male poets while demonstrably adhering to the advice of male treatise-writers. Whether this is because they felt that poetry transcended gender, or whether they felt it was their natural place to follow male examples, would be an important aspect of imitatio to explore. Except in very specific cases, however, the large topic of gender and imitation is beyond the scope of this study.

26. Ackerman, *Origins, Imitation, Conventions*, 137.

27. Ackerman, 135.

28. Bob Dylan, "Joan Baez in Concert, Part 2," reprinted in *Writings and Drawings*, 76, no line numbers (New York: Knopf, 1973).

29. Although Dylan's transmutation from Woody Guthrie imitator to stunning original can seem abrupt, it is more likely that his method of imitation always included something like the apian metaphor's digestive process. One wonders how much credit to give Eve MacKenzie for steering Dylan away from boxcars and railroads.

30. Dylan, "Joan Baez in Concert, Part 2," 76, no line numbers.

31. Dylan, "Joan Baez in Concert, Part 2," 77–78, no line numbers. Discussing the Savoy scene during the 1965 tour, Marianne Faithfull recalls that "[Baez] insisted on singing her high vibrato version[s] of 'Here Comes the Night' and 'Go Now,' which Dylan complained about. He hates her voice and tells her so. At one point he held up a bottle as she sang a high note, and drawled, 'Break that!' She just laughed" (Clinton Heylin, *Bob Dylan: Behind the Shades Revisited, the Biography* [New York: HarperCollins, 2003], 192). So much for his drunken conversion in the Woodstock painter's house: *Joan Baez in Concert, Part 2* and Dylan's jacket notes to the album appeared in 1963, two years before the tour.

32. Dylan, "Joan Baez in Concert, Part 2," 79, no line numbers.

33. Dylan, "Joan Baez in Concert, Part 2," 79–80, no line numbers.

34. Dylan, "Joan Baez in Concert, Part 2," 80, no line numbers.

35. Robert Kelly, "Postscript II," in *A Controversy of Poets: An Anthology of Contemporary Poetry*, eds. Paris Leary and Robert Kelly (Garden City, NY: Anchor Books, 1965), 564.

36. Kelly, "Postscript II," 564.

37. Quoted in John Bauldie, ed., *Wanted Man: In Search of Bob Dylan* (New York: Citadel, 1991), 37. The spelling of the seminal folk venue mentioned here continues to be disputed. Although most sources assert "Gerdes" (no apostrophe), "Gerde's" was also sometimes used, even officially; the venue itself seemed to use the two interchangeably on their own

signage, posters, and documents. Matt [No Last Name], "Gerde's Folk City: The End of a Greenwich Village Icon," *Off the Grid Village Preservation Blog*, www.villagepreservation.org.

38. Bauldie, *Wanted Man*, 37.

39. Richard F. Thomas, "The Streets of Rome: The Classical Dylan," *Oral Tradition* 22, no. 1 (March 2007): 49.

40. Jeff Burger, ed., *Dylan on Dylan: Interviews and Encounters* (Chicago: Chicago Review, 2018), 21.

41. Tim Riley, *Hard Rain: A Dylan Commentary* (New York: Vintage Books, 1993), 218.

42. Riley, *Hard Rain*, 219.

43. See Jean Hagstrum, *The Sister Arts: The Tradition of Literary Pictorialism and English Poetry from Dryden to Gray* (Chicago: University of Chicago Press, 1958), 134.

44. *Bob Dylan: The Beaten Path*, exhibition at the Halcyon Gallery, London, November 5, 2016–January 2, 2017, https://www.halcyongallery.com. I wonder if the gallery intended a message in opening the exhibition on Guy Fawkes Day. See also the link to Dylan's reflections on the exhibition: http://www.bobdylanart.com/beaten-path.asp.

45. Robert Herrick, "The Argument of His Book," in *The Complete Poetry of Robert Herrick*, ed. J. Max Patrick (New York: New York University Press, 1963), 11.

CHAPTER 1

1. Horace Engdahl, "Award Ceremony Speech," December 10, 2016, https://www.nobelprize.org.

2. Anthony Scaduto, *Bob Dylan* (London: Helter Skelter, 1996), 82. The "Smith" family, aka the MacKenzies, wished to remain anonymous for Scaduto's biography. Mrs. Smith's name was Eve.

3. Jonathan Cott, ed. *Bob Dylan: The Essential Interviews* (New York: Wenner Books, 2006), 194.

4. BDA, box 9, folder 1.01. Apuleius, *Metamorphoses*, 2 vols., ed. and trans. by J. Arthur Hanson (Cambridge, MA: Harvard University Press, 1989), I.2.17: "derige, et grassare naviter et occide moriturus" ["Attack zealously and slay, as you are about to die"]. The context is a sex scene; perhaps Dylan refers to the seductiveness of the female speaker.

5. BDA, box 9, folder 1.0208.

6. See my *Conceived Presences: Literary Genealogy in Renaissance England* (Amherst: University of Massachusetts Press, 1994), ch. 1.

7. Seneca, Epistle 84, in *Epistles*, 10 vols., trans. Richard M. Gummere (Cambridge, MA: Harvard University Press, 1917–25), 5:280.

8. See Paul Williams, *Bob Dylan: Performing Artist, 1986–1990 and Beyond, Mind Out of Time* (London: Omnibus, 2005), 122–23. Though there's no citation, Williams quotes this passage from a "500-word essay about Jimi Hendrix for use in a traveling exhibition celebrating Hendrix's work" (122). This exhibition was organized by the Govinda Gallery in July 1993. According to Chris Murray, the gallery director and host of the exhibition, the Jimi Hendrix Exhibition "was the single most popular exhibition in our 35 years in Georgetown. It consisted of 108 Photographs, paintings, drawings ephemera etc." I am grateful to Chris Murray, who generously supplied this information in an email exchange.

9. Wilfrid Mellers, *A Darker Shade of Pale: A Backdrop to Bob Dylan* (New York: Oxford University Press, 1984), 122.

10. Janet Gezari and Charles Hartman, "Dylan's Covers," *Southwest Review* 95, nos. 1–2 (2010): 155–56.

11. Michael Gray, *Song and Dance Man III: The Art of Bob Dylan* (London: Continuum, 2000), 291.

12. Francis James Child anthologized and analyzed the lyrics of 305 traditional English and Scottish ballads and published them in seven volumes in two editions, first in the 1860s

and then 1882–1898 as *The English and Scottish Popular Ballads*, 5 vol. (Boston: Houghton, Mifflin). He published only a few of the tunes, or "airs," in appendices. In 1959–72, Bertrand Bronson published *The Traditional Tunes of the Child Ballads*, 4 vol. (Princeton, NJ: Princeton University Press). Songs from these anthologies, such as "Barbara Allen" and "Lord Randall," became regular fare during the folk revival.

13. Kermode, "Bob Dylan," 25 (see intro, note 9).

14. Betsy Bowden, "Performed Literature: A Case Study of Bob Dylan's 'Hard Rain,'" *Literature in Performance* 3, no. 2 (1982): 35.

15. Arthur Kinney, *Continental Humanist Poetics: Studies in Erasmus, Castiglione, Marguerite de Navarre, Rabelais, and Cervantes* (Amherst: University of Massachusetts Press, 1989), 15.

16. Kinney, *Continental Humanist Poetics*, 17.

17. Du Bellay, *La Défense et illustration de la langue française* (Paris: Librarie Larousse, 1972), 60: "Imitant les meilleurs auteurs grecs, se transformant en eux, les dévorant, et après le avoir bien digérés les convertissant en sang et nourriture"; 61: "D'amplifier la langue française par l'imitation des anciens auteurs grecs et romains." This is just one brief discussion of imitatio among scores of Renaissance treatises and essays. See, inter alia, Bernard Weinberg, ed., *Trattati di poetica e retorica del cinque-cento*, 4 vols. (Bari: Guis. Latuza & Figli, 1970). See also Ackerman, *Origins, Imitation, Conventions*, 129–30 (see intro, n. 24), where he cites prominent discussions of imitatio among such early humanists as Lorenzo Valla, Angelo Poliziano, and Paolo Cortesi, noting that "the most detailed and extensive exchange, written in about 1512, was that of Gianfancesco Pico della Mirandola and Pietro Bembo."

18. Thomas Greene, *The Light in Troy: Imitation and Discovery in Renaissance Poetry* (New Haven, CT: Yale University Press, 1982), 33.

19. Greene, *Light in Troy*, 66. My italics.

20. Kinney, 18.

21. Ricks, *Dylan's Visions of Sin*, 7 (see intro, n. 2).

22. Cott, *Essential Interviews*, 114–15.

23. G. W. Pigman III: "Versions of Imitation in the Renaissance," *Renaissance Quarterly* 33, no. 1 (Spring 1980): 4.

24. Ricks, 7.

25. Scaduto, *Bob Dylan*, 76.

26. Greil Marcus, *Like a Rolling Stone: Bob Dylan at the Crossroads* (New York: Public Affairs, 2005), 137.

27. Scaduto, 82; 108.

28. Seneca, Epistle 84, *Epistles*, 5:279 (my emphasis).

29. Bob Dylan, *Chronicles* (New York: Simon and Schuster, 2004), 1:51.

30. Philip Sidney, *A Defence of Poetry*, ed. J. A. Van Dorsten (Oxford: Oxford University Press, 1989), 23.

31. Gabriel Josipovici, "Off the Grid: Thoughts on the Avant-Garde," *Times Literary Supplement*, August 9, 2019.

32. Catharine Mason and Richard Thomas, "Introduction," *Oral Tradition* 22, no. 1 (March 2007): 3.

33. Virgil, *The Aeneid of Virgil*, 2 vols., ed. R. D. Williams (London: Macmillan, 1972), 6:660–64; my italics.

34. Virgil, *The Aeneid*, trans. Robert Fagles (New York: Penguin Books, 2006), 6:764–69.

35. Virgil, *Aeneid of Virgil*, 1:500 (commentary). Williams also points out that Virgil's Elysium differs from Homer's "in that here the entrance is open not only to those of divine descent but to all those whose merits qualify them." The merit-over-birth distinction, pitting genealogy against meritorious or valorous conduct, resonates in poems and songs from Virgil's *Eclogues* to medieval exempla to Renaissance pastoral and English ballads (including revolutionary exhortations like "Lili-Bulero"). The folk music revival made much of this

conflict, adapting it to American political causes and identifying the working people's voice with merit in a mortal struggle with wealth and institutional privilege. Although in literary history the distinction between birth and merit is more metaphorical—that is, not determined by recourse to a blood myth—an ambitious songwriter like Bob Dylan would, by merit and sheer force of will (not to mention sleight of hand) attach himself to a poetic family tree that implies organic genealogical descent.

36. Thomas Palaima, "Why Bob Dylan Matters," *Bryn Mawr Classical Review* (blog), accessed November 2, 2021, http://bmcr.brynmawr.edu.

37. Ben Jonson, "To the Memory of My Beloved, the Author Mr. William Shakespeare: And What He Hath Left Us," in *The Complete Poems*, ed. George Parfitt (New Haven, CT: Yale University Press, 1975), lines 56–66.

38. John Milton, *The Complete Poetry and Essential Prose of John Milton*, ed. William Kerrigan, John Rumrich, and Stephen M. Fallon (New York: Modern Library, 2007), 34. Except where otherwise noted, all further references to Milton's works will be to this edition. The phrase comes from the editors' headnote to the poem, which originally appeared anonymously in the Second Folio: "It is satisfying in several ways that this should be the first printed of Milton's English poems. The great poet of the age to come begins his career by honoring the great poet of the age just past."

39. David Boucher and Gary Browning, eds., *The Political Art of Bob Dylan* (Exeter, UK: Imprint Academic, 2009), 7.

40. Richard Thomas, *Why Bob Dylan Matters* (New York: HarperCollins, 2017), 174.

41. Thomas, *Why Bob Dylan Matters*, 174. Elsewhere, Thomas had suggested that "Dylan's compositions are only rooted in the prior tradition and are not versions of it *per se*, but the relationship is clear, whether from Guthrie's version of 'Who's Gonna Shoe Your Pretty Little Foot' to Dylan's 'Kingsport Town' or Dylan's appropriation of Charley Patton's 'High Water.' Dylan's composition is of course transformational, and with the exception of all but two of the songs on *Bob Dylan*, and the songs on *World Gone Wrong* and *Good as I Been to You*, is inspired by his various traditions, never or rarely just giving versions of them." See "The Streets of Rome," 48 (see intro, n. 38); and also, "'And I Crossed the Rubicon': Another Classical Dylan," *Dylan Review* 2, no. 1 (2020): 35–64.

42. Wilfred Mellers, "God, Mode and Meaning in Some Recent songs of Bob Dylan," in *The Dylan Companion*, ed. Elizabeth Thomson and David Gutman (London: Papermac, 1991), 248.

43. *Bob Dylan, The Folk Years (The Unauthorized Critical Review)*, directed by Bob Carruthers (Vision Films, 2017).

44. "Pentimento," drawn from visual arts, and "palimpsest," drawn from manuscript paleography, appear regularly. But the textile metaphor tends to hold sway.

45. Dave Van Ronk, with Elijah Wald, *The Mayor of MacDougal Street* (Cambridge, MA: Da Capo Press, 2005), 4. Referring to his grandmother, Van Ronk adds, "Her version was better."

46. M. J. Fitzpatrick, "The Chimes of Trinity," words and music; the lyrics come from sheet music (New York: Howley, Haviland, 1895).

47. Mike Marqusee, *Chimes of Freedom: The Politics of Bob Dylan's Art* (New York: New Press, 2003), 93.

48. Hampton, *Bob Dylan's Poetics*, 91 (see intro, n. 18).

49. Hampton, 94. Hampton is referring to Rimbaud's *Illuminations*. See chapters 2 and 4 for a fuller discussion of Hampton's analysis of Rimbaud and Dylan.

50. In 1972 the poet Stephen Spender, who utterly misunderstood Dylan's transformations from ballad and blues singer, called his late sixties/early seventies lyrics "a bit soft": "They come out of the entertainment industry, and immense sums are being made. Bob Dylan may be sincere in every line he sings, but the atmosphere of the industry soaks

through an awful lot of this, like incontinent urine through pants." See Spender, "Bob Dylan: The Metaphor at the End of the Funnel: But Is It Art?" *Esquire Magazine*, May 1972, 188. As mentioned in the introduction's note 9, *Esquire* printed this Spender essay and an identically named Frank Kermode essay side by side, as if to provide typographical parity.

51. Mark Polizzotti, "Love and Theft: Dylan's Appropriations," *Parnassus: Poetry in Review* 34, nos. 1–2 (2015): 56. This is a review essay and Polizzotti is quoting Sean Wilentz, *Bob Dylan in America* (New York: Doubleday, 2010).

52. Robert Polito, "Bob Dylan's Memory Palace," in *Highway 61 Revisited: Bob Dylan's Road from Minnesota to the World*, ed. Colleen J. Sheehy and Thomas Swiss (Minneapolis: University of Minnesota Press, 2009), 145; 142. Allegations of plagiarism, fraud, and theft are legion among Dylan-watchers. Joni Mitchell, in "a spontaneous indictment of Dylan," reportedly said, "Bob is not authentic at all. He's a plagiarist, and his name and voice are fake. Everything about Bob is a deception" (*Los Angeles Times*, April 22, 2010. Cited in Palaima, "Why Bob Dylan Matters"). Some approaches are more sophisticated than others, but most are still redolent of moral and ethical censure. See, for example, Edward Cook, "Bob Dylan, Carl Sandburg, and the 'Borrowing' Problem," *Ralph the Sacred River* (blog), June 3, 2010, http://ralphriver.blogspot.com, and Scott Warmuth, "Bob Charlatan: Deconstructing Dylan's *Chronicles, Volume One*," *New Haven Review* 6 (January 2008): 70–83.

53. See Pete Seeger, *The Incompleat Folksinger*, ed. Jo Mecalf Schwartz (New York: Simon and Schuster, 1972), 144–49.

54. Mikal Gilmore, "Bob Dylan Unleashed," *Rolling Stone Magazine*, September 27, 2012, https://www.rollingstone.com. Thomas quotes part of this interview: see *Why Bob Dylan Matters*, 166–67.

55. Milton, *Paradise Lost*, 1. 12–16, in *The Complete Poetry and Essential Prose*, 294. My italics.

56. Ludovico Ariosto, *Orlando Furioso*, 2 vols., ed. Marcello Turchi (Milan, Italy: Garzanti, 1974), 1.2.2. Perhaps "cosa non detta" refers to Ariosto's work, whereas Milton's plural shifts away from the work and refers to the deeds: content rather than form. Thanks to Christoph Irmscher for this observation.

57. This practice of quotation is not universal. The recent translations by Guido Waldman (Oxford, 2008, prose) and David Slavitt (Harvard, 2011, verse) do not echo *Paradise Lost*.

58. Milton, *Paradise Lost*, 9.25–33, in *The Complete Poetry and Essential Prose*.

59. C. Crowe, "Bob Dylan. Biograph Booklet," liner notes to *Biograph*, Columbia C3K 38830, 1985, compact disc: "'There was just a clique, you know,' said Dylan, 'Folk music was a strict and rigid establishment. If you sang Southern Mountain Blues, you didn't sing Southern Mountain Ballads and you didn't sing City Blues. If you sang Texas Cowboy songs, you didn't play English ballads. It was really pathetic. You just didn't. If you sang folk songs from the thirties, you didn't do bluegrass tunes or Appalachian Ballads. It was very strict.'" This passage is cited by Christophe Lebold, "I've Got the Judas Complex and the Recycling Blues: Bob Dylan as Cultural Theft," *Recherches anglaises et nord-américaines* 43 (2010): 128.

60. Mellers, *Darker Shade of Pale*, 121.

61. Quoted in Bauldie, *Wanted Man*, 39 (see intro, n. 36).

62. Walter Jackson Bate, *The Burden of the Past and the English Poet* (New York: W. W. Norton, 1970), 61.

63. Quoted in Bauldie, 38.

64. Lebold, "I've Got the Judas Complex," 129.

65. John Hinchey, *Like a Complete Unknown: The Poetry of Bob Dylan's Songs, 1961–1969* (Ann Arbor, MI: Stealing Home, 2002), 38.

66. John Gibbens, *The Nightingale's Code: A Poetic Study of Bob Dylan*, with photographs by Keith Baugh (London: Touched Press, 2001), 3.

67. Van Ronk, *Mayor of MacDougal Street*, 159. Others knew and met with Guthrie before

he became very ill. Ellen Stekert, for instance, reports that she and John Cohen, "a founding member of the New Lost City Ramblers . . . in 1952 . . . visited with Woody Guthrie in Bob Harris's record store on Union Square." This passage appears in Stekert's 1993 introductory remarks preceding the reprint of her 1966 article, "Cents and Nonsense in the Urban Folk-song Movement: 1930–1966," in Neil V. Rosenberg, ed., *Transforming Tradition: Folk Music Revivals Examined* (Urbana: University of Illinois Press, 1993), 85.

68. Quoted by Bauldie, 33.

69. Bauldie, 33. See also Scaduto, 55.

70. Marcus, *Old, Weird America*, 25 (see intro, n. 19). This book was first published in the United States under the title *Invisible Republic: Bob Dylan's Basement Tapes* (New York: Henry Holt, 1997).

71. Daniel Karlin, "My Friend Bob: Dylan's Relationship with JFK," *Times Literary Supplement*, July 6, 2018, 13.

72. Hinchey, *Like a Complete Unknown*, 36.

73. Clinton Heylin, *Revolution in the Air: The Songs of Bob Dylan, 1957–1973* (Chicago: Chicago Review, 2009), 215. "Post-Carmel" refers to a period in 1964 when Dylan was visiting Baez in Big Sur. Heylin points out that Dylan probably set the song aside "only because he duly wrote an even better song along similar lines ('It's All Over Now, Baby Blue')."

74. Seneca, 5:279 (as quoted above, without the emphasis).

75. Clayton Dillard, "Interview: D. A. Pennebaker on *Don't Look Back*, Bob Dylan, and More," *Slant Magazine*, November 24, 2015, https://www.slantmagazine.com.

76. Ian Bell, *Once Upon a Time: The Lives of Bob Dylan*, 2 vols. (New York: Pegasus, 2014), 1:399.

77. D. A. Pennebaker, *Bob Dylan: Don't Look Back* (New York: Ballantine Books, 1968), 5.

78. Pennebaker, *Bob Dylan*, 112–17.

79. Derroll Adams was an American musician who traveled and recorded with Ramblin' Jack Elliott. Both went to England, but Adams stayed, eventually taking Donovan under his wing. Donovan wrote "Epistle to Derroll" for him.

80. Pennebaker recalls that in preparation for filming the famous "Subterranean Home-sick Blues" video that opens *Don't Look Back* they had written words from the lyrics on cards: "We had done the signs the night before, and Donovan had helped—Donovan was a very good artist, it turns out—and Joan Baez." It's hard to imagine that Donovan would have stayed around if he'd felt humiliated, or that Dylan would have let him help draw the cards if either his music or his artistic ability threatened him. Nor does it seem likely that, at this early date, Dylan felt a painterly competitiveness because of Donovan's calligraphic skills. See Dave Itzkoff, "No Direction, No Restriction: D. A. Pennebaker Looks Back at a Dylan Documentary," *New York Times*, May 19, 2016, https://www.nytimes.com.

81. The Buzzard Lope is evidently a strutting dance step, popular, according to Wikipedia, in minstrel shows along with the cakewalk and juba dance. In "Sugar Babe" it might also mean "to make her move along," according to "Mance Lipscomb–Sugar Babe It's All Over Now Lyrics," *Lyrics of Song*, accessed October 31, 2021, https://www.lyricsofsong.com. There's a recording of "The Buzzard Lope" by Bessie Jones and the Georgia Sea Island Singers.

82. John Hinchey, citing Leslie Fiedler, speaks of "Dylan's highly inventive handling of the relationship between the singer and Baby Blue, or, more specifically, between the song's (unstated) 'I' and its 'you.' Beginning with this very song, this 'pronominal romance,' to borrow a term Leslie Fiedler coined to describe the courtship dance of 'I' with 'you' in 'Song of Myself,' moves to the center of Dylan's poetry, where it becomes an extremely volatile and ambiguous affair of sometimes dizzying complexity" (see Hinchey, 99–100).

83. Burger, *Dylan on Dylan*, 2 (see intro, n. 39).

84. Burger, 3.

85. Dylan, *Writings and Drawings*, 105 (see intro, n. 27).

86. Burger, 14–15. Cf. also Cott, 2. In the latter version the passage is edited.

87. See Richard Schoeck, "'Lighting a Candle to the Place': On the Dimensions and Implications of *Imitatio* in the Renaissance," *Italian Culture* 4 (1983): 127–28. In the full passage, Schoeck is quoting Peter Brown, who in turn is quoting H.-I. Marrou. See Brown, *The Making of Late Antiquity* (Cambridge, MA: Harvard University Press, 1978), 8: "[H.-I.] Marrou has likened the impromptu performance of the master rhetoricians of the late classical age to the virtuoso techniques of a Hot Jazz trumpeter: they could bring out themes deeply embedded in their own memory and held at readiness for themselves and their hearers by centuries of tradition and could weave such themes into new combinations."

88. Douglas Brinkley, "Bob Dylan Has a Lot on His Mind," *New York Times*, June 12, 2020, https://www.nytimes.com. See also my column, "The Dylanista," *Dylan Review* 2, no. 1 (Summer 2020), https://thedylanreview.org.

CHAPTER 2

1. Heylin, *Revolution in the Air*, 353 (see ch. 1, n. 72).

2. Marqusee, *Chimes of Freedom*, 218 (see ch. 1, n. 47); Riley, *Hard Rain*, 167 (see intro, n. 40).

3. There was a local urban legend that the name Quinn refers to a policeman who threatened the peace-loving dope-smokers of Woodstock, NY. *The Savage Innocents* shouldn't be seen to replace such possible sources, only to complement them.

4. It has not gone unnoticed that Dean's crown as the Rebel King was stolen in the early sixties by Bob Dylan. But this is as much the result of imitation, even emulation, as of supersession and should be distinguished from Dylan's overhauling of Pete Seeger.

5. Charles Hartman, "Review of Bob Dylan. Rough and Rowdy Ways. Columbia Records, 2020," *Dylan Review* 2, no.1 (Summer 2020): 4.

6. The well-known story is that Dylan privately compensated Clayton for the song and, as Alessandro Carrera suggests, avoided going to court: "Siccome l'appropriazione operata da Dylan era più sostanziosa dell'adattamento di Clayton, sembra che Dylan abbia compensato Clayton in via amichevole, evitando di finire in tribunale." ["Since the appropriation worked by Dylan was more substantial than Clayton's adaption, it seems that Dylan compensated Clayton in a friendly way to avoid ending up in court."] See Alessandro Carrera, "Bob Dylan dall'appropriazione alla trasfigurazione," *Estetica: Studi e ricerche* 1 (2014): 164.

7. See Mark Thompson, "Desire Obscures, Possession Corrupts: The Mind and Work of a Knowing Mid-Century American," *Times Literary Supplement*, March 15, 2019: "[Alfred] Hayes . . . wrote 'I Dreamed I Saw Joe Hill Last Night,' a poem that Earl Robinson turned into a union ballad which passed into folklore."

8. According to Kevin Dettmar, "what's at stake when we talk of a writer's 'orginality' isn't really originality, per se, but intent." He asks, pertinently, "If intentional, did the author mean for readers to recognize the source (hence artful terms like *quotation*, *echo*, *allusion*), or not (the blunt accusation of *plagiarism*)?" See Dettmar, "Borrowing," in *The World of Bob Dylan*, ed. Sean Latham (Cambridge, UK: Cambridge University Press, 2021), 206.

9. This is a reference to the literary legend that, during the Greco-Roman period, educated people knew every line of *The Iliad* and *The Odyssey*: for a poet to use a line from Homer would have been as difficult as stealing Hercules's club.

10. "Fools Rush In (Where Angels Fear to Tread)" (1940), lyrics by Johnny Mercer; music by Rude Bloom. See Alexander Pope, *Pastoral Poetry and An Essay on Criticism*, vol. 1, edited by E. Audra and Aubrey Williams, *The Twickenham Edition of the Poems of Alexander Pope* (New Haven, CT: Yale University Press, 1961), 310.

11. See David Goldstein, "Originality," in *The Princeton Encyclopedia of Poetry and Poetics*, 4th ed. (Princeton, NJ: Princeton University Press, 2012), 981–83. In support of Eliot's remarks, Goldstein cites Northrup Frye: "Any serious study of literature shows that the real

difference between the original and the imitative poet is that the former is more profoundly imitative."

12. The claim is made by von Freytag-Loringhoven's biographer Irene Gemmel, and numerous art critics offer a "convincing rebuttal," according to Alastair Brotchie, in Dawn Adès's "Marcel Duchamp's Fountain: A Continuing Controversy," *Journal of the London Institute of 'Pataphysics* 14 & 15 (2018). See Alastair Brotchie's letter to the editor in *Times Literary Supplement*, September 13, 2019; and also Matthew Brown, "Toilets of Our Time," *Times Literary Supplement*, August 23 and 30, to which Brotchie is responding.

13. R. W. Emerson, "Self-Reliance," in *Selections from Ralph Waldo Emerson: An Organic Anthology*, ed. Stephen E. Whicher (Boston: Houghton Mifflin Company, 1960), 147–48.

14. Milton, *Paradise Lost*, 5.856–61, in *The Complete Poetry and Essential Prose*.

15. See, for example, 5.788–93: "Ye will not, I trust / To know ye right, or of ye know yourselves / Natives and sons of Heav'n possessed before / By none, and if not equal all, yet free, / Equally free; for orders and degrees / Jar not with liberty, but well consist."

16. Emerson, "Self-Reliance," 21.

17. Anthony Kemp, *The Estrangement of the Past: A Study in the Origins of Modern Historical Consciousness* (New York: Oxford University Press, 1991), 150.

18. Rosalind Krauss, "The Originality of the Avant-Garde: A Postmodernist Repetition," *October* 18 (Autumn 1981): 53.

19. Umbro Apollonio, ed., *Futurist Manifestos*, trans. Robert Brain et al. (London: Tate, 2009), 21–22. See Filippo Tommaso Marinetti, *I Manifesti del Futurismo* (Philadelphia: Press at Toad Hall, 2014), 4.

20. Apollonio, *Futurist Manifestos*, 23. See also Marinetti, *Manifesti*, 5.

21. Apollonio, *Futurist Manifestos*, 23.

22. Andy Warhol (1928–87) was among the first to produce what became known as Pop Art. Along with Roy Lichtenstein, Jasper Johns, and Robert Rauschenberg, he pioneered a movement in the sixties and seventies that brought him wealth and worldwide fame. His New York studio, the Factory, attracted a range of people from celebrities to hopeful artists to hangers-on. The Velvet Underground was Warhol's house band. Warhol asked Dylan to do a fifteen-minute screen test, after which Dylan asked for a painting in payment. Reports differ as to whether Warhol was miffed when Dylan took one of the silver *Elvis* paintings or whether Warhol offered it. See Patrick Webster, "In the Factory: Dylan and Warhol's World," in *All Across the Telegraph: A Bob Dylan Handbook*, ed. Michael Gray and John Bauldie (London: Futura, 1988), 57.

23. "Dylan and Warhol," Gerard Malanga interviewed by John Bauldie, in Bauldie, *Wanted Man*, 68 (see intro, n. 36). See also Wendy Steiner, *The Real Real Thing: The Model in the Mirror of Art* (Chicago: University of Chicago Press, 2010), 62: Steiner states "Dylan . . . hated the painting Warhol gave him after the [screen] test," but somewhat counters this in her endnote (199n53), citing a *Rolling Stone* interview in which Dylan praised Warhol as a filmmaker.

24. *The Rolling Thunder Revue: The 1975 Live Recordings*, disc 1, Columbia/Legacy 19075928282, released June 7, 2019. In addition to this changed line, Dylan adds two utterly different impromptu stanzas.

25. Riley, 83.

26. Hampton, *Bob Dylan's Poetics*, 89–100 (see intro, n. 18).

27. Aidan Day, *Jokerman: Reading the Lyrics of Bob Dylan* (Oxford: Basil Blackwell, 1988), 91.

28. Stephen Scobie, *Alias Bob Dylan Revisited* (Calgary, Alberta: Red Deer Press, 2003), 132. He cites Bill Allison for seeing the song as "another account of the singer and the muse" (131); see Allison, "She Belongs to Me: One Possible Hearing," *Telegraph* 19 (Spring 1983): 58–70.

29. Milton, *Paradise Lost*, 9.21–24, in *The Complete Poetry and Essential Prose*.

30. *Bob Dylan: The Asia Series* (New York: Gagosian Gallery, 2011), 8, exhibition catalog.

31. Arthur Rimbaud, *Illuminations*, trans. Louise Varèse (New York: New Directions, 1946;1957), xxx–xxxi. Unfortunately, while the prose poems of the *Illuminations* appear en face in French, the introductory letters are only in English. Rimbaud calls them "Les Lettres du Voyant," mystifyingly translated as "By Way of a Preface."

32. See Hampton's chapter 3, "Absolutely Modern: Electric Music and Visionary Song," 81–117. In a sense, this chapter is the core of Hampton's argument linking Dylan to Modernism and Modernist poetics.

33. Lester Bangs, "Bob Dylan's Dalliance with Mafia Chic," in *The Dylan Companion*, ed. Elizabeth Thomson and David Gutman (London: Papermac, 1991), 215–16; but see 213–22 for a withering comparison of Gallo's twisted violence—from extortion to rape to wife-beating to murder—to Dylan's "romantic, sentimental picture of Joey and his brothers in the gang" (216).

34. Although Bangs is aware that he might be crossing the diegetic line when he attacks Dylan personally as the narrator of "Hurricane" and "Joey," he persists in doing it anyway: "I know I stand at this point in possible danger of plunging quill-first into full-scale Webermanism, but I do think that if you are going to assert that a piece of music is the unburdening of your soul down to the personal pronouns, then you should tell the truth. I also think that if he is capable of lying about and exploiting his own marriage to make himself look a bit more pertinent, he is certainly capable of using the newsy victims of his topical toons with even less attention to moral amenities" (Bangs, "Mafia Chic," 212). So much for Bangs's critical detachment—he feels so indignant and defrauded that he even compares his ad hominem insults to the kind of grotesquely inept readings purveyed by A. J. Weberman. (It might be added, on the subject of exploiting marriage, that if Bangs has his way, we'll have to banish Milton's *Sonnet 23*, "Methought I Saw My Late Espoused Saint" and Longfellow's "The Evening Star," not to mention Millay's sonnet "Gazing upon him now, severe and dead" and, probably, Bishop's "One Art.") Tricky to determine who's telling the "truth" in these poems. And I won't even get into Milton's "protest" *Sonnet 18*, "On the Late Massacre in Piemont."

35. Jonathan Lethem, "The Ecstasy of Influence: A Plagiarism," *Harper's Magazine*, October 2007, 59.

36. Hinchey, *Like a Complete Unknown*, 221fn (marked by an asterisk at the bottom of the page) (see ch. 1, n. 64).

37. Riley, 130, 133.

38. Hinchey, 220 (all quotations in this paragraph). Hinchey adds parenthetically, "The fact that 'horse' is a slang term for heroin is also not unfortuitous." On one hand, this is plausible, as are the suggestions that "rain" in "Visions of Johanna" or "Just Like a Woman" refer to the street lingo for heroin. On the other, sometimes rain is just rain and horses are horses, even if the latter are tropes of a Blind Lemon Jefferson lyric.

39. See chapter 4 for a detailed discussion of "Watchtower." The contrast between John Wesley Harding and the thief as poet-philosopher is complicated by the Texas outlaw's initials, JWH: the tetragrammaton.

40. Lethem, "Ecstasy of Influence," 59–60. Lethem's article, which might be termed ludically confrontational, ranges far beyond Dylan, reaching back to John Donne and encompassing such "appropriators" (my word) as Vladimir Nabokov, Muddy Waters, Dizzy Gillespie, Walt Disney, and André Breton.

41. Robert Shore, *Beg, Steal & Borrow: Artists against Originality* (London: Elephant, 2017), 56–57. This book practices what it preaches: the cover is a duplicate of the old-style Penguin paperbacks, bright orange with a wide white band across the front where the title is printed in a plain black font. A deliberate, playfully defiant copy, the only difference is a little

round sticker in the lower right of the front cover, on which is printed, white on black: "THIS IS NOT A PENGUIN BOOK."

42. The quoted language in this paragraph comes from the Digital Media Law Project page on Fair Use: http://www.dmlp.org. Although this particular page is no longer being updated, the definition of fair use and explanations similar to the one here are available elsewhere. See too the website copyright.gov, "More Information on Fair Use," accessed November 1, 2021, https://www.copyright.gov.

43. Christina Oberstebrink, "Plagiarism and Originality in Painting: Joshua Reynolds's Concept of Imitation and Enlightenment Translation Theory," in *Cultural Transfer through Translation: The Circulation of Enlightened Thought in Europe by Means of Translation*, ed. Stefanie Stockhorst (Amsterdam: Rodopi, 2010), 51.

44. Oberstebrink, "Plagiarism and Originality," 51.

45. Ackerman, *Origins, Imitation, Conventions*: all quotations from Ackerman in the next two paragraphs are from 136–37 (see intro, n. 24).

46. Ackerman, 37.

47. Douglas Heselgrave, "Contents Under Pressure: Bob Dylan's Asia Series," *Restless and Real* (blog), September 30, 2011, https://restlessandreal.blogspot.com.

48. Tony Norman, "More Controversy Finds Dylan as Artist," *Pittsburgh Post-Gazette*, September 30, 2011.

49. David Itzkoff, *ArtsBeat* (blog), *New York Times*, September 26, 2011 [8:20 PM].

50. For copyright reasons, I was unable to reprint images from the Asia Series and Revisionist Art exhibitions. For the Asia Series, see *Bob Dylan: The Asia Series*, Gagosian Galleries, New York, September 20–October 22, 2011, https://gagosian.com. For the Revisionist Art exhibition, see *Revisionist Art: Thirty Works* by Bob Dylan, Gagosian Galleries, New York, November 28, 2012–January 12, 2013, https://gagosian.com. For exhibition catalogs, see bibliography. Dylan is represented by the Halcyon Gallery, London, www.halcyongallery.com.

51. Scott Warmuth, "Deciphering the Asia Series: Dylan, Duchamp and the Letter from Woody," *Goon Talk* (blog), October 1, 2011, http://swarmuth.blogspot.com. But see also the posts for October 8 and 15, 2011.

52. Robert Siegel, "New Paintings Reignite the Bob Dylan Copycat Debate," *All Things Considered*, NPR, October 18, 2011. The title confirms the ubiquity of what Norman calls the "plagiarism meme."

53. Siegel, "New Paintings."

54. Norman, "More Controversy."

55. Oberstebrink, 46.

56. Oberstbrink, 46.

57. Jim Linderman, "Bob Dylan Paints Just Like a Painter," *Expecting Rain* (blog), September 28, 2011, https://expectingrain.com.

58. Heselgrave, "Contents Under Pressure."

59. Robert C. Morgan, "Can Bob Dylan Paint?" *Brooklyn Rail: Critical Perspectives on Arts, Politics, and Culture*, November 2, 2011, https://brooklynrail.org.

60. See Crawford, "Don't Think Twice."

61. This section's heading, "Unique Copy," is plagiarized from the name of a small xerox shop near New York University in the 1980s: the Iron Age before the advent of the internet, PDFs, email, and thumb-drives virtually eliminated the need for hard copies—and before Kinko's cornered the upgraded copier business. "You can still buy on Hong Kong's Hollywood Road . . .": Heselgrave, "Contents Under Pressure."

62. See *The Great Eastern Temple: Treasures of Japanese Buddhist Art from Tōdai-ji* (Tokyo: Dai Nippon Printing 1986), especially fig. 32 (58–59).

63. Miwako Tesuka is the former director of the Japan Society in New York and an independent curator of Japanese art. We had numerous private conversations and exchanged emails about the *Asia Series* paintings. I am grateful to her for the information on Japanese art, photography, and ethnic identity here and in the following paragraphs.

64. See Fabio Fantuzzi, "I dieci comandamenti dell'arte: Bob Dylan e l'antico dilemma tra genio e plagio," *Musica/Realtà* 105 (2014): 77–78. Fantuzzi, who is perhaps the foremost scholar on Dylan and Raeben, makes the fascinating point that the transpositions from one artistic practice to another might well be thought of as a kind of ekphrasis. And he adds something no one else seems to have noticed: within a few days of the scandal Dylan had been in contact with Magnum Photographic Agency and had made arrangements with the legitimate owners of the material.

65. See Priya Wadhera, *Original Copies in Georges Perec and Andy Warhol* (Leiden: Brill, 2017).

66. See Trish Crawford, "Don't Think Twice: Dylan's Paintings in New York Gallery Look Just Like Photos." *Toronto Star*, September 29, 2011:

> "Artists have been doing variations on widely available photos for many decades," said Elizabeth Legge, chair of the University of Toronto's Department of Art. "Warhol would be a big well-known example." It's all right, she said, "provided the artist does something original with the material. Even just changing the context it is seen in, it is usually a non-issue." She acknowledged the art world is tied in knots over the subject, with some, such as Jeff Koons and Damien Hirst, facing frequent challenges of copyright violations. Musicologist Rob Bowman says the sheer celebrity of Dylan has made him a target for criticism (just as it pulls people into the show). . . . A professor at York University, Bowman said, "The art of Bob Dylan creates business for the gallery, whether it is good or not. We are talking fame and celebrity here. You will get people taking shots at him."

67. *Asia Series* catalog, 95.

68. *Asia Series* catalog, 96. Richard Prince published a slightly different version of his essay in the *New York Review of Books*. My guess is that the catalog version is later since there have been minor corrections and a few additions in the Gagosian publication. See Prince, "Bob Dylan's Fugitive Art," *New York Review of Books*, October 5, 2011. https://www.nybooks.com.

69. Ingrid Mössinger, "Prolog/Prologue," in *Bob Dylan: Face Value*, ed. Ingrid Mössinger, (Dresden: Sandstein Verlag, 2016), exhibition catalog, 11. The exhibition was held at the Kuntsammlungen Chemnitz, from May 22–July 31, 2016.

70. Morgan, "Can Bob Dylan Paint?"

71: Alessandro Allemandi Miró, "Lo spettacolo è appena cominciato" ["The Show Has Just Begun"], in Bob Dylan, *Bob Dylan: The Drawn Blank Series* (Turin: Allemandi and C., 2010), 7–8, exhibition catalog. The Italian text precedes the English translations. Two translators are listed on the penultimate page, Nicola Pirulli and Simon Turner; presumably they collaborated on the translations as neither is given credit for specific articles. Miró's remarks appear in a postscript to his contribution.

72. Bob Dylan, *Bob Dylan: The Brazil Series* (Munich: Prestel Verlag, 2010), exhibition catalog, 17.

CHAPTER 3

1. Dylan, *The Brazil Series*, 17 (see ch. 2, n. 71).

2. *Brazil Series*, 152–53.

3. *Brazil Series*, 179–80.

4. Dylan uses the word "glass" eleven times in all his songs, and only once to mean "mirror": "Well, Phaedra with her looking-glass . . . etc.," "I Wanna Be Your Lover" (*Biograph* 1965). See http://konkordans.se/.

5. Bell, *Once Upon a Time*, 1:547 (see ch. 1, n. 75).

6. This might be called *imitatio sui* if there were a Latin parallel to the conventional practice of imitatio. But, to the best of my knowledge, the concept of *imitatio sui* did not exist either in classical or Neo-Latin poetics.

7. Terry Kelly, "Bob Dylan and the Art of Forgery," *Bridge* 2 (Winter 1998): 59, 65.

8. Day, *Jokerman*, 3 (see ch. 2, n. 26).

9. Gray, *Song and Dance Man III*, 201 and 201n11 (see intro, n. 12).

10. Kermode, "Bob Dylan," 188 (see intro, n. 9). Cited by Day, 4.

11. Dylan, *Writings and Drawings* (see intro, n. 27).

12. Karl Shapiro, "The Poetry of Bob Dylan," *New Republic*, June 2, 1973.

13. For what it's worth, Shapiro wrote rhymed metrical poetry almost exclusively. I wonder how much the rhyme and meter of Dylan's songs (though at times a scansion nightmare) influenced Shapiro's judgment of them as "poetry." They make odd bedfellows: Shapiro, the anachronistic metrical rhymer in post-Modernist poetic culture, and Dylan, the celebrated (and sainted) vanguard of lyrical experimentation in popular song.

14. John Wisniewski, "Unrecorded Lyrics by Dylan Published in His Latest Book," *Syracuse Post-Standard*, May 23, 1973. The brief review appears on a page called the Youth Post, one day before Dylan's thirty-second birthday.

15. When asked by Ian Hamilton about Bob Dylan, the poet Robert Lowell said, "Bob Dylan is alloy: he is true folk and fake folk, and he has the Caruso voice. He has lines, but I doubt if he has written whole poems. He leans on the crutch of his guitar." (See *Robert Lowell: Interviews and Memoirs*, ed. Jeffrey Meyers [Ann Arbor: University of Michigan Press], 170.)

16. BDA, box 6, folder 3.01.

17. Michael S. Barrett, "Dylan's 'Writings and Drawings' Certain to 'Please Everybody,'" *Montreal Gazette*, September 7, 1973.

18. Edward Grossman, "Dylan's Odyssey," *Dissent*, October 1, 1973, 492.

19. Grossman, "Dylan's Odyssey," 492.

20. Grossman, 493.

21. Michael Gray notes other anomalies with copyright. Referring to the jacket notes for *Joan Baez in Concert, Part 2*, he points out that the poem appeared first in *Circuit*, ca. 1967, but then "was collected in Bob Dylan *Writings and Drawings* (1972), and is also contained in *Lyrics 1962–85* where, improbably, it is copyrighted 1973, almost a decade after its publication on the back of the Baez album" (*Song and Dance Man III*, 43n32). The 1973 copyright is not so improbable in that the first edition of *Writings and Drawings* was 1973 (not 1972; cf. intro, n. 27). But there's still a lost decade to account for.

22. These poems are listed in the contents of individual albums as well as in the combined index of song titles and first lines.

23. *Writings and Drawings*, 291.

24. *Writings and Drawings*, 28–29.

25. See Nduka Otiono and Josh Toth, eds., *Polyvocal Bob Dylan: Music, Performance, Literature* (Cham, Switzerland: Palgrave Macmillan, 2019).

26. Philippe Margotin and Jean-Michel Guesdon, *Bob Dylan: All the Songs, the Story behind Every Track* (New York: Black Dog and Leventhal, n.d.), 341.

27. There are other versions of the lyric in which the speaker claims "I wish I were a little bird."

28. Adriana G. Proser, "Moral Characters: Calligraphy and Bureaucracy in Han China (206 B.C.E.–C. E. 220)" (PhD diss, Columbia University, 1995), 59.

29. Yūjirō Nakata, ed., *Chinese Calligraphy*, trans. Jeffrey Hunter (New York: Weatherhill, 1983), 184.

30. There are exceptions to this generally accepted idea. Evidently the Swiss physiognomist

Johann Kaspar Lavater once observed that "the more I compare different handwritings, the more am I convinced that handwriting is the expression of the character of him who writes." But Lavater's is a minority view and not a component of artistic production in the West. See Alberto Manguel, Review of Christine Nelson, ed., *The Magic of Handwriting*, *Times Literary Supplement*, March 15, 2019.

31. *Bob Dylan*: *Mondo Scripto* (see intro, n. 3). The language of the title seems to be more fanciful than accurate, although some Dylan aficionados have cited Dante and Byron as possible sources. On the *Expecting Rain* blog there's a pertinent contribution by samu_93: "In the current Italian it would be 'mondo scritto.' However, in the Italian of some centuries ago it was 'Mondo Scripto.'" True enough, but regardless of the temptation to imagine Dylan reading "a book from the thirteenth century" in the original vernacular, it's difficult to image his using the Italian of Dante or Guido Cavalcanti or Petrarch to title the new exhibition (if he's even responsible for the title).

32. David Sexton, "Bob Dylan—*Mondo Scripto* Review: An Unmissable Show for Every Fan," *Evening Standard*, October 9, 2018, https://www.standard.co.uk.

33. See Carrera, "Bob Dylan dall'appropriazione alla trasfigurazione" (see ch. 2, n. 6).

34. Bob Dylan, *Mondo Scripto* (London: Carlotta Cooper), exhibition catalog, 227.

35. Sexton, "*Mondo Scripto* Review."

36. Milton, *Paradise Lost*, 3.45–55, in *The Complete Poetry and Essential Prose*; my italics.

37. Lisa O'Neill Sanders, in private conversation, has told me that the drawings sold to accompany the songs are not always the same. This practice, too, indicates a fluidity in Dylan's approach to the *Mondo Scripto* exhibition and to his association of drawings with songs.

38. John Elderfield, "All These People That You Mention. . . .," in Mössinger, *Bob Dylan: Face Value*, 12 (see ch. 2, n. 68).

39. Elderfield, "All These People," 15.

40. Elderfield, 16.

41. Scobie, *Alias Bob Dylan Revisited*, 71 (see ch. 2, n. 27).

42. Graham Reid, "Bob Dylan: Belle Isle (1970)," *Elsewhere*, June 14, 2012, https://www.elsewhere.co.nz.

43. See Scobie, 67.

44. Hampton, *Bob Dylan's Poetics*, 119, 17 (see intro, n. 18).

45. *Hartford Courant*, August 5, 1973. The review is signed only with the initials H. M.

46. Luc Sante, "Foreword," in Dylan, *Hollywood Foto-Rhetoric: The Lost Manuscript*, photographs by Barry Feinstein (New York: Simon and Schuster, 2008), xvii. The copyrights for Dylan and Feinstein, listed individually on the last page of the book as is common with exhibition catalogs, are dated 2008—which is a bit confusing if the photographs were originally "made for a variety of assignments" (ix).

47. Sante, "Foreword," x.

48. Sante, xiii.

49. *Hollywood Foto-Rhetoric*, 120.

50. *Hollywood Foto-Rhetoric*. This poem runs on the verso pages only, from 130–38. I quote from 130–35.

51. Scobie, 266.

52. Robert Shelton, *No Direction Home: The Life and Music of Bob Dylan* (New York: William Morrow, 1986), 200. Bell, 1:293.

53. Nat Hentoff, "The Crackin,' Shakin,' Breakin,' Sounds," *New Yorker*, October 24, 1964, in Cott, *Essential Interviews*, 26 (see ch. 1, n. 3).

54. Shelton, *No Direction Home*, 201. See Bell, 1:294.

55. Luc Sante, "Introduction," in *Revisionist Art, Thirty Works by Bob Dylan*, ed. John Elderfield (New York: Gagosian Gallery, 2012), 10. The exhibition was held from November 28, 2012–January 12, 2013.

56. Shelton, 200.

57. See Heylin, *Revolution in the Air*, 206 (see ch. 1, n. 72), who reminds us that the working title of "My Back Pages" was "Ancient Memories." The shift from memory to material text is provocative, perhaps indicating Dylan's growing awareness of himself as a both a writer and a performer.

58. Heylin, 206.

59. Hentoff, "Crackin,' Shakin,' Breakin,' Sounds," 26.

60. It sometimes seems disproportionate to level such uncompromising criticism at this young man's choices. In any other context, these so-called momentous decisions might be amusing. Imagine, for example, a college senior changing his mind about the "direction" of his poetry. Even if he were a Keats or Eliot, it would probably be labeled juvenilia and dismissed.

61. Dylan, *Chronicles*, 1:61 (see ch. 1, n. 29).

62. This version of the lyrics is from a 1971 studio outtake, released on *The Essential Bob Dylan*. There is a barebones expressiveness in Dylan's voice and delivery on this recording, with the appropriately stark guitar accompaniment (Happy Traum also plays on the outtake).

63. Gray, 467, enumerates biblical references to vipers: Matthew 3:7 and Luke 3:7, Matthew 12:34 and Matthew 23:33.

64. Clinton Heylin, *Judas! From Forest Hills to the Free Trade Hall, A Historical View of* The Big Boo (New York: Lesser Gods, 2016), 10.

65. *Tyndale's Old Testament, Being the Pentateuch of 1530, Joshua to 2 Chronicles of 1537, and Jonah*, trans. William Tyndale; modern-spelling edition, David Daniell (New Haven, CT: Yale University Press, 1992). Tyndale's translation is not an arbitrary choice, as I discuss in chapter 4 in connection with Dylan's vatic authority.

66. Robert Alter, *The Five Books of Moses: A Translation with Commentary* (New York: W. W. Norton, 2004), 20.

67. David Rosenberg, trans., *The Book of J*, with interpretation by Harold Bloom (New York: Grove Weidenfeld, 1990), 28.

68. Rosenberg, *The Book of J*, 27.

69. William F. Orr and James Arthur Walther, *1 Corinthians: A New Translation* (Garden City, NY: Doubleday, 1976). The italics appear in the original.

70. Eliding the word "God " as "G-d" is a convention followed by some observant Jews: "Judaism does not prohibit writing the Name of God per se; it prohibits only erasing or defacing a Name of God. However, observant Jews avoid writing any Name of God casually because of the risk that the written Name might later be defaced, obliterated or destroyed accidentally or by one who does not know better. Observant Jews avoid writing a Name of God on websites . . . because there is a risk that someone else will print it out and deface it. To avoid writing the Name, Orthodox Jews (and sometimes [members of] other denominations) substitute letters or syllables, for example, writing 'G-d' instead of 'God.'" Jewish Virtual Library, s.v. "Jewish Concepts: The Nature of G-d" (Chevy Chase, MD, American-Israeli Cooperative Enterprise), https://www.jewishvirtuallibrary.org/. Many Jews who do follow this convention nonetheless believe it does not extend to God's name in languages other than Hebrew, so it is therefore not necessary to use the elision in English: "The bulk of Jewish legal opinion agrees that the law applies only to the written name of God when written in Hebrew and not when written in other languages." Victor S. Appell, "Why Do Some Jews Write 'G-d' Instead of 'God'?," "Answers to Jewish Questions," www.reformjudaism.org.

71. BDA, box 82, folder 9.02.

CHAPTER 4

1. Thomas, "'And I Crossed the Rubicon,'" 46 (see ch. 1, n. 41).

2. Sounes, *Down the Highway: The Life of Bob Dylan* (New York: Grove Press, 2001), 2.

3. The quotation comes from Louis Masur's omnibus review of Dylan books, in which he is quoting Greil Marcus's *Like a Rolling Stone*. See Louis P. Masur, "Famous Long Ago: Bob Dylan Revisited," *American Quarterly* 59, no. 1 (March 2007): 176.

4. Max Weber, *Economy and Society*, ed. Guenther Roth and Claus Wittich (Berkeley: University of California Press, 1978), 2:1112.

5. Milton, *Paradise Lost*, 9.21–24, in *The Complete Poetry and Essential Prose*.

6. Cott, *Essential Interviews*, 102 (see ch. 1, n. 3).

7. Cott, 300 (interview with Kurt Loder, *Rolling Stone* [1984]).

8. This is not to say performers have escaped responsibility and either notoriety or (less often) acclamation for their activities beyond the stage. Theo Bikel and Elia Kazan "named names" before the House Un-American Activities Committee. John Wayne avoided serving in the armed forces during World War II to further his career. By contrast, Jennifer Lopez has earned deserved praise for starting several charities and for lending her name to others. Among music stars, social consciousness has led to grandiose political fundraising. George Harrison's memorable Concert for Bangladesh was followed by scores of other benefit concerts hosted by bands like U2. The list is ever-growing. The point, however, is that little of this highly publicized political exposure affected the performers' status ex cathedra in the way Dylan's songs and performances have affected his status among young listeners.

9. Lebold, "I've Got the Judas Complex," 127 (ch. 1, n. 12).

10. Sandy Perlman, "Roto-Rooter," in *The Age of Rock 2*, ed. Jonathan Eisen (New York: Vintage Books, 1970), 327, 328.

11. Hampton, *Bob Dylan's Poetics*, 86 (see intro, n. 18).

12. Hampton, 85.

13. Clinton Heylin, *Still on the Road: The Songs of Bob Dylan, Vol. 2* (London: Constable, 2010), 3.

14. Hampton, 89.

15. Weber, *Economy and Society*, 2:1111 (emphasis in original).

16. Weber, 2:1115.

17. Hampton, 89.

18. Donald McIntosh, "Weber and Freud: On the Nature and Sources of Authority," *American Sociological Review* 35 (1970): 902.

19. See Thomas Spence Smith, *Strong Interaction* (Chicago: University of Chicago Press, 1992), 110–15; 192–97.

20. See, for example, his allusion to Narcissus in "License to Kill": "Now he worships at an altar of a stagnant pool / And when he sees his reflection, he's fulfilled." There's a more complex reference in "Seeing the Real You at Last": "Well, I sailed through the storm / Strapped to the mast, / But the time has come, / And I'm seeing the real you at last." Dylan is (probably) alluding to the Sirens episode from *Odyssey* 12: if so, the introduction of irresistible song being sung to a singer-poet (while everyone else's ears are stuffed with beeswax) offers an interesting reading of a familiar Homeric tableau.

21. Allen Ginsberg, *Howl* (San Francisco: City Lights Books, 1956), lines 1–2.

22. Allen Ginsberg, *Spontaneous Mind: Selected Interviews, 1958–1996*, ed. David Carter (New York: HarperCollins, 2001), 249. See also 248: "I would say Kerouac's poetry is the craftiest of all. And as far as having the most craft of anyone, though those who talk about craft have not yet discovered it, his craft is spontaneity."

23. Stevens was an inveterate horticulturist and flower-arranger, but with actuality always on his mind. According to Samuel French Morse, he would sit admiring the exotic flowers he'd ordered from around the country but speak of "how expensive the garden was, not in an offensive way, but just surprising. [There] was that materialistic streak in him." See Peter Brazeau, *Parts of a World: Wallace Stevens Remembered, an Oral Biography* (New York: Random House, 1983), 152. Stevens wrote a playful poem called "Floral Decorations for

Bananas," but he was also the consummate artist of the actual, as he can grimly remind us: "The only emperor is the emperor of ice-cream." See Stevens, *The Palm at the End of the Mind*, 81–82; 79–80 (see intro, n. 10).

24. Cott, 171.

25. Cott, 197.

26. Elvis Presley recorded this song on his *Spinout* album (1966). He sings the "sunrise" rather than the "rainbow" version of the line. His performance is, as usual, a valuable interpretation: his backup band, though partly electric, retains the simplicity of an audibly strummed guitar. Elvis delivers an unhurried but felt performance. His instantly recognizable voice defies expectations, merely hinting at grace notes and holding the crooning in check. The result is a precise, unsentimental rendition. (This shouldn't come as a surprise to anyone who has heard his exceptional cover of Gordon Lightfoot's "Early Mornin' Rain.")

27. My emphasis.

28. Michael Gilmour, *Tangled Up in the Bible: Bob Dylan & Scripture* (New York: Continuum, 2004), 12.

29. Andrew Muir, *The True Performing of It: Bob Dylan and William Shakespeare* (Penryn, Cornwall: Red Planet Books, 2019), 16.

30. Recognition of Tyndale's influence is not confined to academic critics. The same observation is made, gratuitously in the circumstances, by a character in the British TV series *Midsomer Murders* (season 11, episode 5). What better imprimatur can there be?

31. Colbert Cartwright, *The Bible in the Lyrics of Bob Dylan* (Lancashire, UK: Wanted Man Press, 1985), i.

32. Marqusee, *Chimes of Freedom*, 237 (see ch. 1, n. 47).

33. Marqusee, *Chimes of Freedom*, 237. Dylan's mother, Beattie, made the same observation, claiming to have seen a Bible prominent amid a chaos of other books.

34. See Thomas, "The Streets of Rome," 31 and passim (see intro., n. 38); and *Why Bob Dylan Matters*, esp. chapter 8 (see ch. 1, n. 41).

35. Tyndale translates the phrase: "Ye shall hear of wars, and of the fame of wars." See Tyndale, *Tyndale's New Testament, Translated from the Greek by William Tyndale (1534)*, ed. David Daniell (New Haven, CT: Yale University Press, 1989), 53. The KJV translators changed "fame" to "rumors," but they were simply modernizing the Latin *fama*, rumor. Dylan would not have known the Tyndale translation, though the Latin *fama* and its implications he might well have remembered from studying the *Aeneid*. In any case, as seen in chapter 2, his sense of "fame" has always been ambivalent, and in interviews and songs he has acknowledged the fine line between fame and "the dirt of gossip" ("Restless Farewell").

36. See Virgil, *The Minor Poems of Virgil*, trans. Joseph J. Mooney (Birmingham: Cornish Brothers, 1916), 100 (Latin); 42 (English metrical translation).

37. Margotin and Guesdon, *Bob Dylan, All the Songs*, 596 (see ch. 3, n. 26).

38. That Dylan borrowed the melody for this song from Paul Clayton, who in turn had come across it in his travels through traditional-music backcountry, serves to characterize this imitative practice of this Village folk phase. Evidently Dylan's borrowing was enough to merit a monetary settlement with Clayton when "Don't Think Twice" became so successful.

39. I've omitted the volumes of topical songs, some striving more than others for "traditional" appearance. Phil Ochs's exquisite "There but for Fortune" is more ecumenical than vatic, an appeal to natural egalitarianism.

40. Officially Paul Colby's The Bitter End, this rock club at 147 Bleeker Street in New York City was established in 1961: scores of now-famous artists debuted at the club and came back to play gigs there. On July 3, 1975, Dylan was invited to sing a song during a Ramblin' Jack Elliott show. There is a unique recording on YouTube (but, alas, no film): "Bob Dylan – Abandoned Love (Live) – Unique Version – The Only Recording of This Version," accessed November 1, 2021, https://www.youtube.com.

41. Much ink has been spilled over when Dylan started reading the French poets. See, inter alia, Gray, *Song and Dance Man III*, 201n11 on Baudelaire (see intro, n. 12); Heylin, *Revolution in the Air*, 181–82, 366 and passim (see ch. 1, n. 72); Van Ronk, *Mayor of MacDougal Street*, 206–7: "The parallels between Dylan and people like Rimbaud and Mallarmé were being talked about almost as soon as he started writing, and I don't know if he was aware of them before that, but he checked them out pretty early on. Somewhere in my bookcases I probably still have a paperback collection of modern French poetry with Bobby's underlinings in it" (see ch. 1, n. 45). See Shelton, *No Direction Home*, 99–100 (see ch. 3, n. 51). Ricks mentions Rimbaud and Verlaine, facetiously, as practitioners of a sister art not as engaging to Dylan as butter sculpture (*Dylan's Visions of Sin*, 25, see intro, n. 2). No critic but Hampton gives Rimbaud or Mallarmé as fundamental a role in Dylan's compositional development.

42. Van Ronk, 206. Van Ronk says the song "was not a flawless work . . . but it's overall effect was incredible" (206). And, in comparing Dylan to the other Village songwriters, he adds, perspicaciously, that there were two reactions to Dylan's success. One was jealousy and "the other reaction, even more damaging, was 'I'm gonna be next. All I have to do is find the right agent, the right record company, the right connections, and I can be another Bob Dylan!' Yeah, sure you could. All you had to do was write 'A Hard Rain's A-Gonna Fall'—for the first time. That was what Bobby had done, and none of the rest of us did that. Bobby is not the greatest songwriter in history, but he was far and away the best on our scene" (216).

43. Cf., for example, Buffy Sainte-Marie's version: "What did she give you for supper, my son? / . . . Eels and eel broth, mother / . . . And what color were the skins, Lord Randall, my son? / . . . Oh, brown and speckled, mother / . . . I a-fear you been poisoned, Lord Randall, my son . . . etc."

44. Mt: 14: 26–31. A redaction of the "walking on the sea" story appears in both Mark and John. Neither of those Gospels adopts Tyndale's fuller version.

45. The word "muffled" is Dylan's, used to describe the sound on *John Wesley Harding*: "I heard the sound that Gordon Lightfoot was getting, with Charlie McCoy and Kenny Buttrey. I'd used Charlie and Kenny both before, and I figured if he could get that sound, I could. But we couldn't get it [*laughs*]. It was an attempt to get it, but it didn't come off. We got a different sound . . . I don't know what you'd call that … it's a *muffled* sound" (my emphasis). See Cott (interview with Jann Wenner), 157.

46. Mike Marqusee, *Wicked Messenger: Bob Dylan and the 1960s* (New York: Seven Stories, 2005), 236: "This startlingly concise and deeply mysterious composition begins in medias res."

47. Isaiah 21: 5–9, boldface emphasis mine. Marqusee quotes this passage in full in *Wicked Messenger*, 236.

48. Ezekiel 33:6–7, my italics.

49. Psalm 127.

50. Cott (interview with Nat Hentoff [*Playboy*, March 1966]), 98.

51. Cott (interview with Nat Hentoff), 98.

52. Cott (interview with Nat Hentoff, 98.

53. Van Ronk points out that "when Bobby went in that direction, it opened the floodgates" and probably had an unfortunate effect on many songwriters: "Paxton was a pretty experienced songwriter by that time, but he deferred to Bobby. Ochs worshipped the ground Bobby walked on—it actually became a sort of fixation, and did him a lot of harm. And that's not to mention Eric Anderson [*sic*], David Blue, Patrick Sky" (207). Van Ronk is absolutely right about these other songwriters. Paxton was not as deeply affected, but Patrick Sky, for example, a fine guitarist, humorist, and country-folk songwriter, began releasing records with baffling, pseudo-surrealist lyrics. Sky's poetic gifts, however, were limited in comparison to Dylan's, and the songs fell flat. The Phil Ochs story is more familiar and much sadder. See, inter alia, Heylin, *Behind the Shades Revisited*, 233–34 (see intro, n. 30).

54. Cott (interview with Nat Hentoff), 98.

55. Heylin, *Still on the Road: The Songs of Bob Dylan, Vol. 2*, 305; 308.

56. David Yaffe, "Not Dark Yet: How Bob Dylan Got His Groove Back," in *Highway 61 Revisited*, ed. Colleen Sheehy and Thomas Swiss (Minneapolis: University of Minnesota Press, 2009), 198.

57. David Yaffe, *Bob Dylan: Like a Complete Unknown* (New Haven, CT: Yale University Press, 2011), 60. See chapter 3, "Not Dark Yet: How Bob Dylan Got His Groove Back," for an expansion of Yaffe's 2009 article.

58. Kinney, *Continental Humanist Poetics*, 18 (see ch. 1, n. 15).

59. Tanakh, *The Holy Scriptures*, New JPS Translation (Philadelphia: Jewish Publication Society, 1988), 284.

60. I am grateful to Julia Irmscher and Lauren Bernofsky for their advice on musical matters in this and the following paragraphs.

61. Ricks, 15.

62. Heylin, *Still on the Road: The Songs of Bob Dylan, Vol. 2*, 312.

63. "Ordinary People," lyrics by Danniebelle Hall, begins: "Just ordinary People / God uses ordinary people / He chooses people just like me and you who are willing to do what He command." Dylan construes the title from the second line. (This song was also recorded by Mom Winans.)

64. Clinton Heylin, *Trouble in Mind: Bob Dylan's Gospel Years, What Really Happened* (New York: Lesser Gods, 2017), 303. Dylan is referring to Mona Lisa Young, one of his backup singers on the gospel tour.

65. Heylin, *Trouble in Mind*. Heylin states at the beginning of his appendix containing the spoken intros that "all the raps in this book have been compared with existing transcripts, done by Bob Pook . . . or myself in the eighties, or for Olaf Bjorner's website . . . and in most cases have been re-transcribed from superior audio sources" (302). The result of this process is that, contrary to Dylan's habitual practice in manuscripts, the word "God" is spelled out rather than rendered "G-d."

66. Martin Luther King Jr., "I Have a Dream." August 28, 1963, Washington, DC. Transcript at: https://www.npr.org/2010/01/18/122701268/i-have-a-dream-speech-in-its-entirety.

67. See Sounes, *Down the Highway*, 145.

68. Heylin, *Trouble in Mind*, 304.

69. Andrew McCarron, *Light Come Shining: The Transformations of Bob Dylan* (New York: Oxford University Press, 2017), 91.

70. McCarron, *Light Come Shining*, 90–91.

71. Seth Rogovoy, "Was Bob Dylan at His Best When He Was a Christian?" *Forward*, October 30, 2017. https://forward.com. See Hal Lindsey, with C. C. Carlson, *The Late Great Planet Earth* (Grand Rapids, MI: Zondervan, 1970).

72. Stephen H. Webb, *Redeemed: From Highway 61 to Saved* (New York: Continuum, 2006), 87.

73. Heylin, *Trouble in Mind*, 38.

74. Paul Williams, *Dylan—What Happened?* (South Bend, IN: And Books / Entwhistle Books, 1980), 86.

75. Williams, *Dylan—What Happened?*, 86.

76. Webb, *Redeemed*, 87.

77. Bob Dylan, *Saved! The Gospel Speeches of Bob Dylan* (New York: Hanuman Books, 1991). McCarron gives the publication date as 1990, but his book does not include a bibliography. Amazon lists the publication date as January 1, 1991. See also Heylin, *Trouble in Mind*, appendix 2, "Some Alternate Raps," 302–11.

78. Williams, *Dylan—What Happened?*, 8.

79. This is a reference to Matthew 12:29–30: "Are not two sparrows sold for a farthing?

And one of them shall not fall on the ground without your Father. But the very hairs on your head are numbered" (Cf. Luke 12:6–7). Gray discusses a possible mistranslation, suggesting "fall to ground" might mean "caught in a snare." See *Song and Dance Man III*, 406n9.

80. Gayle Wald, "Gospel Music," in *The World of Bob Dylan*, ed. Sean Latham (Cambridge, UK: Cambridge University Press, 2021), 88.

81. Wald, "Gospel Music," 89.

82. Wald, 94.

83. Jeffrey Lamp, "The Hal Lindsey Effect: Bob Dylan's Christian Eschatology," *Dylan Review* 3, no. 1 (Summer 2021), 62. Lamp adds that "Lindsey's emphasis on the role of Jews and the current state of Israel in God's end time program provided Dylan with a heuristic that allowed him to integrate the Judaism of his background with his new Christian faith" (62).

84. This document is rife with misspellings, as in "Perserverance," "Defilment," "Insincerety," "Integrety," "Intemperence," and "Rightiousness."

85. This is the only entry with the word "God," and it is highly uncharacteristic for Dylan to spell out the name rather than writing "G-d."

86. Hal Lindsey raises the notion of being ready, but in the context of what he calls "putting it all together," an oracular reading of current events through a biblical lens. He warns of the threat from the alliance of Russian authority, Israeli control of Jerusalem, Egyptian leadership, and the Black African nations' false liberation by the Arabs: "It's happening. God is putting it all together. God may have His meaning for the 'now generation' which will have a greater effect on mankind than anything since Genesis 1. Will you be ready if we are to be a part of the prophetic 'now generation'?" (*Late Great Planet Earth*, 69).

87. Webb, *Redeemed*, 6.

88. Dettmar, "Borrowing," 210 (see ch. 2, n. 8).

89. My emphasis.

90. Gibbens, *The Nightingale's Code*, 202 (see ch. 1, n. 65).

91. Thomas, *Why Bob Dylan Matters*, 117.

92. See Thomas, *Why Bob Dylan Matters*, 116, on Dylan's 2004 Rome press conference.

93. Muir speculates that there's a connection between the title and the time-bending: "In the misty past of linguistic derivation, the root word for tempest was *tempus*, which means 'time.' The work 'tempest' perhaps originally signified a storm so severe that it appeared to disrupt time, bringing chaos and flux in its wake" (*Performing of It*, 339). Muir recognizes that an etymology that "perhaps originally signified" something is a bit too tentative. But it's a tempting proposition nonetheless.

94. I am grateful to Mark Davidson at the Bob Dylan Archive for confirming Dylan's use of "G-d" in the *Tempest* manuscripts and other recent acquisitions. More recently, the spelling "G-d" also appears online in the official lyrics for "Goodbye Jimmy Reed" and "Murder Most Foul," both from *Rough and Rowdy Ways* (see bobdylan.com).

95. For discussion of this point see Mikal Gilmore's 2012 *Rolling Stone* interviews with Dylan. In the September publication, he quotes Dylan: "Shakespeare's last play was called *The Tempest*. It wasn't called just plain *Tempest*. The name of my record is just plain *Tempest*. It's two different titles." And see also Muir, 285: "Dylan is perfectly correct in highlighting the dissimilarity in the titles. The definite article makes a vital distinction, as would an indefinite one. 'The Tempest,' 'Tempest' and 'A Tempest' are all different. However, we have seen how regularly Dylan draws comparisons of himself to Shakespeare and, consequently, he would surely have been aware that his title would strike people this way, regardless of the obvious disparity."

96. William Shakespeare, *The Tempest*, ed. Stephen Orgel (Oxford: Oxford University Press, 1987), 1.2.301–4.

97. The phrase *ubique naufragium est* from Petronius's *Satyricon* became the epigraph for

Justa Edouardo King (Obsequies for Edward King, 1638), the collection of elegies in which Milton's *Lycidas* appeared.

98. Shakespeare, *The Tempest*, 1.2.193–206.

99. Shakespeare, *The Tempest*, 1.2.224–28; 230; 232–37.

100. In fact, it's Caliban, not Prospero, who issues a curse: "You taught me language, and my profit on't / Is I know how to curse. The red plague rid you / For learning me your language" (1.2.366–68). This passage and the kind of language Prospero taught Caliban, including the use of cursing, have spawned a good deal of critical analysis. See, among others, Stephen Greenblatt, *Learning to Curse: Essays in Early Modern Culture* (New York: Routledge, 1990).

101. Thomas, *Why Bob Dylan Matters*, 116.

102. Dylan in response to a Gilmore question: "This country is just too fucked up about color. It's a distraction. People at each other's throats just because they are of a different color. It's the height of insanity, and it will hold any nation back—or any neighborhood back. Or any anything back. Blacks know that some whites didn't want to give up slavery—that if they had their way, they would still be under the yoke, and they can't pretend they don't know that. If you got a slave master or Klan in your blood, blacks can sense that. That stuff lingers to this day. Just like Jews can sense Nazi blood and the Serbs can sense Croatian blood. It's doubtful that America's ever going to get rid of that stigmatization. It's a country founded on the backs of slaves. You know what I mean? Because it goes way back. It's the root cause. If slavery had been given up in a more peaceful way, America would be far ahead today. Whoever invented the idea 'lost cause . . . .' There's nothing heroic about any lost cause. No such thing, though there are people who still believe it." (*Rolling Stone*, September 27, 2012)

103. Thomas, *Why Bob Dylan Matters*, 117.

104. Thomas, *Why Bob Dylan Matters*, 117.

AFTERWORD

1. Jack Kroll, Untitled review of *Renaldo and Clara*, *Newsweek*, January 30, 1978, 56.

2. Dave Marsh, "Ballad in Plain Dull," *Rolling Stone Magazine*, March 9, 1978. Dylan wrote the song in the sixties and recorded it in June and October 1967 in the basement of Big Pink, a house rented by members of the Band in West Saugerties, New York. Columbia released the song on *Dylan* (1973) and then released *The Basement Tapes* in 1975.

3. Riley, *Hard Rain*, 209 (see intro, n. 40).

4. Kermode, "Bob Dylan," 188 (see intro, n. 9).

5. Sam Shepard, *Rolling Thunder Logbook* (New York: Viking Press, 1977), 100.

DISCOGRAPHY
Compiled by Nicole Font

The following discography includes only Dylan's albums and the dates of their American release. For information on singles, films, videos, British releases, and album outtakes I would recommend Brian Hinton's *Bob Dylan: Complete Discography* (2006) and Margotin and Guesdon, *Bob Dylan: All the Songs: The Story behind Every Track.*

1962

Bob Dylan, **Columbia CL-1779 (mono) / Columbia CS-8579 (stereo). Released March 19, 1962**
SIDE 1: You're No Good; Talkin' New York; In My Time of Dyin'; Man of Constant Sorrow; Fixin' to Die; Pretty Peggy-O; Highway 51 Blues
SIDE 2: Gospel Plow; Baby, Let Me Follow Me Down; House of the Risin' Sun; Freight Train Blues; Song to Woody; See That My Grave Is Kept Clean

1963

The Freewheelin' Bob Dylan, **Columbia CL-1986 (mono) / Columbia CS-8786 (stereo). Released May 27, 1963**
SIDE 1: Blowin' in the Wind; Girl from the North Country; Masters of War; Down the Highway; Bob Dylan's Blues; A Hard Rain's A-Gonna Fall
SIDE 2: Don't Think Twice, It's All Right; Bob Dylan's Dream; Oxford Town; Talkin' World War III Blues; Corrina, Corrina; Honey, Just Allow Me One More Chance; I Shall Be Free

1964

The Times They Are A-Changin', **Columbia CL-2105 (mono) / Columbia CS-8905 (stereo). Released January 13, 1964**
SIDE 1: The Times They Are A-Changin'; Ballad of Hollis Brown; With God on Our Side; One Too Many Mornings; North Country Blues
SIDE 2: Only a Pawn in Their Game; Boots of Spanish Leather; When the Ship Comes In; The Lonesome Death of Hattie Carroll; Restless Farewell

Another Side of Bob Dylan, **Columbia CL-2193 (mono) / Columbia CS-8993 (stereo). Released August 8, 1964**
SIDE 1: All I Really Want to Do; Black Crow Blues; Spanish Harlem Incident; Chimes of Freedom; I Shall Be Free no. 10; To Ramona
SIDE 2: Motorpsycho Nitemare; My Back Pages; I Don't Believe You (She Acts Like We Never Have Met); Ballad in Plain D; It Ain't Me Babe

1965

Bringing It All Back Home, **Columbia CL-2328 (mono) / Columbia CS-9128 (stereo). Released March 22, 1965**
SIDE 1: Subterranean Homesick Blues; She Belongs to Me; Maggie's Farm; Love Minus Zero/No Limit; Outlaw Blues; On the Road Again; Bob Dylan's 115th Dream

SIDE 2: Mr. Tambourine Man; Gates of Eden; It's Alright, Ma (I'm Only Bleeding); It's All Over Now, Baby Blue

Highway 61 Revisited, **Columbia CL-2389 (mono) / Columbia CS-9189 (stereo). Released August 30, 1965**
SIDE 1: Like a Rolling Stone; Tombstone Blues; It Takes a Lot to Laugh, It Takes a Train to Cry; From a Buick 6; Ballad of a Thin Man
SIDE 2: Queen Jane Approximately; Highway 61 Revisited; Just Like Tom Thumb's Blues; Desolation Row

1966

Blonde on Blonde, **Columbia C2L-41 (mono) / Columbia C2S-841 (stereo). Released June 20, 1966**
SIDE 1: Rainy Day Women ♯12 & 35; Pledging My Time; Visions of Johanna; One of Us Must Know (Sooner or Later)
SIDE 2: I Want You; Stuck Inside of Mobile with the Memphis Blues Again; Leopard-Skin Pill-Box Hat; Just Like a Woman
SIDE 3: Most Likely You Go Your Way (and I'll Go Mine); Temporary Like Achilles; Absolutely Sweet Marie; Fourth Time Around; Obviously Five Believers
SIDE 4: Sad-Eyed Lady of the Lowlands

1967

Bob Dylan's Greatest Hits, **Columbia C 9463. Released March 27, 1967**
SIDE 1: Rainy Day Women ♯12 & 35; Blowin' in the Wind; The Times They Are A-Changin'; It Ain't Me Babe; Like a Rolling Stone
SIDE 2: Mr. Tambourine Man; Subterranean Homesick Blues; I Want You; Positively 4th Street; Just Like a Woman

John Wesley Harding, **Columbia CL-2804 (mono) / Columbia CS-9604 (stereo). Released December 27, 1967**
SIDE 1: John Wesley Harding; As I Went Out One Morning; I Dreamed I Saw St. Augustine; All Along the Watchtower; The Ballad of Frankie Lee and Judas Priest; Drifter's Escape
SIDE 2: Dear Landlord; I Am a Lonesome Hobo; I Pity the Poor Immigrant; The Wicked Messenger; Down along the Cove; I'll Be Your Baby Tonight

1969

Nashville Skyline, **Columbia 9825. Released April 9, 1969**
SIDE 1: Girl from the North Country; Nashville Skyline Rag; To Be Alone with You; I Threw It All Away; Peggy Day
SIDE 2: Lay, Lady, Lay; One More Night; Tell Me That It Isn't True; Country Pie; Tonight I'll Be Staying Here with You

1970

Self Portrait, **Columbia 30050. Released June 8, 1970**
SIDE 1: All the Tired Horses; Alberta #1; I Forgot More Than You'll Ever Know; Days of 49; Early Mornin' Rain; In Search of Little Sadie
SIDE 2: Let It Be Me; Little Sadie; Woogie Boogie; Belle Isle; Living the Blues; Like a Rolling Stone
SIDE 3: Copper Kettle; Gotta Travel On; Blue Moon; The Boxer; The Mighty Quinn (Quinn the Eskimo); Take Me as I Am (Or Let Me Go)

SIDE 4: Take a Message to Mary; It Hurts Me Too; Minstrel Boy; She Belongs to Me; Wigwam; Alberta #2

New Morning, Columbia 30290. Released October 21, 1970
SIDE 1: If Not for You; Day of the Locusts; Time Passes Slowly; Went to See the Gypsy; Winterlude; If Dogs Run Free
SIDE 2: New Morning; Sign on the Window; One More Weekend; The Man in Me; Three Angels; Father of Night

1971

Bob Dylan's Greatest Hits Volume II, Columbia 31120. Released November 17, 1971
SIDE 1: Watching the River Flow; Don't Think Twice, It's All Right; Lay, Lady, Lay; Stuck Inside of Mobile with the Memphis Blues Again
SIDE 2: I'll Be Your Baby Tonight; All I Really Want to Do; My Back Pages; Maggie's Farm; Tonight I'll Be Staying Here with You
SIDE 3: She Belongs to Me; All Along the Watchtower; The Mighty Quinn (Quinn the Eskimo); Just Like Tom Thumb's Blues; A Hard Rain's A-Gonna Fall
SIDE 4: If Not for You; It's All Over Now, Baby Blue; Tomorrow Is a Long Time; When I Paint My Masterpiece; I Shall Be Released; You Ain't Goin' Nowhere; Down in the Flood

1973

Pat Garrett & Billy the Kid, Columbia 32460. Released July 13, 1973
SIDE 1: Main Title Theme (Billy); Cantina Theme (Workin' for the Law); Billy 1; Bunkhouse Theme; River Theme
SIDE 2: Turkey Chase; Knockin' on Heaven's Door; Final Theme; Billy 4; Billy 7

Dylan, Columbia 32747. Released November 16, 1973
SIDE 1: Lily of the West; Can't Help Falling in Love; Sarah Jane; The Ballad of Ira Hayes
SIDE 2: Mr. Bojangles; Mary Ann; Big Yellow Taxi; A Fool Such as I; Spanish Is the Loving Tongue

1974

Planet Waves, Asylum 1003. Originally released January 17, 1974. Rereleased 1982, Columbia PC/CK 37637
SIDE 1: On a Night Like This; Going, Going, Gone; Tough Mama; Hazel; Something There Is About You; Forever Young
SIDE 2: Forever Young; Dirge; You Angel You; Never Say Goodbye; Wedding Song

Before the Flood, Asylum AB 201. Released June 20, 1974. Reissued in 1982, Columbia KG 37661
SIDE 1: Most Likely You Go Your Way (and I'll Go Mine); Lay, Lady, Lay; Rainy Day Women #12 & 35; Knockin' on Heaven's Door; It Ain't Me, Babe; Ballad of a Thin Man
SIDE 2: Up on Cripple Creek; I Shall Be Released; Endless Highway; The Night They Drove Old Dixie Down; Stage Fright
SIDE 3: Don't Think Twice, It's All Right; Just Like a Woman; It's Alright, Ma (I'm Only Bleeding); The Shape I'm In; When You Awake; The Weight
SIDE 4: All Along the Watchtower; Highway 61 Revisited; Like a Rolling Stone; Blowin' in the Wind

1975

Blood on the Tracks, **Columbia 33235. Released January 20, 1975**
SIDE 1: Tangled Up in Blue; Simple Twist of Fate; You're a Big Girl Now; Idiot Wind;
You're Gonna Make Me Lonesome When You Go
SIDE 2: Meet Me in the Morning; Lily, Rosemary and the Jack of Hearts; If You See Her,
Say Hello; Shelter from the Storm; Buckets of Rain

The Basement Tapes, **Columbia 33682. Released June 26, 1975. Recorded June and
October 1967**
SIDE 1: Odds and Ends; Orange Juice Blues (Blues for Breakfast); Million Dollar Bash;
Yazoo Street Scandal; Goin' to Acapulco; Katie's Been Gone
SIDE 2: Lo and Behold!; Bessie Smith; Clothes Line Saga; Apple Suckling Tree; Please,
Mrs. Henry; Tears of Rage
SIDE 3: Too Much of Nothing; Yea! Heavy and a Bottle of Bread; Ain't No More Cane;
Crash on the Levee (Down in the Flood); Ruben Remus; Tiny Montgomery
SIDE 4: You Ain't Goin' Nowhere; Don't Ya Tell Henry; Nothing Was Delivered; Open the
Door, Homer; Long Distance Operator; This Wheel's on Fire

1976

Desire, **Columbia 33893. Released January 5, 1976**
SIDE 1: Hurricane; Isis; Mozambique; One More Cup of Coffee; Oh, Sister
SIDE 2: Joey; Romance in Durango; Black Diamond Bay; Sara

Hard Rain, **Columbia PC 34349. Released September 10, 1976**
SIDE 1: Maggie's Farm; One Too Many Mornings; Stuck Inside of Mobile with the Memphis
Blues Again; Oh, Sister; Lay, Lady, Lay
SIDE 2: Shelter from the Storm; You're a Big Girl Now; I Threw It All Away; Idiot Wind

1978

Street-Legal, **Columbia 35453. Released June 15, 1978**
SIDE 1: Changing of the Guards; New Pony; No Time to Think; Baby, Stop Crying
SIDE 2: Is Your Love in Vain?; Señor (Tales of Yankee Power); True Love Tends to Forget;
We Better Talk This Over; Where Are You Tonight? (Journey through Dark Heat)

1979

Bob Dylan at Budokan, **Columbia C2 36067. Released April 23, 1979**
SIDE 1: Mr. Tambourine Man; Shelter from the Storm; Love Minus Zero/No Limit; Ballad
of a Thin Man; Don't Think Twice, It's All Right
SIDE 2: Maggie's Farm; One More Cup of Coffee (Valley Below); Like a Rolling Stone; I
Shall Be Released; Is Your Love in Vain?; Going, Going, Gone
SIDE 3: Blowin' in the Wind; Just Like a Woman; Oh, Sister; Simple Twist of Fate; All
Along the Watchtower; I Want You
SIDE 4: All I Really Want to Do; Knockin' on Heaven's Door; It's Alright, Ma (I'm Only
Bleeding); Forever Young; The Times They Are A-Changin'

Slow Train Coming, **Columbia 36120. Released August 20, 1979**
SIDE 1: Gotta Serve Somebody; Precious Angel; I Believe in You; Slow Train
SIDE 2: Gonna Change My Way of Thinking; Do Right to Me Baby (Do unto Others);
When You Gonna Wake Up; Man Gave Names to All the Animals; When He Returns

1980

Saved, Columbia 36553. **Released June 20, 1980**
SIDE 1: A Satisfied Mind; Saved; Covenant Woman; What Can I Do for You?; Solid Rock
SIDE 2: Pressing On; In the Garden; Saving Grace; Are You Ready

1981

Shot of Love, Columbia 37496. **Released August 12, 1981**
SIDE 1: Shot of Love; Heart of Mine; Property of Jesus; Lenny Bruce; Watered-Down Love
SIDE 2: The Groom's Still Waiting at the Altar; Dead Man, Dead Man; In the Summertime; Trouble; Every Grain of Sand

1983

Infidels, Columbia 38819. **Released October 27, 1983**
SIDE 1: Jokerman; Sweetheart Like You; Neighborhood Bully; License to Kill
SIDE 2: Man of Peace; Union Sundown; I and I; Don't Fall Apart on Me Tonight

1985

Real Live, Columbia 39944. **Released November 29, 1984**
SIDE 1: Highway 61 Revisited; Maggie's Farm; I and I; License to Kill; It Ain't Me, Babe
SIDE 2: Tangled Up in Blue; Masters of War; Ballad of a Thin Man; Girl from the North Country; Tombstone Blues

Empire Burlesque, Columbia 40110. **Released June 8, 1985**
SIDE 1: Tight Connection to My Heart (Has Anybody Seen My Love); Seeing the Real You at Last; I'll Remember You; Clean Cut Kid; Never Gonna Be the Same Again
SIDE 2: Trust Yourself; Emotionally Yours; When the Night Comes Falling from the Sky; Something's Burning, Baby; Dark Eyes

Biograph, Columbia C3K 38830 (CD). **Released November 7, 1985**
SIDE 1: Lay, Lady, Lay; Baby, Let Me Follow You Down; If Not for You; I'll Be Your Baby Tonight; I'll Keep It with Mine
SIDE 2: The Times They Are A-Changin'; Blowin' in the Wind; Masters of War; The Lonesome Death of Hattie Carroll; Percy's Song
SIDE 3: Mixed-Up Confusion; Tombstone Blues; The Groom's Still Waiting at the Altar; Most Likely You Go Your Way (and I'll Go Mine); Like a Rolling Stone; Jet Pilot
SIDE 4: Lay Down Your Weary Tune; Subterranean Homesick Blues; I Don't Believe You; Visions of Johanna; Every Grain of Sand
SIDE 5: Quinn the Eskimo (The Mighty Quinn); Mr. Tambourine Man; Dear Landlord; It Ain't Me, Babe; You Angel You; Million Dollar Bash
SIDE 6: To Ramona; You're a Big Girl Now; Abandoned Love; Tangled Up in Blue; It's All Over Now, Baby Blue
SIDE 7: Can You Please Crawl Out Your Window?; Positively 4th Street; Isis; Caribbean Wind; Up to Me
SIDE 8: Baby, I'm in the Mood for You; I Wanna Be Your Lover; I Want You; Heart of Mine; On a Night Like This; Just Like a Woman
SIDE 9: Romance in Durango; Señor (Tales of Yankee Power); Gotta Serve Somebody; I Believe in You; Time Passes Slowly
SIDE 10: I Shall Be Released; Knockin' on Heaven's Door; All Along the Watchtower; Solid Rock; Forever Young

1986

Knocked Out Loaded, **Columbia 40439. Released July 14, 1986**
SIDE 1: You Wanna Ramble; They Killed Him; Driftin' Too Far from Shore; Precious
    Memories; Maybe Someday
SIDE 2: Brownsville Girl; Got My Mind Made Up; Under Your Spell

1988

Dylan and the Dead, **Columbia CK 45056 (CD). Released February 6, 1989**
SIDE 1: Slow Train; I Want You; Gotta Serve Somebody; Queen Jane Approximately
SIDE 2: Joey; All Along the Watchtower; Knockin' on Heaven's Door

Down in the Groove, **Columbia 40957. Released May 31, 1988**
SIDE 1: Let's Stick Together; When Did You Leave Heaven?; Sally Sue Brown; Death Is
    Not the End; Had a Dream about You, Baby
SIDE 2: Ugliest Girl in the World; Silvio; Ninety Miles an Hour (Down a Dead End
    Street); Shenandoah; Rank Strangers to Me

1989

Oh Mercy, **Columbia 45281. Released September 18, 1989**
SIDE 1: Political World; Where Teardrops Fall; Everything Is Broken; Ring Them Bells;
    Man in the Long Black Coat
SIDE 2: Most of the Time; What Good Am I?; Disease of Conceit; What Was It You
    Wanted; Shooting Star

1990

Under the Red Sky, **Columbia 46794. Released September 11, 1990**
SIDE 1: Wiggle Wiggle; Under the Red Sky; Unbelievable; Born in Time; T. V. Talkin' Song
SIDE 2: 10,000 Men; 2 × 2; God Knows; Handy Dandy; Cat's in the Well

1991

The Bootleg Series, Vol. 1–3: Rare and Unreleased 1961–1991, **Columbia C3K 65302 (3
CD version). Released March 26, 1991**
DISC 1: Hard Times in New York Town; He Was a Friend of Mine; Man on the Street; No
    More Auction Block; House Carpenter; Talkin' Bear Mountain Picnic Massacre Blues;
    Let Me Die in My Footsteps; Rambling, Gambling Willie; Talkin' Hava Negeilah Blues;
    Quit Your Low Down Ways; Worried Blues; Kingsport Town; Walkin' Down the Line;
    Walls of Red Wing; Paths of Victory; Talkin' John Birch Paranoid Blues; Who Killed
    Davey Moore?; Only a Hobo; Moonshiner; When the Ship Comes In; The Times They
    Are A-Changin'; Last Thoughts on Woody Guthrie
DISC 2: Seven Curses; Eternal Circle; Suze (The Cough Song); Mama, You Been on My
    Mind; Farewell, Angelina; Subterranean Homesick Blues; If You Gotta Go, Go Now
    (Or Else You Got to Stay All Night); Sitting on a Barbed Wire Fence; Like a Rolling
    Stone; It Takes a Lot to Laugh, It Takes a Train to Cry; I'll Keep It with Mine; She's
    Your Lover Now; I Shall Be Released; Santa-Fe; If Not for You; Wallflower; Nobody
    'Cept You; Tangled Up in Blue; Call Letter Blues; Idiot Wind
DISC 3: If You See Her, Say Hello; Golden Loom; Catfish; Seven Days; Ye Shall Be
    Changed; Every Grain of Sand; You Changed My Life; Need a Woman; Angelina;
    Someone's Got a Hold of My Heart; Tell Me; Lord Protect My Child; Foot of Pride;
    Blind Willie McTell; When the Night Comes Falling from the Sky; Series of Dreams

1992

Good as I Been to You, Columbia 53200. Released October 27, 1992
SIDE 1: Frankie & Albert; Jim Jones; Blackjack Davey; Canadee-i-o; Sittin' on Top of the World; Little Maggie; Hard Times
SIDE 2: Step It Up and Go; Tomorrow Night; Arthur McBride; You're Gonna Quit Me; Diamond Joe; Froggie Went a Courtin'

1993

The 30th Anniversary Concert, Columbia C2K 53230. Released August 24, 1993
DISC 1: Like a Rolling Stone; Leopard-Skin Pill-Box Hat; Introduction; Blowin' in the Wind; Foot of Pride; Masters of War; The Times They Are A-Changin'; It Ain't Me Babe; What Was It You Wanted; I'll Be Your Baby Tonight; Highway 61 Revisited; Seven Days; Just Like a Woman; When the Ship Comes In; You Ain't Going Nowhere; Don't Think Twice, It's All Right
DISC 2: Just Like Tom Thumb's Blues; All Along the Watchtower; I Shall Be Released; Don't Think Twice, It's All Right; Emotionally Yours; When I Paint My Masterpiece; Absolutely Sweet Marie; License to Kill; Rainy Day Women #12 & 35; Mr. Tambourine Man; It's Alright, Ma (I'm Only Bleeding); My Back Pages; Knockin' on Heaven's Door; Girl from the North Country; I Believe in You

World Gone Wrong, Columbia 57590. Released October 26, 1993
SIDE 1: World Gone Wrong; Love Henry; Ragged & Dirty; Blood in My Eyes; Broke Down Engine
SIDE 2: Delia; Stack a Lee; Two Soldiers; Jack-A-Roe; Lone Pilgrim

1994

Bob Dylan's Greatest Hits Volume 3, Columbia CK 66783 (CD). Released November 15, 1994
Tangled Up in Blue; Changing of the Guards; The Groom's Still Waiting at the Altar; Hurricane; Forever Young; Jokerman; Dignity; Silvio; Ring Them Bells; Gotta Serve Somebody; Series of Dreams; Brownsville Girl; Under the Red Sky; Knockin' on Heaven's Door

1995

Bob Dylan Unplugged, Columbia CK 67000 (CD). Released April 25, 1995
Tombstone Blues; Shooting Star; All Along the Watchtower; The Times They Are A-Changin'; John Brown; Rainy Day Women #12 & 35; Desolation Row; Dignity; Knockin' on Heaven's Door; Like a Rolling Stone; With God on Our Side

1997

Time Out of Mind, Columbia 68556. Released September 30, 1997
Love Sick; Dirt Road Blues; Standing in the Doorway; Million Miles; Tryin' to Get to Heaven; Til I Fell in Love with You; Not Dark Yet; Cold Irons Bound; Make You Feel My Love; Can't Wait; Highlands

1998

The Bootleg Series, Vol. 4: Bob Dylan Live 1966, Columbia/Legacy C2K 65759 (2CD). Released October 13, 1998

DISC 1: She Belongs to Me; Fourth Time Around; Visions of Johanna; It's All Over Now, Baby Blue; Desolation Row; Just Like a Woman; Mr. Tambourine Man

DISC 2: Tell Me, Momma; I Don't Believe You (She Acts Like We Never Have Met); Baby, Let Me Follow You Down; Just Like Tom Thumb's Blues; Leopard-Skin Pill-Box Hat; One Too Many Mornings; Ballad of a Thin Man; Like a Rolling Stone

2000

The Essential Bob Dylan, **Columbia C2K 85168. Released October 31, 2000**

DISC 1: Blowin' in the Wind; Don't Think Twice, It's All Right; The Times They Are A-Changin'; It Ain't Me, Babe; Maggie's Farm; It's All Over Now, Baby Blue; Mr. Tambourine Man; Subterranean Homesick Blues; Like a Rolling Stone; Positively 4th Street; Just Like a Woman; Rainy Day Women #12 & 35; All Along the Watchtower; Quinn the Eskimo (The Mighty Quinn); I'll Be Your Baby Tonight

DISC 2: Lay, Lady, Lay; If Not for You; I Shall Be Released; You Ain't Goin' Nowhere; Knockin' on Heaven's Door; Forever Young; Tangled Up in Blue; Shelter from the Storm

DISC 3 (limited edition 3.0 version): Thunder on the Mountain; Mississippi; Blind Willie McTell; Make You Feel My Love; Beyond Here Lies Nothin'; Dark Eyes

2001

"Love and Theft", **Columbia 85975. Released September 11, 2001**

DISC 1: Tweedle Dee & Tweedle Dum; Mississippi; Summer Days; Bye and Bye; Lonesome Day Blues; Floater (Too Much to Ask); High Water (For Charley Patton); Moonlight; Honest with Me; Po' Boy; Cry a While; Sugar Baby

2002

The Bootleg Series, Vol. 5: Bob Dylan Live 1975, **Columbia/Legacy C2K 87047 (2CD). Released November 26, 2002**

DISC 1: Tonight I'll Be Staying Here with You; It Ain't Me Babe; A Hard Rain's a-Gonna Fall; The Lonesome Death of Hattie Carroll; Romance in Durango; Isis; Mr. Tambourine Man; Simple Twist of Fate; Blowin' in the Wind; Mama, You Been on My Mind; I Shall Be Released

DISC 2: It's All Over Now, Baby Blue; Love Minus Zero/No Limit; Tangled Up in Blue; The Water Is Wide; It Takes a Lot to Laugh, It Takes a Train to Cry; Oh, Sister; Hurricane; One More Cup of Coffee (Valley Below); Sara; Just Like a Woman; Knockin' on Heaven's Door

2004

The Bootleg Series, Vol. 6: Bob Dylan Live 1964, **Columbia/Legacy C2K 86882 (2CD). Released March 30, 2004**

DISC 1: The Times They Are A-Changin'; Spanish Harlem Incident; Talkin' John Birch Paranoid Blues; To Ramona; Who Killed Davey Moore?; Gates of Eden; If You Gotta Go, Go Now (Or Else You Got to Stay All Night); It's Alright, Ma (I'm Only Bleeding); I Don't Believe You (She Acts Like We Never Have Met); Mr. Tambourine Man; A Hard Rain's a-Gonna Fall

DISC 2: Talkin' World War III Blues; Don't Think Twice, It's All Right; The Lonesome Death of Hattie Carroll; Mama, You Been on My Mind; Silver Dagger; With God on Our Side; It Ain't Me, Babe; All I Really Want to Do

2005

The Bootleg Series, Vol. 7: No Direction Home, Columbia/Legacy C2K 93937 (2CD). **Released August 30, 2005**
DISC 1: When I Got Troubles; Rambler, Gambler; This Land Is Your Land (live); Song to Woody; Dink's Song; I Was Young When I Left Home; Sally Gal; Don't Think Twice, It's All Right; Man of Constant Sorrow; Blowin' in the Wind (live); Masters of War (live); A Hard Rain's A-Gonna Fall (live); When the Ship Comes In (live); Mr. Tambourine Man; Chimes of Freedom (live); It's All Over Now, Baby Blue (take 1)
DISC 2: She Belongs to Me (take 2); Maggie's Farm (live); It Takes a Lot to Laugh, It Takes a Train to Cry (take 9); Tombstone Blues; Just Like Tom Thumb's Blues (alternate take); Desolation Row (take 1); Highway 61 Revisited (take 6); Leopard-Skin Pill-Box Hat (take 1); Stuck Inside of Mobile with the Memphis Blues Again (take 5); Visions of Johanna (take 8); Ballad of a Thin Man (live); Like a Rolling Stone (live)

The Best of Bob Dylan, Columbia (US, Canada). **Released November 15, 2005**
Blowin' in the Wind; The Times They Are A-Changin'; Mr. Tambourine Man; Like a Rolling Stone; Rainy Day Women #12 & 35; All Along the Watchtower; Lay, Lady, Lay; Knockin' on Heaven's Door; Tangled Up in Blue; Hurricane; Forever Young; Gotta Serve Somebody; Jokerman; Not Dark Yet; Things Have Changed; Summer Days

2006

Modern Times, Columbia 82876 87606 2. **Released August 29, 2006**
Thunder on the Mountain; Spirit on the Water; Rollin' and Tumblin'; When the Deal Goes Down; Someday Baby; Workingman's Blues #2; Beyond the Horizon; Nettie Moore; The Levee's Gonna Break; Ain't Talkin'

2007

Dylan, Columbia 88697 11420 2. **Released October 2, 2007**
DISC 1: Song to Woody; Blowin' in the Wind; Masters of War; Don't Think Twice, It's All Right; A Hard Rain's A-Gonna Fall; The Times They Are A-Changin'; All I Really Want to Do; My Back Pages; It Ain't Me, Babe; Subterranean Homesick Blues; Mr. Tambourine Man; Maggie's Farm; Like a Rolling Stone; It's All Over Now, Baby Blue; Positively 4th Street; Rainy Day Women #12 & 35; Just Like a Woman; Most Likely You Go Your Way (And I'll Go Mine); All Along the Watchtower
DISC 2: You Ain't Goin' Nowhere; Lay, Lady, Lay; If Not for You; I Shall Be Released; Knockin' on Heaven's Door; On a Night Like This; Forever Young; Tangled Up in Blue; Simple Twist of Fate; Hurricane; Changing of the Guards; Gotta Serve Somebody; Precious Angel; The Groom's Still Waiting at the Altar; Jokerman; Dark Eyes
DISC 3: Blind Willie McTell; Brownsville Girl; Silvio; Ring Them Bells; Dignity; Everything Is Broken; Under the Red Sky; You're Gonna Quit Me; Blood in My Eyes; Not Dark Yet; Things Have Changed; Make You Feel My Love; High Water (For Charley Patton); Po' Boy; Someday Baby; When the Deal Goes Down

2008

The Bootleg Series, Vol. 8: Tell Tale Signs, Columbia/Legacy 88697 35795 2. **Released October 7, 2008**
DISC 1: Mississippi; Most of the Time; Dignity; Someday Baby; Red River Shore; Tell Ol' Bill; Born in Time; Can't Wait; Everything Is Broken; Dreamin' of You; Huck's Tune; Marchin' to the City; High Water (For Charley Patton)

DISC 2: Mississippi; 32–20 Blues; Series of Dreams; God Knows; Can't Escape from You; Dignity; Ring Them Bells; Cocaine Blues; Ain't Talkin'; The Girl on the Greenbriar Shore; Lonesome Day Blues; Miss the Mississippi; The Lonesome River; Cross the Green Mountain; Love Sick

BONUS DISC: Duncan & Brady; Cold Irons Bound; Mississippi; Most of the Time; Ring Them Bells; Things Have Changed; Red River Shore; Born in Time; Tryin' to Get to Heaven; Marchin' to the City; Can't Wait; Mary and the Soldier

2009

Together Through Life, **Columbia 88697 43893 2. Released April 28, 2009**
Beyond Here Lies Nothin'; Life Is Hard; My Wife's Home Town; If You Ever Go to Houston; Forgetful Heart; Jolene; This Dream of You; Shake Shake Mama; I Feel a Change Comin' On; It's All Good

Christmas in the Heart, **Columbia 88697 57323 2. Released October 13, 2009**
Here Comes Santa Claus; Do You Hear What I Hear?; Winter Wonderland; Hark the Herald Angels Sing; I'll Be Home for Christmas; Little Drummer Boy; The Christmas Blues; O' Come All Ye Faithful (Adeste Fideles); Have Yourself a Merry Little Christmas; Must Be Santa; Silver Bells; The First Noel; Christmas Island; The Christmas Song; O Little Town of Bethlehem

2010

The Original Mono Recordings, **Columbia MONO-88697761051. Released October 19, 2010**
DISC 1: You're No Good; Talkin' New York; In My Time of Dyin'; Man of Constant Sorrow; Fixin' to Die; Pretty Peggy-O; Highway 51; Gospel Plow; Baby, Let Me Follow You Down; House of the Risin' Sun; Freight Train Blues; Song to Woody; See That My Grave Is Kept Clean

DISC 2: Blowin' in the Wind; Girl from the North Country; Masters of War; Down the Highway; Bob Dylan's Blues; A Hard Rain's A-Gonna Fall; Don't Think Twice, It's All Right; Bob Dylan's Dream; Oxford Town; Talkin' World War III Blues; Corrina, Corrina; Honey, Just Allow Me One More Chance; I Shall Be Free

DISC 3: The Times They Are A-Changin'; Ballad of Hollis Brown; With God on Our Side; One Too Many Mornings; North Country Blues; Only a Pawn in Their Game; Boots of Spanish Leather; When the Ship Comes In; The Lonesome Death of Hattie Carroll; Restless Farewell

DISC 4: All I Really Want to Do; Black Crow Blues; Spanish Harlem Incident; Chimes of Freedom; I Shall Be Free no. 10; To Ramona; Motorpsycho Nightmare; My Back Pages; I Don't Believe You (She Acts Like We Never Have Met); Ballad in Plain D; It Ain't Me, Babe

DISC 5: Subterranean Homesick Blues; She Belongs to Me; Maggie's Farm; Love Minus Zero/No Limit; Outlaw Blues; On the Road Again; Bob Dylan's 115th Dream; Mr. Tambourine Man; Gates of Eden; It's Alright, Ma (I'm Only Bleeding); It's All Over Now, Baby Blue

DISC 6: Like a Rolling Stone; Tombstone Blues; It Takes a Lot to Laugh, It Takes a Train to Cry; From a Buick 6; Ballad of a Thin Man; Queen Jane Approximately; Highway 61 Revisited; Just Like Tom Thumb's Blues; Desolation Row

DISC 7: Rainy Day Women #12 & 35; Pledging My Time; Visions of Johanna; One of Us Must Know (Sooner or Later); I Want You; Stuck Inside of Mobile with the Memphis Blues Again; Leopard-Skin Pill-Box Hat; Just Like a Woman

DISC 8: Most Likely You Go Your Way (and I'll Go Mine); Temporary Like Achilles; Absolutely Sweet Marie; Fourth Time Around; Obviously Five Believers; Sad-Eyed Lady of the Lowlands

DISC 9: John Wesley Harding; As I Went Out One Morning; I Dreamed I Saw St. Augustine; All Along the Watchtower; The Ballad of Frankie Lee and Judas Priest; Drifter's Escape; Dear Landlord; I Am a Lonesome Hobo; I Pity the Poor Immigrant; The Wicked Messenger; Down Along the Cove; I'll Be Your Baby Tonight

The Bootleg Series, Vol. 9: The Witmark Demos: 1962–1964, **Columbia/Legacy 88697 76179 2 (2CD). Released October 19, 2010**

DISC 1: Man on the Street; Hard Times in New York Town; Poor Boy Blues; Ballad for a Friend; Rambling, Gambling Willie; Talkin' Bear Mountain Picnic Massacre Blues; Standing on the Highway; Man on the Street; Blowin' in the Wind; Long Ago, Far Away; A Hard Rain's A-Gonna Fall; Tomorrow Is a Long Time; The Death of Emmett Till; Let Me Die in My Footsteps; Ballad of Hollis Brown; Quit Your Low Down Ways; Baby, I'm in the Mood for You; Bound to Lose, Bound to Win; All Over You; I'd Hate to Be You on That Dreadful Day; Long Time Gone; Talkin' John Birch Paranoid Blues; Masters of War; Oxford Town; Farewell

DISC 2: Don't Think Twice, It's All Right; Walkin' Down the Line; I Shall Be Free; Bob Dylan's Blues; Bob Dylan's Dream; Boots of Spanish Leather; Girl from the North Country; Seven Curses; Hero Blues; Whatcha Gonna Do?; Gypsy Lou; Ain't Gonna Grieve; John Brown; Only a Hobo; When the Ship Comes In; The Times They Are A-Changin'; Paths of Victory; Guess I'm Doing Fine; Baby, Let Me Follow You Down; Mama, You Been on My Mind; Mr. Tambourine Man; I'll Keep It with Mine

The Best of the Original Mono Recordings, **Columbia 88697791672. Released October 19, 2010**

Song to Woody; Blowin' in the Wind; The Times They Are A-Changin'; Chimes of Freedom; It Ain't Me, Babe; Subterranean Homesick Blues; Mr. Tambourine Man; Like a Rolling Stone; Tombstone Blues; Positively 4th Street; Rainy Day Women #12 & 35; Just Like a Woman; I Want You; I'll Be Your Baby Tonight; All Along the Watchtower

2011

Bob Dylan in Concert: Brandeis University 1963, **Columbia 88697 84742 2. Released April 11, 2011**

FIRST SET: Honey, Just Allow Me One More Chance; Talkin' John Birch Paranoid Blues; Ballad of Hollis Brown; Masters of War

SECOND SET: Talkin' World War III Blues; Bob Dylan's Dream; Talkin' Bear Mountain Picnic Massacre Blues

2012

Tempest, **Columbia 88725 45760 2. Released September 11, 2012**

Duquesne Whistle; Soon After Midnight; Narrow Way; Long and Wasted Years; Pay in Blood; Scarlet Town; Early Roman Kings; Tin Angel; Tempest; Roll on John

2013

Another Self Portrait, the Bootleg Series, Vol. 10, **Columbia/Legacy 88883 73487 2. Released August 23, 2013**

DISC 1: Went to See the Gypsy; Little Sadie; Pretty Saro; Alberta # 3; Spanish Is the Loving Tongue; Annie's Going to Sing Her Song; Time Passes Slowly #1; Only a Hobo;

Minstrel Boy; I Threw It All Away; Railroad Bill; Thirsty Boots; This Evening So Soon; These Hands; In Search of Little Sadie; House Carpenter; All the Tired Horses

DISC 2: If Not for You; Wallflower; Wigwam; Days of '49; Working on A Guru; Country Pie; I'll Be Your Baby Tonight; Highway 61 Revisited; Copper Kettle; Bring Me a Little Water; Sign on The Window; Tattle O'Day; If Dogs Run Free; New Morning; Went to See the Gypsy; Belle Isle; Time Passes Slowly #2; When I Paint My Masterpiece

DISC 3 (Deluxe Edition): She Belongs to Me; I Threw It All Away; Maggie's Farm; Wild Mountain Time; It Ain't Me, Babe; To Ramona; Mr. Tambourine Man; I Dreamed I Saw St. Augustine; Lay, Lady, Lay; Highway 61 Revisited; One Too Many Mornings; I Pity the Poor Immigrant; Like a Rolling Stone; I'll Be Your Baby Tonight; (Quinn the Eskimo) The Mighty Quinn; Minstrel Boy; Rainy Day Women #12 & 35

DISC 4 (Deluxe Edition; *Self Portrait* Remastered): All the Tired Horses; Alberta #1; I Forgot More Than You'll Ever Know; Days of '49; Early Mornin' Rain; In Search of Little Sadie; Let It Be Me; Little Sadie; Woogie Boogie; Belle Isle; Living the Blues; Like a Rolling Stone; Copper Kettle; Gotta Travel On; Blue Moon; The Boxer; The Mighty Quinn (Quinn the Eskimo); Take Me as I Am (Or Let Me Go); Take a Message to Mary; It Hurts Me Too; Minstrel Boy; She Belongs to Me; Wigwam; Alberta #2

2014

The 30th Anniversary Concert Celebration—Deluxe Edition, Columbia/Legacy 88843034102 (USA). Released March 4, 2014

DISC 1: Like a Rolling Stone; Leopard-Skin Pill-Box Hat; Introduction by Kris Kristofferson; Blowin' in the Wind; Foot of Pride; Masters of War; The Times They Are A-Changin'; Introduction by Kris Kristofferson (2); It Ain't Me Babe; What Was It You Wanted; I'll Be Your Baby Tonight; Highway 61 Revisited; Seven Days; Just Like a Woman; When the Ship Comes In; Introduction by Johnny Cash; You Ain't Going Nowhere; Don't Think Twice, It's All Right

DISC 2: Just Like Tom Thumb's Blues; All Along the Watchtower; I Shall Be Released; Don't Think Twice, It's All Right; Emotionally Yours; When I Paint My Masterpiece; Absolutely Sweet Marie; License to Kill; Rainy Day Women #12 & 35; Mr. Tambourine Man; It's Alright, Ma (I'm Only Bleeding); My Back Pages; Knockin' on Heaven's Door; Girl from the North Country; I Believe in You

The Bootleg Series, Vol. 11: The Basement Tapes Complete, Columbia/Legacy 88875016122. Released November 4, 2014

DISC 1: Edge of the Ocean; My Bucket's Got a Hole in It; Roll on Train; Mr. Blue; Belshazzar; I Forgot to Remember to Forget; You Win Again; Still in Town; Waltzing with Sin; Big River (take 1); Big River (take 2); Folsom Prison Blues; Bells of Rhymney; Spanish Is the Loving Tongue; Under Control; Ol' Roisin the Beau; I'm Guilty of Loving You; Cool Water; The Auld Triangle; Po' Lazarus; I'm a Fool for You (take 1); I'm a Fool for You (take 2)

DISC 2: Johnny Todd; Tupelo; Kickin' My Dog Around; See You Later Allen Ginsberg (take 1); See You Later Allen Ginsberg (take 2); Tiny Montgomery; Big Dog; I'm Your Teenage Prayer; Four Strong Winds; The French Girl (take 1); The French Girl (take 2); Joshua Gone Barbados; I'm in the Mood; Baby Ain't That Fine; Rock, Salt and Nails; A Fool Such As I; Song for Canada; People Get Ready; I Don't Hurt Anymore; Be Careful of Stones That You Throw; One Man's Loss; Lock Your Door; Baby, Won't You Be My Baby; Try Me Little Girl; I Can't Make It Alone; Don't You Try Me Now

DISC 3: Young but Daily Growing; Bonnie Ship the Diamond; The Hills of Mexico; Down on Me; One for the Road; I'm Alright; Million Dollar Bash (take 1); Million Dollar Bash (take 2); Yea! Heavy and a Bottle of Bread (take 1); Yea! Heavy and a Bottle of

Bread (take 2); I'm Not There; Please, Mrs. Henry; Crash on the Levee (Down in the Flood) (take 1); Crash on the Levee (Down in the Flood) (take 2); Lo and Behold! (take 1); Lo and Behold! (take 2); You Ain't Goin' Nowhere (take 1); You Ain't Goin' Nowhere (take 2); I Shall Be Released (take 1); I Shall Be Released (take 2); This Wheel's on Fire; Too Much of Nothing (take 1); Too Much of Nothing (take 2)

DISC 4: Tears of Rage (take 1); Tears of Rage (take 2); Tears of Rage (take 3); Quinn the Eskimo (The Mighty Quinn) (take 1); Quinn the Eskimo (The Mighty Quinn) (take 2); Open the Door, Homer (take 1); Open the Door, Homer (take 2); Open the Door, Homer (take 3); Nothing Was Delivered (take 1); Nothing Was Delivered (take 2); Nothing Was Delivered (take 3); All American Boy; Sign on the Cross (take 3); Odds and Ends (take 1); Odds and Ends (take 2); Get Your Rocks Off; Clothes Line Saga; Apple Suckling Tree (take 1); Apple Suckling Tree (take 2); Don't Ya Tell Henry; Bourbon Street

DISC 5: Blowin' in the Wind; One Too Many Mornings; A Satisfied Mind; It Ain't Me, Babe; Ain't No More Cane (take 1); Ain't No More Cane (take 2); My Woman She's A-Leavin'; Santa Fe; Mary Lou, I Love You Too; Dress It Up, Better Have It All; Minstrel Boy; Silent Weekend; What's It Gonna Be When It Comes Up; 900 Miles from My Home; Wildwood Flower; One Kind Favor; She'll Be Coming Round the Mountain; It's the Flight of the Bumblebee; Wild Wolf; Goin' to Acapulco; Gonna Get You Now; If I Were a Carpenter; Confidential; All You Have to Do Is Dream (take 1); All You Have to Do Is Dream (take 2)

DISC 6: 2 Dollars and 99 Cents; Jelly Bean; Any Time; Down by the Station; Hallelujah, I've Just Been Moved; That's the Breaks; Pretty Mary; Will the Circle Be Unbroken; King of France; She's on My Mind Again; Goin' Down the Road Feeling Bad; On a Rainy Afternoon; I Can't Come in with a Broken Heart; Next Time on the Highway; Northern Claim; Love Is Only Mine; Silhouettes; Bring It on Home; Come All Ye Fair and Tender Ladies; The Spanish Song (take 1); The Spanish Song (take 2); 900 Miles from My Home/Confidential

The Bootleg Series, Vol. 11: The Basement Tapes Raw, **Columbia/Legacy 88875019672 (2CD). Released November 4, 2014**
DISC 1: Open the Door, Homer; Odds and Ends; Million Dollar Bash; One Too Many Mornings; I Don't Hurt Anymore; Ain't No More Cane; Crash on the Levee; Tears of Rage; Dress It Up, Better Have It All; I'm Not There; Johnny Todd; Too Much of Nothing; Quinn the Eskimo (The Mighty Quinn); Get Your Rocks Off ; Santa-Fe; Silent Weekend; Clothes Line Saga; Please, Mrs. Henry; I Shall Be Released

DISC 2: You Ain't Goin' Nowhere; Lo and Behold!; Minstrel Boy; Tiny Montgomery; All You Have to Do Is Dream; Goin' to Acapulco; 900 Miles from My Home; One for the Road; I'm Alright; Blowin' in the Wind; Apple Suckling Tree; Nothing Was Delivered; Folsom Prison Blues; This Wheel's on Fire; Yea! Heavy and a Bottle of Bread; Don't Ya Tell Henry; Baby, Won't You Be My Baby; Sign on the Cross; You Ain't Goin' Nowhere

2015

Shadows in the Night, **Columbia 88875051242. Released February 3, 2015**
I'm a Fool to Want You; The Night We Called It a Day; Stay with Me; Autumn Leaves; Why Try to Change Me Now; Some Enchanted Evening; Full Moon and Empty Arms; Where Are You?; What'll I Do; That Lucky Old Sun

The Bootleg Series, Vol. 12: The Best of the Cutting Edge 1965–1966, **Columbia/Legacy 88875124422. Released November 6, 2015**
DISC 1: Love Minus Zero/No Limit; I'll Keep It with Mine; Bob Dylan's 115th Dream;

She Belongs to Me; Subterranean Homesick Blues; Outlaw Blues; On the Road Again; Farewell, Angelina; If You Gotta Go, Go Now (Or Else You Got to Stay All Night); You Don't Have to Do That; California; Mr. Tambourine Man; It Takes a Lot to Laugh, It Takes a Train to Cry; Like a Rolling Stone (short version); Like a Rolling Stone; Sitting on a Barbed-Wire Fence; Medicine Sunday; Desolation Row (take 2); Desolation Row (take 1)

DISC 2: Tombstone Blues; Positively 4th Street; Can You Please Crawl Out Your Window?; Just Like Tom Thumb's Blues; Highway 61 Revisited (take 3); Queen Jane Approximately; Visions of Johanna; She's Your Lover Now; Lunatic Princess; Leopard-Skin Pill-Box Hat; One of Us Must Know (Sooner or Later); Stuck Inside of Mobile with the Memphis Blues Again; Absolutely Sweet Marie; Just Like a Woman; Pledging My Time; I Want You; Highway 61 Revisited (take 7)

***The Bootleg Series, Vol. 12: The Cutting Edge 1965–1966 Deluxe Edition**, Columbia/Legacy 88875124412. Released November 6, 2015*

DISC 1: Love Minus Zero/No Limit (take 1, breakdown); Love Minus Zero/No Limit (take 2, acoustic); Love Minus Zero/No Limit (take 3 remake, complete); Love Minus Zero/No Limit (take 1 remake, complete); I'll Keep It with Mine; It's All Over Now, Baby Blue; Bob Dylan's 115th Dream (take 1, fragment); Bob Dylan's 115th Dream (take 2, complete); She Belongs to Me (take 1, complete); She Belongs to Me (take 2 remake, complete); She Belongs to Me (take 1 remake, complete); Subterranean Homesick Blues (take 1); Subterranean Homesick Blues (take 1 remake, complete); Outlaw Blues (take 1, complete); Outlaw Blues (take 2 remake, complete); On the Road Again (take 1, complete); On the Road Again (take 4, complete); On the Road Again (take 1 remake, complete); On the Road Again (take 7 remake, complete); Farewell, Angelina (take 1); If You Gotta Go, Go Now (take 1, complete); If You Gotta Go, Go Now (take 2, complete); You Don't Have to Do That (take 1, incomplete)

DISC 2: California (take 1, complete); It's Alright, Ma (I'm Only Bleeding) (take 1, false start); Mr. Tambourine Man (takes 1–2, false starts); Mr. Tambourine Man (take 3, breakdown); It Takes a Lot to Laugh, It Takes a Train to Cry (take 1, complete); It Takes a Lot to Laugh, It Takes a Train to Cry (take 8, complete); It Takes a Lot To Laugh, It Takes a Train to Cry (take 3, incomplete); It Takes a Lot to Laugh, It Takes a Train to Cry (take 3 remake, complete); Sitting on a Barbed-Wire Fence (take 2, complete); Tombstone Blues (take 1, complete); Tombstone Blues (take 9); Positively 4th Street (takes 1–3, false starts); Positively 4th Street (take 4, complete); Positively 4th Street (take 5, complete); Desolation Row (take 1, complete); Desolation Row (take 2, rehearsal); Desolation Row (take 5 remake, complete); From a Buick 6 (take 1, false start); From a Buick 6 (take 4)

DISC 3: Like a Rolling Stone (takes 1–3, rehearsal); Like a Rolling Stone (take 4, rehearsal); Like a Rolling Stone (take 5, breakdown); Like a Rolling Stone (rehearsal remake); Like a Rolling Stone (take 1 remake, rehearsal); Like a Rolling Stone (takes 2–3 remake, false starts); Like a Rolling Stone (take 4, remake); Like a Rolling Stone (take 5 remake, rehearsal); Like a Rolling Stone (take 6 remake, false Start); Like a Rolling Stone (take 8 remake, breakdown); Like a Rolling Stone (takes 9–10 remake, false starts); Like a Rolling Stone (take 11 remake, complete); Like a Rolling Stone (take 12 remake, false start); Like a Rolling Stone (take 13 remake, breakdown); Like a Rolling Stone (take 14 remake, false start); Like a Rolling Stone (take 15 remake, breakdown); Like a Rolling Stone (master take, guitar); Like a Rolling Stone (master take, vocals, guitar); Like a Rolling Stone (master take, piano, bass); Like a Rolling Stone (master take, drums, organ)

DISC 4: Can You Please Crawl Out Your Window? (take 1, complete); Can You Please Crawl Out Your Window? (take 17); Highway 61 Revisited (take 3, complete);

Highway 61 Revisited (take 5, complete); Highway 61 Revisited (take 7, false start); Just Like Tom Thumb's Blues (take 1, breakdown); Just Like Tom Thumb's Blues (take 3, complete); Just Like Tom Thumb's Blues (take 13, complete); Queen Jane Approximately (take 2, complete); Queen Jane Approximately (take 5, complete); Ballad of a Thin Man (take 2, breakdown); Medicine Sunday (take 1, incomplete); Jet Pilot (take 1); I Wanna Be Your Lover (take 1, fragment); I Wanna Be Your Lover (take 6, complete); Instrumental (take 2, complete); Can You Please Crawl Out Your Window? (take 6, complete); Visions of Johanna (take 1, rehearsal); Visions of Johanna (take 5, complete)

DISC 5: Visions of Johanna (take 7, complete); Visions of Johanna (take 8); Visions of Johanna (take 14, complete); She's Your Lover Now (take 1, breakdown); She's Your Lover Now (take 6, complete); She's Your Lover Now (take 15); She's Your Lover Now (take 16, complete); One of Us Must Know (Sooner or Later) (take 2, rehearsal); One of Us Must Know (Sooner or Later) (take 4, rehearsal); One of Us Must Know (Sooner or Later) (take 19, complete); Lunatic Princess (take 1, incomplete); Fourth Time Around (take 11, complete); Leopard-Skin Pill-Box Hat (take 3, complete); Leopard-Skin Pill-Box Hat (take 8, complete); Rainy Day Women #12 & 35 (take 1, rehearsal and finished track)

DISC 6: Stuck Inside of Mobile with the Memphis Blues Again (take 1, rehearsal); Stuck Inside of Mobile with the Memphis Blues Again (rehearsal); Stuck Inside of Mobile with the Memphis Blues Again (take 5); Stuck Inside of Mobile with the Memphis Blues Again (take 13, breakdown); Stuck Inside of Mobile with the Memphis Blues Again (take 14, complete); Absolutely Sweet Marie (take 1, complete); Just Like a Woman (take 1, complete); Just Like a Woman (take 4, complete); Just Like a Woman (take 8, complete); Pledging My Time (take 1, breakdown); Most Likely You Go Your Way (and I'll Go Mine) (take 1, complete); Temporary Like Achilles (take 3, complete); Obviously Five Believers (take 3, complete); I Want You (take 4, complete); Sad-Eyed Lady of the Lowlands (take 1, complete)

2016

Fallen Angels, Columbia 88985316001. Released May 20, 2016
Young at Heart; Maybe You'll Be There; Polka Dots and Moonbeams; All the Way; Skylark; Nevertheless; All or Nothing at All; On a Little Street in Singapore; It Had to Be You; Melancholy Mood; That Old Black Magic; Come Rain or Come Shine

2017

Triplicate, Columbia 88985413492 RD 1–3. Released March 31, 2017
DISC 1: I Guess I'll Have to Change My Plans; September of My Years; I Could Have Told You; Once Upon a Time; Stormy Weather; This Nearly Was Mine; That Old Feeling; It Gets Lonely Early; My One and Only Love; Trade Winds
DISC 2: Braggin'; As Time Goes By; Imagination; How Deep Is the Ocean; P. S. I Love You; The Best Is Yet to Come; But Beautiful; Here's That Rainy Day; Where Is the One; There's a Flaw in My Flue
DISC 3: Day In, Day Out; I Couldn't Sleep a Wink Last Night; Sentimental Journey; Somewhere along the Way; When the World Was Young; These Foolish Things; You Go to My Head; Stardust; It's Funny to Everyone but Me; Why Was I Born

Trouble No More—The Bootleg Series, Vol. 13/1979–1981, Columbia/Legacy 88985454652. Released November 3, 2017
DISC 1: Slow Train; Gotta Serve Somebody; I Believe in You; When You Gonna Wake Up?; When He Returns; Man Gave Names to All the Animals; Precious Angel;

Covenant Woman; Gonna Change My Way of Thinking; Do Right to Me Baby (Do unto Others); Solid Rock; What Can I Do for You?; Saved; In the Garden

DISC 2: Slow Train; Ain't Gonna Go to Hell for Anybody; Gotta Serve Somebody; Ain't No Man Righteous, No Not One; Saving Grace; Blessed Is the Name; Solid Rock; Are You Ready?; Pressing On; Shot of Love; Dead Man, Dead Man; Watered-Down Love; In the Summertime; The Groom's Still Waiting at the Altar; Caribbean Wind; Every Grain of Sand

Deluxe Version Additional Discs

DISC 3: Slow Train; Do Right to Me Baby (Do unto Others); Help Me Understand; Gonna Change My Way of Thinking; Gotta Serve Somebody; When He Returns; Ain't No Man Righteous, No Not One; Trouble in Mind; Ye Shall Be Changed; Covenant Woman; Stand by Faith; I Will Love Him; Jesus Is the One; City of Gold; Thief on the Cross; Pressing On

DISC 4: Slow Train; Gotta Serve Somebody; Making a Liar Out of Me; Yonder Comes Sin; Radio Spot for January 1980, Portland, OR show; Cover Down, Pray Through; Rise Again; Ain't Gonna Go to Hell for Anybody; The Groom's Still Waiting at the Altar; Caribbean Wind; You Changed My Life; Shot of Love; Watered-Down Love; Dead Man, Dead Man; Every Grain of Sand

DISC 5: Gotta Serve Somebody; I Believe in You; Covenant Woman; When You Gonna Wake Up?; When He Returns; Ain't Gonna Go to Hell for Anybody; Cover Down, Pray Through; Man Gave Names to All the Animals; Precious Angel

DISC 6: Slow Train; Do Right to Me Baby (Do unto Others); Solid Rock; Saving Grace; What Can I Do for You?; In the Garden; Band Introductions; Are You Ready?; Pressing On

DISC 7: Gotta Serve Somebody; I Believe in You; Like a Rolling Stone; Man Gave Names to All the Animals; Maggie's Farm; I Don't Believe You (She Acts Like We Never Have Met); Dead Man, Dead Man; Girl from the North Country; Ballad of a Thin Man

DISC 8: Slow Train; Let's Begin; Lenny Bruce; Mr. Tambourine Man; Solid Rock; Just Like a Woman; Watered-Down Love; Forever Young; When You Gonna Wake Up?; In the Garden; Band Introductions; Blowin' in the Wind; It's All Over Now, Baby Blue; Knockin' on Heaven's Door

Bonus DVD

DISC 9: Trouble No More—A Musical Film

DVD EXTRAS: Shot of Love; Cover Down, Pray Through; Jesus Met the Woman at the Well (alternate version); Ain't Gonna Go to Hell for Anybody (complete version); Precious Angel (complete version); Slow Train (complete version)

Limited Edition Exclusive Bonus Discs

DISC 10: Gotta Serve Somebody; I Believe in You; When You Gonna Wake Up?; When He Returns; Man Gave Names to All the Animals; Precious Angel; Slow Train; Covenant Woman

DISC 11: Gonna Change My Way of Thinking; Do Right to Me Baby (Do unto Others); Solid Rock; Saving Grace; Saved; What Can I Do for You?; In the Garden (from November 27); Band introduction; Blessed Be the Name; Pressing On; In the Garden (incomplete, from November 28)

2018

Live 1962–1966—Rare Performances from the Copyright Collections, Columbia/Sony Legacy 19075865322. Released July 20, 2018

DISC 1: Blowin' in the Wind; Corrina, Corrina; John Brown; Don't Think Twice, It's All Right; Bob Dylan's Dream; Seven Curses; Boots of Spanish Leather; Masters of War; The Lonesome Death of Hattie Carroll; When the Ship Comes in; The Times They Are A-Changin'; Girl from the North Country; Mr. Tambourine Man; It Ain't Me, Babe; To Ramona; Chimes of Freedom

DISC 2: One Too Many Mornings; It's Alright, Ma (I'm Only Bleeding); Love Minus Zero/No Limit; Gates of Eden; It's All Over Now, Baby Blue; She Belongs to Me; Maggie's Farm; It Takes a Lot to Laugh, It Takes a Train to Cry; Desolation Row; Baby, Let Me Follow You Down; I Don't Believe You (She Acts Like We Never Have Met); Ballad of a Thin Man; Visions of Johanna

More Blood, More Tracks—The Bootleg Series, Vol. 14, **Columbia/Legacy 19075858971. Released November 2, 2018**

Tangled Up in Blue; Simple Twist of Fate; Shelter from the Storm; You're a Big Girl Now; Buckets of Rain; If You See Her, Say Hello; Lily, Rosemary and the Jack of Hearts; Meet Me in the Morning; Idiot Wind; You're Gonna Make Me Lonesome When You Go; Up to Me

More Blood, More Tracks—The Bootleg Series, Vol. 14 Deluxe Edition, **Columbia/Legacy 19075858962. Released November 2, 2018**

DISC 1: If You See Her, Say Hello (take 1); If You See Her, Say Hello (take 2); You're a Big Girl Now (take 1); You're a Big Girl Now (take 2); Simple Twist of Fate (take 1); Simple Twist of Fate (take 2); You're a Big Girl Now (take 3); Up to Me (rehearsal); Up to Me (take 1); Lily, Rosemary and the Jack of Hearts (take 1); Lily, Rosemary and the Jack of Hearts (take 2)

DISC 2: Simple Twist of Fate (take 1A); Simple Twist of Fate (take 2A); Simple Twist of Fate (take 3A); Call Letter Blues (take 1); Meet Me in the Morning; Call Letter Blues (take 2); Idiot Wind (take 1); Idiot Wind (take 1, remake); Idiot Wind (take 3 with insert); Idiot Wind (take 5); Idiot Wind (take 6); You're Gonna Make Me Lonesome When You Go (rehearsal and take 1); You're Gonna Make Me Lonesome When You Go (take 2); You're Gonna Make Me Lonesome When You Go (take 3); You're Gonna Make Me Lonesome When You Go (take 4); You're Gonna Make Me Lonesome When You Go (take 5); You're Gonna Make Me Lonesome When You Go (take 6); You're Gonna Make Me Lonesome When You Go (take 6, remake); You're Gonna Make Me Lonesome When You Go (take 7); You're Gonna Make Me Lonesome When You Go (take 8)

DISC 3: Tangled Up in Blue (take 1); You're a Big Girl Now (take 1, remake); You're a Big Girl Now (take 2, remake); Tangled Up in Blue (rehearsal); Tangled Up in Blue (take 2, remake); Spanish Is the Loving Tongue; Call Letter Blues (rehearsal); You're Gonna Make Me Lonesome When You Go (take 1); Shelter from the Storm (take 1); Buckets of Rain (take 1); Tangled Up in Blue (take 3, remake); Buckets of Rain (take 2); Shelter from the Storm (take 2); Shelter from the Storm (take 3); Shelter from the Storm (take 4)

DISC 4: You're Gonna Make Me Lonesome When You Go (take 1, remake 2); You're Gonna Make Me Lonesome When You Go (take 2, remake 2); Buckets of Rain (take 1, remake); Buckets of Rain (take 2, remake); Buckets of Rain (take 3, remake); Buckets of Rain (take 4, remake); Up to Me (take 1, remake); Up to Me (take 2, remake); Buckets of Rain (take 1, remake 2); Buckets of Rain (take 2, remake 2); Buckets of Rain (take 3, remake 2); Buckets of Rain (take 4, remake 2); If You See Her, Say Hello (take 1, remake); Up to Me (take 1, remake 2); Up to Me (take 2, remake 2); Up to Me (take 3, remake 2); Buckets of Rain (rehearsal); Meet Me in the Morning (take 1, remake); Meet Me in the Morning (Take 2, Remake); Buckets of Rain (take 5, remake 2)

DISC 5: Tangled Up in Blue (rehearsal and take 1, remake 2); Tangled Up in Blue (take 2, remake 2); Tangled Up in Blue (take 3, remake 2); Simple Twist of Fate (take 2, remake); Simple Twist of Fate (take 3, remake); Up to Me (rehearsal and take 1, remake 3); Up to Me (take 2, remake 3); Idiot Wind (rehearsal and takes 1–3, remake); Idiot Wind (take 4, remake); Idiot Wind (take 4, remake with organ overdub); You're a Big Girl Now (take 1, remake 2); Meet Me in the Morning (take 1, remake 2); Meet Me in the Morning (takes 2–3, remake 2)

DISC 6: You're a Big Girl Now (takes 3–6, remake 2); Tangled Up in Blue (rehearsal and takes 1–2, remake 3); Tangled Up in Blue (take 3, remake 3); Idiot Wind (Minneapolis remake); You're a Big Girl Now (Minneapolis remake); Tangled Up in Blue (Minneapolis remake); Lily, Rosemary and the Jack of Hearts (Minneapolis remake); If You See Her, Say Hello (Minneapolis remake)

2019

The Rolling Thunder Revue: The 1975 Live Recordings, **Columbia/Legacy 19075928282. Released June 7, 2019**

DISC 1: Rake and Ramblin' Boy; Romance in Durango; Rita May; I Want You; Love Minus Zero/No Limit; She Belongs to Me; Joey; Isis; Hollywood Angel; People Get Ready; What Will You Do When Jesus Comes?; Spanish Is the Loving Tongue; The Ballad of Ira Hayes; One More Cup of Coffee (Valley Below); Tonight I'll Be Staying Here with You; This Land Is Your Land; Dark As a Dungeon

DISC 2: She Belongs to Me; A Hard Rain's A-Gonna Fall; Isis; This Wheel's on Fire; Hurricane; All Along the Watchtower; One More Cup of Coffee (Valley Below); If You See Her, Say Hello; One Too Many Mornings; Patty's Gone to Laredo; Gwenevere; Lily, Rosemary and the Jack of Hearts; It's Alright, Ma (I'm Only Bleeding)

DISC 3: Tears of Rage; I Shall Be Released; Easy and Slow; Ballad of a Thin Man; Hurricane; One More Cup of Coffee (Valley Below); Just Like a Woman; Knockin' on Heaven's Door

DISC 4: When I Paint My Masterpiece; It Ain't Me, Babe; The Lonesome Death of Hattie Carroll; It Takes a Lot to Laugh, It Takes a Train to Cry; Romance in Durango; Isis; Blowin' in the Wind; Wild Mountain Thyme; Mama, You Been on My Mind; Dark As a Dungeon; I Shall Be Released

DISC 5: Tangled Up in Blue; Oh, Sister; Hurricane; One More Cup of Coffee (Valley Below); Sara; Just Like a Woman; Knockin' on Heaven's Door; This Land Is Your Land

DISC 6: When I Paint My Masterpiece; It Ain't Me, Babe; The Lonesome Death of Hattie Carroll; It Takes a Lot to Laugh, It Takes a Train to Cry; Romance in Durango; Isis; Blowin' in the Wind; Wild Mountain Thyme; Mama, You Been on My Mind; Dark As a Dungeon; I Shall Be Released

DISC 7: Simple Twist of Fate; Oh, Sister; Hurricane; One More Cup of Coffee (Valley Below); Sara; Just Like a Woman; Knockin' on Heaven's Door; This Land Is Your Land

DISC 8: When I Paint My Masterpiece; It Ain't Me, Babe; The Lonesome Death of Hattie Carroll; A Hard Rain's A-Gonna Fall; Romance in Durango; Isis; The Times They Are A-Changin'; I Dreamed I Saw St. Augustine; Mama, You Been on My Mind; Never Let Me Go; I Shall Be Released

DISC 9: Mr. Tambourine Man; Oh, Sister; Hurricane; One More Cup of Coffee (Valley Below); Sara; Just Like a Woman; Knockin' on Heaven's Door; This Land Is Your Land

DISC 10: When I Paint My Masterpiece; It Ain't Me, Babe; The Lonesome Death of Hattie Carroll; It Takes a Lot to Laugh, It Takes a Train to Cry; Romance in Durango; Isis; Blowin' in the Wind; The Water Is Wide; Mama, You Been on My Mind; Dark As a Dungeon; I Shall Be Released

DISC 11: I Don't Believe You (She Acts Like We Never Have Met); Tangled Up in Blue; Oh, Sister; Hurricane; One More Cup of Coffee (Valley Below); Sara; Just Like a Woman; Knockin' on Heaven's Door; This Land Is Your Land

DISC 12: When I Paint My Masterpiece; It Ain't Me, Babe; The Lonesome Death of Hattie Carroll; Tonight I'll Be Staying Here with You; A Hard Rain's A-Gonna Fall; Romance in Durango; Isis; Blowin' in the Wind; Dark as a Dungeon; Mama, You Been on My Mind; Never Let Me Go; I Dreamed I Saw St. Augustine; I Shall Be Released

DISC 13: It's All Over Now, Baby Blue; Love Minus Zero/No Limit; Tangled Up in Blue; Oh, Sister; Hurricane; One More Cup of Coffee (Valley Below); Sara; Just Like a Woman; Knockin' on Heaven's Door; This Land Is Your Land

DISC 14: One Too Many Mornings; Simple Twist of Fate; Isis; With God on Our Side; It's Alright, Ma (I'm Only Bleeding); Radio Announcement for Niagara Falls Shows; The Ballad of Ira Hayes; Your Cheatin' Heart; Fourth Time Around; The Tracks of My Tears; Jesse James; It Takes a Lot to Laugh, It Takes a Train to Cry

Travelin' Thru—The Bootleg Series, Vol. 15 1967–1969, **Sony Legacy 19075981932. Released November 1, 2019**

DISC 1: Drifter's Escape; I Dreamed I Saw St. Augustine; All Along the Watchtower; John Wesley Harding; As I Went Out One Morning; I Pity the Poor Immigrant; I Am a Lonesome Hobo; I Threw It All Away; To Be Alone with You; Lay, Lady, Lay; One More Night; Western Road; Peggy Day; Tell Me That It Isn't True; Country Pie

DISC 2: I Still Miss Someone (take 5); Don't Think Twice, It's All Right/Understand Your Man; One Too Many Mornings; Mountain Dew (Take 1); Mountain Dew (take 2); I Still Miss Someone (take 2); Careless Love; Matchbox; That's All Right, Mama; Mystery Train/This Train Is Bound for Glory; Big River; Girl from the North Country (rehearsal); Girl from the North Country (take 1); I Walk the Line; Guess Things Happen That Way (rehearsal); Guess Things Happen That Way (take 3); Five Feet High and Rising; You Are My Sunshine; Ring of Fire

DISC 3: Studio Chatter; Wanted Man; Amen; Just a Closer Walk with Thee; Jimmie Rodgers Medley no. 1; Jimmie Rodgers Medley no. 2; I Threw It All Away; Living the Blues; Girl from the North Country; Ring of Fire; Folsom Prison Blues; Earl Scruggs Interview; East Virginia Blues; To Be Alone with You; Honey, Just Allow Me One More Chance; Nashville Skyline Rag

2020

Rough and Rowdy Ways, **Columbia 19439780982. Released June 19, 2020**

DISC 1: I Contain Multitudes; False Prophet; Own Version of You; Made Up My Mind to Give Myself to You; Black Rider; Goodbye Jimmy Reed; Mother of Muses; Crossing the Rubicon; Key West (Philosopher Pirate)

DISC 2: Murder Most Foul

2021

The Bootleg Series, Vol. 16: Springtime in New York 1980–1985, **Sony Legacy 19439865791. Released September 17, 2021**

DISC 1: Señor (Tales of Yankee Power); To Ramona; Jesus Met the Woman at the Well; Mary of the Wild Moor; Need a Woman; A Couple More Years; Mystery Train; This Night Won't Last Forever; We Just Disagree; Let's Keep It Between Us; Sweet Caroline; Fever; Abraham, Martin and John

DISC 2: Angelina; Price of Love; I Wish It Would Rain; Let It Be Me; Cold, Cold Heart; Don't Ever Take Yourself Away; Fur Slippers; Borrowed Time; Is It Worth It?; Lenny Bruce; Yes Sir, No Sir

DISC 3: Jokerman; Blind Willie McTell; Don't Fall Apart on Me Tonight (version 1); Don't Fall Apart on Me Tonight (version 2); Neighborhood Bully; Someone's Got a Hold of My Heart; This Was My Love; Too Late (acoustic version); Too Late (band version); Foot of Pride

DISC 4: Clean Cut Kid; Sweetheart Like You; Baby What You Want Me to Do; Tell Me; Angel Flying Too Close to the Ground; Julius and Ethel; Green, Green Grass of Home; Union Sundown; Lord Protect My Child; I and I; Death Is Not the End (full version)

DISC 5: Enough Is Enough (live); License to Kill (live); I'll Remember You; Tight Connection to My Heart (Has Anybody Seen My Love); Seeing the Real You at Last; Emotionally Yours; Clean Cut Kid; Straight A's in Love; When the Night Comes Falling from the Sky (slow version); When the Night Comes Falling from the Sky (fast version); New Danville Girl; Dark Eyes

BIBLIOGRAPHY

The bibliography comprises works cited in the text as well as other sources on which I relied while researching this book. Further, as is well known to Dylan watchers, the internet continues to provide voluminous information on all aspects of Dylan's career. The official Dylan website, www.bobdylan.com, contains the lyrics to all the songs, images of album covers, tour information, and a shop. Important unofficial websites are Karl Erik Andersen's Expecting Grain (https://www.expectingrain.com) and Olaf Bjorner's site, in particular the page titled "Olaf's Files" and the "Bringing It All Back Home" button (http://www.bjorner.com /bob.htm): this link contains separate downloadable PDFs of Dylan's musical activities, organized year to year, from 1959 until 2017 (as of this writing).

Ackerman, James S. *Origins, Imitation, Conventions: Representation in the Visual Arts*. Cambridge, MA: MIT Press, 2002.

Adès, Dawn. "Marcel Duchamp's Fountain: A Continuing Controversy." *Journal of the London Institute of 'Pataphysics* 14 & 15 (2018).

Allison, Bill. "She Belongs to Me: One Possible Hearing." *Telegraph* 19 (Spring 1983): 58–70.

Alter, Robert. *The Five Books of Moses: A Translation with Commentary*. New York: W. W. Norton, 2004.

Apollonio, Umbro, ed. *Futurist Manifestos*. Translated by Robert Brain, R. W. Flint, J. C. Higgitt, and Caroline Tisdall. London: Tate, 2009.

Apuleis, *Metamorphoses*, 2 vols., Edited and translated by J. Arthur Hanson. Cambridge, MA: Harvard University Press, 1989.

Ariosto, Ludovico. *Orlando Furioso*, 2 vols., ed. Marcello Turchi. Milan, Italy: Garzanti, 1974.

Bangs, Lester. "Bob Dylan's Dalliance with Mafia Chic." In Thomson and Gutman, *Dylan Companion*, 210–22.

Barrett, Michael S. "Dylan's 'Writings and Drawings' Certain to 'Please Everybody.'" *Montreal Gazette*, September 7, 1973.

Bate, Walter Jackson. *The Burden of the Past and the English Poet*. New York: W. W. Norton, 1970.

Bauldie, John, ed. *Wanted Man: In Search of Bob Dylan*. New York: Citadel, 1991.

Bell, Ian. *Once Upon a Time: The Lives of Bob Dylan*. Vol. 1. New York: Pegasus Books, 2012.

———. *Time Out of Mind: The Lives of Bob Dylan*. Vol. 2. New York: Pegasus Books, 2014.

Bono. "Dylan's 70 Greatest Songs." *Rolling Stone Magazine*, May 26, 2011, 56–78.

Boucher, David, and Gary Browning, eds. *The Political Art of Bob Dylan*. Exeter, UK: Imprint Academic, 2009.

Bowden, Betsy. "Performed Literature: A Case Study of Bob Dylan's 'Hard Rain.'" *Literature in Performance* 3, no. 2 (1982): 35–48.

Brazeau, Peter. *Parts of a World: Wallace Stevens Remembered, an Oral Biography*. New York: Random House, 1983.

Brinkley, Douglas. "Bob Dylan Has a Lot on His Mind," *New York Times*, June 12, 2020. https://www.nytimes.com.

Bronson, Bertrand. *The Traditional Tunes of the Child Ballads*. 4 vols. Princeton, NJ: Princeton University Press, 1959–72.

Brotchie, Alastair. "Letter to the Editor." *Times Literary Supplement*, September 13, 2019.

Brown, Matthew. "Toilets of Our Time." *Times Literary Supplement*, August 23 and 30, 2019. https://www.the-tls.co.uk.

Brown, Peter. *The Making of Late Antiquity*. Cambridge, MA: Harvard University Press, 1978.

Burger, Jeff, ed. *Dylan on Dylan: Interviews and Encounters*. Chicago: Chicago Review, 2018.

Carrera, Alessandro. "Bob Dylan dall'appropriazione alla trasfigurazione." *Estetica: Studi e ricerche* 1 (2014): 161–75.

Carruthers, Bob, dir. *Bob Dylan, The Folk Years (The Unauthorized Critical Review)*. 2017. Vision Film.

Cartwright, Colbert. *The Bible in the Lyrics of Bob Dylan*. Lancashire, UK: Wanted Man Press, 1985.

Child, Francis James. *The English and Scottish Popular Ballads*. 5 vols. Boston: Houghton, Mifflin, 1882–98.

Concordance. "Bob Dylan Lyrics without Multiple Refrains." Accessed January 13, 2022. http://konkordans.se.

Cook, Edward. "Bob Dylan, Carl Sandburg, and the 'Borrowing' Problem." *Ralph the Sacred River* (blog), June 3, 2010. http://ralphriver.blogspot.com/.

Cott, Jonathan, ed. *Bob Dylan: The Essential Interviews*. New York: Wenner Books, 2006.

Crawford, Trish. "Don't Think Twice: Dylan's Paintings in New York Gallery Look Just Like Photos." *Toronto Star*, September 29, 2011.

Crowe, C. "Bob Dylan. Biograph Booklet." Liner notes to *Biograph*. Columbia C3K 38830, 1985, compact disc.

Day, Aidan. *Jokerman: Reading the Lyrics of Bob Dylan*. Oxford: Basil Blackwell, 1988.

Dettmar, Kevin. "Borrowing." In Latham, *World of Bob Dylan*, 205–13.

Dillard, Clayton. "Interview: D. A. Pennebaker on *Don't Look Back*, Bob Dylan, and More." *Slant Magazine*, November 24, 2015. https://www.slantmagazine.com.

Du Bellay, J. *La défense et illustration de la langue française*. Paris: Librairie Larousse, 1972.

Dylan, Bob. *The Asia Series*. New York: Gagosian Gallery, 2011. Exhibition catalog.

———. *The Beaten Path*. Exhibition organized by and presented at the Halcyon Gallery, London, November 5, 2016–January 2, 2017.

———. *Bob Dylan: The Brazil Series*. Munich: Prestel Verlag, 2010. Exhibition catalog.

———. *Bob Dylan: The Drawn Blank Series*. Turin: Allemandi, 2010. Exhibition catalog.

———. *Chronicles*. Vol. 1. New York: Simon and Schuster, 2004.

———. *Hollywood Foto-Rhetoric: The Lost Manuscript*. Photographs by Barry Feinstein. New York: Simon and Schuster, 2008.

———. Jacket notes to *Joan Baez in Concert, Part 2*. Vanguard VSD-2123, 1963, LP.

———. *The Lyrics, 1961–2012*. New York: Simon and Schuster, 2016.

———. *Mondo Scripto*. Exhibition organized by and presented at the Halcyon Gallery, London, October 9–December 23, 2018. Exhibition catalog, Carlotta Cooper, 2018.

———. *Revisionist Art: Thirty Works by Bob Dylan*. Exhibition organized and presented at the Gagosian Gallery, New York, November 28–January 12, 2013.

———. *Revisionist Art: Thirty Works by Bob Dylan*. Edited by John Elderfield. Introduction by Luc Sante. New York: Gagosian Gallery, 2012. Exhibition catalog.

———. *Saved! The Gospel Speeches of Bob Dylan*. New York: Hanuman Books, 1991.

———. *Writings and Drawings*. New York: Knopf, 1973.

Eisen, Jonathan. Ed. *The Age of Rock 2*. New York: Vintage Books, 1970.

Elderfield, John. "All These People That You Mention. . . ." In Mössinger, *Bob Dylan: Face Value*, 9–17.

Emerson, R. W. *Selections from Ralph Waldo Emerson: An Organic Anthology*. Edited by Stephen E. Whicher. Boston: Houghton Mifflin, 1960.

Falco, Raphael. *Conceived Presences: Literary Genealogy in Renaissance England*. Amherst, MA: University of Massachusetts Press, 1994.

———. "The Dylanista." *Dylan Review* 2, no. 1 (Summer 2020). https://thedylanreview.org.

Fantuzzi, Fabio. "I dieci comandamenti dell'arte: Bob Dylan e l'antico dilemma tra genio e Plagio." *Musica/Realtà* 105 (2014): 75–95.

Filene, Benjamin. *Romancing the Folk: Public Memory and American Roots Music.* Chapel Hill: University of North Carolina Press, 2000.

Fitzpatrick, M. J. "The Chimes of Trinity." New York: Howley, Haviland, 1895.

Gezari, Janet, and Charles Hartman. "Dylan's Covers." *Southwest Review* 95, nos. 1–2 (2010): 155–56.

Gibbens, John. *The Nightingale's Code: A Poetic Study of Bob Dylan.* Photographs by Keith Baugh. London: Touched Press, 2001.

Gilmore, Mikal. "Bob Dylan Unleashed." *Rolling Stone Magazine,* September 27, 2012. https://www.rollingstone.com.

Gilmour, Michael. *Tangled Up in the Bible: Bob Dylan and Scripture.* New York: Continuum, 2004.

Ginsberg, Allen. *Howl.* San Francisco: City Lights Books, 1956.

———. *Spontaneous Mind: Selected Interviews, 1958–1996.* Edited by David Carter. New York: HarperCollins, 2001.

Goldstein, David. "Originality." In *The Princeton Encyclopedia of Poetry and Poetics,* 4th ed., 981–83. Princeton, NJ: Princeton University Press, 2012.

Gray, Michael. *Song and Dance Man III: The Art of Bob Dylan.* London: Continuum, 2000.

Gray, Michael, and John Bauldie, eds. *All Across the Telegraph: A Bob Dylan Handbook.* London: Futura, 1988.

The Great Eastern Temple: Treasures of Japanese Buddhist Art from Tōdai-ji. Tokyo: Dai Nippon, 1986. Exhibition catalog.

Greenblatt, Stephen. *Learning to Curse: Essays in Early Modern Culture.* New York: Routledge, 1990.

Greene, Andy. "Bob Dylan's Lost 1970 Gem 'Pretty Saro' – Premiere." *Rolling Stone,* August 7, 2013. https://www.rollingstone.com.

Greene, Thomas. *The Light in Troy: Imitation and Discovery in Renaissance Poetry.* New Haven, CT: Yale University Press, 1982

Grossman, Edward. "Dylan's Odyssey." *Dissent,* October 1, 1973, 491–92.

Hagstrum, Jean. *The Sister Arts: The Tradition of Literary Pictorialism and English Poetry from Dryden to Gray.* Chicago: University of Chicago Press, 1958.

Hampton, Timothy. *Bob Dylan's Poetics: How the Songs Work.* New York: Zone Books, 2019.

Hartman, Charles. "Review of *Bob Dylan. Rough and Rowdy Ways.* Columbia Records, 2020." *Dylan Review* 2, no. 1 (Summer 2020): 3–15.

Hentoff, Nat. "The Crackin,' Shakin,' Breakin,' Sounds." *New Yorker,* October 24, 1964. In Cott, *Essential Interviews,* 13–28.

Herrick, Robert. "The Argument of His Book." In *The Complete Poetry of Robert Herrick,* edited by J. Max Patrick, 12. New York: New York University Press, 1963.

Heselgrave, Douglas. "Contents under Pressure: Bob Dylan's Asia Series." *Restless and Real* (blog), September 30, 2011. https://restlessandreal.blogspot.com.

Heylin, Clinton. *Bob Dylan: Behind the Shades Revisited, the Biography.* New York: HarperCollins, 2003.

———. *Judas! From Forest Hills to the Free Trade Hall, A Historical View of* The Big Boo. New York: Lesser Gods, 2016.

———. *Revolution in the Air: The Songs of Bob Dylan, 1957–1973.* Chicago: Chicago Review, 2009.

———. *Still on the Road: The Songs of Bob Dylan, Vol. 2: 1974–2008.* London: Constable, 2010.

———. *Trouble in Mind: Bob Dylan's Gospel Years, What* Really *Happened.* New York: Lesser Gods, 2017.

Hinchey, John. *Like a Complete Unknown: The Poetry of Bob Dylan's Songs, 1961–1969*. Ann Arbor, MI: Stealing Home Press, 2002.

Hinton, Brian. *Bob Dylan: Complete Discography*. New York: Universe, 2006.

Itzkoff, Dave. "No Direction, No Restriction: D. A. Pennebaker Looks Back at a Dylan Documentary." *New York Times*, May 19, 2016. https://www.nytimes.com/.

———. *ArtsBeat* (blog), *New York Times*, September 26, 2011 [8:20 PM].

Jonson, Ben. "To the Memory of My Beloved, the Author Mr. William Shakespeare: And What He Hath Left Us." In *The Complete Poems*, edited by George Parfitt, 263–65. New Haven, CT: Yale University Press, 1975.

Josipovici, Gabriel. "Off the Grid: Thoughts on the Avant-Garde." *Times Literary Supplement*, August 9, 2019.

Karlin, Daniel. "My Friend Bob: Dylan's Relationship with JFK." *Times Literary Supplement*, July 6, 2018.

Kelly, Robert. "Postscript II." In Leary and Kelly, *Controversy of Poets*, 563–67.

Kelly, Terry. "Bob Dylan and the Art of Forgery." *Bridge* 2 (Winter 1998): 58–67.

Kemp, Anthony. *The Estrangement of the Past: A Study in the Origins of Modern Historical Consciousness*. New York: Oxford University Press, 1991.

Kermode, Frank. "Bob Dylan: The Metaphor at the End of the Funnel: But Is It Art?" *Esquire Magazine*, May 1972, 109–18.

King, Martin Luther, Jr. "I Have a Dream." August 28, 1963, Washington, DC. Transcript at: https://www.npr.org/2010/01/18/122701268/i-have-a-dream-speech-in-its-entirety.

Kinney, Arthur. *Continental Humanist Poetics: Studies in Erasmus, Castiglione, Marguerite de Navarre, Rabelais, and Cervantes*. Amherst: University of Massachusetts Press, 1989.

Krauss, Rosalind. "The Originality of the Avant-Garde: A Postmodernist Repetition." *October* 18 (Autumn 1981): 47–66.

Kroll, Jack. "Untitled Review of *Renaldo and Clara*." *Newsweek*, January 30, 1978.

Lamp, Jeffrey. "The Hal Lindsey Effect: Bob Dylan's Christian Eschatology." *Dylan Review* 3, no. 1 (Summer 2021): 61–85.

Latham, Sean, ed., *The World of Bob Dylan*. Cambridge, UK: Cambridge University Press, 2021.

Leary, Paris, and Robert Kelly, eds. *A Controversy of Poets: An Anthology of Contemporary Poetry*. Garden City, NY: Anchor Books, 1965.

Lebold, Christophe. "I've Got the Judas Complex and the Recycling Blues: Bob Dylan as Cultural Theft." *Recherches anglaises et nord-américaines* 43 (2010): 127–35.

Lethem, Jonathan. "The Ecstasy of Influence: A Plagiarism." *Harper's Magazine*, October 2007, 59–71.

Linderman, Jim. "Bob Dylan Paints Just Like a Painter." *Expecting Rain* (blog), September 28, 2011. https://expectingrain.com.

Lindsey, Hal, with C. C. Carlson. *The Late Great Planet Earth*. Grand Rapids, MI: Zondervan, 1970.

Lott, Eric. *Black Mirror: The Cultural Contradictions of American Racism*. Cambridge, MA: Harvard University Press, 2017.

Lowell, Robert. *Robert Lowell: Interviews and Memoirs*. Edited by Jeffrey Meyers. Ann Arbor: University of Michigan Press, 1988.

M., H. Untitled article in *Hartford Courant*, August 5, 1973.

Malanga, Gerard. "Dylan and Warhol." Interview by John Bauldie. In Bauldie, *Wanted Man*, 67–71.

Manguel, Alberto. Review of Christine Nelson, ed., *The Magic of Handwriting*, *Times Literary Supplement*, March 15, 2019.

Marcus, Greil. *Invisible Republic: Bob Dylan's Basement Tapes*. New York: Henry Holt, 1997.

———. *Like a Rolling Stone: Bob Dylan at the Crossroads*. New York: Public Affairs, 2005.

———. *The Old, Weird America: The World of Bob Dylan's Basement Tapes.* New York: Picador, 2011.

Margotin, Philippe, and Jean-Michel Guesdon. *Bob Dylan: All the Songs, the Story behind Every Track.* New York: Black Dog and Leventhal, n.d.

Marinetti, Filippo Tommaso. *I Manifesti del Futurismo.* Philadelphia: Press at Toad Hall, 2014.

Marqusee, Mike. *Chimes of Freedom: The Politics of Bob Dylan's Art.* New York: New Press, 2003.

———. *Wicked Messenger: Bob Dylan and the 1960s.* New York: Seven Stories, 2005.

Marsh, Dave. "Ballad in Plain Dull." *Rolling Stone Magazine,* March 9, 1978.

Masur, Louis P. "Famous Long Ago: Bob Dylan Revisited." *American Quarterly* 59, no. 1 (March 2007): 165–77.

Matthews, J. H., ed. *An Anthology of French Surrealist Poetry.* London: University of London Press, 1966.

McCarron, Andrew. *Light Come Shining: The Transformations of Bob Dylan.* New York: Oxford University Press, 2017.

McIntosh, Donald. "Weber and Freud: On the Nature and Sources of Authority." *American Sociological Review* 35, no. 2 (October 1970): 901–11.

McLuhan, Marshall. *Understanding Media: The Extensions of Man.* 2nd critical edition. Edited by W. Terrence Gordon. Corte Madera, CA: Gingko Press, 1994.

Mellers, Wilfrid. *A Darker Shade of Pale: A Backdrop to Bob Dylan.* New York: Oxford University Press, 1984.

———. "God, Mode and Meaning in Some Recent Songs of Bob Dylan." In Thomson and Gutman, *Dylan Companion,* 247–59.

Miller, Karl Hagstrom. *Segregating Sound: Inventing Folk and Pop Music in the Age of Jim Crow.* Durham, NC: Duke University Press, 2010.

Milton, John. *The Complete Poetry and Essential Prose of John Milton.* Edited by William Kerrigan, John Rumrich, and Stephen M. Fallon. New York: Modern Library, 2007.

Miró, Alessandro Allemandi. "Lo spettacolo è appena cominciato." In Dylan, *Bob Dylan: The Drawn Blank Series,* 6–8.

Moon, Tom. "Trickster Treat: Bob Dylan's New Song Sounds Awfully Old … and Familiar." NPR, May 12, 2020. https://www.npr.org.

Morgan, Robert C. "Can Bob Dylan Paint?" *Brooklyn Rail: Critical Perspectives on Arts, Politics, and Culture,* November 2, 2011. https://brooklynrail.org.

Mössinger, Ingrid, "Prolog/Prologue." In *Bob Dylan: Face Value.*, edited by Ingrid Mössinger, 10–13. Dresden: Sandstein Verlag, 2016. Exhibition catalog.

Muir, Andrew. *The True Performing of It: Bob Dylan and William Shakespeare.* Penryn, Cornwall: Red Planet, 2019.

Nakata, Yūjirō, ed. *Chinese Calligraphy.* Translated by Jeffrey Hunter. New York: Weatherhill, 1983.

Norman, Tony. "More Controversy Finds Dylan as Artist." *Pittsburgh Post-Gazette* (PA), September 30, 2011.

Oberstebrink, Christina. "Plagiarism and Originality in Painting: Joshua Reynolds's Concept of Imitation and Enlightenment Translation Theory." In *Cultural Transfer through Translation: The Circulation of Enlightened Thought in Europe by Means of Translation,* edited by Stefanie Stockhorst, 45–59. Amsterdam: Rodopi, 2010.

Orr, William F., and James Arthur Walther. *1 Corinthians: A New Translation.* Garden City, NY: Doubleday, 1976.

Otiono, Nduka, and Josh Toth, eds. *Polyvocal Bob Dylan: Music, Performance, Literature.* Cham, Switzerland: Palgrave Macmillan, 2019.

Palaima, Thomas. "Why Bob Dylan Matters." *Bryn Mawr Classical Review* (blog). Accessed November 2, 2021. http://bmcr.brynmawr.edu.

Pennebaker, D. A. *Bob Dylan: Don't Look Back*. New York: Ballantine Books, 1968.

Perlman, Sandy. "Roto-Rooter." In Eisen, *Age of Rock 2*, 327–35.

Pigman, G. W., III. "Versions of Imitation in the Renaissance." *Renaissance Quarterly* 33, no. 1 (Spring 1980): 1–32.

Polito, Robert. "Bob Dylan's Memory Palace." In Sheehy and Swiss, *Highway 61 Revisited*, 140–53.

Polizzotti, Mark. "Love and Theft: Dylan's Appropriations." *Parnassus: Poetry in Review* 34, nos. 1–2 (2015): 50–73.

Pope, Alexander. *Pastoral Poetry and An Essay on Criticism*. Edited by E. Audra and Aubrey Williams. New Haven, CT: Yale University Press, 1961.

Prince, Richard. "Bob Dylan's Fugitive Art." *New York Review of Books*, October 5, 2011. https://www.nybooks.com.

Proser, Adriana G. "Moral Characters: Calligraphy and Bureaucracy in Han China (206 B.C.E.–C. E. 220)." PhD diss., Columbia University, 1995.

Reid, Graham. "Bob Dylan: Belle Isle (1970)." *Elsewhere*, June 14, 2012. https://www.elsewhere.co.nz.

Ricks, Christopher. *Dylan's Visions of Sin*. New York: HarperCollins, 2004.

Riley, Tim. *Hard Rain: A Dylan Commentary*. New York: Vintage Books, 1993.

Rimbaud, Arthur. *Illuminations*. 1946. Translated by Louise Varèse. New York: New Directions, 1957.

Rogovoy, Seth. "Was Bob Dylan at His Best When He Was a Christian?" *Forward*, October 30, 2017.

Rosenberg, David, trans. *The Book of J*. Interpreted by Harold Bloom. New York: Grove Weidenfeld, 1990.

Rosenberg, Neil V., ed. *Transforming Tradition: Folk Music Revivals Examined*. Urbana: University of Illinois Press, 1993.

Sante, Luc. "Foreword." In Dylan, *Hollywood Foto-Rhetoric*, ix–xvii.

———. "Introduction." In Dylan, *Revisionist Art*, 7–10.

Scaduto, Anthony. *Bob Dylan*. London: Helter Skelter, 1996.

Schoeck, Richard. "'Lighting a Candle to the Place': On the Dimensions and Implications of *Imitatio* in the Renaissance." *Italian Culture* 4 (1983): 123–43.

Scobie, Stephen. *Alias Bob Dylan Revisited*. Calgary: Red Deer Press, 2003.

Seeger, Pete. *The Incompleat Folksinger*. Edited by Jo Mecalf Schwartz. New York: Simon and Schuster, 1972.

Seneca. *Moral Epistles*. Vol. 5. Translated by Richard M. Gummere. Cambridge, MA: Harvard University Press, 1920.

Sexton, David. "Bob Dylan—*Mondo Scripto* Review: An Unmissable Show for Every Fan." *Evening Standard*, October 9, 2018. https://www.standard.co.uk.

Shakespeare, William. *The Tempest*. Edited by Stephen Orgel. Oxford: Oxford University Press, 1987.

———. *The Winter's Tale*. Edited by Stephen Orgel. Oxford: Oxford University Press, 1996.

Shapiro, Karl. "The Poetry of Bob Dylan." *New Republic*, June 2, 1973.

Sheehy, Colleen J., and Thomas Swiss, eds. *Highway 61 Revisited: Bob Dylan's Road from Minnesota to the World*. Minneapolis: University of Minnesota Press, 2009.

Shelton, Robert. "The Charisma Kid." *Cavalier*, July 1965, n.p.

———. *No Direction Home: The Life and Music of Bob Dylan*. New York: William Morrow, 1986.

Shepard, Sam. *Rolling Thunder Logbook*. New York: Viking Press, 1977.

Shore, Robert. *Beg, Steal and Borrow: Artists against Originality*. London: Elephant Books, 2017.

Sidney, Philip. *A Defense of Poetry*. Edited by J. A. Van Dorsten. Oxford: Oxford University Press, 1989.

Siegel, Robert. "New Paintings Reignite the Bob Dylan Copycat Debate." *All Things Considered*, NPR, October 18, 2011.

Simon, Ron. "Jokerman Meets Mad Man." *PopMatters*, September 14, 2008. https://www.popmatters.com.

Smith, Thomas Spence. *Strong Interaction*. Chicago: University of Chicago Press, 1992.

Spender, Stephen. "Bob Dylan: The Metaphor at the End of the Funnel: But Is It Art?" *Esquire Magazine*, May 1972, 109–18.

Steiner, Wendy. *The Real Real Thing: The Model in the Mirror of Art*. Chicago: University of Chicago Press, 2010.

Stekert, Ellen. "Cents and Nonsense in the Urban Folksong Movement: 1930–1966." In Rosenberg, *Transforming Tradition*, 84–106.

Stevens, Wallace. *The Palm at the End of the Mind: Selected Poems and a Play*. Edited by Holly Stevens. New York: Vintage Books, 1972.

Sounes, Howard. *Down the Highway: The Life of Bob Dylan*. New York: Grove Press, 2001.

Tanakh. *The Holy Scriptures*. The New JPS Translation. Philadelphia: Jewish Publication Society, 1988.

Thomas, Richard F. "'And I Crossed the Rubicon': Another Classical Dylan." *Dylan Review* 2, no. 1 (2020): 35–64.

———. "The Streets of Rome: The Classical Dylan." *Oral Tradition* 22, no. 1 (March 2007): 30–56.

———. *Why Bob Dylan Matters*. New York: HarperCollins, 2017.

Thomas, Richard F., and Catharine Mason. "Introduction." *Oral Tradition* 22, no. 1 (March 2007): 3–13.

Thompson, Mark. "Desire Obscures, Possession Corrupts: The Mind and Work of a Knowing Mid-Century American." *Times Literary Supplement*, March 15, 2019.

Thomson, Elizabeth, and David Gutman, eds. *The Dylan Companion*. London: Papermac, 1991.

Tyndale, William. *Tyndale's New Testament, Translated from the Greek by William Tyndale (1534)*. Edited by David Daniell. New Haven, CT: Yale University Press, 1989.

———. *Tyndale's Old Testament, Being the Pentateuch of 1530, Joshua to 2 Chronicles of 1537, and Jonah*. Edited by David Daniell, modern spelling edition. New Haven, CT: Yale University Press, 1992.

Van Ronk, Dave, with Elijah Wald. *The Mayor of MacDougal Street*. Cambridge, MA: Da Capo Press, 2005.

Virgil. *The Aeneid*. Translated by Robert Fagles. New York: Penguin Books, 2006.

———. *The Aeneid of Virgil*. 2 vols. Edited by R. D. Williams. London: Macmillan, 1972.

———. *The Minor Poems of Virgil*. Translated by Joseph J. Mooney. Birmingham: Cornish Brothers, 1916.

Wadhera, Priya. *Original Copies in Georges Perec and Andy Warhol*. Leiden: Brill, 2017.

Wald, Gayle, "Gospel Music." In Latham, *World of Bob Dylan*, 88–99.

Warmuth, Scott. "Bob Charlatan: Deconstructing Dylan's *Chronicles, Volume One*." *New Haven Review* 6 (January 2008): 70–83.

———. "Deciphering the Asia Series: Dylan, Duchamp and the Letter from Woody." *Goon Talk* (blog), October 1, 2011. http://swarmuth.blogspot.com.

Webb, Stephen H. *Redeemed: From Highway 61 to Saved*. New York: Continuum, 2006.

Weber, Max. *Economy and Society*. 2 vols. Edited by Guenther Roth and Claus Wittich. Berkeley: University of California Press, 1978.

Webster, Patrick J. "In the Factory: Dylan and Warhol's World." In Gray and Bauldie, *All Across the Telegraph*, 55–62.

Weinberg, Bernard, ed. *Trattati di poetica e retorica del cinque-cento*. 4 vols. Bari: Guis. Latuza & Figli, 1970.

Wilentz, Sean. *Bob Dylan in America*. New York: Doubleday, 2010.

Williams, Paul. *Bob Dylan: Performing Artist, 1986–1990 and Beyond, Mind Out of Time*. London: Omnibus, 2005.

———. *Dylan—What Happened?* South Bend, IN: And Books / Entwhistle Books, 1980.

Wisniewski, John. "Unrecorded Lyrics by Dylan Published in His Latest Book." *Syracuse Post-Standard*, May 23, 1973.

Yaffe, David. *Bob Dylan: Like a Complete Unknown*. New Haven, CT: Yale University Press, 2011.

———. "Not Dark Yet: How Bob Dylan Got His Groove Back." In Sheehy and Swiss, *Highway 61 Revisited*, 197–212.

COPYRIGHT INFORMATION

COPYRIGHT INFORMATION

INDEX

Page numbers in italics indicate figures.